AF580308

PICTURING THE SOUTH

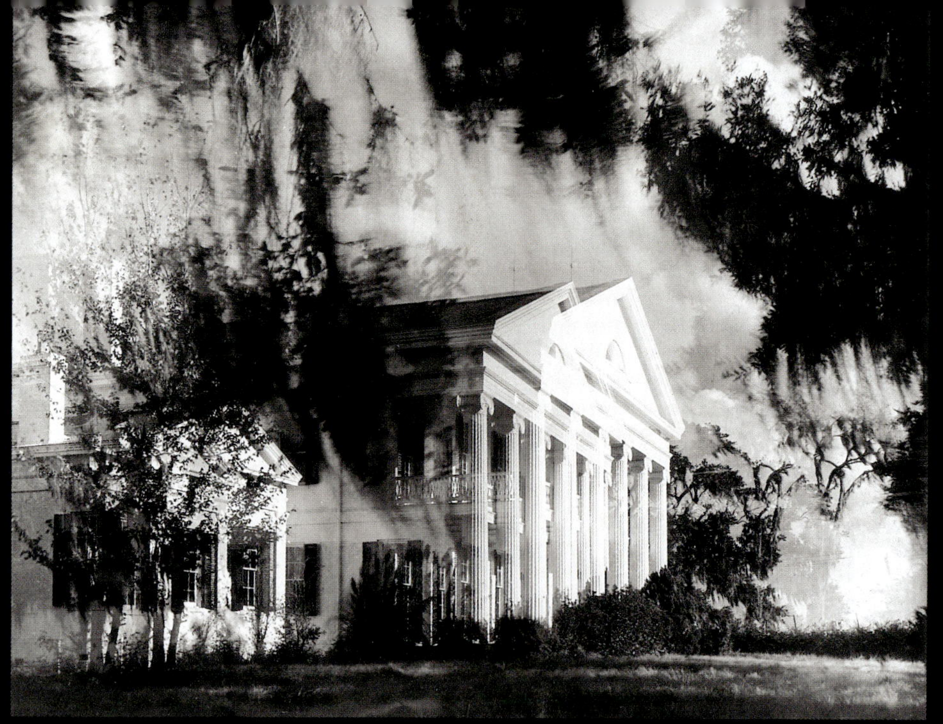

PHOTOGRAPHERS AND WRITERS

PICTURING

WILLIAM BALDWIN

A. J. VERDELLE

CLYDE EDGERTON

WILLIE MORRIS

BOBBIE ANN MASON

JOSEPHINE HUMPHREYS

ESSAY BY

CHARLES REAGAN WILSON

THE SOUTH

1860 TO THE PRESENT

EDITED BY

ELLEN DUGAN

HIGH MUSEUM OF ART

CHRONICLE BOOKS

The High Museum of Art is grateful for the generous support of Georgia-Pacific Corporation.

Additional support has been provided by National Data Corporation.

Picturing the South: 1860 to the Present
was on view at the High Museum of Art
Folk Art and Photography Galleries
Atlanta, Georgia
June 15–September 14, 1996.

The exhibition was organized by the High Museum of Art
and presented in collaboration with
The Atlanta Committee for the Olympic Games Cultural Olympiad.

Compilation copyright © 1996 by High Museum of Art. All rights reserved.
No part of this book may be reproduced in any form without written
permission from the publisher.

Library of Congress Cataloging-in-Publication Data
Picturing the South : 1860 to the present : photographers and writers
/ [compiled by] Ellen Dugan.
p. cm.
Exhibition held at the High Museum of Art, Folk Art and Photography Galleries, Atlanta, Georgia, June 15–Sept. 14, 1996.
ISBN 0-8118-1323-1 (hc). —ISBN 0-8118-1343-6 (pb)
1. Southern States—History—1865–1951—Pictorial works—Exhibitions. 2. Southern States—History—1951– —Pictorial works—Exhibitions. 3. Southern States—History—1865–1951—Exhibitions. 4. Southern States—History—1951– —Exhibitions. I. Dugan, Ellen. II. High Museum of Art, Folk Art and Photography Galleries.
F245.P56 1996
975.04—dc20 96-10493

Designed by Brian Ellis Martin, with assistance by Noreen Ryan
Produced by Marquand Books, Inc., Seattle
Printed and bound in Hong Kong

Distributed in Canada by Raincoast Books
8680 Cambie Street
Vancouver, BC V6P 6M9

10 9 8 7 6 5 4 3 2 1

Chronicle Books
275 Fifth Street
San Francisco, CA 94103

Cover: Walker Evans. *Roadside Stand Near Birmingham, Alabama,* 1936
Title page: Clarence John Laughlin. *The Waters of Memory,* 1946

CONTENTS

PREFACE

As a young boy—born in Alabama and having spent a few years in rural Tennessee before moving with my family to New York City—I found among my parents' library a book on the Confederate prison at Andersonville. I was about eight years old and, other than a few cowboy and war movies and television programs, I had never seen a depiction of a dead person. I will never forget the images of randomly strewn corpses, the portraits of boys dressed awkwardly for combat, hopelessly misfit and miscast. I still marvel at how these photographs register the immutable stillness of death.

The South, long a source of inspiration for artists and writers, became available to greater numbers of people with the invention of photography in the middle of the nineteenth century. The topography, architecture, social conditions, and faces of residents were widely disseminated. And, for this country, the Civil War was the first to be chronicled by the camera, yielding the first indelible images of mass destruction and brutal violence on the fields of battle.

The High Museum of Art is profoundly proud to have an ongoing corporate friend and patron in the Georgia-Pacific Corporation. On behalf of the Board of Directors and the staff, I thank A. D. "Pete" Correll, Chairman of the Board and Chief Executive Officer, for his strong commitment to the visual arts and culture and for Georgia-Pacific's sponsorship of this exhibition. Georgia-Pacific and Metropolitan Life, Inc., the co-owners of the Georgia-Pacific Center, have been major catalysts in Atlanta and have significantly undergirded efforts to advance the appreciation and understanding of the visual arts. I also wish to extend my gratitude to Honorary Chairman of the Board of Georgia-Pacific Corporation, T. Marshall Hahn, Jr. Curley M. Dossman, Jr., President of The Georgia-Pacific Foundation and Senior Director of Community Affairs, has been integral to the partnership with Georgia-Pacific for this exhibition. The Museum is also immensely grateful to Robert A. Yellowlees, Chairman and Chief Executive Officer of National Data Corporation, for his leadership and involvement with *Picturing the South.* The shareholders and employees of National Data Corporation have enabled the High to fulfill a major aspect of its Olympic goals, providing visitors with an opportunity to witness the evolution of this region. I thank Harriet Sanford, Executive Director of the Fulton County Arts Council, for her support, leadership, and involvement. Many thanks also to the Fulton County Commission and to the seven elected officials who represent the interests of the taxpayers of Fulton County.

The High is proud to present *Picturing the South: 1860 to the Present* in conjunction with our colleagues of the Cultural Olympiad of the Atlanta Committee for the Olympic Games. I would like to extend thanks to William Porter "Billy" Payne, President and Chief Executive Officer; his Director of Programs, Linda Stephenson; Dr. Jeffrey N. Babcock, Director of the Cultural Olympiad; and Annette Carlozzi, Visual Arts Producer, for helping make this project successful.

I want to recognize the extraordinary job that Ellen Dugan, the Museum's Curator of Photography, has done in creating this exhibition. Not only did she throw herself into the research immediately upon assuming the position of curator, she also managed an unrelenting schedule of photography exhibitions. *Picturing the South* will endure, thanks to this handsome publication. The High is very pleased to have worked with Chronicle Books in co-publishing this collection of original writings and reproductions of compelling original prints.

Picturing the South will have achieved a measure of success if the images we have presented remain with you after seeing the exhibition or after you have read through this book. We welcome you to the South for the celebration of the centenary of the modern Olympic Games in Atlanta.

—NED RIFKIN
Director
High Museum of Art

LIST OF LENDERS

CORPORATE COLLECTIONS, GALLERIES, AND PHOTOGRAPHY ART DEALERS

Agnes Gallery, Birmingham, Alabama
Deborah Bell Photographs, New York
Bonni Benrubi Gallery, New York
James Corcoran Gallery, Venice, California
James Danziger Gallery, New York
Catherine Edelman Gallery, Chicago
Fraenkel Gallery, San Francisco
Gilman Paper Company Collection, New York
Fay Gold Gallery, Atlanta
Howard Greenberg Gallery, New York
Houk Friedman, New York
Jackson Fine Art, Atlanta
The McIntosh Gallery, Atlanta
PaceWildensteinMacGill, New York
Panopticon Gallery, Boston
P·P·O·W, Inc., New York
Turner Entertainment Company, Los Angeles
Wach Gallery, Cleveland, Ohio

PRIVATE LENDERS

Derrick Joshua Beard, Atlanta
Lucinda W. Bunnen, Atlanta
Stanley B. Burns, M.D., and The Burns Archive, New York
Gregory Conniff, Madison, Wisconsin
Steve Folio, Atlanta
Lynda Frese, Scott, Louisiana
Ernst Haas Studio, New York
Chester Higgins Jr., New York
Dr. Benjamin A. Hill, Atlanta
Paul R. Jones, Atlanta
Stuart D. Klipper, Madison, Wisconsin
Ferne Koch, Dallas
James "Spider" Martin, Birmingham, Alabama
John McWilliams, Atlanta
Estate of Ralph Eugene Meatyard, Lexington, Kentucky
Al and Claudia Niemiec, LaGrange, Illinois
The Roger Houston Ogden Collection, New Orleans
John Pfahl, Buffalo, New York
Private Collection, New York
Dr. and Mrs. Barry S. Ramer, Santa Rosa, California
Estate of Richard Samuel Roberts, Washington, D.C.
Virginia Warren Smith, Atlanta
Melissa Springer, Birmingham, Alabama
William A. Turner, La Plata, Maryland
George S. Whiteley IV, Atlanta

PUBLIC INSTITUTIONS

Alabama Department of Archives and History, Montgomery
The Art Institute of Chicago
Atlanta History Center
Boston Athenaeum
The Brooklyn Museum
Center for Creative Photography, University of Arizona, Tucson
Center for Southern Folklore, Memphis, Tennessee
The Charleston Museum, South Carolina
Fogg Art Museum, Harvard University Art Museums, Cambridge, Massachusetts
George Arents Research Library for Special Collections, Syracuse University, Syracuse, New York
George Eastman House, International Museum of Photography and Film, Rochester, New York
Henry E. Huntington Library and Art Gallery, San Marino, California
High Museum of Art, Atlanta
The Historic New Orleans Collection
International Center of Photography, New York
Louisiana State Museum, New Orleans
The Medford Historical Society, Massachusetts
Memphis Brooks Museum of Art, Memphis, Tennessee
The Metropolitan Museum of Art, New York
The Museum of The Confederacy, Richmond, Virginia
The Museum of Modern Art, New York
National Gallery of Art, Washington, D.C.
New Orleans Museum of Art
The New-York Historical Society
The New York Public Library
North Carolina Collection, University of North Carolina Library at Chapel Hill
The Oakland Museum of California
Penn School Collection, Penn Center, Inc., St. Helena, South Carolina
Philadelphia Museum of Art
Photographic Archives, University of Louisville, Kentucky
Prints and Photographs Division, Library of Congress, Washington, D.C.
Schomburg Center for Research in Black Culture, The New York Public Library
Southeastern Architectural Archive, Tulane University Library, New Orleans
Southern Historical Collection, University of North Carolina Library at Chapel Hill
The Saint Louis Art Museum, Missouri
The Valentine Museum, Richmond, Virginia
The Virginia Historical Society, Richmond, Virginia
William Ransom Hogan Jazz Archive, Tulane University Library, New Orleans
Xavier University Archives and Special Collections, New Orleans

ACKNOWLEDGMENTS

The realization of an exhibition and catalogue of this size and complexity would be unthinkable without the committed cooperation, goodwill, and assistance of artists, museum professionals, archivists, collectors, and dealers around the country, and working in every part of the High Museum of Art.

I am greatly indebted to the numerous lenders listed on pages 8–9, who were willing to part with their works for the Atlanta presentation of *Picturing the South*. Without their generosity and collegiality, this exhibition would not have been possible. Space does not permit me to mention all the individuals at museums, archives, corporate collections, and libraries who gave unstintingly of their time in securing loans and providing research materials and reproductions. Special thanks, however, are due to Carolyn Davis, George Arents Research Library, Syracuse University; Kristen S. Nagel and Pamela Studemann, The Art Institute of Chicago; Rodney Armstrong, Sally Pierce, and Catharina Slautterback, Boston Athenaeum; Barbara Millstein, The Brooklyn Museum; Anne Sullivan and Diane Nilsen, Center for Creative Photography; Judy Peiser, Center for Southern Folklore; Therese Mulligan, Janice Madhu, Joseph Struble, and Del Zogg, George Eastman House, International Museum of Photography and Film; Deborah Martin Kao, Fogg Art Museum; Pierre Apraxine and Maria Umali, Gilman Paper Company Collection; John H. Lawrence, Jude Solomon, and John Magill, The Historic New Orleans Collection; Miles Barth, International Center of Photography; Tambra Johnson, Prints and Photographs Division, Library of Congress; Claudia Kheel, Louisiana State Museum; James Anderson and Bill Garner, Photographic Archives, University of Louisville; Christopher Meatyard, Estate of Ralph Eugene Meatyard; Noah Dennen and Jay Griffin, The Medford Historical Society; Patty Bladon Lawrence, Memphis Brooks Museum of Art; Maria Morris Hambourg, Jeff Rosenheim, Beatrice Epstein, and Eileen Sullivan, The Metropolitan Museum of Art; Peter Galassi, Virginia Dodier, Thomas Grischkowsky, and Renee Coppola, The Museum of Modern Art; Barbara Barnard, National Gallery of Art; Steven Maklansky, New Orleans Museum of Art; Dale Neighbors, Diana Arecco, and Wendy Haynes, The New-York Historical Society; Tony Troncale, The New York Public Library; Jerry Cotten, North Carolina Collection, University of North Carolina Library at Chapel Hill; Drew Johnson, Janice A. Capecci, and Joy Tahan, The Oakland Museum of California; Gerald E. Roberts, Estate of Richard Samuel Roberts; Kenneth W. Barnes, The Roger Houston Ogden Collection; Emory S. Campbell and Joseph McGill, Penn Center, Inc.; Mary Yearwood, Schomburg Center for Research in Black Culture; Richard A. Schrader and John E. White, Southern Historical Collection, University of North Carolina Library at Chapel Hill; Daniel T. Williams and Cynthia Wilson, Tuskegee University Archives; Adrianne Proeller and Beth Lilly, Turner Broadcasting System; Kathy Lendech, Turner Entertainment Company; Barbara C. Batson, The Valentine Museum; and Lester Sullivan and Raymond Berthelot, Xavier University Archives and Special Collections.

I would also like to acknowledge the efforts of the owners and staff members of the galleries that supported *Picturing the South*—in particular, Jon Coffelt, Agnes Gallery; Deborah Bell, Deborah Bell Photographs; Bonni Benrubi and Karen Marks, Bonni Benrubi Gallery; Tracy Lew, James Corcoran Gallery; James Danziger, James Danziger Gallery; Catherine Edelman, Catherine Edelman Gallery; Jeffrey Fraenkel and Deborah Berne, Fraenkel Gallery; Fay Gold and Alex Barlow, Fay Gold Gallery; Howard Greenberg, Howard Greenberg Gallery; Jenni Holder, Houk Friedman; Jane Jackson and Betsy Brucker, Jackson Fine Art; Louisa McIntosh, The McIntosh Gallery; Laurence Miller, Laurence Miller Gallery; Howard Read and Mary Doerhofer, Robert Miller Gallery; Peter MacGill and Margaret Kelly, PaceWildensteinMacGill; Antony Decaneas, Panopticon Gallery; Scott A. Catto, P·P·O·W, Inc.; and Peter and Judy Wach, Wach Gallery.

In addition, I would like to convey my appreciation to all the artists and private lenders to *Picturing the South,* especially Dr. Stanley Burns and Sara Cleary, The Burns Archive, Harry Callahan, Gregory Conniff, Lynda Frese, Benjamin A. Hill, Paul R. Jones, Stuart D. Klipper, Jay B. Leviton, Lynn Marshall-Linnemeier, Ezra Mack, James "Spider" Martin, John McWilliams, Moneta Sleet, Jr., Virginia Warren Smith, Melissa Springer, and William A. Turner.

I would also like to extend my warmest thanks to Lucinda W. Bunnen, Wanda and Lindsey Hopkins, III, Dr. Joe and Adair Massey and The Massey Charitable Trust, the law firm of Powell, Goldstein, Frazer & Murphy, and the Robert Ferst Memorial Fund for their ongoing generosity and support of the Photography Department at the High Museum of Art. These benefactors have made possible the recent acquisition of many of the fine works in this exhibition for our permanent collection, and they have my profound gratitude.

I am also indebted to those colleagues who made an extraordinary effort in helping locate works beyond those in their own collections, or in offering new research to us. For their generosity with their time and expertise, I wish to especially thank consultants and lenders Derrick Joshua Beard and George S. Whiteley IV, and Guy Arello, Tom Bamberger, Matthew Bruccoli, John T. Hill, Steven Kasher, Josh Paillet, and Carole Thompson.

My deepest appreciation goes to the staff of the High Museum of Art, whose professionalism and commitment are unmatched. Above all, director Ned Rifkin early on recognized the importance of this project, and I cannot sufficiently thank him for his confidence and advice, which led to its fruition. Michael Shapiro, Director for Museum Programs/Chief Curator, and Bill Bodine, former Director for Museum Programs and now Chief Curator at the Columbia Museum, South Carolina, provided essential guidance throughout the project, from the moment of the exhibition proposal through every phase of the development of the show and its publications. For their help in obtaining financial assistance for this exhibition, I wish to thank Anne Baker, Director of External Affairs, and her staff, particularly Keira Ellis, Manager of Foundation and Government Support; Betsy Hamilton, Manager of Individual Support; and Susan Hyde Brown, Manager of Corporate Support. Consultant Elisa Glazer coordinated specific aspects of corporate support of the exhibition with unusual clarity and grace in the heat of countless demands and menacing deadlines. Rhonda Matheison, Director for Business Affairs, and her staff are also to be recognized for their critical assistance in the areas of facility operations, shop merchandising, and other areas of budgeting and administration. Jackie King, Manager of Folk Art and Photography Galleries, and her staff have also made important contributions to the show's organization. The efforts of Helen James, Chief of Security, and Dean Wolcott, Security Supervisor, and their staff are often unsung, but I wish to acknowledge them for their constant vigilance and efforts on behalf of this exhibition.

The myriad responsibilities that attended the framing, crating, shipping, and receiving of works and countless other matters pertaining to the show fell to Jody Cohen, Associate Registrar. She fulfilled her job, as she has so often, with consummate professionalism and calm astuteness, and it has been a pleasure to again work with her on this project. Marjorie Harvey, Manager of Exhibitions and Design, and Nancy Roberts, Chief Preparator, and her talented crew, as well as Karen Giles, Graphics Technician, are to be commended for their outstanding work on the exhibition design and graphics. Thanks also to Larry Miller, Works on Paper Technician, for his sensitive and careful attention to the matting and framing of much of the work in this exhibition, and to Kate Flores, our former librarian, who was extremely helpful in various research matters.

Shaping the impact of the exhibition on the visiting public is an area of critical importance, and the particular responsibility of two Museum departments. First, for getting out the word and for their careful attention to the best presentation of this exhibition on all media fronts, great thanks are owed to Ann Wilson, Manager of Public Relations and Marketing; Wilma Eisenlau, Public Relations Coordinator; and their entire staff. Luisa Kreisberg and Anne Edgar of The Kreisberg Group served as expert and energetic consultants on national and international publicity, and I am greatly appreciative of their work. Karen Luik, Eleanor McDonald Storza Chair of Education, and the many other staff members in the Department of Education have done so much to guide the museum visitor to a greater appreciation and understanding of the ideas and images that the exhibition presents. I thank them all for their invaluable advice and assistance. The staff was supported by many volunteers who contributed countless hours to the project, led by Kay Weiss and Jeff Hinson, Chairs, Docent Committee; Pat D'Alba, President, Members Guild; and Marti Rainbow, Manager of Volunteer Services.

In the production of the *Picturing the South* book, my coauthors Charles Reagan Wilson, William Baldwin, Clyde Edgerton, Josephine Humphreys, Bobbie Ann Mason, Willie Morris, and A. J. Verdelle must be recognized not only for their superb and insightful essays, but also for their other important writings, which have had such an indelible impact on contemporary Southern literature and scholarship. We are honored by their participation in this project. The book's editor, Kelly Morris, was a tireless and patient collaborator whose characteristically scrupulous attention to matters of quality has kept this project from veering off track at critical moments. In the face of exceptional pressures with other Olympic publication projects, Kelly and Margaret Wallace, Associate Editor, dedicated themselves to every phase of the editing and production of the book, and I am truly grateful to them for their exemplary work. Ed Marquand oversaw the design of the book with exceptional sensitivity and intelligence, and the staff at Chronicle Books, particularly Annie Barrows, did a superb job in managing the complexities of production, distribution, and promotion. Finally, a special thanks to Katharine Walton at Algonquin Books for her assistance with the project.

While there is no part of the Museum that did not feel, at one time or another, the demands and pressures of this exhibition, it is those who work most closely with me to whom I owe my deepest thanks. Eleanor Roper, Exhibition Assistant, tackled the mountainous paperwork, countless phone calls, intricate arrangements, and so many other organizational aspects of the project with great energy, professionalism, and an indefatigable sense of humor. Trish Vlastnik's thorough research, creative initiative, and willingness to go the extra mile also made signal contributions to the shaping of the exhibition. Our talented interns, Chandler Oldham, Eleanor Driver, Christen White, and Cathy Sylte, are to be commended for their able assistance in many areas of the project. I owe a particular debt to Anna Bloomfield, Curatorial Assistant, Department of Photography. She not only supervised and contributed to the writing, editing, and production of the exhibition brochure and wall texts and worked on countless other aspects of the show, but also organized the business of the office in such a manner as to allow me to stay focused on the exhibition and maintain day-to-day management of an extremely busy department. As always, she has done outstanding work and has well earned the professional admiration and warm thanks of all who were involved in the exhibition.

Finally, I wish to thank my family for their constant and loving support. I dedicate this book to them and to Vladimir Fleurov, whose own journey from Moscow to the American South has taught me so very much about this fascinating, often bewildering, and deeply affecting place we both now call home.

—ELLEN DUGAN

INTRODUCTION

"Tell about the South," asks the Canadian Shreve McCannon, a character in William Faulkner's *Absalom, Absalom!*. "What's it like there. What do they do there. Why do they live there. Why do they live at all?"[1] And Quentin Compson, Shreve's Southern-born roommate at Harvard in 1910, later answers, "You cant understand it. You would have to be born there."[2] Nevertheless, Quentin goes on to recount the long and violent story of Thomas Sutpen, who came to Yoknapatawpha County with his French architect and Haitian slaves in the early 1830s to build a grand plantation out of the muddy swamps of the northern Mississippi wilderness. Sutpen's tragedy leaves its impress, not only on his immediate kin and townsfolk, but also on several generations of their descendants, including Quentin Compson himself, whose obsession with it reveals something essential about the making of Southern history in which "nothing ever happens once and is finished."

It has been exactly sixty years since the publication of Faulkner's greatest literary achievement. Yet there still seems to be no limit to the questions that can be asked about the South, even as the unremitting pace of change renders the notion of a homogeneous place—"another land," to use W. J. Cash's phrase—tenuous or at least highly debatable.[3] Economic diversification, urbanization, population growth, and political change have radically transformed the region, especially in the postwar era, and contributed to what one writer has aptly called "the Americanization of Dixie."[4] For the more optimistic observers, from outside and inside the region, it appeared that the South had finally discarded its fractious, sectional identity, its "peculiar past" forged from the legacy of slavery, military defeat, racial disenfranchisement, and relative privation. In the words of historian John Egerton, "the South was no longer simply a colony of the nation, an inferior region, a stepchild: it is now rushing to rejoin the Union and in the process it is becoming indistinguishable from North and East and West."[5]

Traditionalists, on the other hand, viewed the twin forces of modernization and modernity, which threatened to eradicate Southern values, with a deep sense of apprehension and regret, if not moral crisis. In the 1930s, the Agrarian writer John Crowe Ransom perceived the region as succumbing "to a foreign invasion of Southern soil, which is capable of doing more devastation than was wrought when Sherman marched to the sea."[6] In a similarly bellicose tone, a contemporary writer fifty years later would also lament the continued flattening of regional differences: "On any given day . . . in Atlanta or Richmond or Raleigh or New Orleans or Birmingham or Houston, it would be easy to believe not only that the South [had] thoroughly lost the War, but since then it has been effaced, ploughed under, and covered with asphalt. Has vanished forever in a total and final Yankee triumph."[7]

Today, the ever-increasing nationalization of the Southern community has probably entered its terminal stages. Interstate superhighways, fast-food chains, shopping malls, suburban subdivisions, and sleek, glass-curtained corporate towers now dominate much of the landscape, where there once existed wetland marshes, cultivated fields, two-lane blacktops, and county seats boasting their courthouse and library, drugstore and barber shop, tavern and civic monuments. "Signs of the times," thinks one of Lee Smith's characters in the book *Fancy Strut,* as she looks at a soft-drink ad casting its neon light on the Confederate statue in the center of her Alabama town. "Everywhere you looked, you saw them."[8] From the contemporary photographs of Harry Callahan, Thomas Tulis, Joel Meyerowitz, William Eggleston, and Stuart D. Klipper, among others, we can also discern much about how the region's social and economic fabric has been rewoven into a bold new design whose forms have assumed more characteristically American arrangements and whose aspirations now more fully partake in the superordinate dreams of never-ending abundance, liberty, and progress. In the 1990s, it would appear that the older Southern patterns of life have been irretrievably broken, beyond restitution. And yet, despite the perceptible and unbridgeable changes in the material and social conditions of Southern existence, there still persist, for better and ill, the vestiges of a coherent and distinctive regional character and identity.

The question of what constitutes the determinants of Southern cultural resiliency in an age of mass consumption and uniformity has been the subject of extensive and systematic scholarly attention, popular debate, and creative exploration. While many commentators agree that "the mind of the South" has never been a monolithic entity available for complete explication, nonetheless there are important cultural traits that continue to distinguish this region from the rest of the country.[9] Among the abiding characteristics most frequently cited are: a distinctive commitment to family, tradition, and community, "an allegiance and love for one small place," as Willie Morris expressed it;[10] the predominance of evangelical Protestantism that has endured all the major events in Southern history; and a proclivity for violence linked from the first to a defense of individual "rights" or honor, and rooted in the survival of military and hunting traditions. Most important, perhaps, is an urgent, dramatized sense of history, the defining moment being the Civil War, which permeates the consciousness of this region, as in no other American place. As Allen Tate once put it, there is a recognition among Southerners "that the future and the past are part of the same passage."[11]

Out of the tragic experience of military defeat, white Southerners, in particular, sought to valorize and redeem their history—an act, as Richard Gray has stated, "not so much a recovery as a reinvention of the past."[12] The various myths of the Lost Cause—constructed to affirm and validate a bloodied, if unbowed, identity soon after the Civil War's end—persist, but not without repercussions, today. Confederate symbolism, for example, can be found on bumper stickers, the kitsch memorabilia available at any truck stop or souvenir stand, in the lyrics of some country songs, and on the flags that are still raised over several Southern state capitols. For some, the Stars and Bars is a defiant symbol of pride and remembrance; for others, it is a vexing emblem of the refusal to extirpate bigotry. Public controversies swirl around the latter issue, as well as the recent polarizing debates on the proposal to erect a bronze statue of the pioneering black tennis star Arthur Ashe, a native of Richmond, on Monument Avenue, that city's and the South's grandest commemorative precinct dedicated to the heroes of the Confederacy. These are but two of many recent examples that could be drawn to show how the mythicized Southern past constantly roils the present. The notion of a vanished, halcyon "Dixie" still enthralls the popular imagination, even as its imputed meanings are increasingly contested by those whose historical voices have often been muted by the din of older, revisionist interpretations.

Southern reality, a curious conflation of fact and fiction, has been vigorously recorded, defined, and re-created through literature, music, film, the mass media, and other agencies of popular and high culture. It has been photography, however, which has arguably had the most sustained, wide-ranging, and indelible role in chronicling how the region has perceived itself and been understood (or misapprehended) by others, particularly in its most crucial periods of transition and crisis—the Civil War and its aftermath, the Depression years, and the "Second Reconstruction," the civil rights era of the 1950s and 1960s.

The purpose of this book, *Picturing the South: 1860 to the Present,* and its accompanying exhibition is to examine how our understanding of Southern history, identity, and character has been mediated through photography since the mid-nineteenth century. It is not intended to be, in any sense, a definitive historic or aesthetic survey, as anything along those lines would take up several museums or volumes. Rather, this book looks at how selected photographers, spanning thirteen decades and encompassing a wide range of genres, artistic styles, and political viewpoints, helped to shape the changing and often dichotomous idea of the South in the very act of seeing and describing it.

This book contains nearly 180 images: some are among the classic works of nineteenth- and twentieth-century art, some are by a younger generation of artists, and some have been created by important (though undervalued) regional photographers whose intimate knowledge of their own communities yielded work that often differed considerably in perspective and tenor from that of outsiders. Among the lesser-known Southern photographers or studios represented are Mother St. Croix, Arthur P. Bedou, and Fonville Winans (New Orleans and Baton Rouge, Louisiana); John Horgan, Jr., James "Spider" Martin, Prentice H. Polk, and Cornelius M. Battey (Birmingham and Tuskegee, Alabama); Reverend Lonzie Odie Taylor and Ernest C. Withers (Memphis, Tennessee); Kate Matthews and Stern J. Bramson (Louisville and Lexington, Kentucky); Richard Samuel Roberts, Bayard Wootten, and Michael Miley (Columbia, South Carolina; New Bern, North Carolina; and Richmond, Virginia).

Besides a richly provocative array of photographs by more than eighty artists and commercial studios, this volume also includes many references to the world of the vernacular—those family portraits, snapshots, and albums made and owned by anonymous and identifiable Southerners. These lovingly preserved photographs have an undeniable immediacy and evocative power, and they reveal, perhaps most poignantly, the pervasive and compelling need to construct our own histories from the raw material of the objective.

"There are images—especially, it seems to Southerners—that never go away; they do not even fade," observed the writer Elizabeth Spencer.[13] The pictures to which Spencer alludes and the photographs presented here may have a special resonance and more private meaning for those who claim some blood knowledge of the South. Certainly, this has been true for the six Southern authors—William Baldwin, Clyde Edgerton, Josephine Humphreys, Bobbie Ann Mason, Willie Morris, and A. J. Verdelle—who, after looking at these photographs, were moved to write the deeply felt and searching stories and recollections that grace this book by their presence. However, while these images (whether literary or visual) are indeed rooted in the heritage and traditions of a particular place and people, their cultural significance transcends geographic and temporal bounds. Photographers and writers have long recognized that compressed and magnified within Southern history are many of the key events and underlying issues that have dramatically shaped American society as a whole, and that will continue to exert their convulsive pressures well into the twenty-first century. Many of those salient themes embodied in and engendered by the Southern experience emerge with a stunning lucidity, taut beauty, and resounding power in their work: the search for sustaining traditions and values at times of wrenching change and discontinuity; the struggle to realize historic precepts and ideals in a society weighted by the distinctions of race, gender, and social class; the need to establish a more responsible balance between human endeavors and fragile, natural ecologies; and the role of myth, memory, and history in defining individual and collective identity in a global era.

In *Picturing the South,* generations of photographers have discovered a complex and distinctive, albeit shifting, culture shaped by circumstances, failures, and pressures often peculiar to itself, which continues to fascinate, confound, and enrich people throughout the world. At the same time, their formidable visual record (like its literary counterpart) touches upon larger, shared concerns that extend far beyond the Mason-Dixon line. If we look carefully and reflect upon this collective vision of the South, certain truths, both discomfiting and ennobling, will be revealed about our American past that remain profoundly important and relevant to understanding the promises and challenges of both our immediate present and the beckoning future.

NOTES

1. William Faulkner, *Absalom, Absalom!* (1936; New York, 1990), 142.
2. Ibid, 289.
3. W. J. Cash, *The Mind of the South* (1941; New York, 1960), vii.
4. See John Egerton, *The Americanization of Dixie: The Southernization of America* (New York, 1974).
5. Ibid., xix–xx.
6. Quoted in Richard Gray, *Writing the South: Ideas of an American Region* (Cambridge, Mass., 1986), 143.
7. George Garrett, "Southern Literature Here and Now," in *Fifteen Southerners: Why the South Will Survive* (Athens, Ga., 1981), 123.
8. Lee Smith, *Fancy Strut* (New York, 1973), 6.
9. For an excellent synthesis of current scholarship on these topics, see the extensive articles and bibliographies in Charles Reagan Wilson and William Ferris, eds., *Encyclopedia of Southern Culture* (Chapel Hill, N.C., 1989).
10. Willie Morris, *Good Old Boy: A Delta Boyhood* (London, 1974), 143.
11. Quoted in Gray, 179.
12. Ibid., 76. For further background on Southern myths, see especially Charles Reagan Wilson, *Baptized in Blood: The Religion of the Lost Cause, 1865–1920* (Athens, Ga., 1980) and Catherine Clinton, *Tara Revisited: Women, War & The Plantation Legend* (New York, 1995).
13. Quoted in Sheree Hightower and Cathie Stanga, *Mississippi Observed* (Jackson, Miss., 1994), vii.

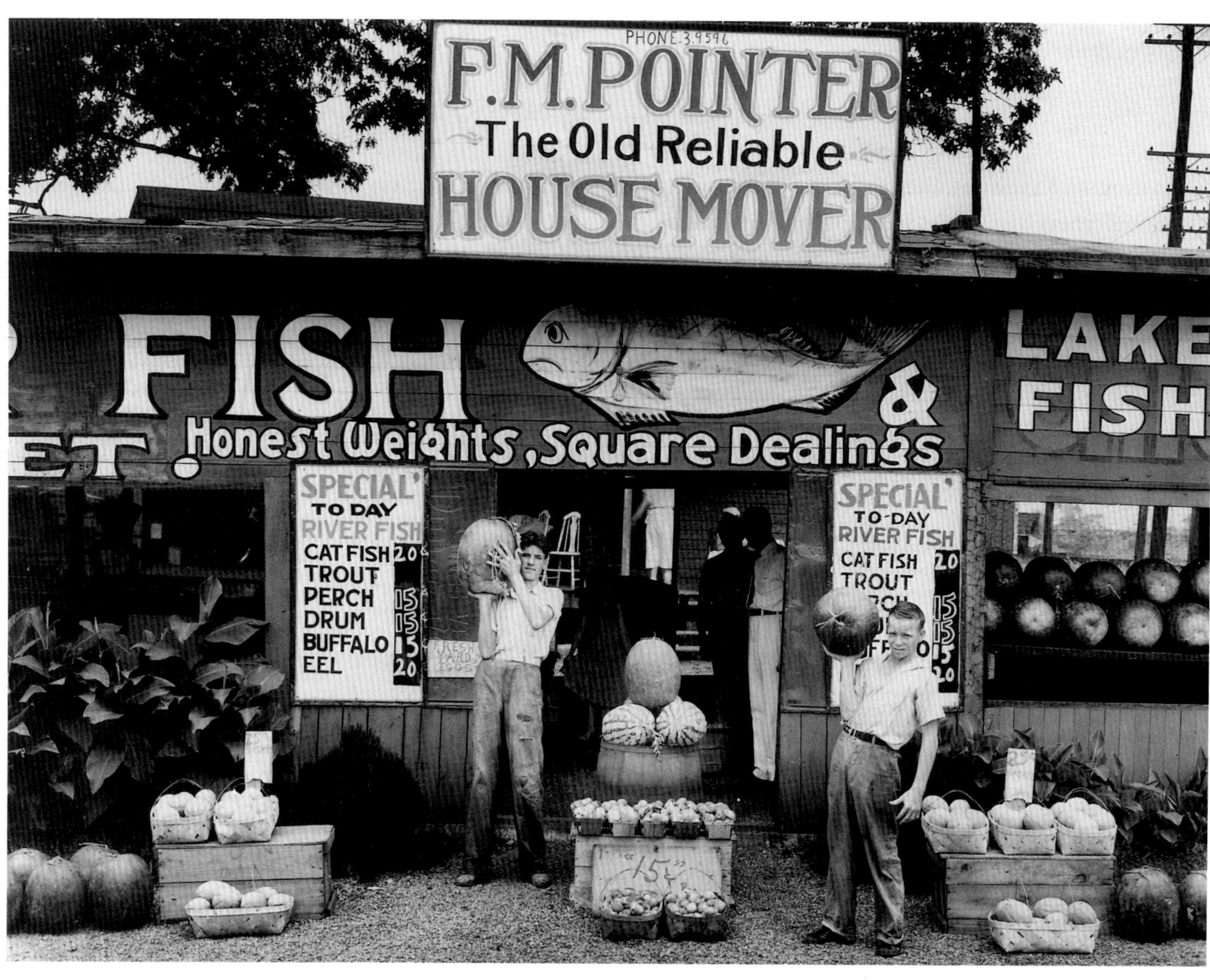

WALKER EVANS

Roadside Stand Near Birmingham, Alabama

1936

WORRIED MIND, SINGING HEART: SOUTHERN HISTORY IN GOOD TIMES AND BAD

Land & People

The American South has long evoked powerful imaginative responses. Writers explore the psychology of its people, and scholars wrestle with defining its distinctiveness. Travelers sketch their insights on the customs of the people in the region, and Southerners themselves seem given to brooding upon their inheritance and their destiny. Country ballads and blues probe the South's complexities and tragedies but celebrate the joy of life in the region as well.

Early promoters of settlement in the South advertised it as a Garden of Eden, a lush world requiring little work and offering much leisure. This appealing legend is the beginning point for understanding the image of the South and also the ironies of its history. The first European colonists were charmed by the sights and smells of the Southern environment. The fragrance of honeysuckle, the pesky presence of mosquitoes, the charm of fireflies on a summer night, the electrifying power of a spring thunderstorm—all have continued to be part of the texture of everyday life in the South.

"Let us begin by discussing the weather," wrote the Southern historian U. B. Phillips in the early twentieth century, and Southerners would still put much faith in that view, especially when outside in the hot and humid July afternoon. The states of the Old Confederacy are characterized by plentiful rainfall, much humidity, and a bright sun. Temperatures do not get hotter than in other parts of the nation, but the heat typically lasts longer. Given these conditions, vegetation can indeed be abundant, overgrown throughout much of the South in a semitropical outcropping.

Compared to the rest of the United States, the South is given to the turbulence of tornadoes and hurricanes and the obfuscation of fog. The seemingly beneficent environment also has been the nation's "hot zone," harboring microbes that once brought epidemics of yellow fever, malaria, and other plagues. If the South's effusive natural landscape has promoted its image as a sensuous place of ease, it also reminds one that dangers abide there, potential threats lurking in the woods and swamps and down the mountain hollers.

The hill country and mountains of the upper South are not tropical at all, but the idea of a tropical South became a prime image used by non-Southerners to interpret the region, nurturing a gothic fear of what lurked in this exotic landscape. The photographs of the Wilderness battlefield (pages 46–47) capture the overgrown quality of the environment, portraying a thicket of vines, briars, tree limbs, and shrubs. The images take on added meaning when we know that they were taken after the Civil War battle there; the Southern landscape is invested with complexity by the history of humans and their marks on the land.

The land sustained a distinctive group of regional citizens. Native-American cultures established many of the patterns involving use of resources, the location of settlements, and the transportation routes that Europeans later exploited. Southern tribes introduced Europeans and Africans to New World ways of living. Modern Southerners sometimes still use folk remedies first discovered by Native Americans. Indian names mark the land.

Colonists from the British Isles brought their institutions and ways to the South and became a second great demographic group shaping the region. They included the predominant English but also the Scotch-Irish, Irish, and Scots, who made up a group of Celtic origins. Africans were a crucial element in the Southern ethnic mix. An African Southern identity emerged from the meeting of many diverse African groups who had been brought to the region as far back as the early 1600s. Their toil and their ideas have helped energize regional life ever since.

Agrarian Republic

Southerners have been agrarians, a rural farm people, through most of their history. A long growing season supported such commercial crops as tobacco, rice, sugar, and, above all, cotton. In the early nineteenth century, Southerners moved into what was then called the Old Southwest—the states of Alabama, Mississippi, and Arkansas—and the rich lands there became known as the Cotton Kingdom. Steamboats loaded with cotton became common sights. When South Carolina Senator James H. Hammond loudly proclaimed on the floor of Congress in the 1850s that "Cotton is King!," Southern ideology became fixed on defending this monarch and his system.

Many Southerners before the Civil War lived as small farmers, planters, or slaves on a rural frontier. This way of life promoted both individualism and neighborliness; it resulted in impatience with formal institutions and allegiance to family; it encouraged hard work, promoted violence, and yet evangelical religion flourished there—establishing enduring Southern paradoxes. Southerners built log cabins and, in the Deep South, dogtrots with walkthrough breezeways to fight the heat, creating early symbols of country-living Southerners.

The plantation became the distinctive Southern rural institution. Before the Civil War, a planter (such as the one pictured on page 32) was known as such if he possessed twenty slaves or more—a benchmark of power even more important than acres of land or amount of crops shipped. Being a slaveowner, however, was uncommon. In 1850, only 384,000 Southerners (out of eight million whites in fifteen slave states) owned any slaves. Planters nonetheless dominated the political, economic, and social life of the Old South.

The planter ideology was a conservative vision of the good society, represented as an orderly, semifeudal world of harmonious, little-changing, hierarchical relationships between master and slave. The plantation ideal fired the imaginations of Southerners. Intellectuals and writers created a myth of the planter as a noble, honorable figure; the plantation lady was chaste, saintly, sacrificial, and spiritual. Slaves were childlike and loyal in this happy fantasyland.

The planter had a genealogical basis for superiority: Northerners and Southerners came to believe that Southerners descended from aristocratic, royalist exiles from Oliver Cromwell's Puritan England. Northerners, according to legend, were Puritan by origin. The belief was that these two types had generated two distinct peoples in North America, with differing temperaments, psychologies, and concerns.

The plain white farmers, the yeomen, sustained a different version of agrarianism than that of the plantation. They were subsistence farmers before the Civil War, located in greatest numbers not on the richest farmlands but in the isolated rural districts of the hill country, mountains, and piney woods. They raised crops to eat, with King Corn their monarch and King Hog wandering the open range on common lands.

The yeoman ethic was an individualistic one of self-reliance, material acquisition, valuation of private property, and honorable behavior. These people relied on one another, especially on kin. Plain farmers tended to live near family, so all could provide mutual aid and share in times of droughts, windstorms, floods, and other disasters that threatened their livelihoods. A pronounced sense of community appeared in such rural rituals as logrollings, house-raisings, dances, camp meetings, political gatherings, and visiting neighbors and kin. These farmers sometimes owned slaves, but, unlike larger planters, they worked beside them in the fields, ate similar food, and lived in similar structures. Yeomen in the South, unlike their kindred neighbors in the Midwest, typically aspired to own slaves, which defined social success in their society, a Southern version of the American Dream.

Whether planter or yeoman, Southern whites asserted the importance of republicanism as a ruling political ideology. The region's political rhetoric said that all men were created equal with inalienable rights, and Southern whites asserted their democratic rights. But this belief rested on the assumption of black subjugation. It was democracy for white men only. Seeing black slaves around them, in fact, apparently led whites to value their own freedom all the more and to celebrate their bond with whites in other classes.

Slaves represented the final ingredient in the antebellum agrarian republic. White ideologues called them the "mudsill," the laboring class that provided the hard work to make the plantations and small farms operate. Slavery was a system of much brutality, resting ultimately on force. *Slave Pen, Alexandria, Virginia* (page 33) shows us a building. It could have been any Victorian era business, a countinghouse, perhaps. Slavery is chilling to contemplate, not only because of the physical violence associated with it, but also because it was a business, a countinghouse of human souls.

African Americans themselves responded in many ways to slavery—some openly rebelling, some simply not cooperating, others acquiescing to its realities. Slaves developed a rich culture that saw them through the dark days. Religious faith gave a secure worldview above and beyond any plantation owner. The spirituals gave a vision of freedom and the hope of eventual eternal peace. While slave marriage was illegal throughout the South, slaves developed a "fictive family" tradition, combining parents, grandparents, extended kin, and communal caring and responsibility within the slave quarters for all children. The slave quarters (page 27) rank with the log cabin and the mansion as a hearth of Southern culture.

The War & Cultural Myths

The Civil War grew out of issues related to slavery and stands at the center of Southern history, the unmistakable monument to regional distinctiveness. For whites it cemented regional identity, creating a history forever different from those of other Americans. The Confederate States of America tried to preserve a traditional life that seemed threatened by outside intervention, a conservative political revolution aimed at preventing social and economic changes in its fundamental institutions. White Southerners justified the war as one for local control, righteous holiness, and constitutional rights. The racial dimensions of a war fought by a slave society were hard to miss. Confederate Vice President Alexander Stephens even admitted that slavery was the cornerstone of the Confederacy. White Southerners, however, developed only a limited sense of political nationalism around the slavery ideology. As the war and its suffering went on, deep social cleavages became apparent. Bread riots occurred in Southern cities, and yeoman farmers came to believe that they were suffering more than wealthy plantation families. George N. Barnard's *Ruins in Charleston, South Carolina* (page 24) shows the final result: a burned landscape, humans seemingly shellshocked, and the end of a cause.

For African Americans, the Civil War was a watershed, because through it they gained their freedom after two centuries of enslavement. Gable's *Summer Scene* (page 54) is surely one of the most poignant photographs picturing the South; the hopes and dreams of the postwar period shine through as one imagines what seems like a bright future with slavery forever gone.

Although the postwar years would see deep frustrations, emancipation bequeathed to black Americans the rights of equality and self-determination. Achieving those goals would remain primarily a Southern story for generations. Freed blacks mostly stayed in the South after the war, seeking full incorporation into Southern society. During Reconstruction, they served in political offices, helped to establish the first widespread public school system in the region, and defined the black church as the central institution of a separate culture that would grow in importance as whites suppressed black aspirations.

Southern black life reached a nadir in the years between the Civil War and World War I, a troubled time for the South in general. Political disenfranchisement took away black political power beginning in the 1890s, the same decade that saw passage of the Jim Crow segregation laws establishing separate-but-equal facilities for blacks. The landscape literally changed: "colored" signs now marked off a group of people as inferior. Lynching and other forms of violence against blacks rose to new heights, as Southern whites used whatever tactics were necessary to ensure that blacks would remain "in their place," the phrase used to describe the unchanging social position of a suppressed racial caste.

Sharecropping trapped Southern blacks economically. The defeat of the Confederacy had devastated the Southern agricultural economy. Confederate money was now worthless, and physical destruction was widespread, since most of the fighting during the Civil War had taken place on Southern soil.

In this crisis situation, the crop-lien system emerged. Sharecroppers, the farm tenants, would work the crop, and instead of paying rent would give the landowner part of the crop at the end of the year. Since the sharecropper likely had little money, the landowner might advance funds for food, clothing, seed, agricultural implements, even a mule to work the land. At the end of the year, the sharecropper could owe a great deal indeed, sometimes going into so much debt that he and his family lived in virtual peonage, bound legally by their debts.

Southerners in general have been noteworthy as people who appreciate the value of a sense of place, but sharecroppers were frustrated in their desires for a physical place to call home and a social place of dignity and security. As the decades went on, the cotton economy spread further throughout the South, exposing its people to the vagaries of cotton commodity prices. Increasing numbers of once-independent white yeoman farmers fell into the poverty of sharecropping, joining blacks. "Cotton with us is almost human," wrote journalist Ben Robertson in a 1942 memoir about upcountry South Carolina. He pictured cotton as "like some member of the family that the folks have had a lot of trouble with, but in whom they still believe." Robertson suggested that "a Southerner's idea of heaven is a fine cotton-growing country with the price of cotton pegged at twenty cents a pound."

The agrarian society established from the South's earliest days, then, was reconstituted after the Civil War, with new institutions like sharecropping and the crop-lien but with older symbols like planter families, black folks working the land, and cotton crops surviving in the transformation. The region's people were the poorest in the nation and would long continue to be so. In the 1930s, the federal government officially announced that the South was "the Nation's number one economic problem," bringing considerable shame to a proud people. Race relations were at a new low, with commonplace scenes of dreadful violence.

The South sometimes met these realities indirectly, through the creation of cultural myths. Myths are stories about the past, the tales the tribe tells itself, embodied in heroic figures and narratives. All societies develop myths about themselves, but the South seems especially given to them, perhaps because its complex history makes the simplicities of myth appealing.

The postbellum South lived for generations in a romantic haze, embodied in several legends. Southern writers after the Civil War developed fully, for example, the myth of the Old South as a land of cavaliers and a moonlight-and-magnolias charm. As Thomas Nelson Page wrote, "even the moonlight was richer and mellower before the war." The myth of the Lost Cause was a related saga, the story of the Confederates leaving their plantations and farms to wage war against the evil empire of the Yankees. As Robert Penn Warren noted, the Confederacy became immortal after its death, a "city of the soul." Ministers and religious groups sacralized the Lost Cause, tying regional patriotism and religion together so that the remembered Confederate cause took on spiritual significance. Robert E. Lee became a saint and Stonewall Jackson a martyr. Images of the Confederate heroes became pervasive in the postwar South; prints of Michael Miley's *General Robert E. Lee on Traveller* (page 58) probably hung on the walls in many Southern homes and classrooms. In a ritual celebration of the Lost Cause, the unveiling of a monument to Jeb Stuart in Richmond drew tens of thousands of people to the former Confederate capital a generation after the war. Southern whites created a long-lasting culture of ruin and remembrance.

Another myth that reinforced the sense of a common white Southern identity was the legend of Reconstruction, the memory of which set white Southerners against Northerners externally and against blacks internally. The Southern white view of Reconstruction portrayed greedy and malicious carpetbaggers, treacherous white scalawags, and vicious, ignorant freedmen—all exploiting the defeated South for their own corrupt purposes. Remembering Reconstruction became for whites a moral lesson about the evils of allowing blacks to vote and the necessity for whites to retain control of Southern society, despite external or internal threats. Official history books, literature, and family stories passed on the legend for generations. In the early twentieth century, Kentuckian D. W. Griffith's film *Birth of a Nation* refurbished the myth for new generations.

The New South

Southerners facing the twentieth century, though, were not just looking backward. Defeat had opened the way for forces of change and led to new symbols. The railroad became a vital force in the South after the Civil War. Atlanta became a city, *the* city of the New South, because of the railroad. Birmingham had been only a series of meadows and farms at the end of the Civil War, but when two rail lines met there, the iron and coal industries began to prosper and a new city appeared by 1900. The railroad released a Southern booster spirit that led the region's communities to compete vigorously, often giving generous subsidies, land grants, and easy operating charters to railroads that would locate nearby.

The railroad also entered the Southern imagination, symbolizing mobility and escape from the isolation of rural life. Musicians sang of the rails. Mississippian Jimmie Rodgers, "the Singing Brakeman," was the son of a section foreman and became the first star of country music partly through his train songs. Blues singer Peg Leg Sam also sang of the railroad, stories with added authenticity because he had lost a leg falling from a freight train. The train brought new heroes like Casey Jones and John Henry, who represented Southerners interacting with technology, an increasingly important force in Southern life in the early twentieth century.

Railroads had begun to play a more active role in the region in the 1870s, and the next decade had seen the proclamation of a New South, an ideology for modernization. Newspapermen, led by Atlanta's Henry Grady, preached an uplifting gospel to Southerners in the 1880s. The region needed to industrialize and diversify, to get beyond the cotton economy. The New South creed called for more factories, different crops, more scientific farming techniques, good work habits, increased education in general, harmonious race relations, and good relations with non-Southerners.

Results of the New South crusade included growth in towns and cities and a developing gap between those places and the rural countryside, where most Southerners continued to live. Merchants became key figures in the regional economy, sometimes the only sources of credit in the countryside and sometimes heading up giant new corporations that competed nationally.

The symbol that best represented this stage of Southern modernization was the textile mill. Wilbur J. Cash noted that the drive to bring cotton manufacturing to the South in the 1880s was "a mighty folk movement" and the "dream of virtually the whole southern people." Factories especially appeared in the Carolina Piedmont, where hydroelectric power made it desirable to locate mills in rural areas, near the source of the unskilled labor that the mills needed.

Mill villages became the locale where countless rural Southerners met the modern world, or at least a version of it. The old paternalism of the plantation became intertwined with the new logic of industrial capitalism. The mills used child labor, offered long, often grueling workweeks, and paid low wages (see page 82). They offered cash, though, and probably a better life than many had known as sharecroppers or struggling landowning small farmers. Many of the mill workers would later remember the sense of community and fellowship in the villages and their pride in work.

The twentieth-century South has been a peculiar combination of the traditional and the modern. The region's poverty and rural isolation led to retention of traditional ways and attitudes, despite the inroads of modernization symbolized by textile mills. With racial laws and customs hardening at the turn of the twentieth century, Southerners acted out a ritual of racial caste behavior, in which blacks were deferential and whites superior in all things. Although of recent historical origins, rigid racial segregation came to be seen by white Southerners as a long-established tradition.

Localism was a truer tradition. People learned values, ways to work and relax, courtship habits, and countless other behaviors from family and neighbors. Lives were lived out in the context of family, with household matters and kin relations of central importance to personal identity. Southern families prayed together, sang inherited songs together, ate distinctive regional food together, gossiped about the community, and sometimes fought one another, figuratively and literally. They upheld an ancient ethic of honor. If race relations were rigid, so were gender roles. Patriarchy characterized well-off and poor families, rural and urban, until changes in the economy and society after World War II brought dramatic change.

Evangelical religion has provided an enduring worldview for most Southerners, black and white, in the twentieth century as well as in the nineteenth. Evangelical Protestantism testifies that religious experience is the essence of the faith. Theology is important, key doctrines must be affirmed, worship services are vital for a congregation to thrive. But none of those dimensions matter if you have not been born again, if you have not "seen Jesus" and had your sins washed clean in the waters of baptism. Human nature is sinful, but salvation is within the grasp of the righteous, who then must live upright lives to show others the way.

The Baptist and Methodist churches, the embodiments of Evangelicalism, emerged in the early nineteenth century as the largest churches of the South, and their predominance has survived all the key events and social forces of Southern history. The pentecostal-holiness faith emerged in the late nineteenth and early twentieth centuries to reaffirm that the South was, to many believers, sacred ground for cultivating the religion of the spirit.

Despite the abiding impact of Southern traditionalism, dramatic change continued to characterize the twentieth-century South. The federal government played a key role, pushing the region to modernize through New Deal crop-reduction programs. These programs promoted a Southern enclosure movement, as landowners took land out of cultivation, collected their government checks, and left their sharecroppers to fend for themselves. Farm mechanization also pushed tenants and small farmers off the land and promoted migration to cities.

Modern Southerners have been migrants. Blacks began leaving the South in increasing numbers around World War I, as racial conflict and increasing economic hardship in the 1920s pushed them out of the rural South and toward industrial employment in the North and West. Three million African Americans fled the South from 1910 to 1960. Hundreds of thousands of whites from the Southern mountains, the hill country, and the Southern plains also left the region, most between 1930 and 1960, seeking opportunities elsewhere. Dorothea Lange's *Family on the Road, Oklahoma* (page 116) pictures people hitchhiking to a new life. The migration of such families transported Southern culture to the rest of the nation, establishing enclaves of regional culture in the soul food restaurants of south Chicago, the honky-tonk bars of Detroit, and the stock car tracks of Bakersfield.

City streets became the new places for Southerners to work out their destinies. A civic elite, made up of bankers, builders, insurance brokers, real estate agents, merchants, and professionals—a newly strong middle class—governed cities and pushed for growth. Chambers of Commerce and Rotary Clubs became fixtures of a South dedicated to progress, the word that city dwellers seemed to imbibe from the air, at least when it was not too polluted to breathe.

New Orleans was traditionally the South's leading urban area, but the twentieth century saw proliferating cities and the emergence of Atlanta, Charlotte, Memphis, Nashville, Miami, Dallas, Houston, and San Antonio as among the nation's most populous places. Rural culture moved to the city and became commercialized. This was most apparent in music. Nashville made mountain and hill musical traditions into the country music industry. Memphis's Beale Street nurtured the blues and then helped give birth to rock and roll in the 1950s.

World War II, which accelerated change in the South and proved to be the most memorable experience in the life of a generation, decisively broke the economic backwardness, isolation of country life, and the culture of poverty that had characterized the region since the Civil War. Southerners worked in the shipyards of the Atlantic and Gulf coasts, or gained jobs in the expanding aircraft, chemical, petroleum, machinery, and metals industries. *Fortune* magazine intoned that for the first time since the Civil War, "almost any native of the Deep South who wants a job can get one." Half of the nation's military installations were in the South, and about six million non-Southerners trained at them, introducing new influences into the region at the same time that millions of Southerners found themselves in once-unimagined European, Asian, or North African locales.

If World War II changed the South's traditional economic plight, the Civil Rights Movement helped temper the region's traditional racial obsessions. The National Association for the Advancement of Colored People had long pursued a strategy of challenging the legality of racial discrimination, and the Supreme Court's *Brown v. Board of Education* (1954) was a landmark victory, undermining any claim to the constitutionality of the Southern way of race relations.

The racial caste system remained in place, though, until the aggressive challenge of Southern blacks themselves, which began with the Montgomery Bus Boycott (1955–56) and the emergence of the charismatic Martin Luther King, Jr. Local black communities throughout the South launched grassroots organizing efforts that challenged white power through disciplined campaigns of nonviolent resistance. The new Southern symbols were lunch counters, swimming pools, school buses, and voting booths.

Whites responded with a resurgence of Confederate symbolism, evoking the Southern rebelliousness of a previous century. Terrorist groups like the Ku Klux Klan and its middle class equivalent, the Citizens' Council, led a campaign of massive resistance to desegregation. An image of screaming white teenagers (page 157) protesting the sight of black students suggests as well as anything can the wild emotions unleashed in the troubled South of the 1950s and 1960s.

Between 1963 and 1968, ninety-seven civil rights advocates were murdered in a frenzy that hallowed the efforts of those pushing a recalcitrant white South toward change. Eventually, the power of the federal government, combined with internal pressures in local Southern communities, brought down Jim Crow racial segregation and removed the obstacles to black voting rights.

By the 1970s, Southerners were wondering whether their region was still distinctive. Landmarks of Southern uniqueness within the nation had toppled: cotton was no longer king, replaced by the soybean, which was economically profitable but an uninspiring symbol; the Democratic party had been the basis of a Solid South for a hundred years, but when Richard Nixon's Republican party swept the region in 1972 it represented the rise of a two-party political system; the peculiar institution of Jim Crow legal segregation was over and the South's race relations, while still troubled, seemed indistinct from those of the rest of the nation.

Journalists talked of the Americanization of the South. Such homogenizing forces as interstate highways, shopping malls, and airports undermined regional differences. Americans now ate the same McDonald's hamburger in Macon as in Sausalito. Transportation and communication links not only drew regions into tighter national networks but made everyone a part of a global village.

By this time Southerners had laid claim to considerable renown for their cultural achievements, especially in such fields as literature and music. Nobel laureate William Faulkner was only the most acclaimed of the writers of the Southern Literary Renaissance, which had emerged in the years between the first and second World Wars. The Renaissance went beyond literature and included Pulitzer Prize–winning journalists, accomplished social scientists, respected historians, and popular musicians.

Developments in music were especially revealing of broader patterns. Singing had long been a part of the South's folk culture, a shared ritual of families, church members, and neighbors. In the twentieth century, this folk culture evolved into a popular culture that may now best represent the South's continuing distinctiveness. A poor white boy from Mississippi, who grew up listening to Nashville's Grand Ole Opry and to Memphis's black radio station, Elvis Presley became one of the major celebrities of the modern age. Presley helped to synthesize white country music, black blues, and Southern gospel. He was a result of the cultural integration that had slowly taken place between the region's two predominant ethnic groups—whites of British ancestry and blacks of African heritage. The twentieth-century South remained a biracial society, as it had been from the beginning.

But a quieter, less-noticed story was that blacks and whites shaped a common culture in the South. In the course of occupying the same soil for three-and-a-half centuries, Southern blacks and whites had exchanged cultural knowledge. One saw it in everyday life, in the food they ate. Barbecued ribs, fried chicken, grits, cornbread, okra, black-eyed peas—these went into a cauldron of racial amalgamation, in which meat and vegetables, recipes, and ways of cooking boiled down into a new stew distinctive to the South. One saw cultural interaction in recreation, as males—black and white—hunted the South's forests and trails, while the region's women appreciated the social life and aesthetic accomplishments of the quilting bee.

One saw cultural interaction in religion but also religion's tragic limitations. Blacks and whites both valued spiritual life, sharing a moralistic Protestant outlook and an otherworldly theology. Yet they worshiped in segregated congregations, so that, as Dr. King said, 11 A.M. on Sunday morning remains the most segregated time in the South.

As the United States and the rest of the world prepare for the twenty-first century, a time in which the Western nations will increasingly interact with peoples from many cultures around the globe, the Southern story will likely continue to resonate. The Southern saga is of peoples from dramatically different cultures trying to live together and build a society. The story includes injustice and tragic moments, but it also reveals heroic struggle and the possibility of change and reconciliation. It is the South's legacy to the world.

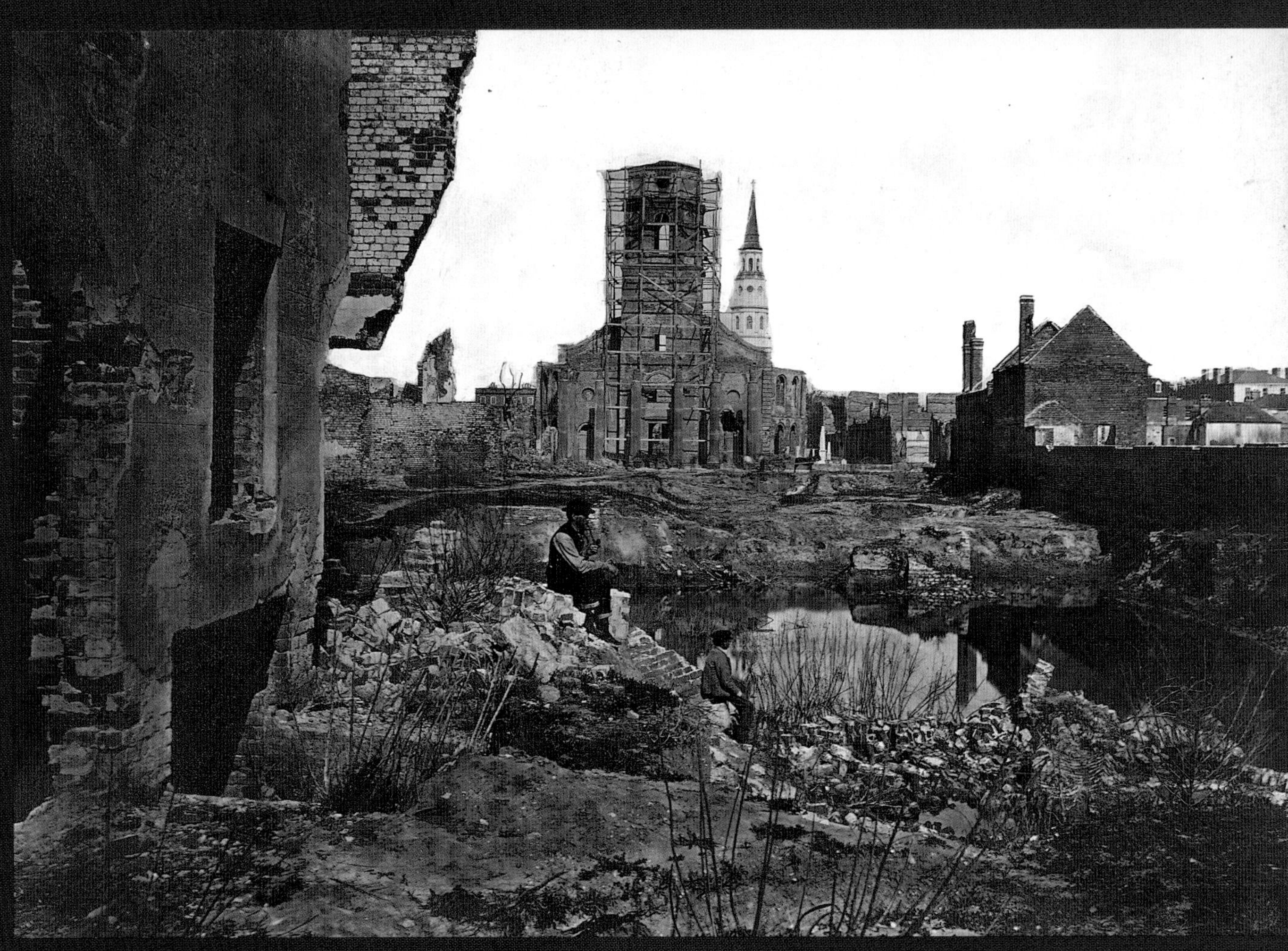

GEORGE N. BARNARD

Ruins in Charleston, South Carolina from the album "Photographic Views of Sherman's Campaign" 1865 or 1866

WILLIAM BALDWIN

POSSESSIONS

In 1952 or thereabouts, our family was living in the small town of Bluffton, South Carolina. We had put Savannah behind us—twenty miles behind us. My father, a U.S. Fish and Wildlife biologist, still drove to the city to work, but we were out of the crackerbox duplex in treeless "Oakwood" subdivision. We had a home of our own. Small but new, and on the salt marsh with great moss-spangled live oaks on every side. I was eight years old and my mother became a partner in an antiques shop. And she took me on as an assistant . . . of sorts.

The new house had been a wild extravagance and left no money for purchasing antiques, so my mother and her cousin Anne searched the Salvation Army and Goodwill stores in Savannah for misplaced heirlooms. A bedraggled china-headed doll bought for a dime sold for eighty dollars. Some battered tin plates turned out to be pewter. A pewter mug turned out to be a silver cup made in London two centuries earlier. My mother kept that. There was magic in old things.

My mother and her cousin Anne would load us children (six in all) in the back of Anne's station wagon and take the ferry to Hilton Head Island.

Only two white families on the island that I recall and three or four automobiles. Black men straddled marsh tacky ponies. The bare feet of these men brushed the ground. Orange trees growing wild. A semi-lost world.

But we hadn't come as tourists. We children were driven to old Fort Walker on the north end of the island and put to work combing the concrete ruins, the beach, and the adjoining creek banks. We filled bushel baskets with cannon balls, musket balls, wine bottles, china, and even coins. Some of this was Spanish-American War debris. Most dated from the Civil War.

In November of 1861 a Union fleet of seventy-seven vessels had sailed into view. On neighboring St. Helena Island the local militia got drunk and had a lancing tournament in preparation for battle, but here on Hilton Head a thousand grim-faced reinforcements dug in to defend Fort Walker's artillery batteries. To no avail. The Northern fleet represented the largest concentration of firepower ever known since the beginning of time, and in a matter of hours strategic Port Royal Sound was lost and Hilton Head was abandoned. The plantation owners escaped to Bluffton. Then, realizing that their mansions would give comfort to the enemy, the most zealous slipped back to the island and burned down their own homes—and those of their neighbors as well. Such buffoonery. Such lethal buffoonery. By April of 1865 it had killed 600,000 men.

On the mainland trips I would go alone with my mother. She would drive into the black neighborhoods ten miles away. Twenty miles away. Fifty miles away. She was a small woman. She would slide over against the driver's-side door and prop me, an eight-year-old, behind the steering wheel of the slowly moving automobile. Then she would extend herself half out of the window but somehow manage to keep her toe on the accelerator.

"You got any old things?" That's what she shouted at the black inhabitants. Then back at me she'd shout, "Stay on the road!" Then back out the window: "You got any old things?"

They did. Black women with wizened or cherubic faces and all with kerchiefed heads waved her over and led us past the scrap-lumber shanties and into their backyard sheds. Antebellum furniture. Bottomless three-legged chairs. Broken-back lowboys. Chicken droppings on top and the legs eaten away by termites. Most of these things were bought for next to nothing, washed off, patched up, and sold for a few dollars more.

"When the big houses burned, they carried this furniture out." That was my mother's explanation, one that made sense . . . sort of. She didn't bother to add that she and I were systematically following the path of Sherman's March. Sherman, as the old joke goes, said "War is hell!" and set out to prove it. He burned Atlanta, marched to the sea, bivouacked in an unharmed Savannah for Christmas of 1865, and headed off for Columbia. Once in South Carolina, his men burned practically everything they came to. The white residents fled and the freed slaves emptied the houses of furniture before they were lit. And eighty-five years later a white woman came by shouting "You got any old things?" An eight-year-old boy was driving the car.

Actually, it took me another forty years to figure this out. I was working on a tour guidebook and traveling those same roads with my aging father. Since leaving the government in 1955, he'd been working with modern-day plantation owners as a wildlife management consultant and selling plantations as well. He knew poor old Jasper County like the back of his Wilmington, Delaware, carpetbagging hand. He muttered, "Sherman, that bastard." We stayed in a motel. He sat up in the middle of the night, looked straight at me, and said, "The plantation. You understand. The place." He was still sound asleep. I said "Yes," which was only a partial lie, and he lay down.

I'm a sucker for old photographs. Once I bought a secondhand copy stand and tried to copy every family album in the vicinity. Another time I rode the train to Washington, D.C., to look at the "Southern" WPA photographs in the Library of Congress. It took three-and-a-half days of steady flipping.

Every picture tells a story. That's oh so true. One in *Picturing the South* is labeled *Hamilton, a Slave at the Legare Plantation, Capers Island, South Carolina* (page 27). A man is shown climbing into a carriage. A house in the background with women occupants. A second man holds the horse steady. I assume that the humble horse-holder is "Hamilton, a Slave."

Now, the census records of 1820 put my great-great-great-grandfather on Capers Island. He married one of the Legare daughters and they went to the Indian frontier of Alabama. She went insane and died. He came back with his family to McClellanville, South Carolina, which is where I live today—which is where I sit studying the picture of Hamilton the slave and reflecting on the fact that my mother's people owned this man.

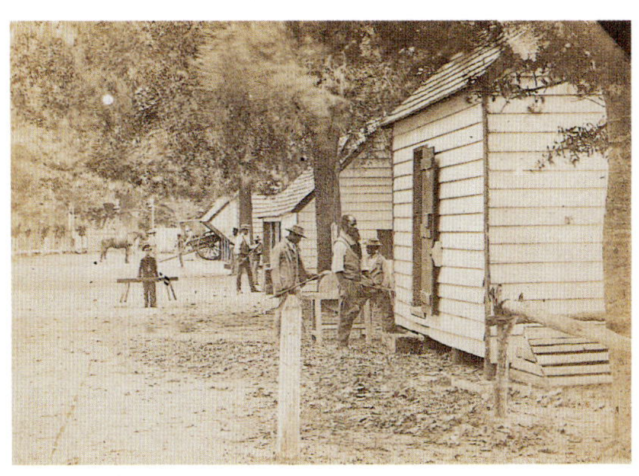

UNIDENTIFIED PHOTOGRAPHER
Negro Quarters, Perseverance Plantation, Goose Creek Parish, South Carolina
ca. 1860–63

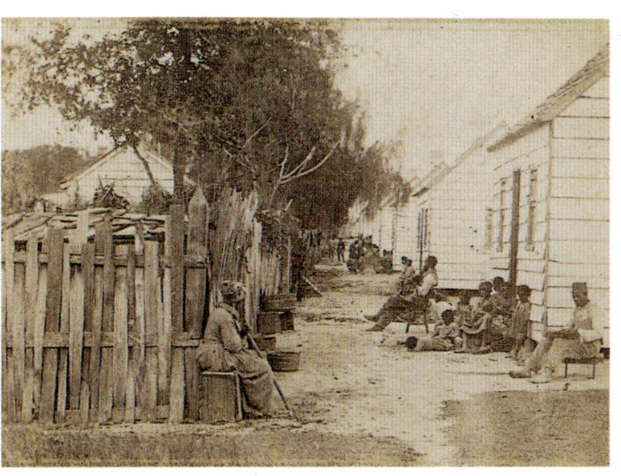

UNIDENTIFIED PHOTOGRAPHER
Negro Quarters, Perseverance Plantation, Goose Creek Parish, South Carolina
ca. 1860–63

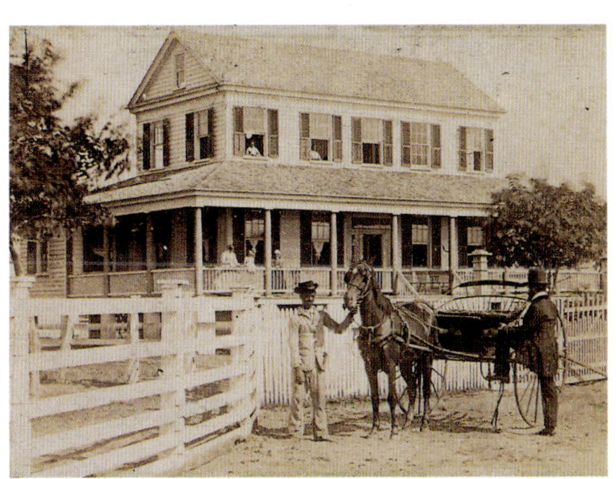

UNIDENTIFIED PHOTOGRAPHER
Hamilton, a Slave at the Legare Plantation, Capers Island, South Carolina
ca. 1860–63

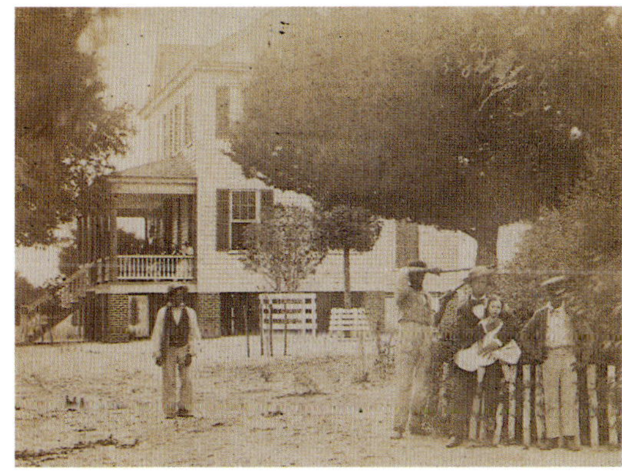

UNIDENTIFIED PHOTOGRAPHER
Slaves Going to Church, Bryan Plantation, Folly Island, South Carolina
ca. 1860–63

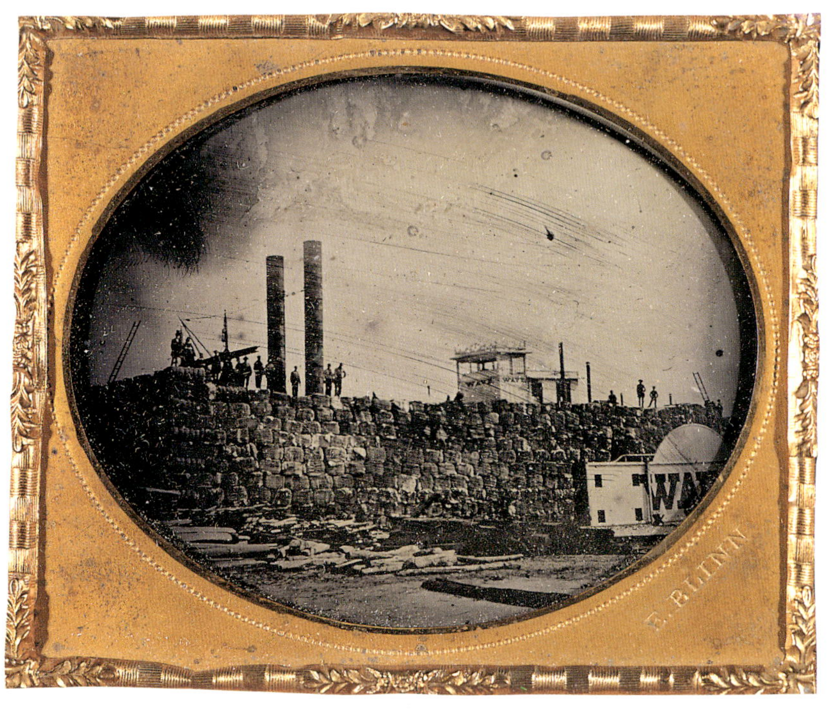

E. B. LINN

Cotton on the Steamboat Wave

ca. 1860

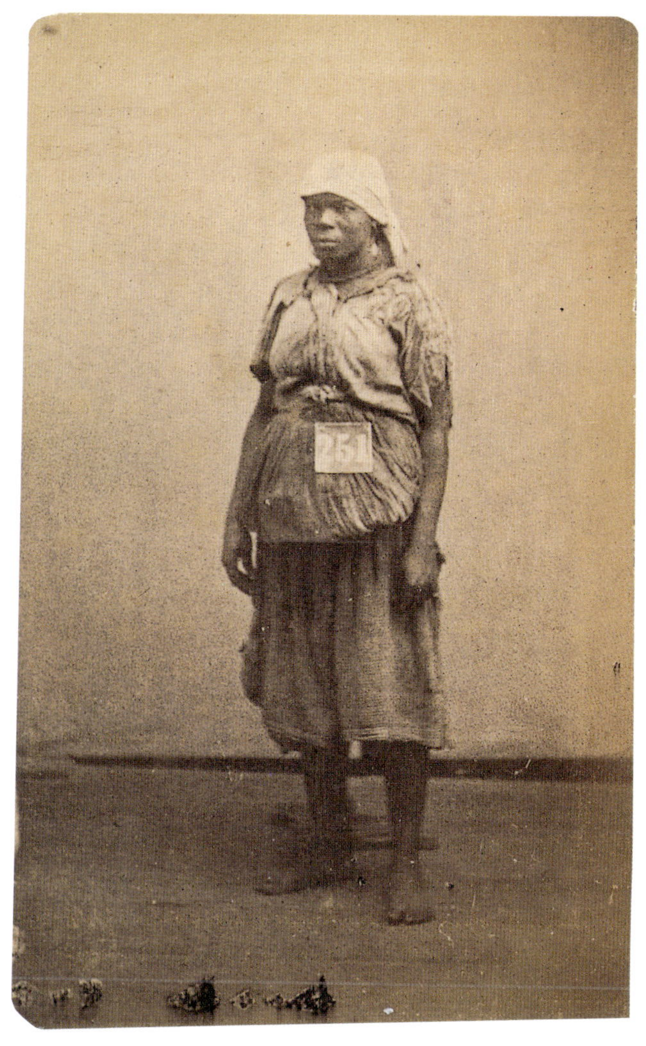

UNIDENTIFIED PHOTOGRAPHER
Slave with Inventory Number
ca. 1860

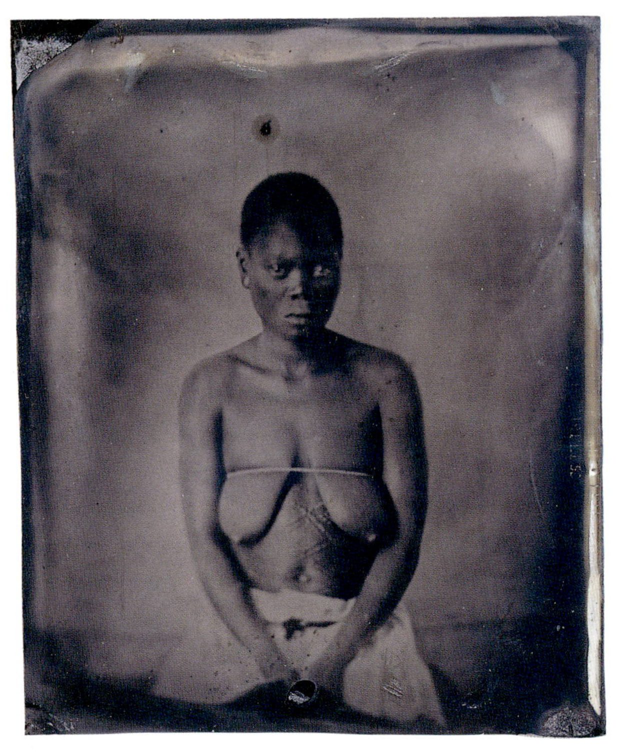

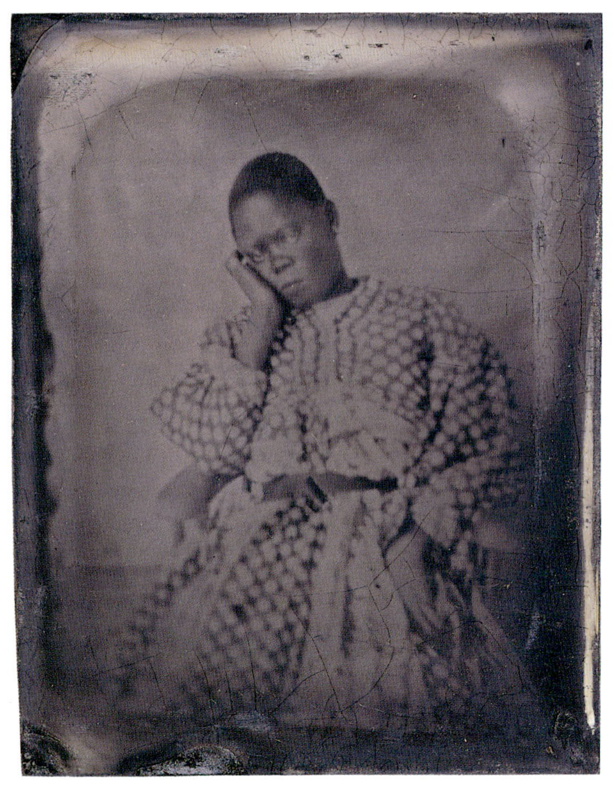

UNIDENTIFIED PHOTOGRAPHER

Portraits of an Unidentified Slave

ca. 1860–63

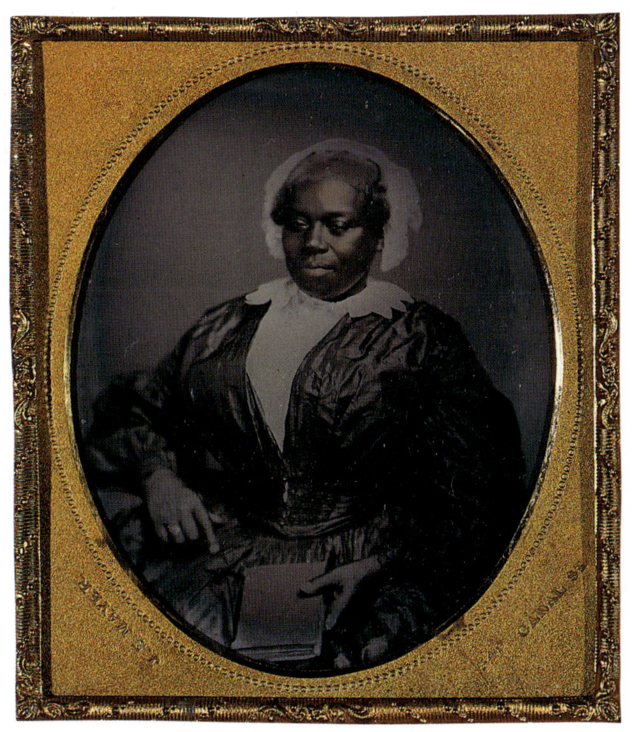

J. S. MAYER
Free Woman of Color, New Orleans, Louisiana
1850–60

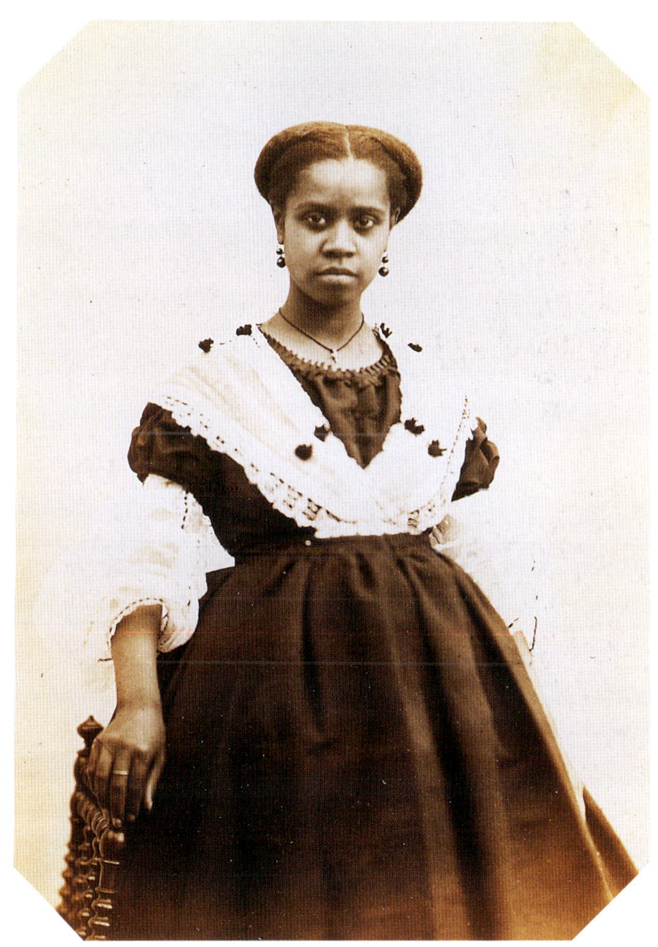

LOUIS ROUSSEAU
Portrait of Marie Lassus, New Orleans
1860

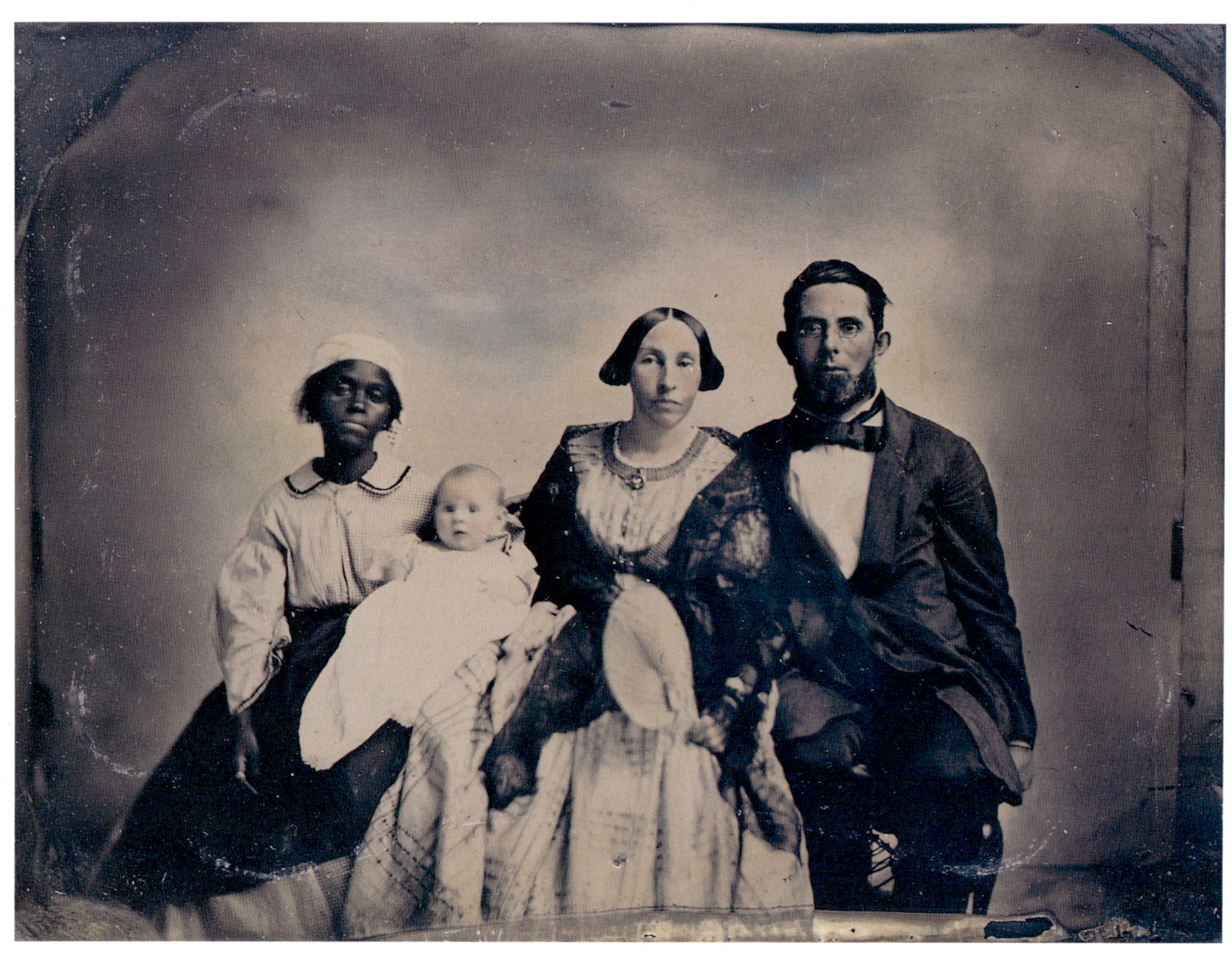

UNIDENTIFIED PHOTOGRAPHER

Portrait of a Planter's Family and Slave, New Market, Virginia

ca. 1859–64

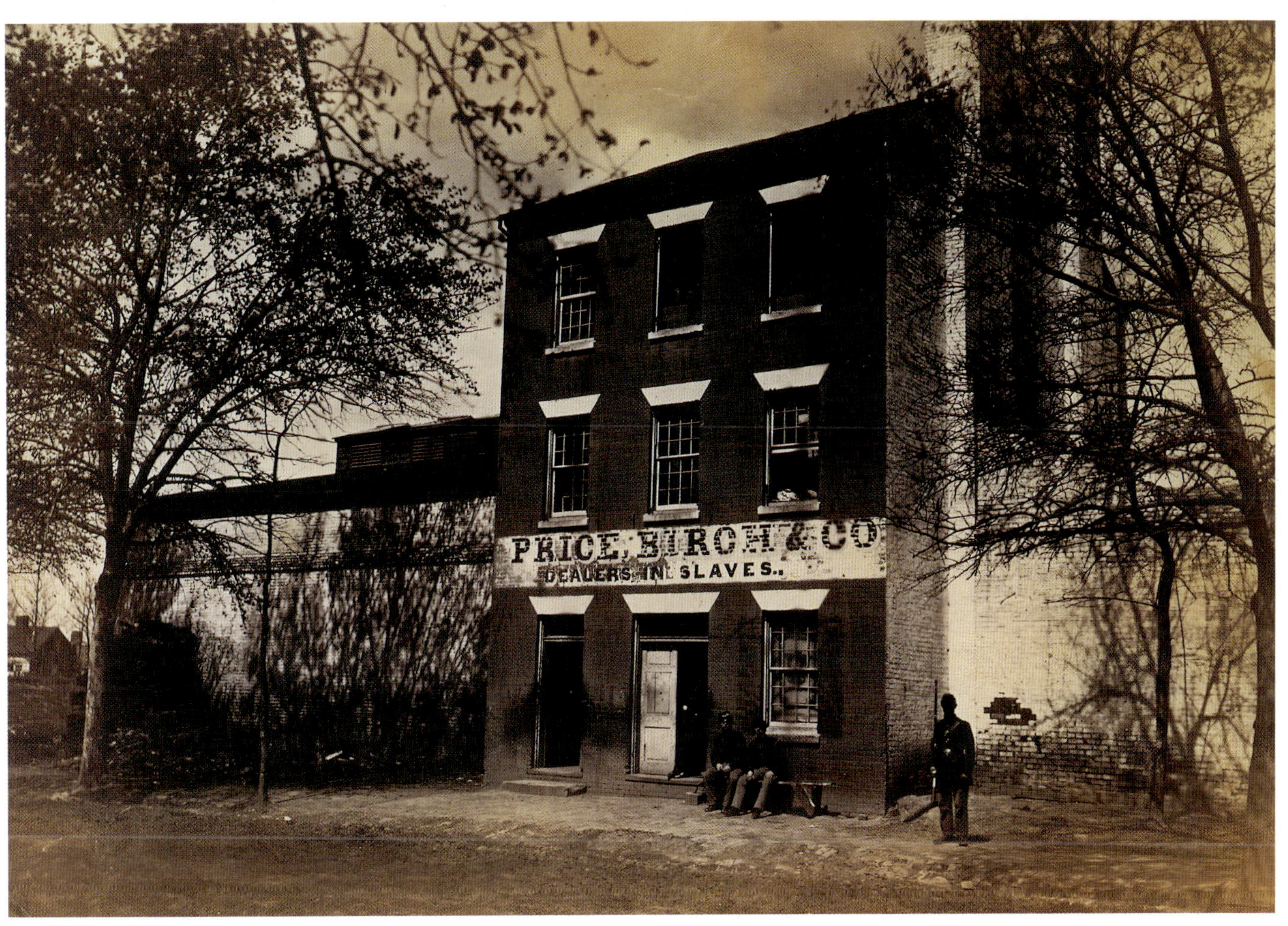

ANDREW JOSEPH RUSSELL

Slave Pen, Alexandria, Virginia

ca. 1863

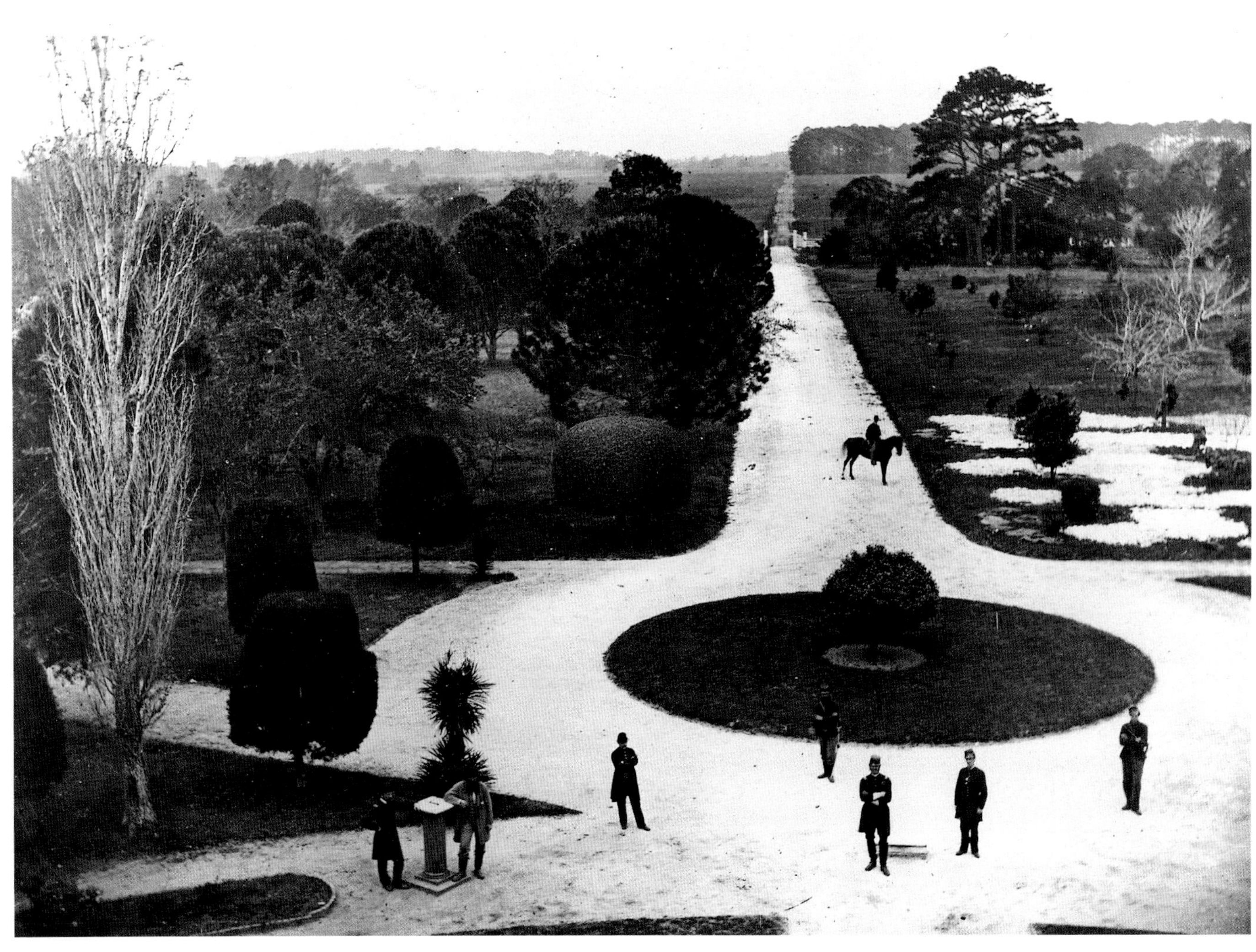

UNIDENTIFIED PHOTOGRAPHER

View of Park, James E. Seabrook's Plantation, Edisto Island, South Carolina

1862

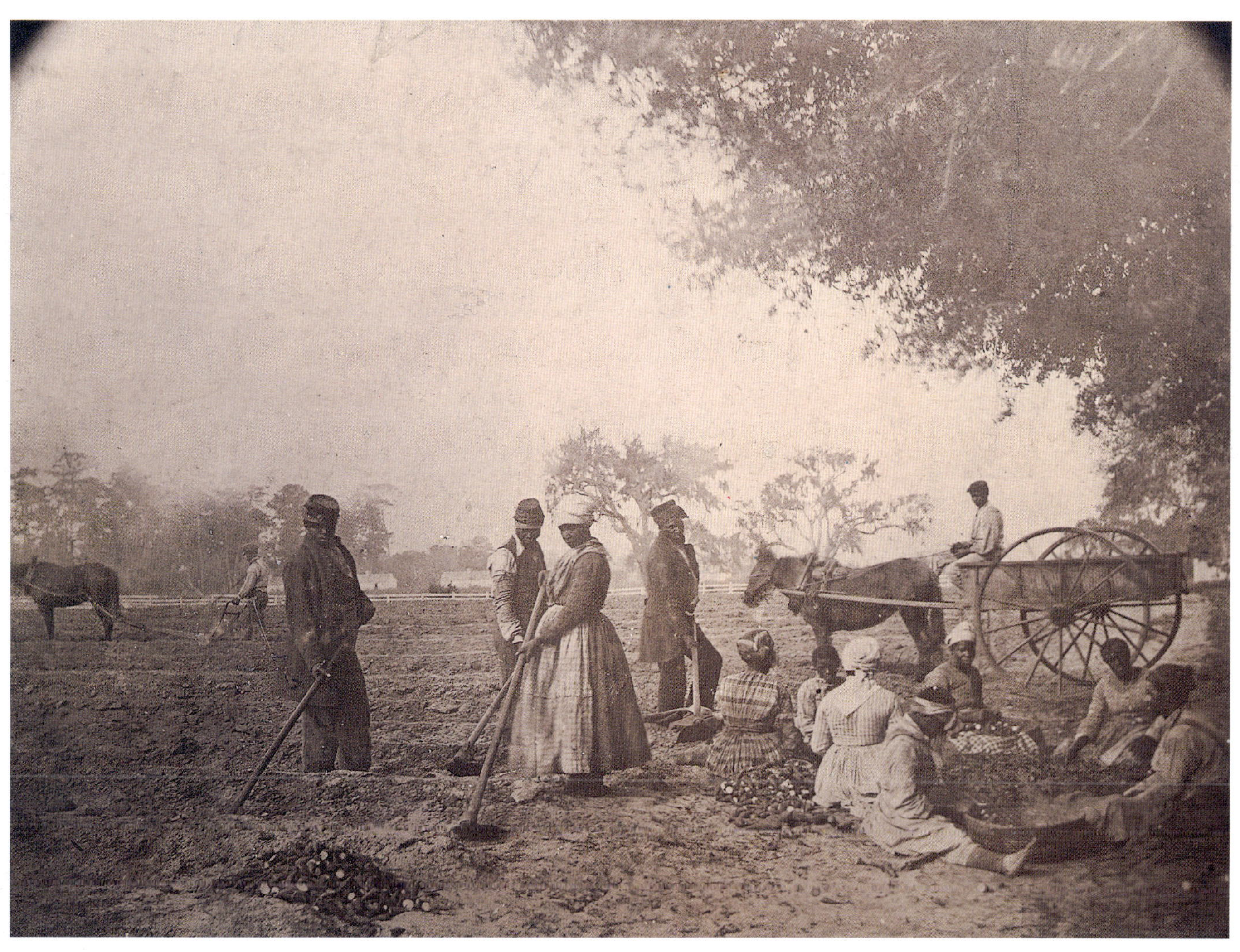

HENRY P. MOORE

Planting Sweet Potatoes, James Hopkinson's Plantation, Edisto Island, South Carolina

1862

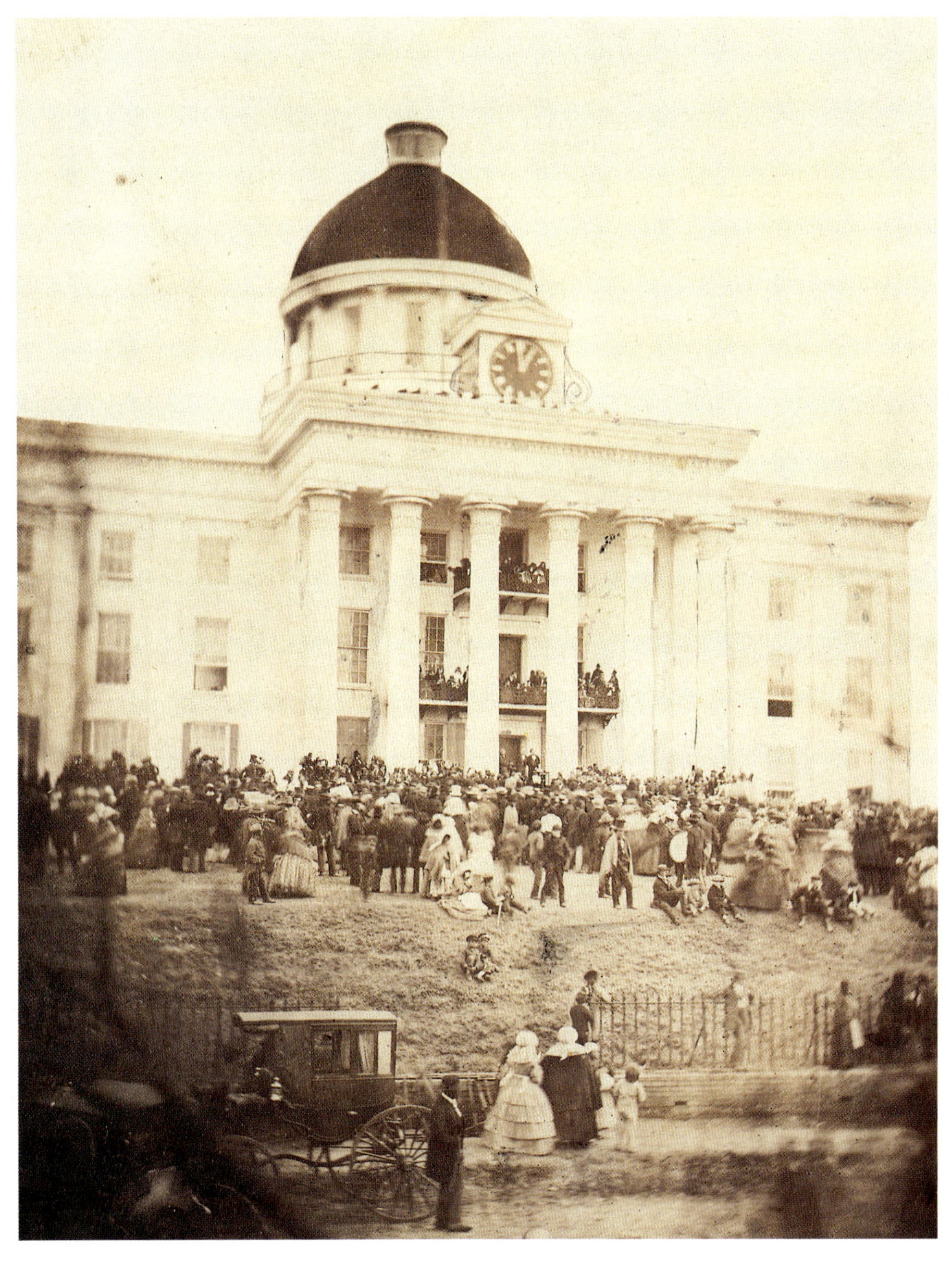

ARCHIBALD CROSSLAND MC INTYRE

First Inauguration of Jefferson Davis as President of the Confederate States of America at Montgomery, Alabama

February 18, 1861

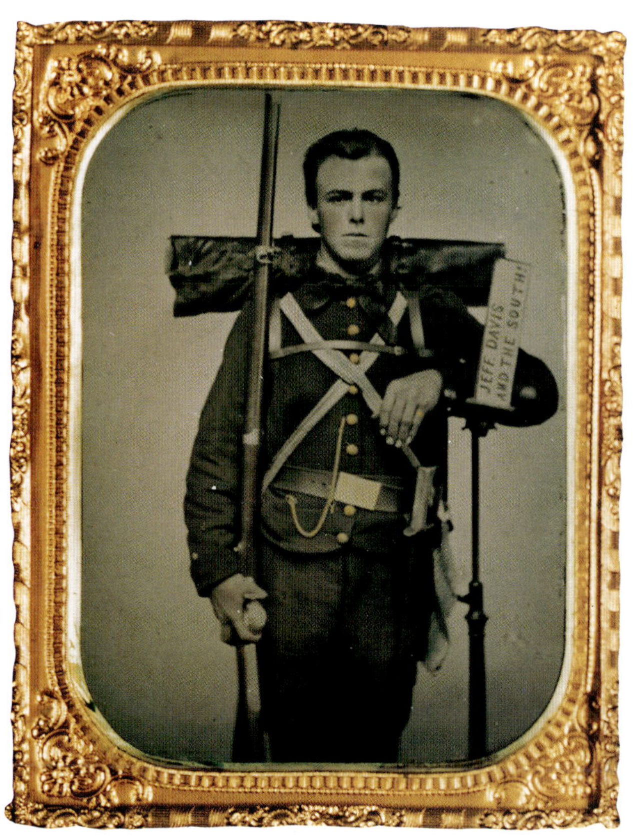

UNIDENTIFIED PHOTOGRAPHER

Portrait of an Alabama Infantryman

ca. 1861

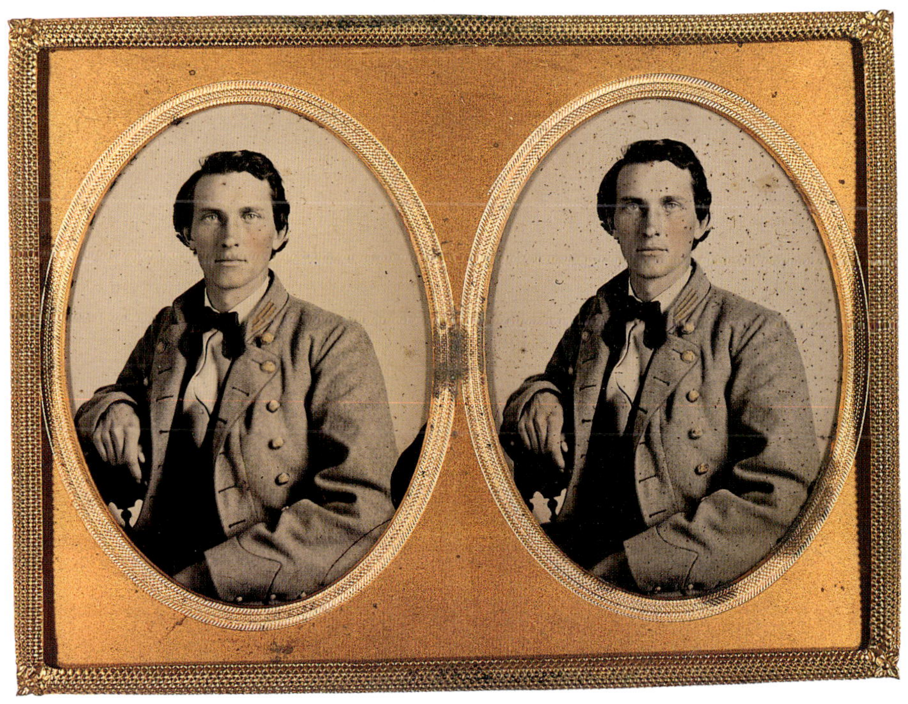

UNIDENTIFIED PHOTOGRAPHER

Portrait of Columbus W. Motes, Troup Artillery

1861–65

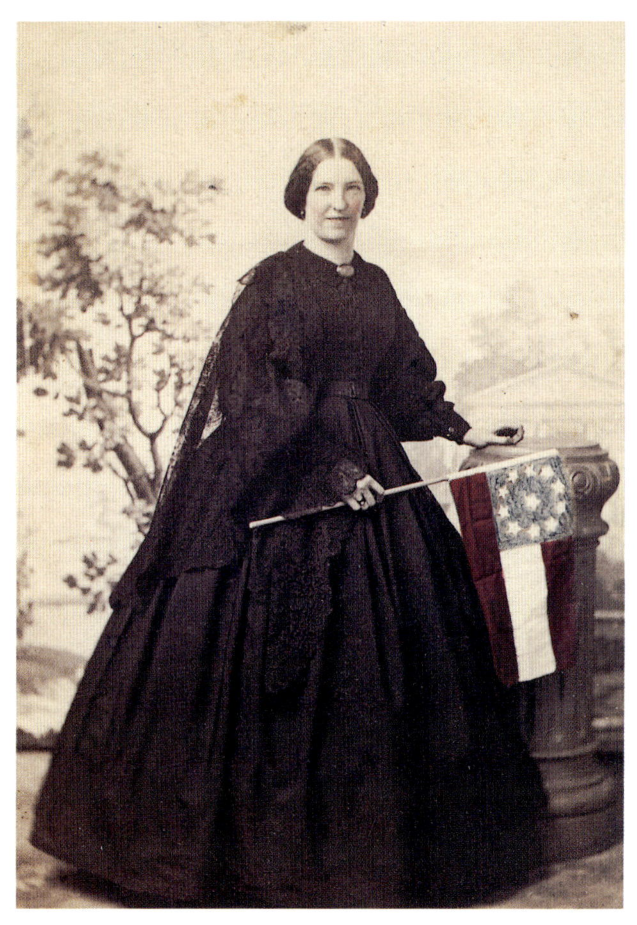

UNIDENTIFIED PHOTOGRAPHER

Portrait of Mrs. Ridgley-Brown

1861–65

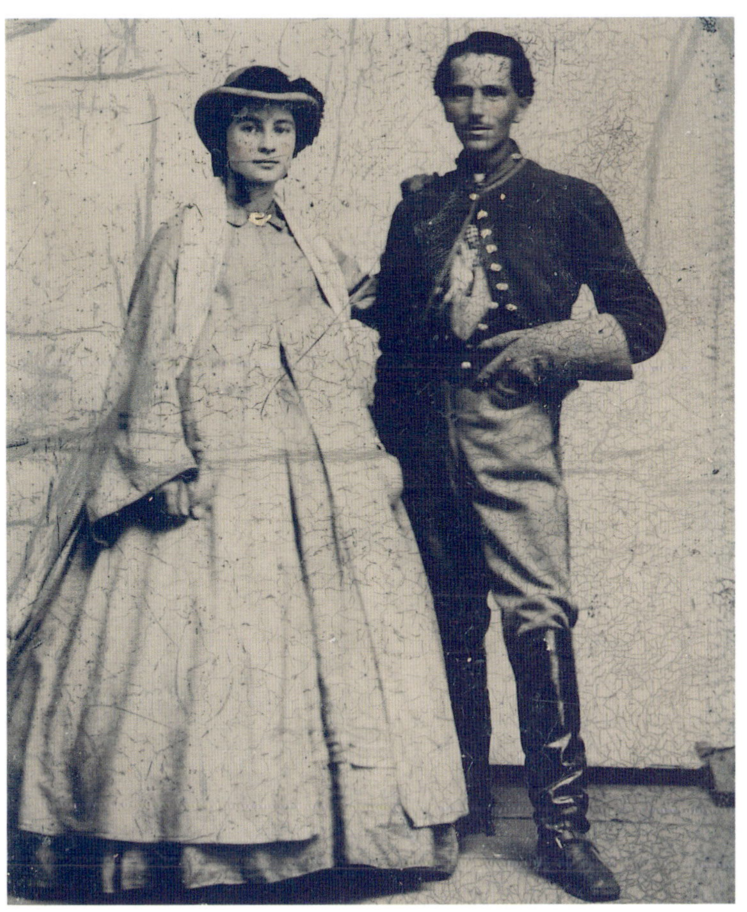

UNIDENTIFIED PHOTOGRAPHER
Portrait of an Unidentified Woman and a Confederate Cavalryman
1861–65

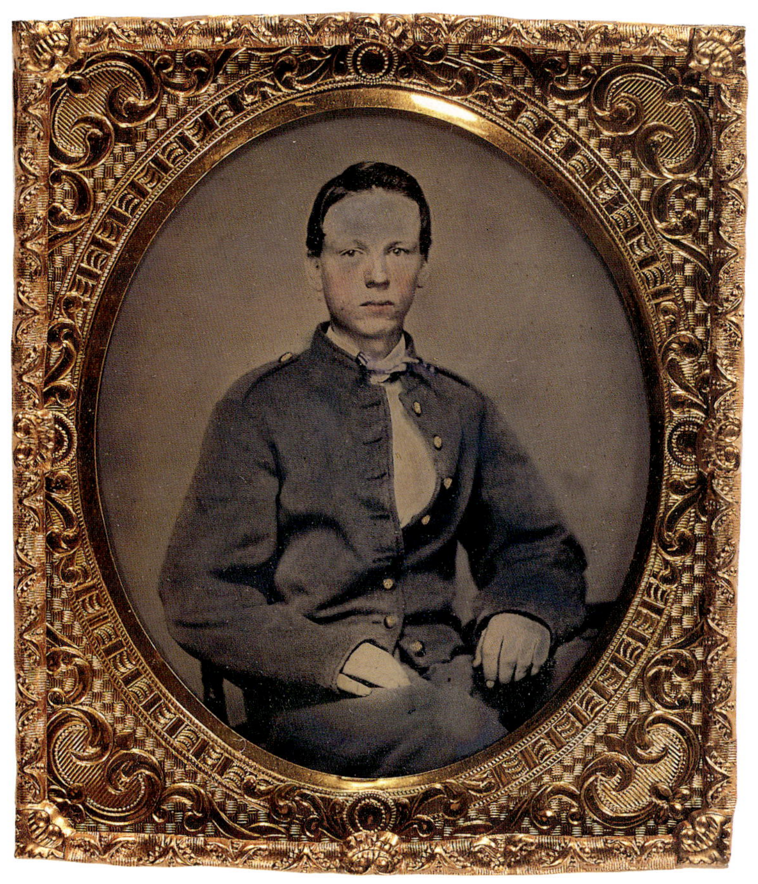

UNIDENTIFIED PHOTOGRAPHER

Portrait of Private Alexander Harris, Parker's Virginia Battery

1861–65

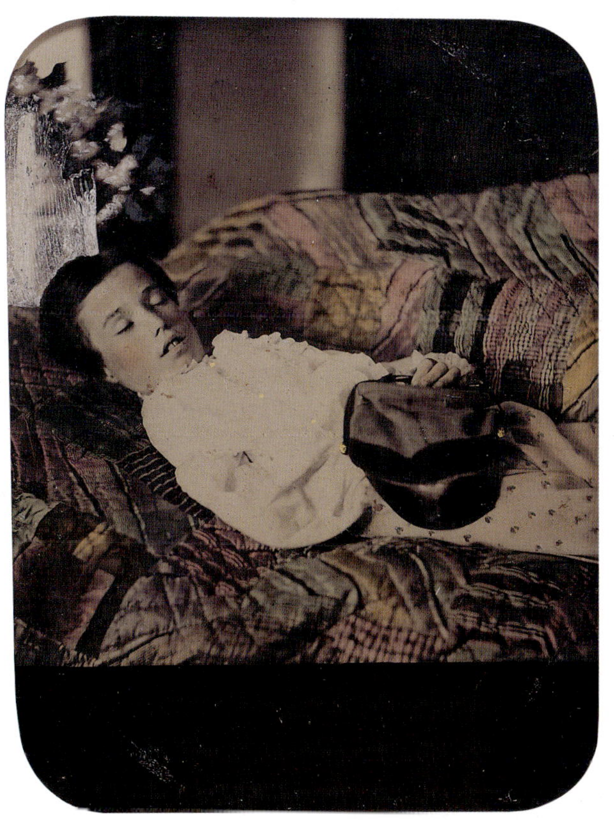

UNIDENTIFIED PHOTOGRAPHER

Post-Mortem Portrait of Charles Bostrick Marshall, Mobile, Alabama

1861–65

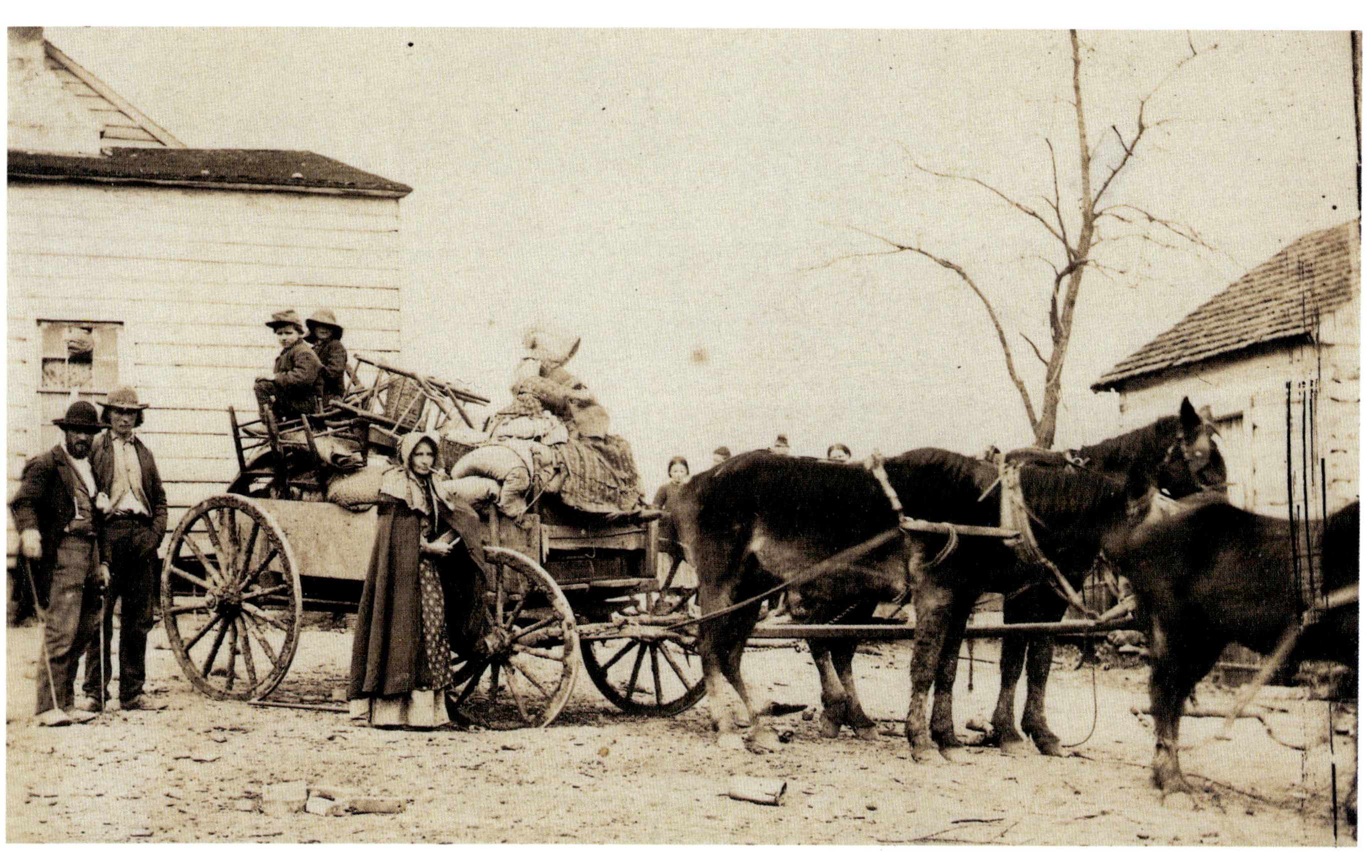

BARNARD & GIBSON

Departure from the Old Homestead, Centreville, Virginia from the series "Brady's Album Gallery"
1862

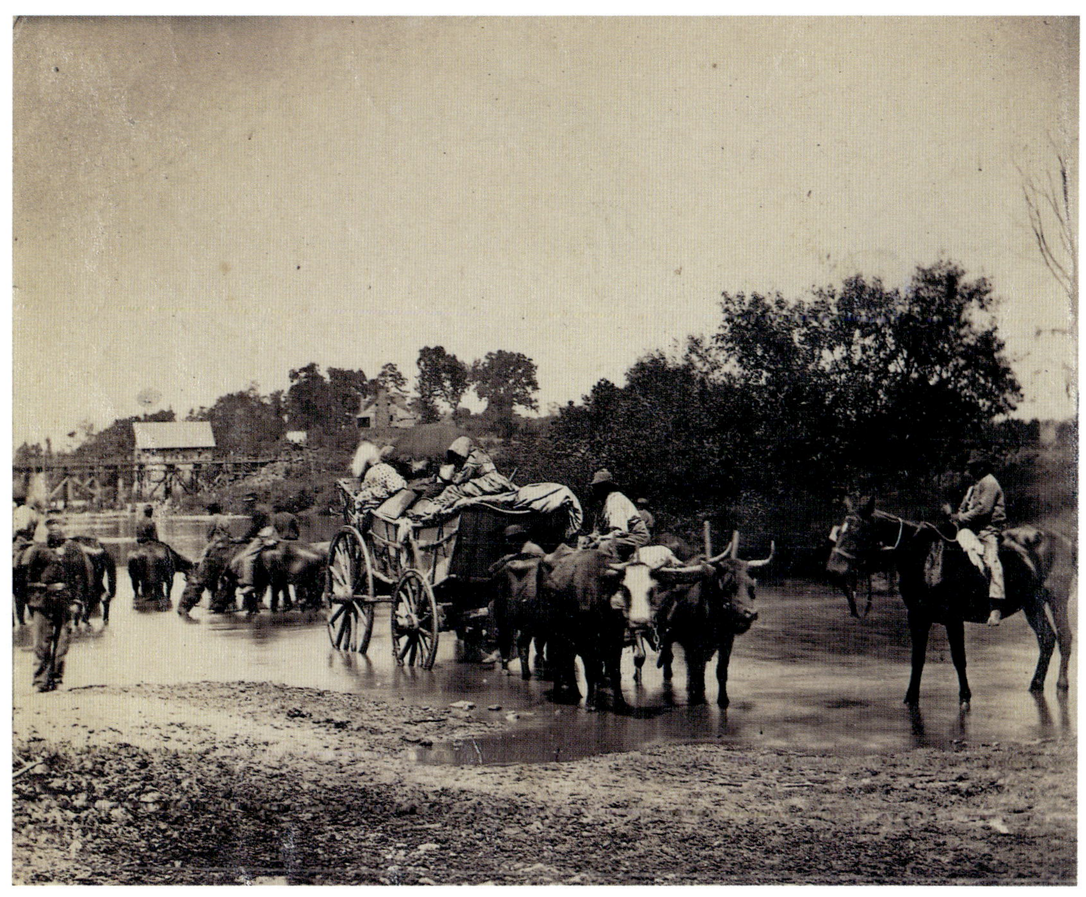

TIMOTHY O'SULLIVAN

Fugitive Slaves Fording the Rappahannock River, Virginia (detail)

1862

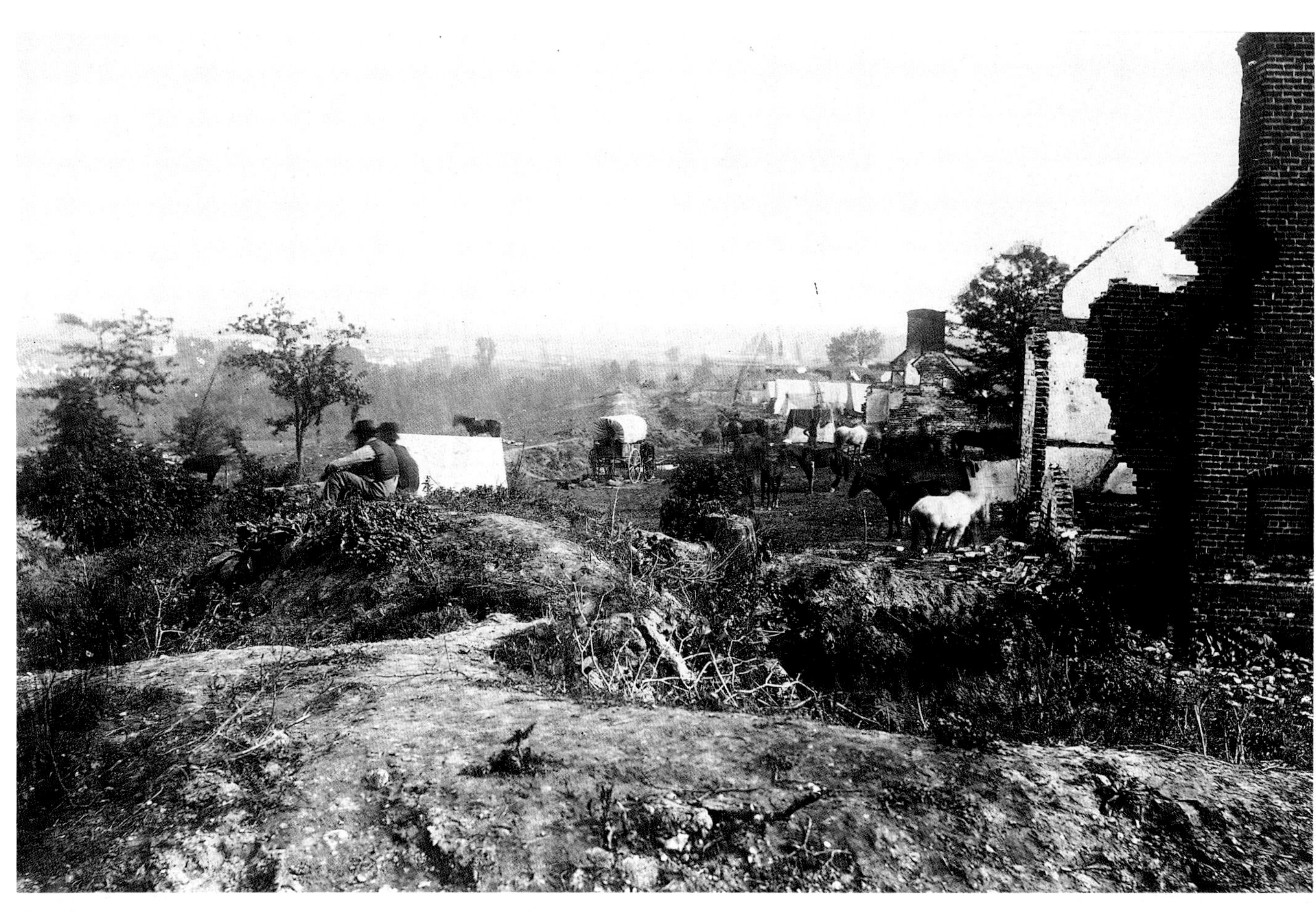

ATTRIBUTED TO MATHEW BRADY STUDIO

Ruins of the Willis House, Marye's Heights, Fredericksburg, Virginia

ca. 1864

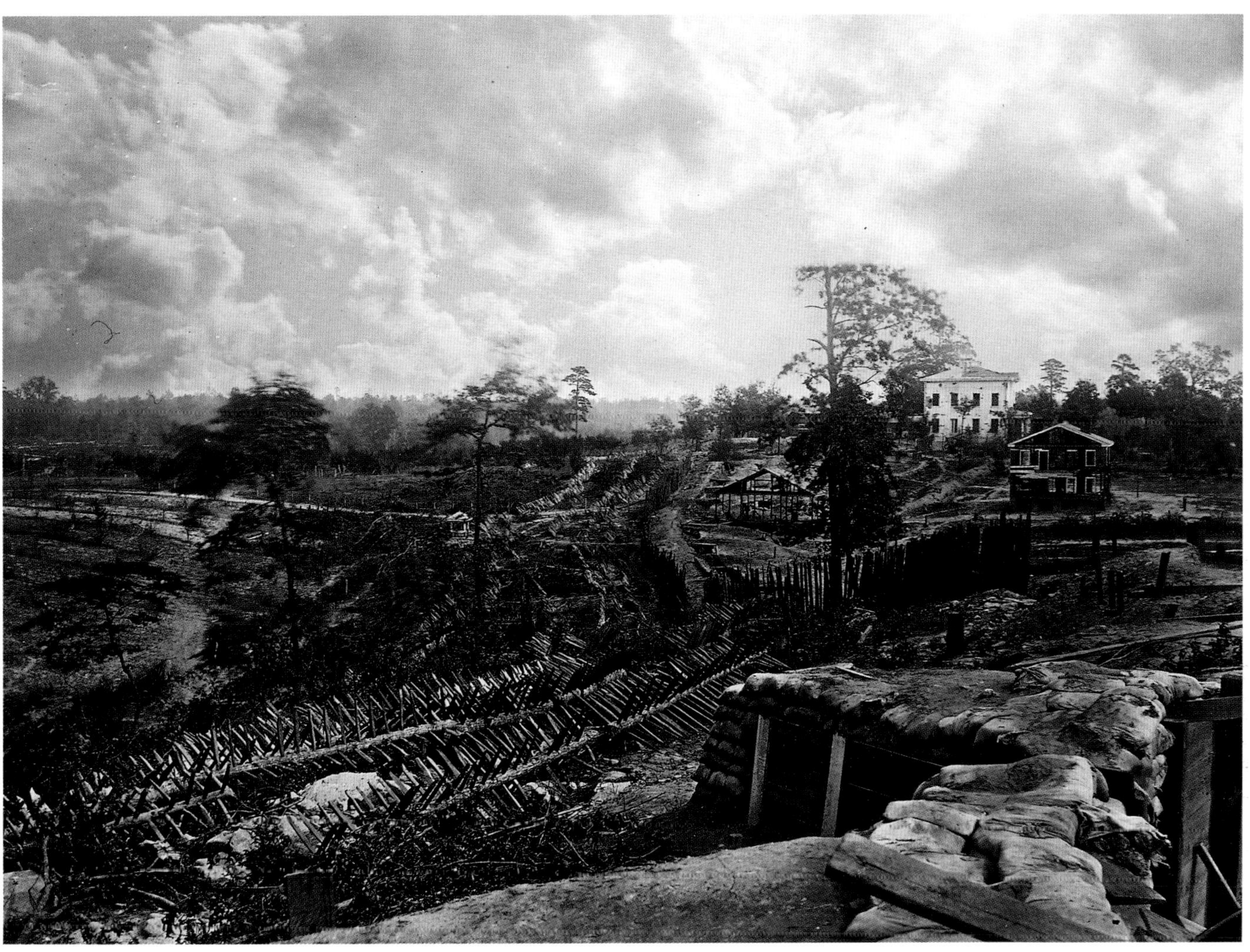

GEORGE N. BARNARD

Rebel Works in Front of Atlanta, Georgia, No. 1 from the album "Photographic Views of Sherman's Campaign"
1864

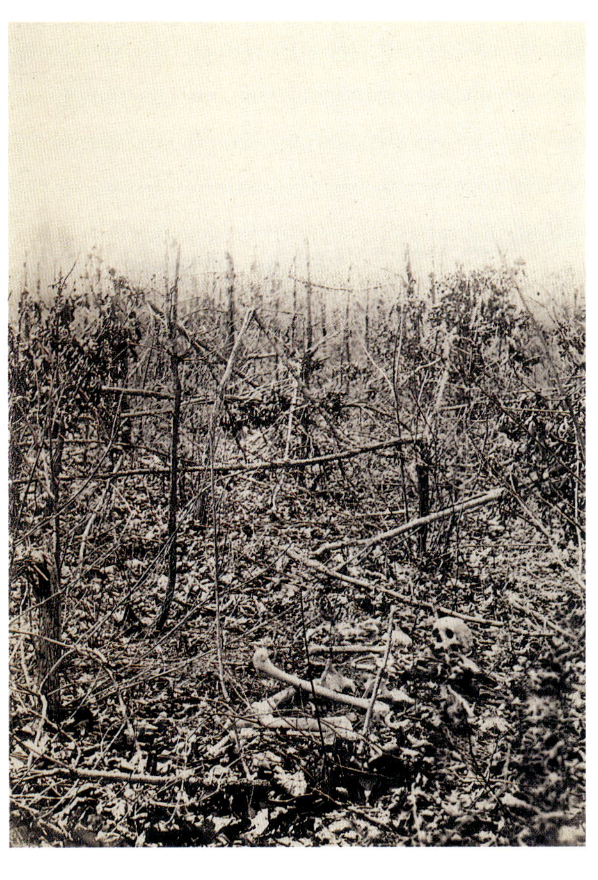

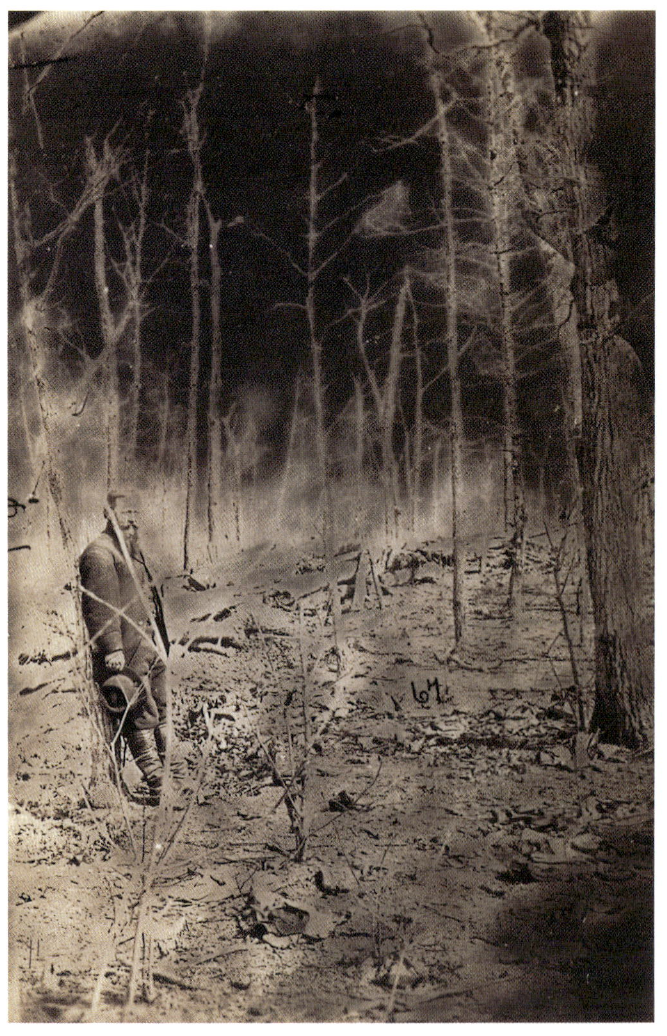

UNIDENTIFIED PHOTOGRAPHER
The Wilderness Battlefield
1865–67

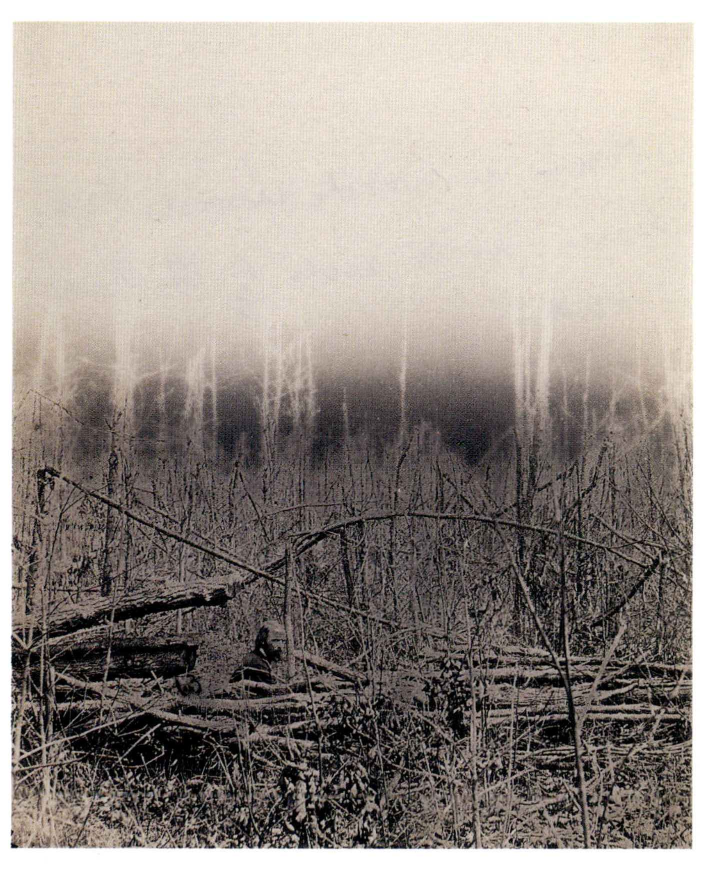

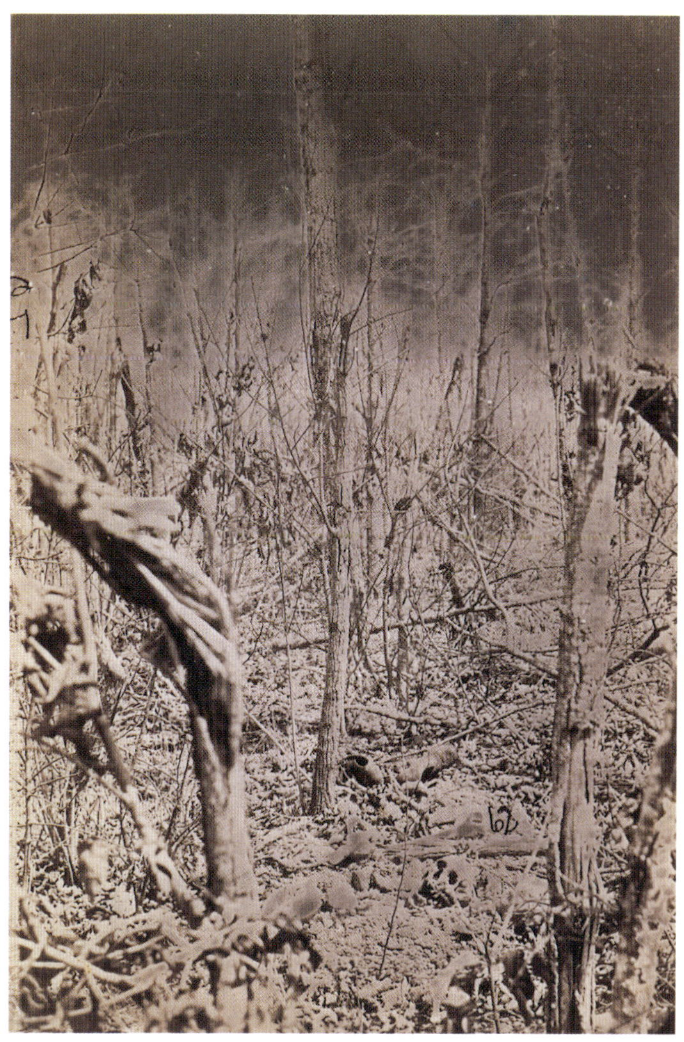

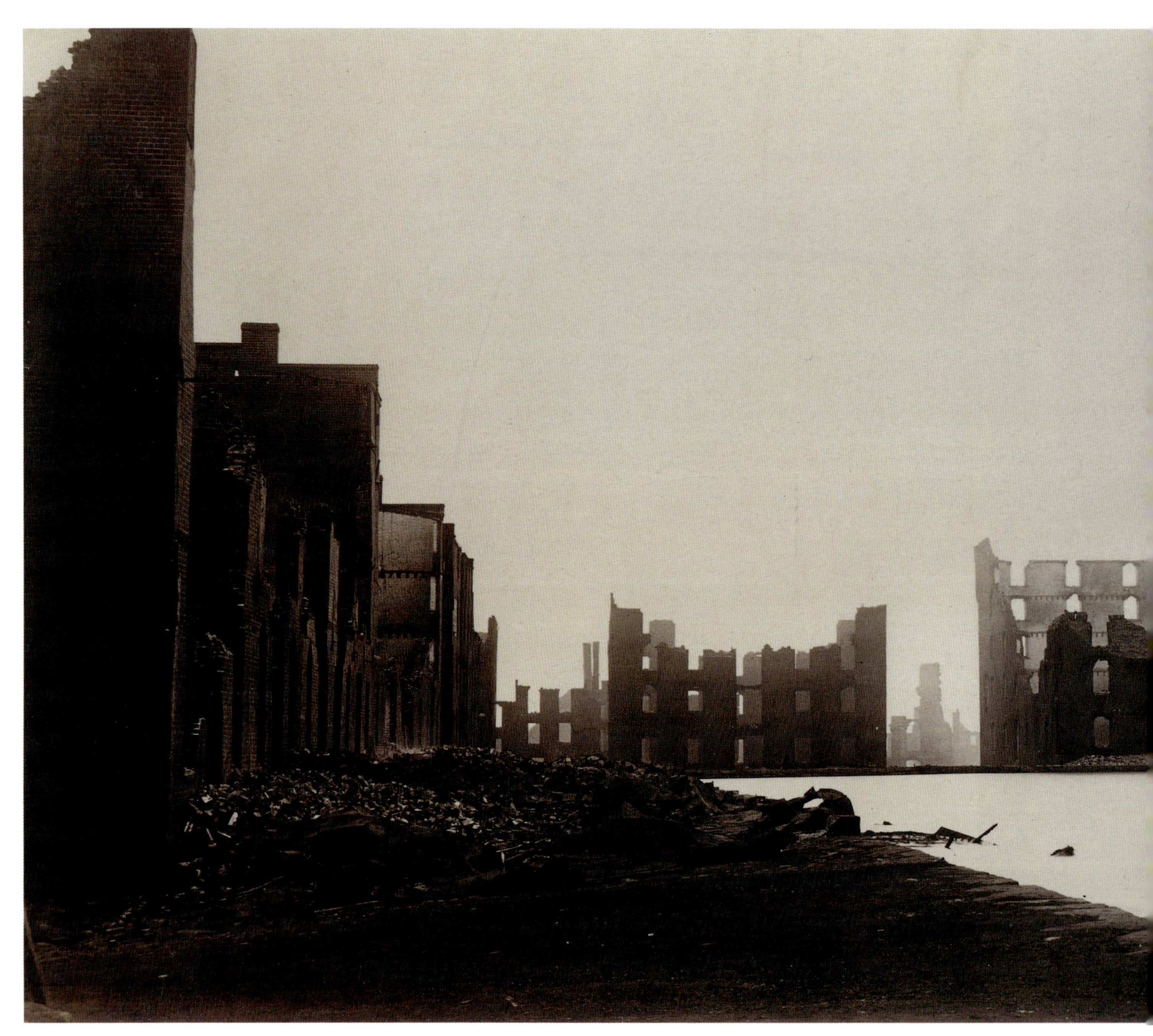

ALEXANDER GARDNER

Ruins of Gallego Flour Mills, Richmond, Virginia

1865

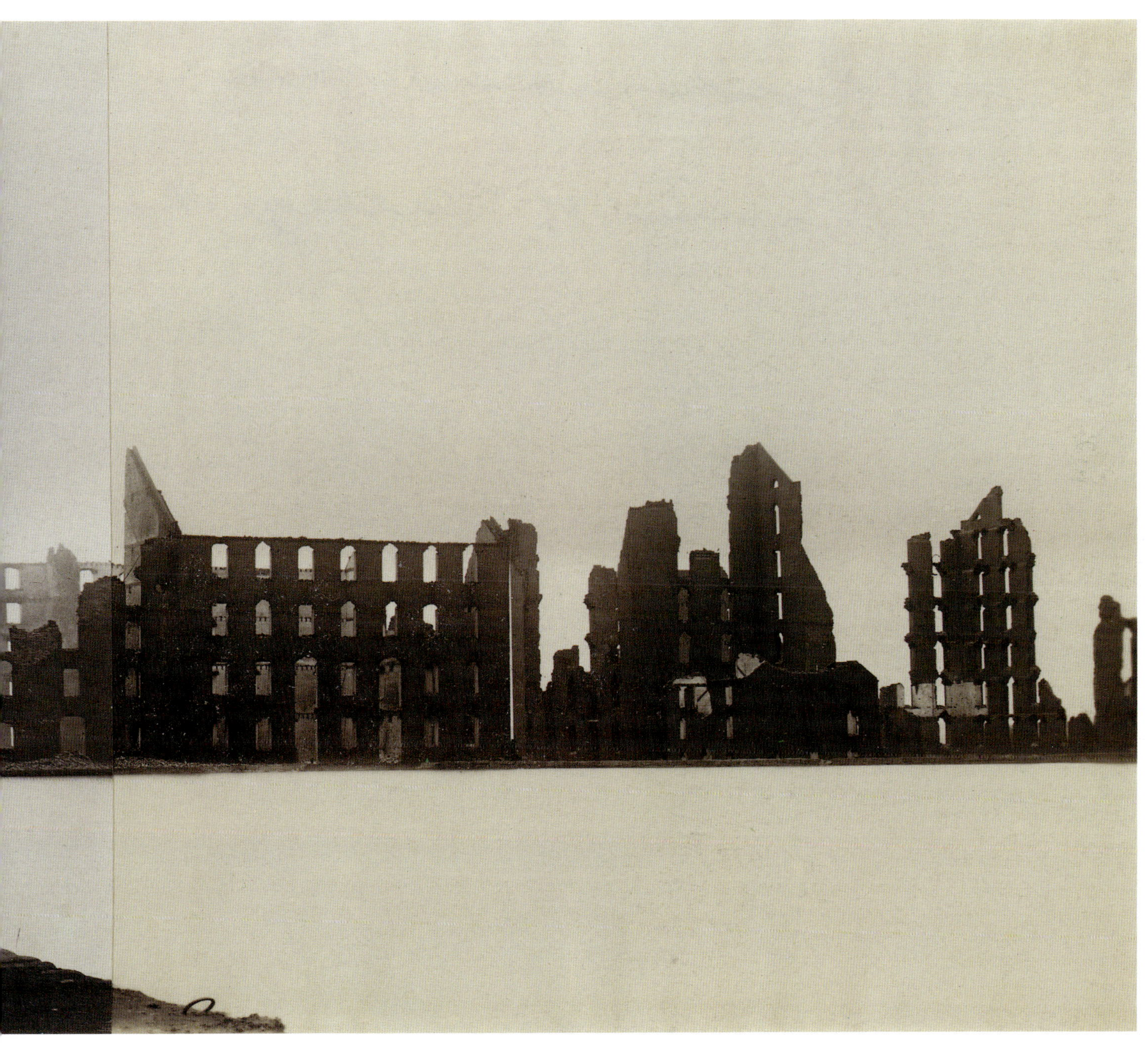

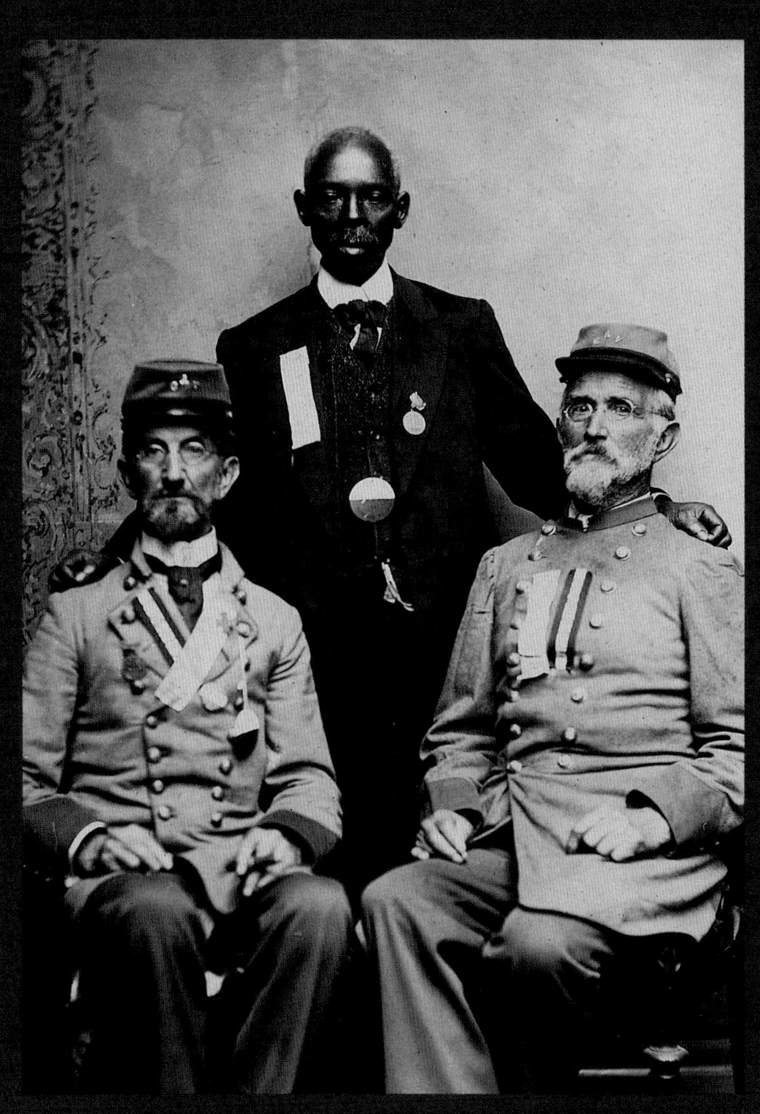

GEORGE SMITH COOK

"Comrades" (Portrait of W. M. Ellis, Black Body Servant, and T. B. Ellis)

ca. 1870s

A. J. VERDELLE

THE HALF-LIGHT OF MANUMISSION

The nineteenth century had its own science—slavery—which was a reckless, nasty field experiment. Under slavery, dark people were partial people, until Emancipation intervened. Emancipation put the slave dealerships out of business. It doled out comeuppance to the black-sheep South. Emancipation released the slaves and disabled the vicious punishments—the whips, the chains, the bit, the yoke. Only the rope remained.

Few slaves rose above the venom. Few were seen as capable slaves. Those who proved they could build, or solder, or create the ornate—they were given tools, and time. These were the legendary slaves.

During Reconstruction, slaves made Negroes of themselves. They reclaimed their right to personality, their entitlement to psychology, to human need, human heart. But slavery had mauled both its owners and its subjects. Slavery had manufactured half-minds. So, Emancipation created only half a light. Freedom magnified the damage, all around.

A nameless tall Negro stands between the marses. He has no chair. The men who flank him have returned from overseeing the war. They have been scratched and starved and scurvied and pockmarked and well-near froze to death. The tall Negro in the center cares deeply about their exploits, even though these were undertaken to protect their vicious science, their pernicious way of life.

He, in the center of the picture, now looks through the lens of his future. His history of service is his only stepping stone.

Woe is she, the young laundress who has reached the age to agitate. Her back starts its chronic ache at this young age. She concentrates on the bluing, trying to agitate it white. Hers is steady heat, all day. She is preoccupied with these questions: *Is the clothes white enough? Is they boiled clean yet? How long must I stand here, stirring?*

Reconstruction altered the vision of the South. Southern whitefolk had romanticized the land, seeing it in panorama, when it was neatly lined and cultivated, managed by tireless hands, countless slaves. Now they saw the free nigras out of the side of their eyes. They plotted to constrict the manumission. To retain or regain their landed fantasies.

They saw themselves as if telescoped. The wealth they had seized from the labor of the beaten was at the far end of a tunnel, out of reach. The war had made tatters all around.

The lie of chattel history had held that Negroes would not learn: not to write, not to measure, or to add. But methods of counting had been kept a quiet secret. Slaves had had no money to keep track of. Slaves had no account ledgers. Slaves had no possessions, and did not have access to the weight of their children, except to note that they weighed less or more than the cotton crop sack. Slaves had no number skills, or literacy. Reconstruction ended this wicked silence toward the slaves, and Negro schools were born. Then all the many Negroes were all at once becoming. They made doorways, door frames, doors.

During Reconstruction, Negroes put clothes on themselves. Under slavery, nakedness had been enforced at will, used for deprivation, punishment, control. To wear clothes like people was half the prize of manumission. It was a cause for grateful pause, among the newly free.

The baby girl is pretty in her lavish new dress, and her boots are laced and ready for the walk. She has a ready mind, and her eyes are daring. Still she is a specimen, minimally understood.

Other babies ride atop the full crop sacks. This way they can rest and see the wide fields. Their little feet hang off the sides of the reaping gone to scales. Like children tend to be, they are hungry. Under Reconstruction, there are provisions to be bought, or owed for. Under slavery, food had been stingily meted out.

Negroes cannot exchange their labor for much that can be used, or kept. The crops will turn to cash without the Negroes seeing drip or drop of it. It's the move out that the Negroes come to relish: slack, empty sacks; deserted fields; a ride for the children; the noon lunch.

Whole groups of Negroes were liable to up and ford a river. They figured ways to travel on. The prejudice of the past had presumed they couldn't figure. But whole communities struck out, with just the tin cups they had and the belief that they could conjure up. Hope had not been a plantation crop, but Reconstruction grew it wildly, hope seed thrown out alongside the roads.

For some years after Emancipation, the Negro future will mimic the slave past. The Southern chattel tradition will not easily give way. The routine for Southern Negroes has thus turned to sharecropping, which was more of the slave same: bending, seizing, loading, burning in the Southern sun.

Reconstruction cannot birth a new science of Negro humanity. The Negro did not hold that power. Neither language nor perception nor photography will really honor Reconstruction. Freedom becomes an impasto atop the canvas of the worn-out South. Freedom will seem an impostor sometimes.

Reconstruction did nurture a new Negro personality. Daring Negro baby girls were allowed to live. Negroes became parents who could keep their children. Builders, farmers, mathematicians wore the skin of the despised. Teachers took to classrooms, and orators took the podium. Fiddlers played, and hats were made. Presidents and their successors were considered, voted for. Some Negroes became futurists, or pessimists, or perpetual servants.

Under Reconstruction, the free sit together, looking forward. They enjoy the cool breeze of America's flag. For some reason, the flag doesn't show in this picture. And neither does the man who holds the flag. But you see this idealized backdrop: the sun, the breeze, the flag, the South. It is a summer scene. The former slaves have clothes, and purpose, and a direct look for whatever the black box and poof light create. These are manumitted people. Set for new lives, the next century. It is unclear from here which of the doors will stay open, which of life's boxes will remain unsealed. But centuries to come are not pressing, in this idealized moment. This season, there is manumission. In this half-light of the last century, the Negroes are finally free.

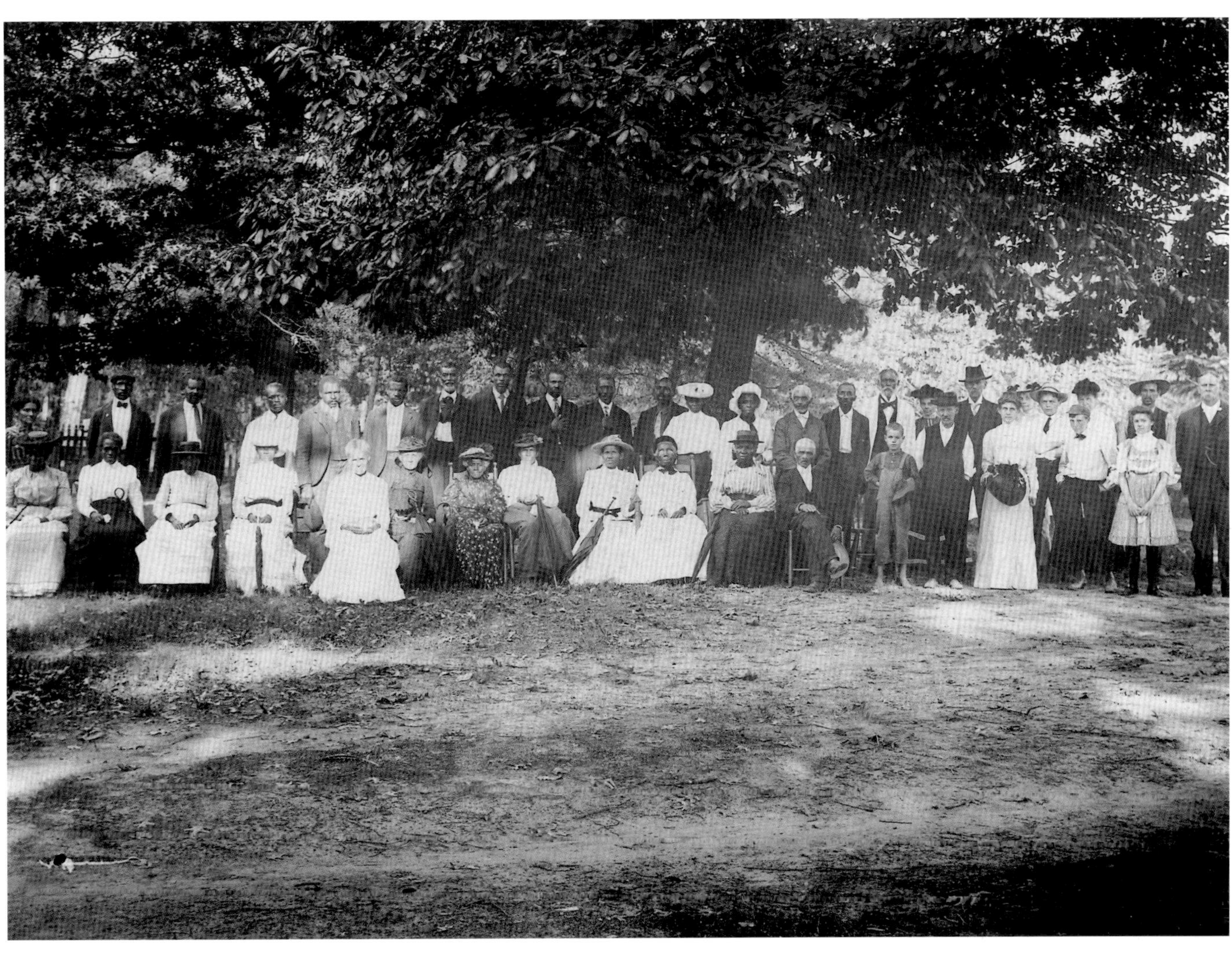

UNIDENTIFIED PHOTOGRAPHER

Reunion of Nathaniel Burwell's Slaves at Sherwood Plantation near Salem, in Roanoke County, Virginia

1903

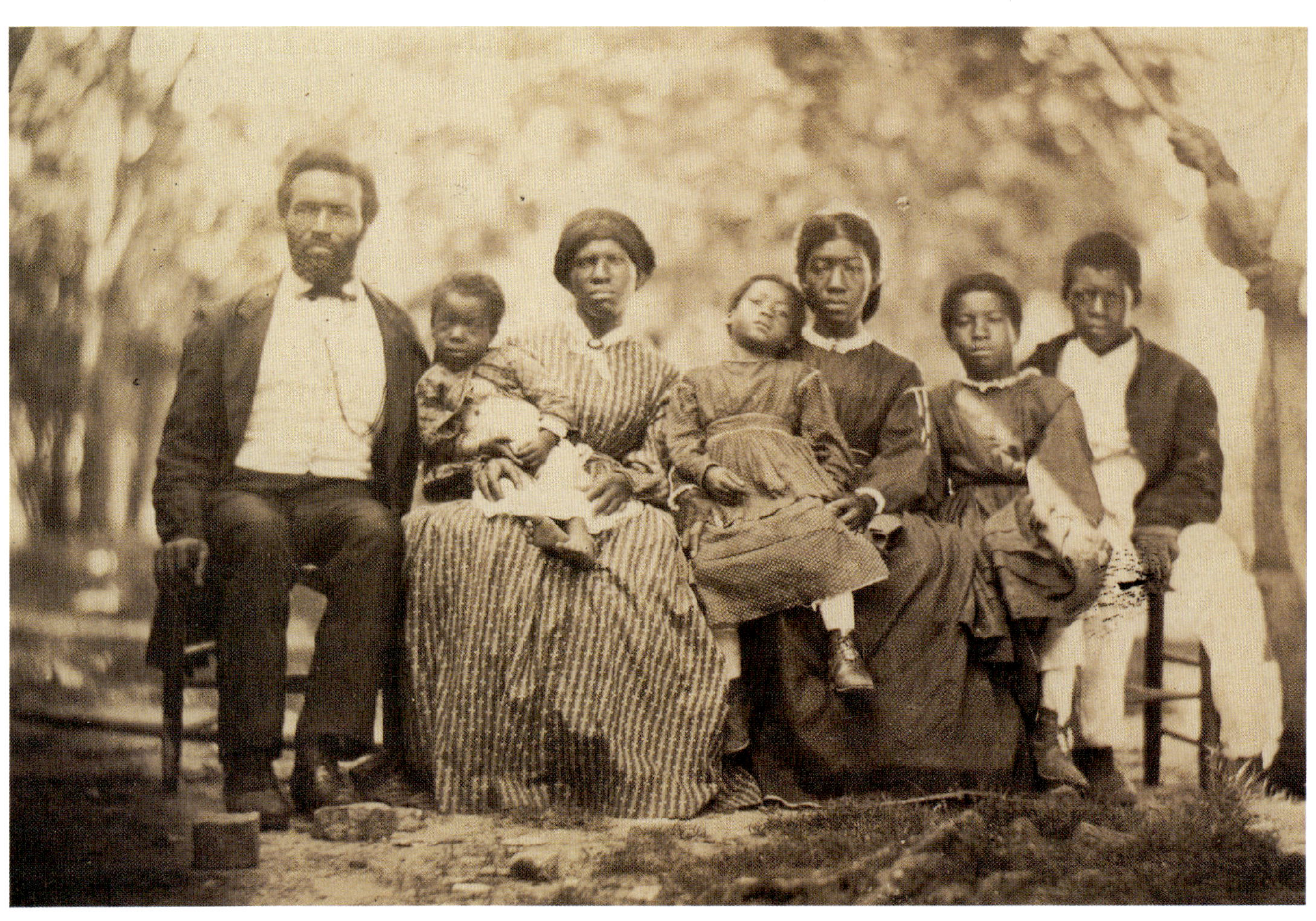

G. GABLE

Summer Scene (The Harry Stephens Family)

1866

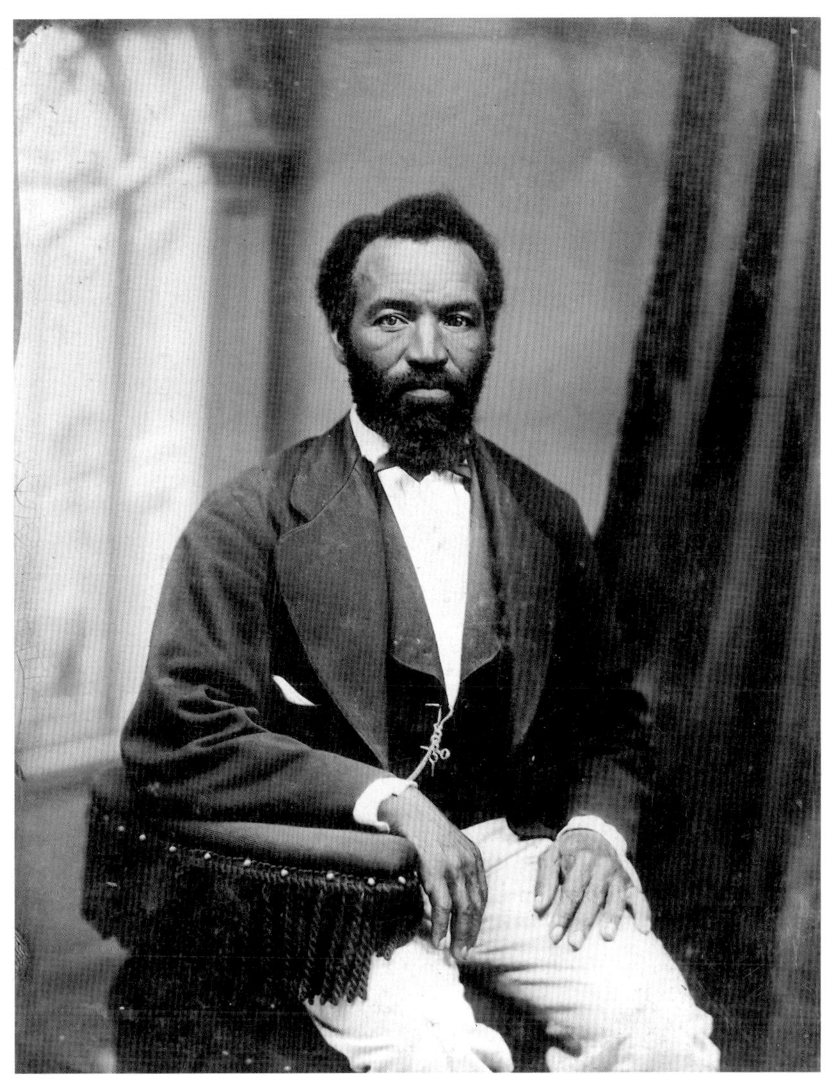

WILLIAM KUHN
Portrait of Harry Stephens
ca. 1875

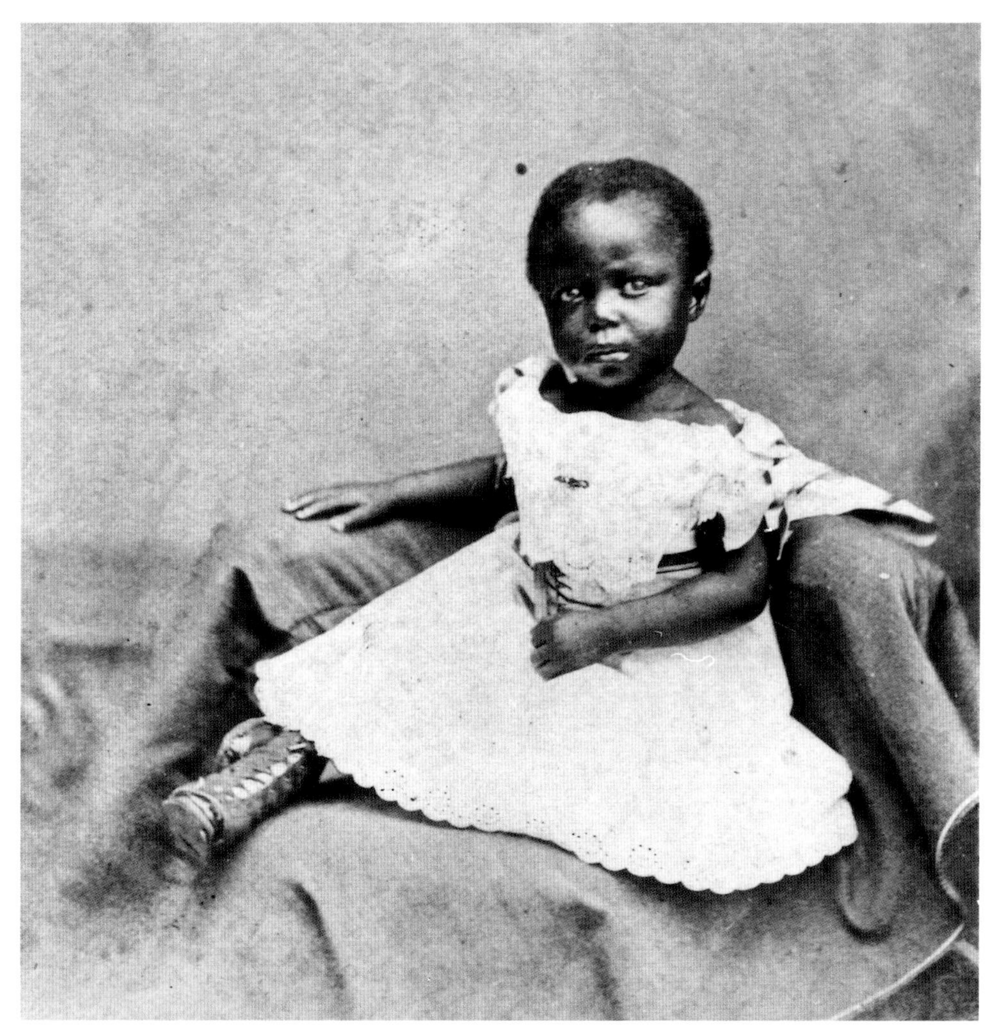

GEORGE N. BARNARD

Fifteenth Amendment—A Good Specimen (stereographic detail)
ca. 1874–75

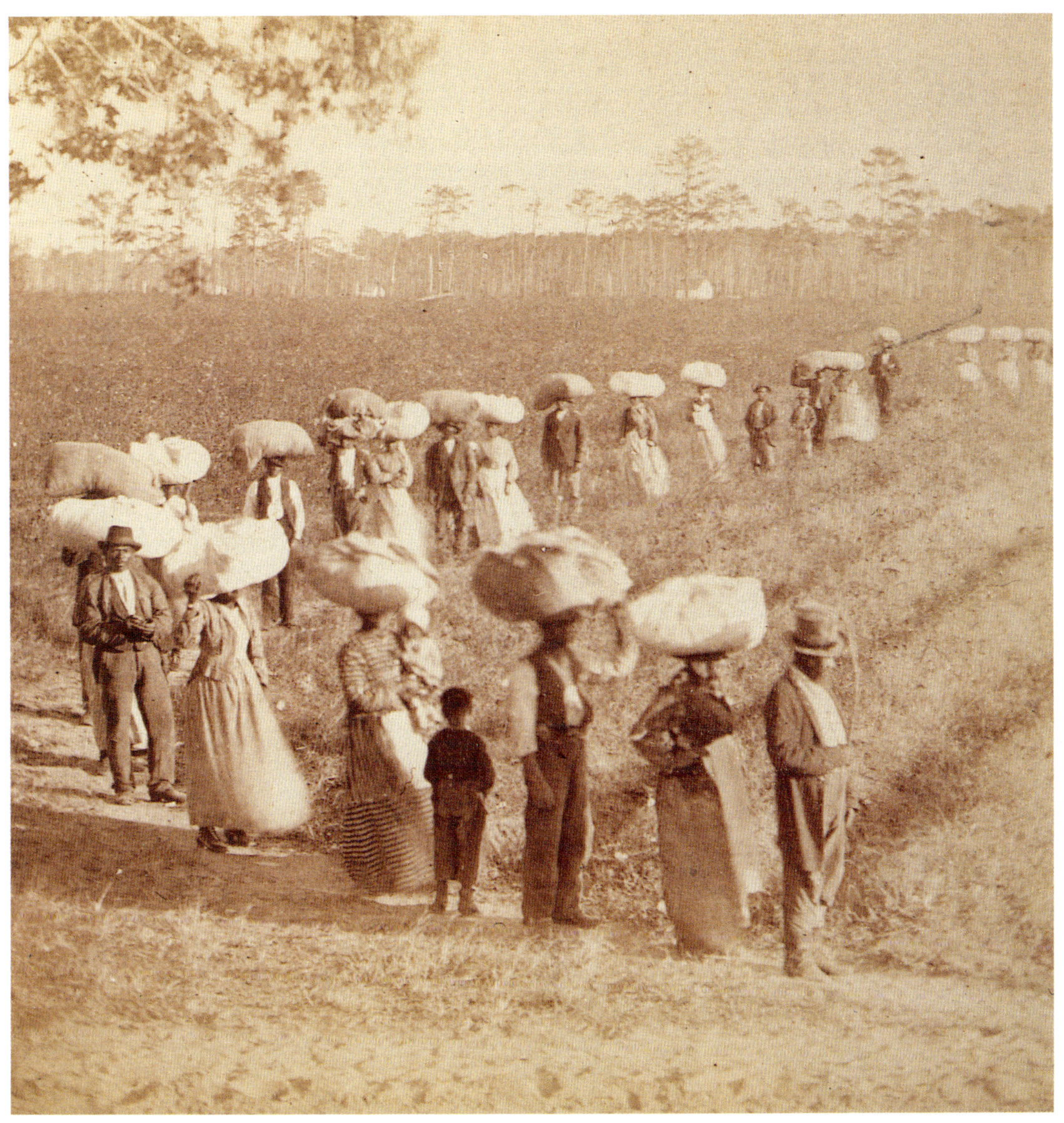

GEORGE N. BARNARD

Laborers Returning at Sunset from Picking Cotton on Alex. Knox's Plantation, Mt. Pleasant, near Charleston, South Carolina from the series "South Carolina Views" (stereographic detail)
ca. 1874

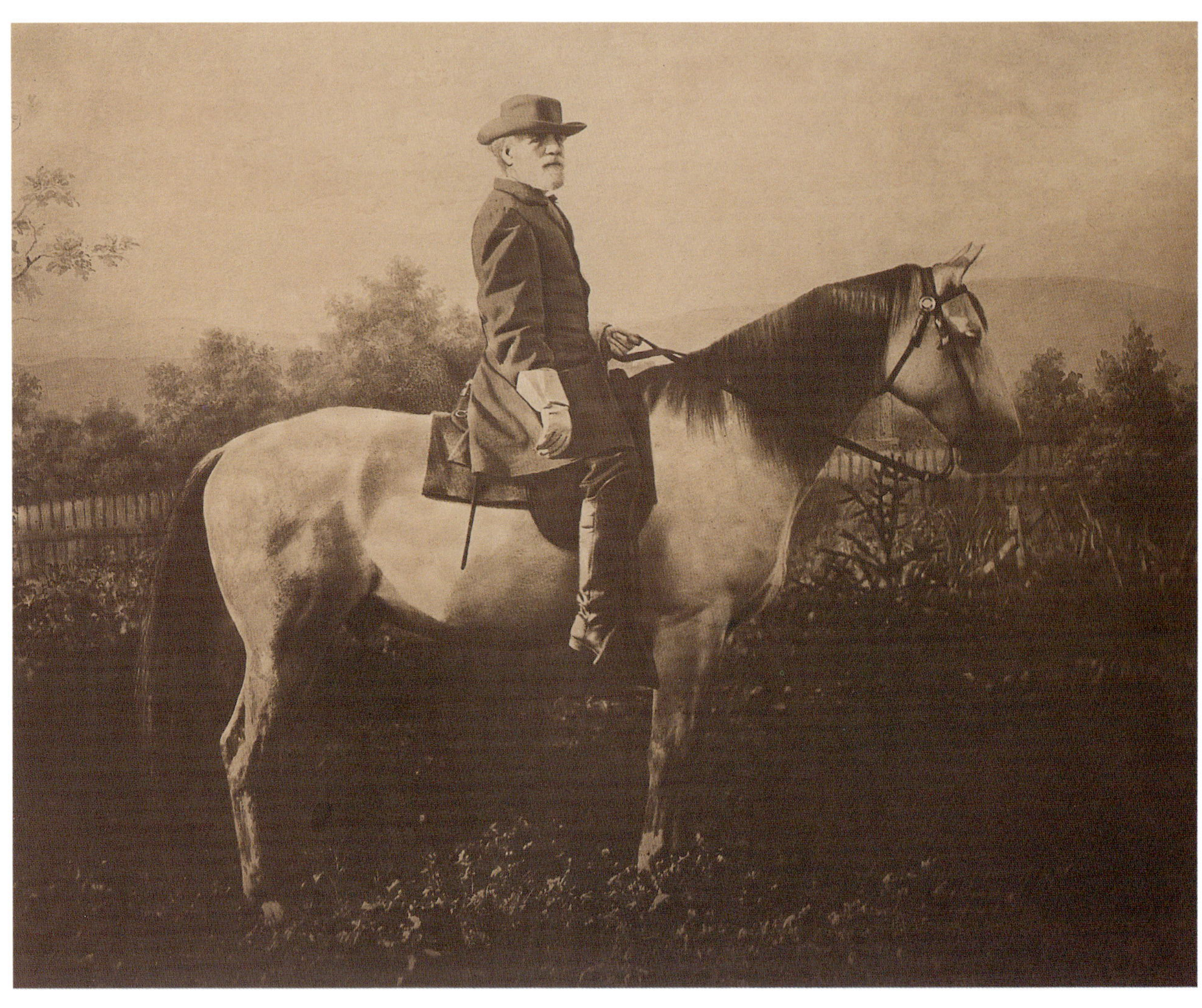

MICHAEL MILEY

General Robert E. Lee on Traveller

1867

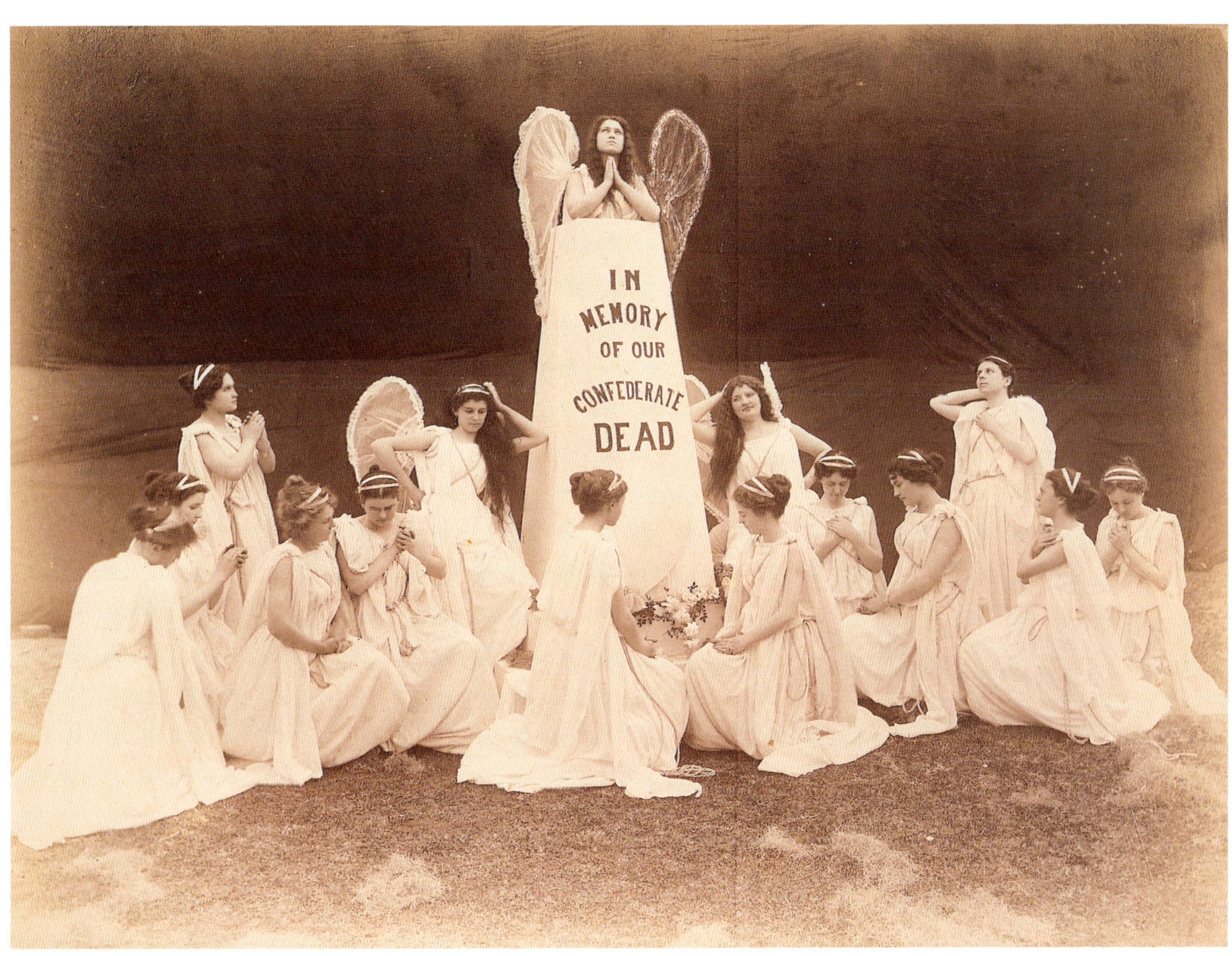

UNIDENTIFIED PHOTOGRAPHER

In Memory of Our Confederate Dead

ca. 1880s

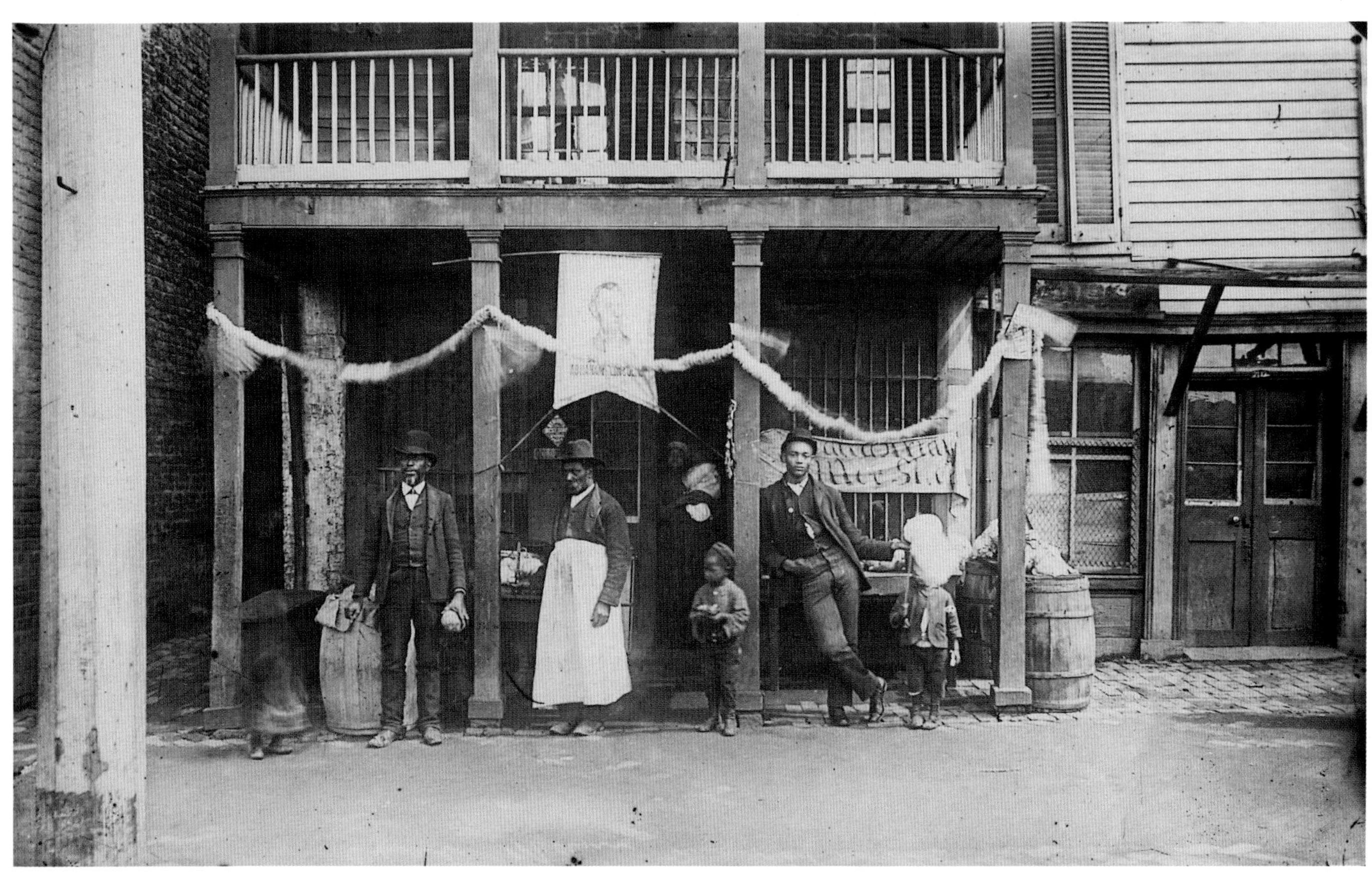

GEORGE SMITH COOK

Emancipation Day Celebration, Richmond, Virginia

1888

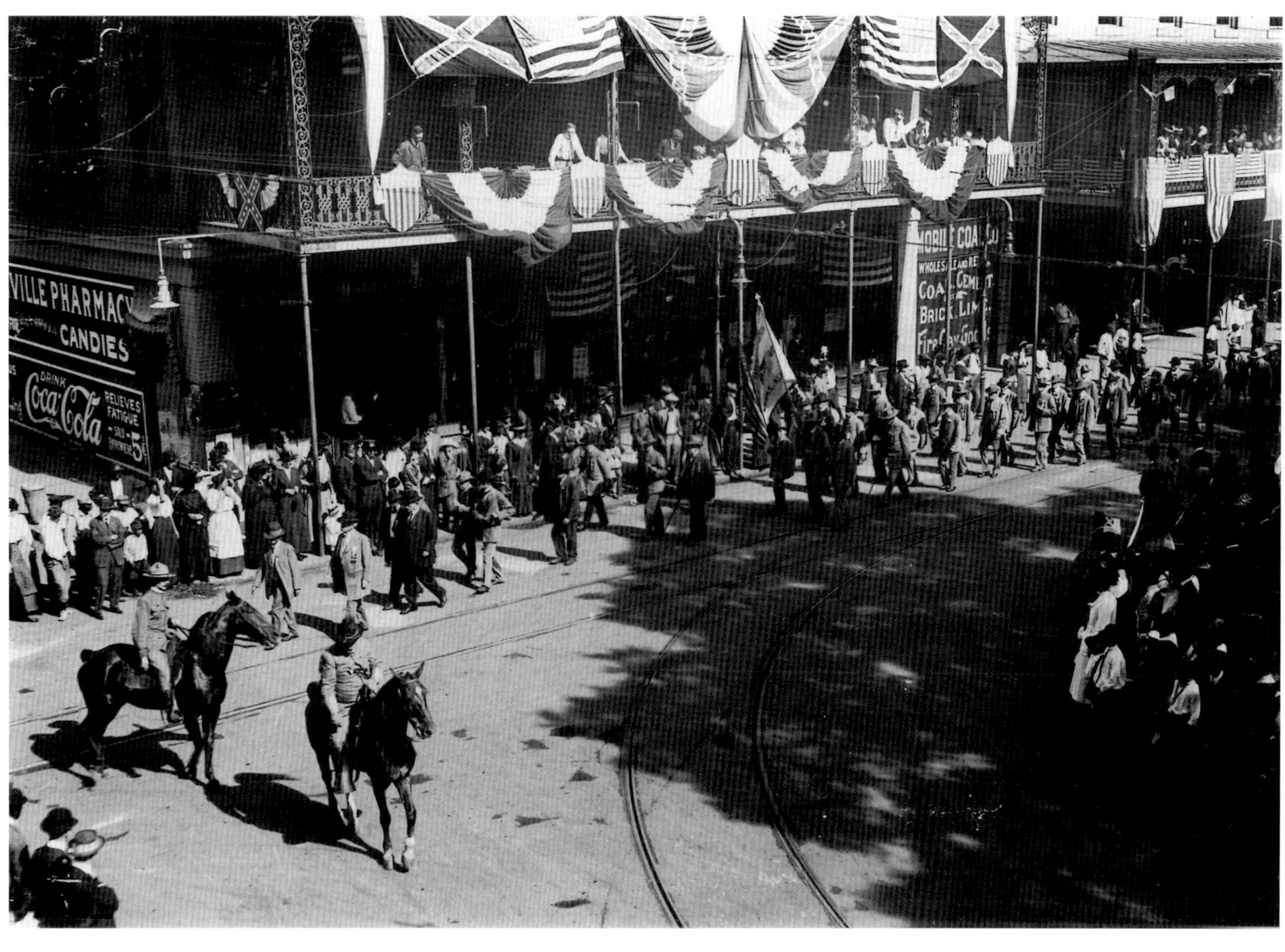

LEWIS W. HINE

The Last Stand of the Confederacy, Mobile, Alabama

1914

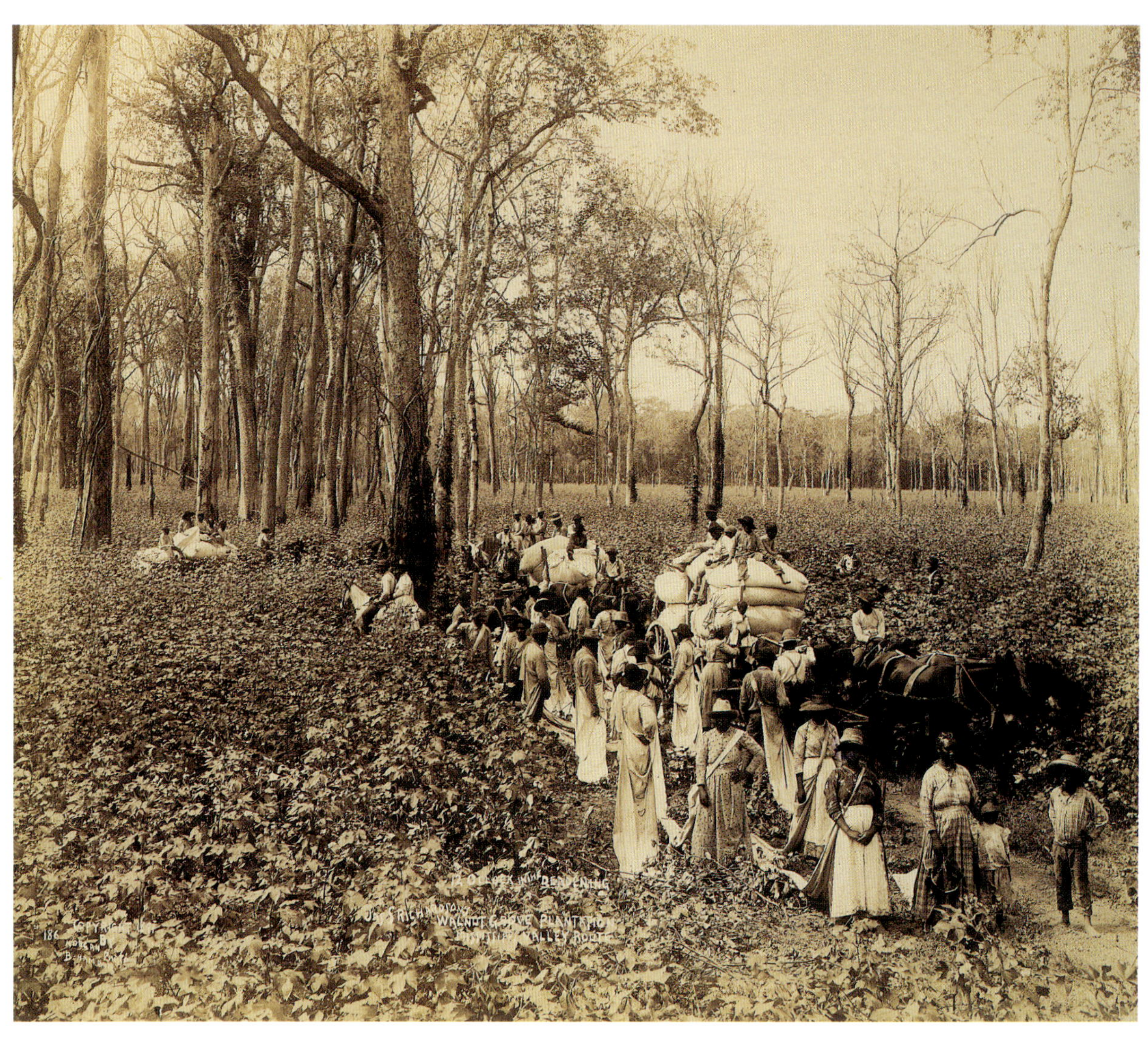

JOHN HORGAN, JR.

12 o'Clock in the Deadening, Jas. S. Richardson's Walnut Grove Plantation, Mississippi Valley Route

ca. 1891

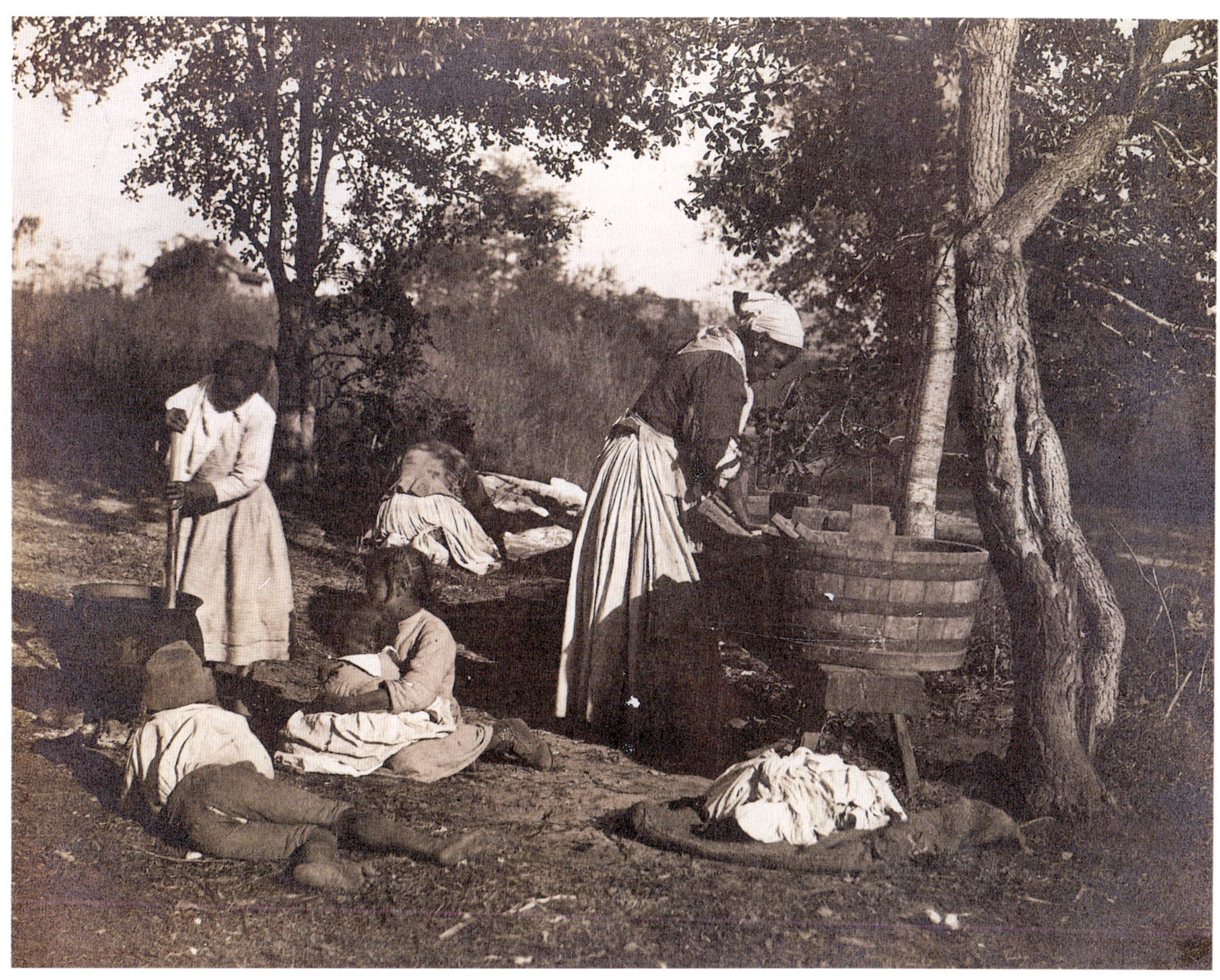

RUDOLF EICKEMEYER, JR.
Wash Day on the Plantation, Mt. Meigs, Alabama
ca. 1887

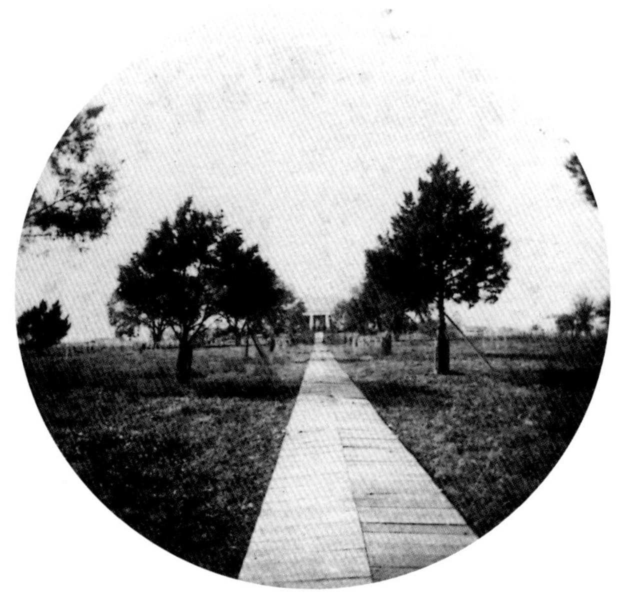

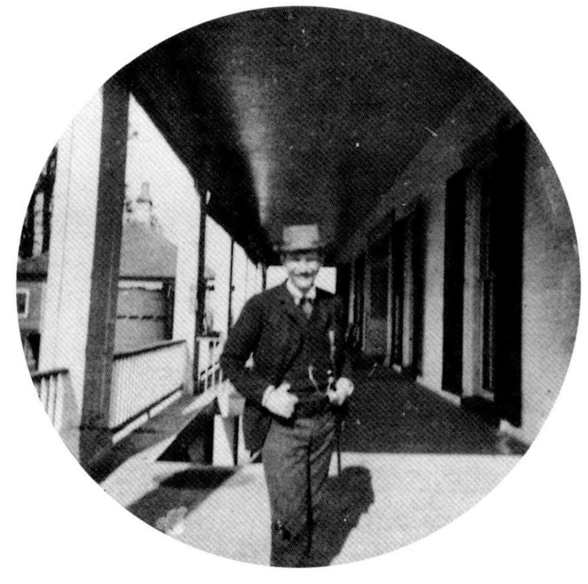

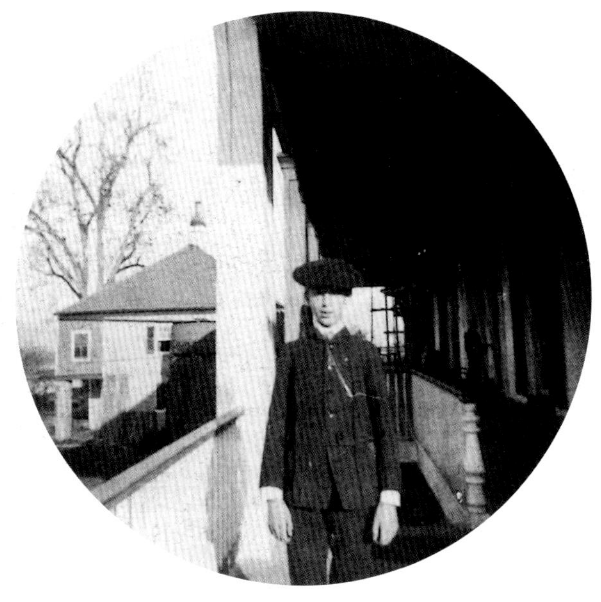

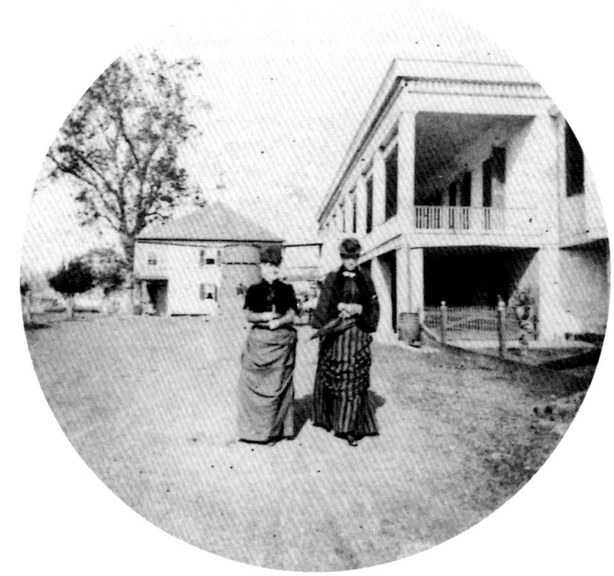

UNIDENTIFIED PHOTOGRAPHER

Members of the Henry McCall and Meta McCall Diesback Families and Their Servants at Evan Hall Plantation, Donaldsonville, Louisiana

1888

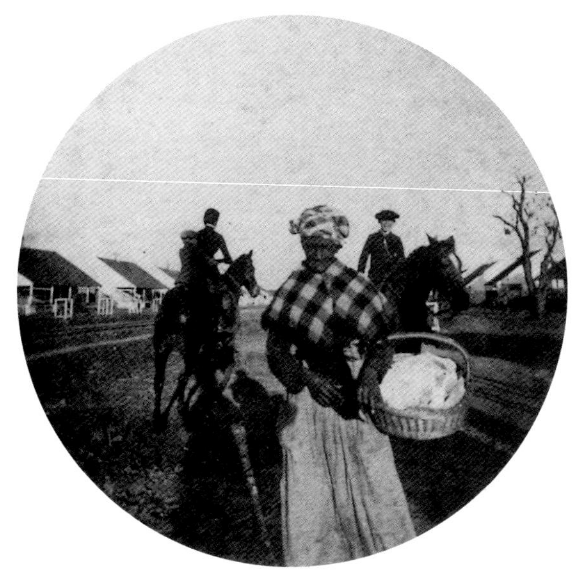

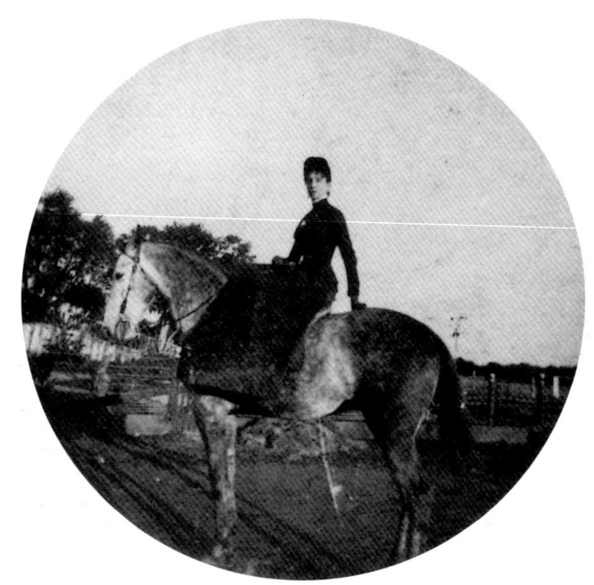

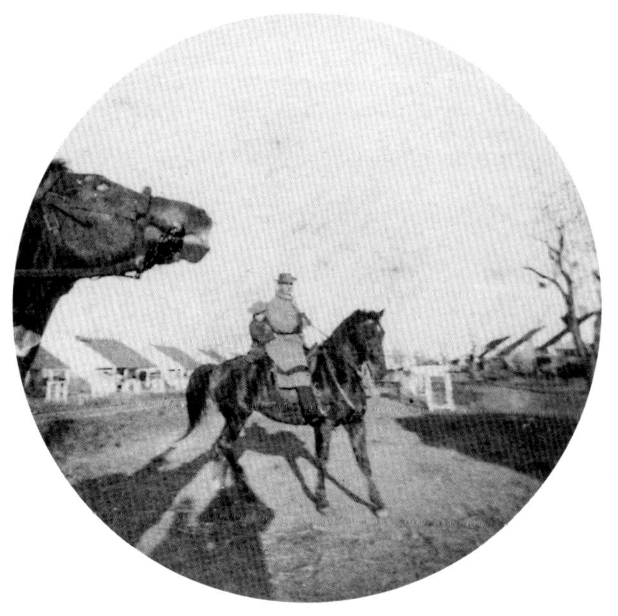

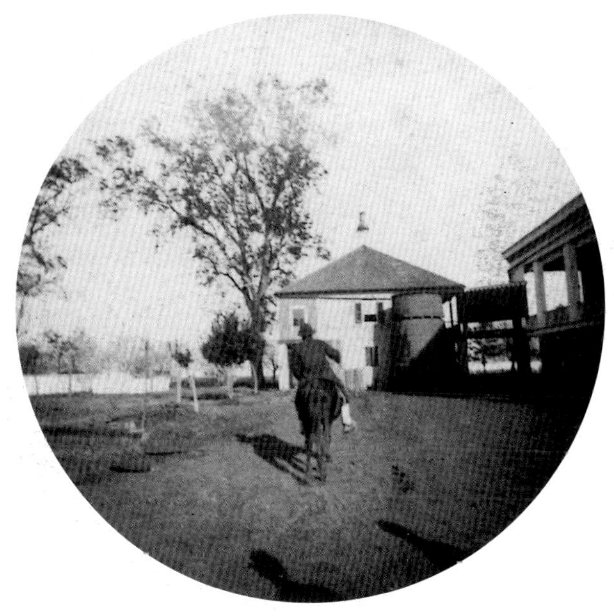

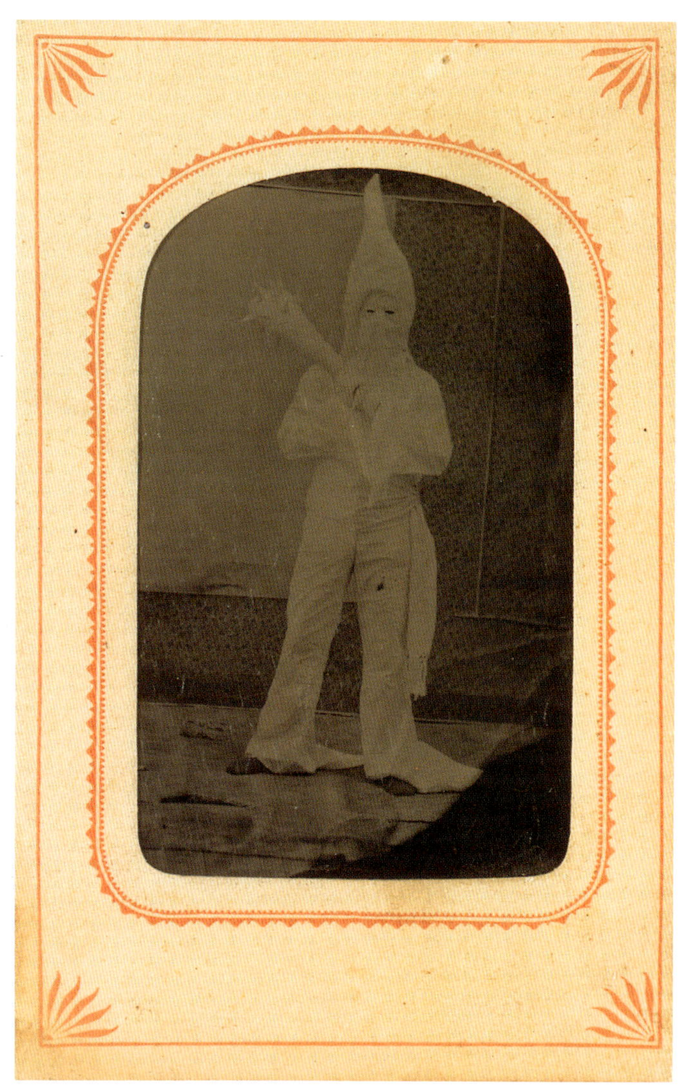

UNIDENTIFIED PHOTOGRAPHER

Ku Klux Klansman

ca. 1869

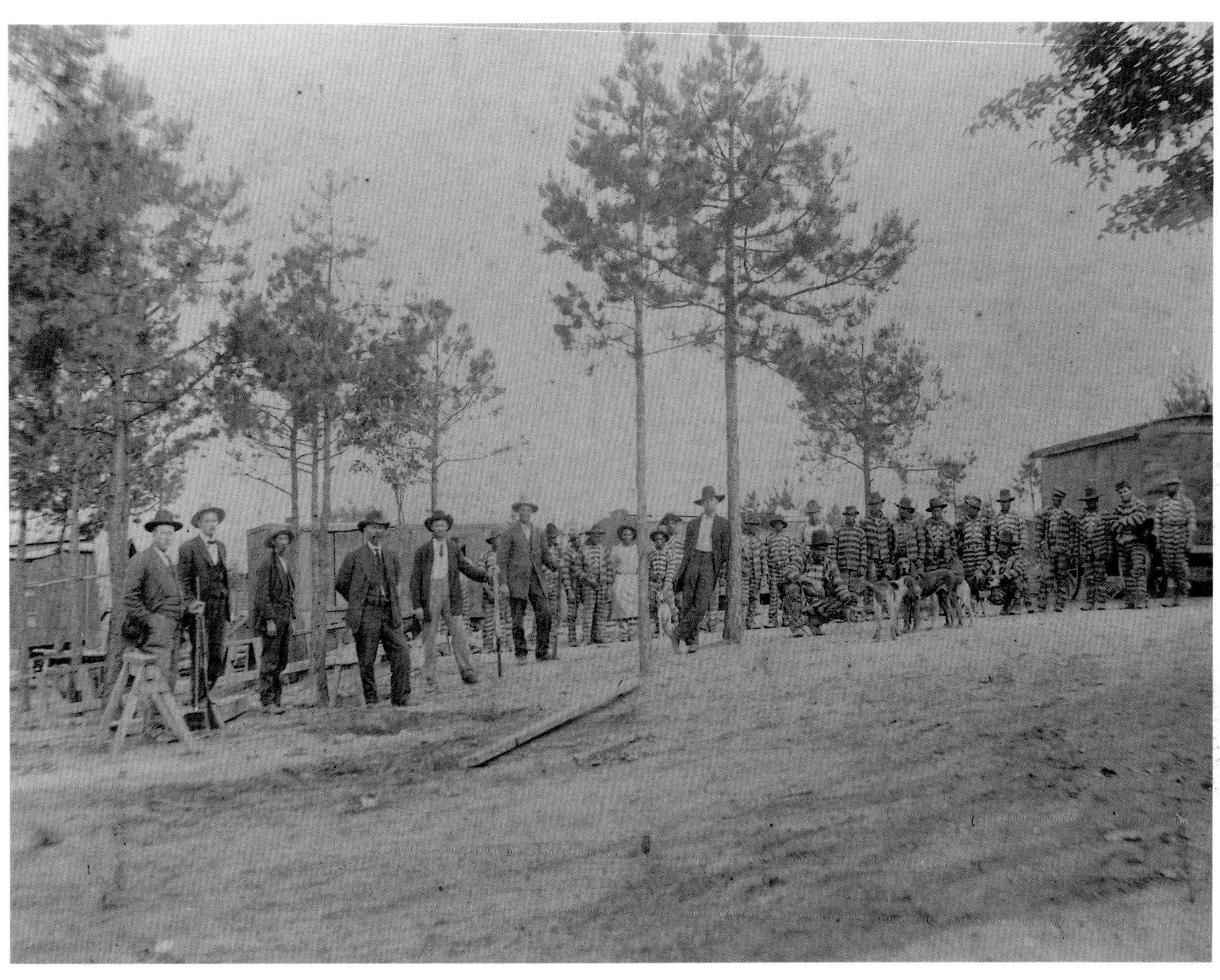

UNIDENTIFIED PHOTOGRAPHER

Men Guarding Prisoners, Campbell County, Georgia

ca. 1890

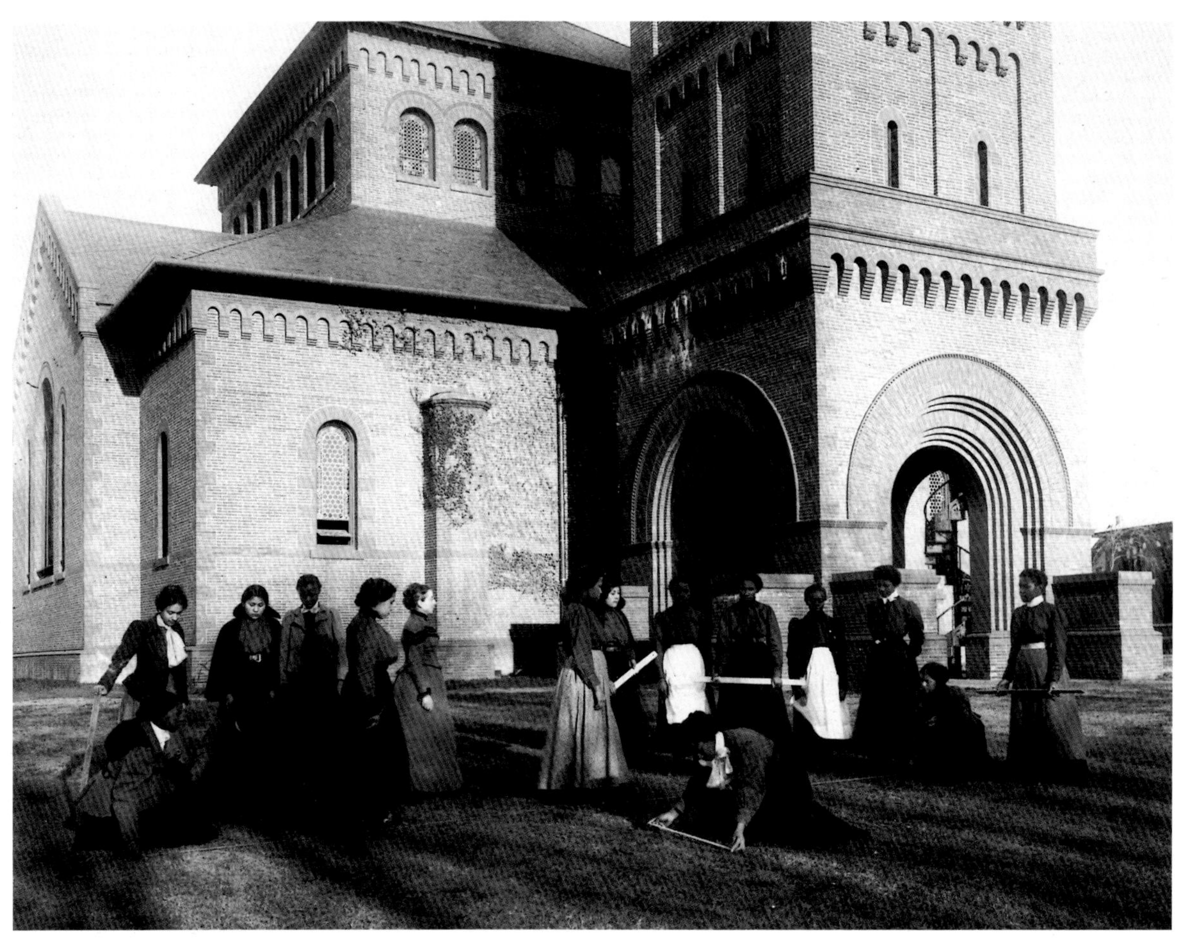

FRANCES BENJAMIN JOHNSTON

Arithmetic. Measuring and Pacing from "The Hampton Album"

1899–1900

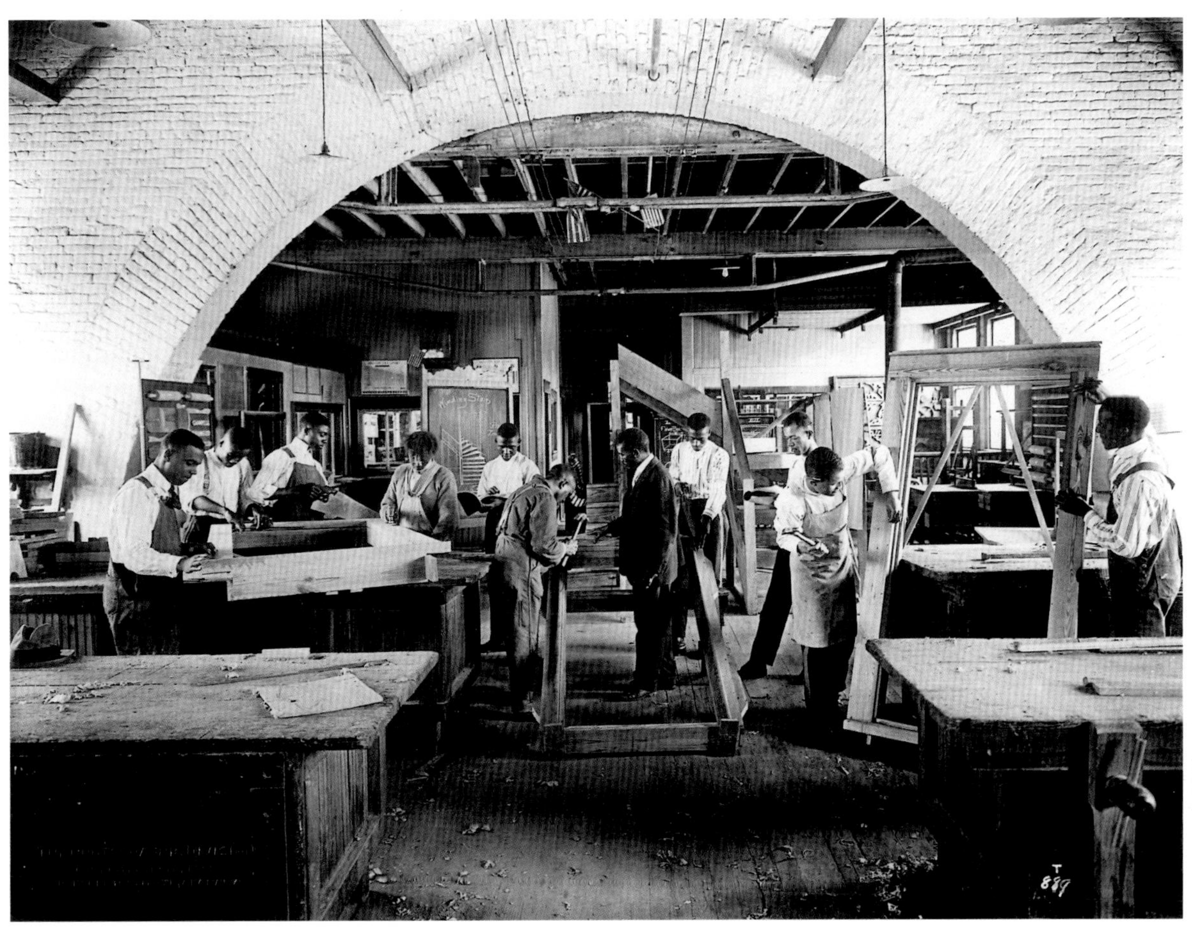

CORNELIUS MARION BATTEY

Carpentry Class, Tuskegee Institute, Tuskegee, Alabama

ca. 1920

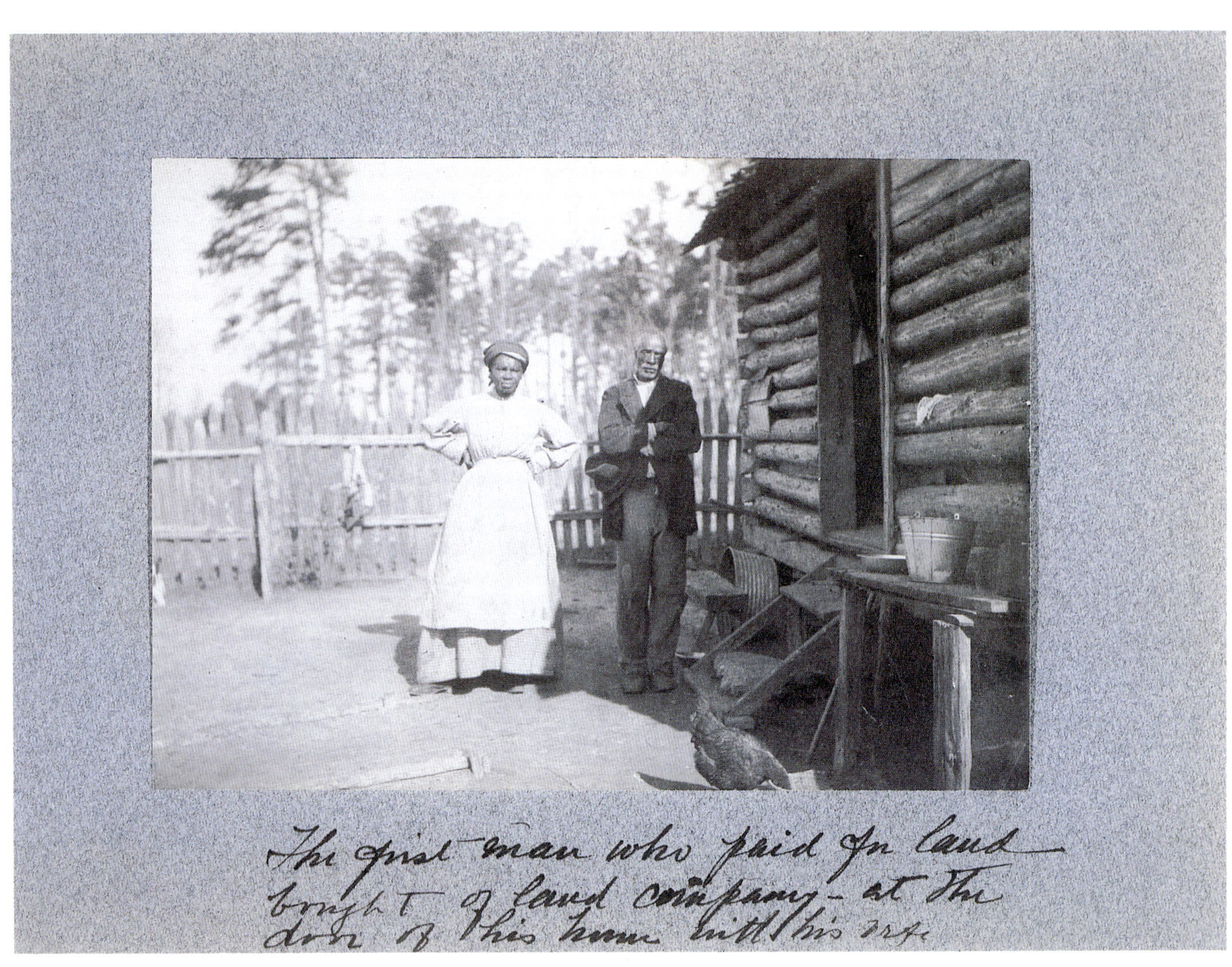

UNIDENTIFIED PHOTOGRAPHER

Untitled from the "Calhoun School and Settlement Album, Calhoun, Alabama"
ca. 1900

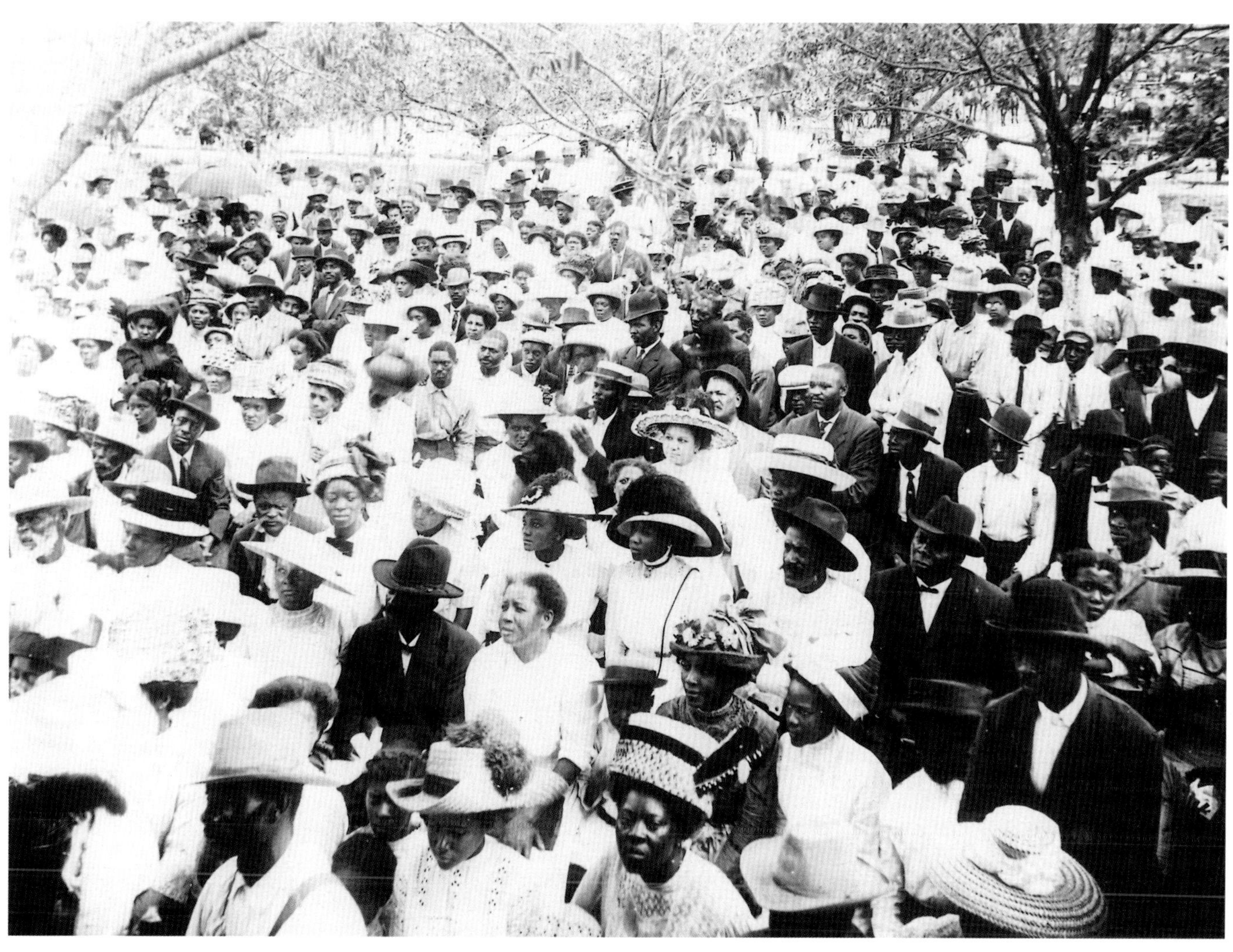

ARTHUR P. BEDOU
Booker T. Washington's Last Tour of Louisiana
1915

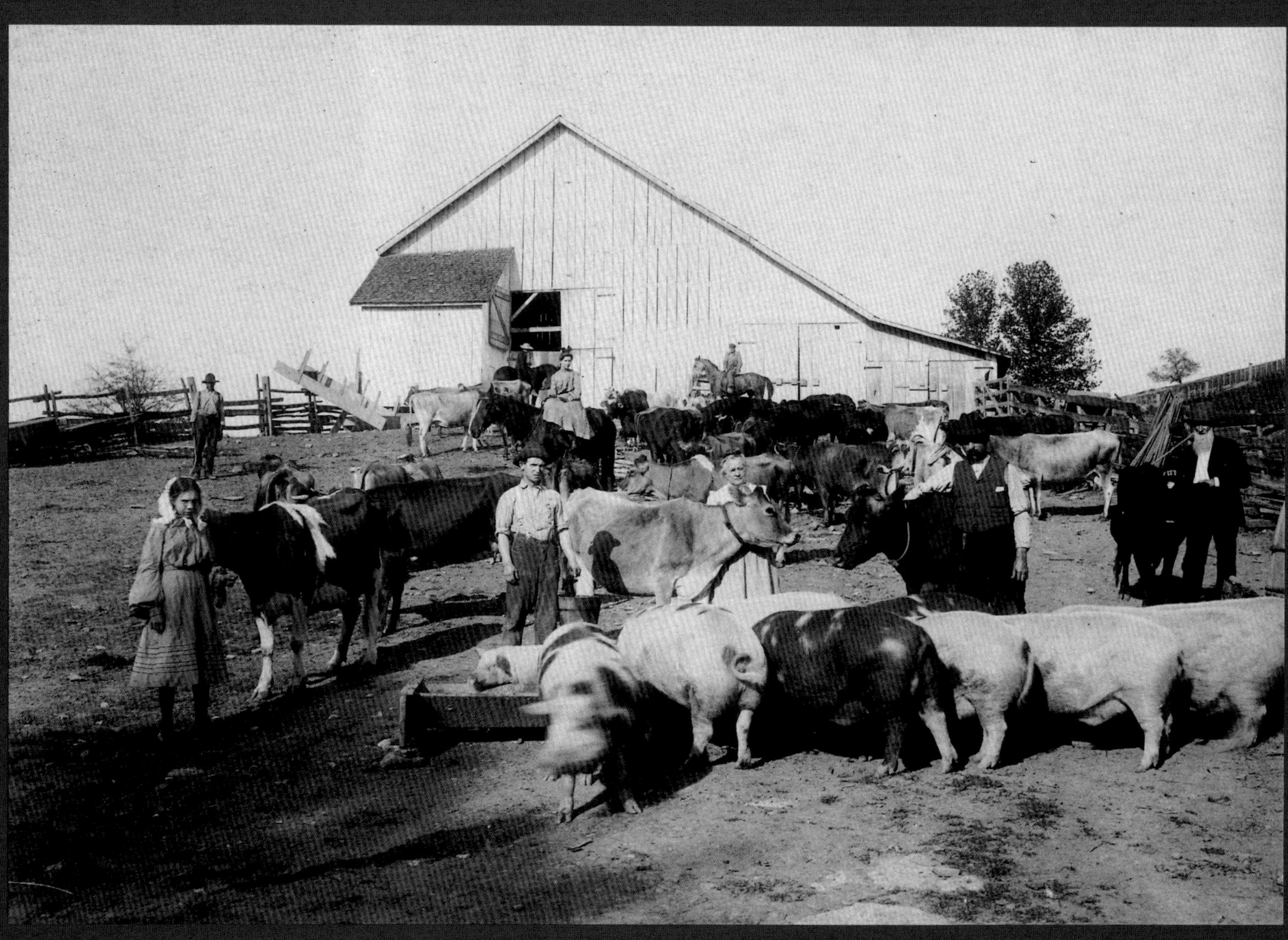

A. J. EARP

Cliff Owen Dairy Farm, Clark County, Kentucky from the "Arthur Y. Ford Album"
ca. 1900–1904

CLYDE EDGERTON

EVOCATIONS FROM THE PHOTOGRAPHS

Part I. Memory

My 1996 memory holds pieces of my mother's memory, my father's, aunts', and uncles'—white people—whose memories long ago collected memories from older kinfolks. Thus I remember the Yankees coming through, what was said on that day, and I somehow remember and feel unstated guilt, shame, and anger left from that war. If I were an African American, I'd perhaps remember what was said on a day that my feet and hands and eyes and tongue and ears were owned by another member of our species—or on the day of a lynching.

Part II. Twenty-Second-Century Anthropology

Anthropologists of the 2100s will study the 1900–1930 South. They will report:

The Cornbread Eaters, the largest group of Southerners, 1900–1930, were divided into dark-skins and light-skins. The dark-skins suffered indignity, pain, horror, and inhumanity as a consequence of light-skinned racial hatred. The light-skins suffered, but generally not as a result of direct, unabridged evil.

Each day almost all of the Cornbread Eaters made and ate a bread made of cornmeal, salt, and water. They also had in common: fried fatback, buttermilk, non-taxed whiskey, hot weather, vegetable gardens, chickens, blackberries, dogs, extended families, several taboos, certain similar language habits and religious practices, and little or no political or economic power.

In those days—all over America—it was about blood. The blood of European-Americans and African-Americans, but also Asian-Americans, Latin-Americans, Hebrew-Americans, Native-Americans, Spanish-Americans, Canadian-Americans, Eskimo-Americans.

In those thirty years of that century in the southern United States, it was mostly "white" and "colored." Blood. That's about all it's been since. Back then many coloreds and whites sang, proclaimed—some shouted, danced—proclaimed that the blood of Jesus was shed for salvation from their sins.

The music of these subgroups was different.

We know about these 1900–1930 Cornbread Eaters from film, but mainly through written words and photographs—and quotes such as the following, gathered scientifically from certain wood grains (sono-retrieval):

1. "What God granted us in buckets and tubs and tin pitchers and on tin plates and in tin cups was in some cases by God one hell of a lot better—'them is good oysters'—than what the old man was eating up in his fancy carved mahogany breakfast room like something you see in Bible pictures that had to do with the Roman Empire. And even if it tasted the same, we sure had more fun eating it. That's something God gave us. And we had a place to swim and enough to get by on. What we didn't know never hurt us. Except I do wish Mama and Brother could have lived longer."

2. "I won't eat a cucumber. Pigs won't eat 'em./—Will too./—No they won't./Will./—Won't./—I don't care. I like 'em."

3. "You know, Miss Mae Roberts had so many cousins and nieces and grandchildren that when her grandson David introduced himself at the reunion after a thirty-year absence, she said, 'Now, who'd you say you was?' And he said, 'I'm David.' She looked at him. He said, 'You know your daughter Betty?' and she said, 'Yes,' and he said, 'Well, I'm Betty's son, and that makes *me . . . your . . . grandson*.' And she leaned over, looked him in the eye and said, 'That's too deep for me.'

"But she remembered making $1.86 the first week she worked full-time in the hosiery mill—back around 1908. She was ten years old then. That one particular amount of money was a sharp memory."

4. (It was thought that if a woman kept nursing her baby, she couldn't get pregnant. Some children nursed while standing.) "Cousin Sis told her third boy youngin that if he'd just stop taking titty, for gracious sakes, he could start smoking."

5. "'Sitting here a thousand miles from nowhere, in this one-room country shack. My only worldly possession is this eleven-foot raggedy old cotton sack.' (Old blues song.) Those cotton sacks were yep eleven feet long and you stuff and stuff and stuff and then dump cotton at the end of a row where it's picked up and put into bales and taken to the gin and finally made into something for somebody to wear."

Part III. Music

How much better for us all—the world over—that the blues and gospel stay with us, clear our hearts of the hatred that is fate.

And in the end, I mean the *very* end, that music might be the best thing the South ever produced, and some significant pieces of the blues, gospel, jazz will escape gravity and float forever and ever toward the void—float along on indestructible sound waves—until the ear of an angel picks it up, and she hums along, tapping her foot and nodding her head, eyes closed.

Part IV. Heroes

In 1907 the Jeb Stuart monument was unveiled in Richmond, Virginia. The Arthur Ashe monument was unveiled a few years later. What the hell is a hero anyway? A hero is an image saying Be Like Me. Jesus was a hero, as was the sheeted horseman. Who said we were different in the South? Jesus is a villain, you know? To some people. We defined—define—our villains by how we lived, what we thought, did, do, failed to do.

You learn a lot about what to revere if you're seven years old and you see a black man with painted white lips and a white man with a black face and painted white lips—and they're making fools out of themselves. You learn a lot from what your culture prompts you to laugh at.

Part V. The Economy

My daddy started smoking in 1914. Bull Durham tobacco wrecked his lungs and finally killed him when he was 77. Emphysema. Uncle Clem lost his arm in 1918 in Germany and became an alcoholic and shot himself in the heart when he was 83 because his drugged brain would not allow sleep. But if we act against tobacco or alcohol, why my lord, then the economy will suffer. We need a strong economy. Always have.

One of the strongest, most reasonable arguments for maintaining slavery in the South was that without it our economy would suffer. We Southerners, we human beings, had—still have—an odd feel for what to protect. Where to place our bets.

Part VI. Questions

Raise your hand. How many of you were raised on a farm?/Picked cotton?/How many were raised by Protestant fundamentalists?/How many raised in a home where standard English was not the home dialect?/How many had no parents, aunts, or uncles go to college?/Used an outhouse until you left home?/Chopped wood?/Were raised in a home where you could not say damn?/Had more than 20 aunts and uncles, with 90 percent living within a few miles of your home?/ How many of you have eaten meat that was kept in a smokehouse?/How many had not traveled more than 25 miles from home by the time you were 18?/ How many of you have gotten paper money out of a machine—this week—and watched television and used a computer?/ How many of you just raised your hand for the first time?

Part VII. Facts

Between 1900 and 1930, several thousands of African Americans were lynched in the South. The blessed good will of Jesus and the guidance of God was sought daily. It was the worst of times. The poverty of the poor matched the poverty of the rich. Humor, affection, and love resided in families and among friends.

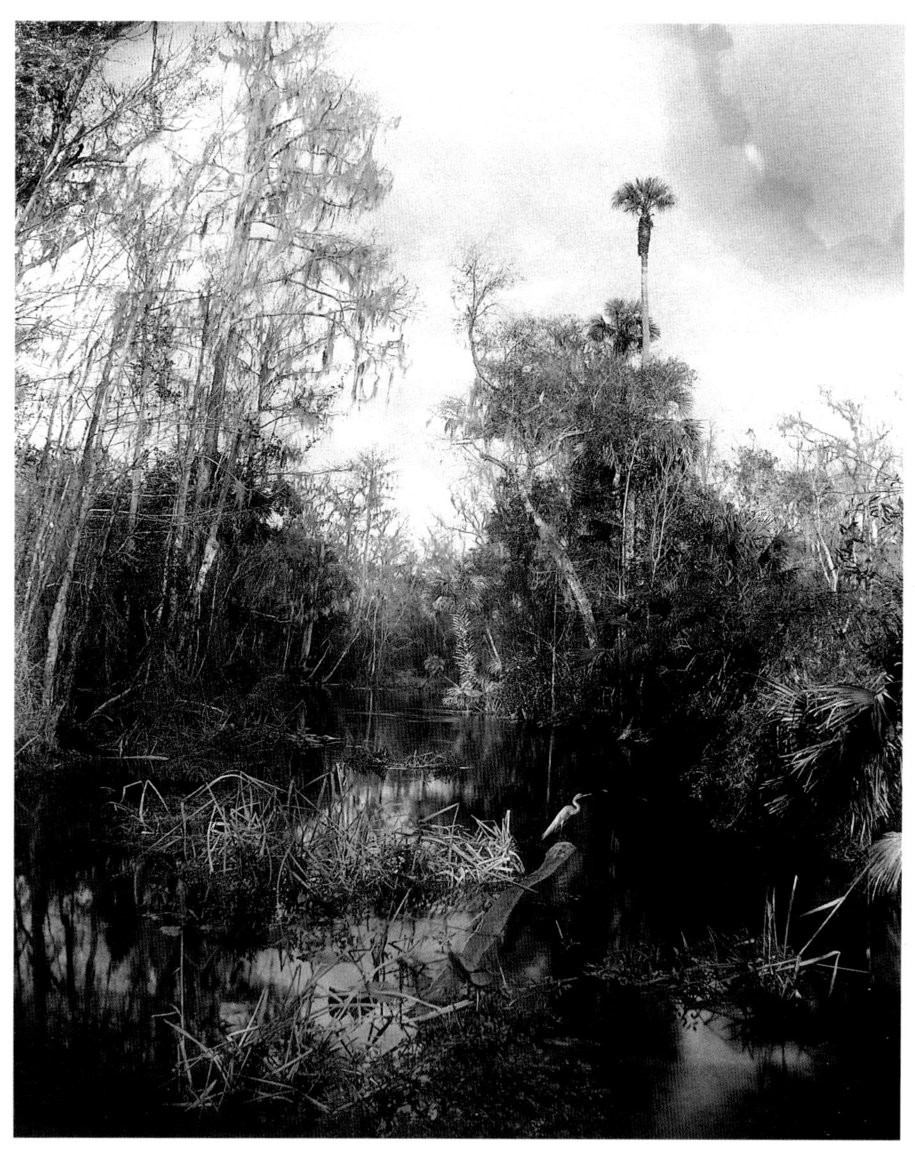

GEORGE BARKER

Oklawaha River, Florida (with bird standing on log)
ca. 1886

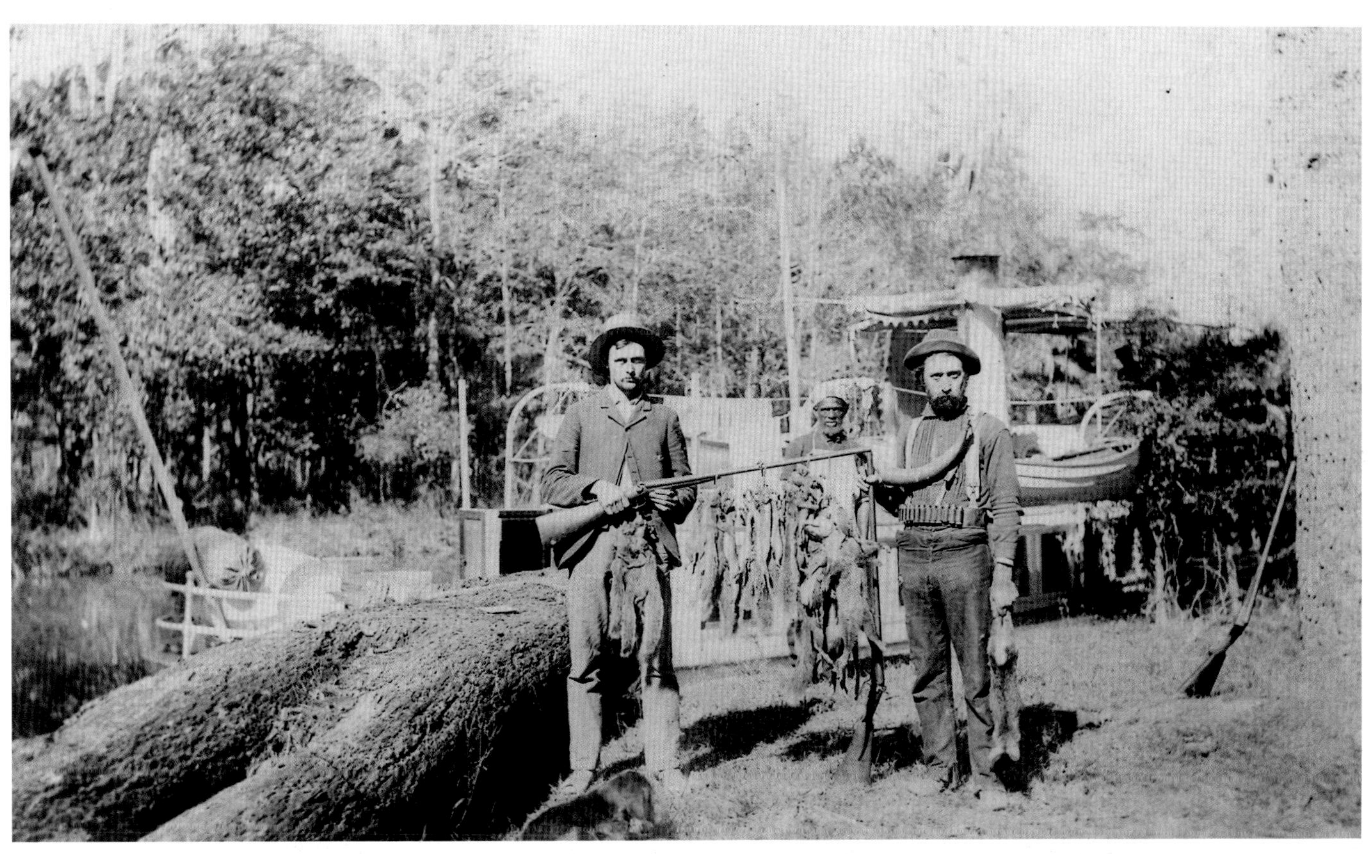

THOMAS SULLY

Portrait of Two Hunters

ca. 1890

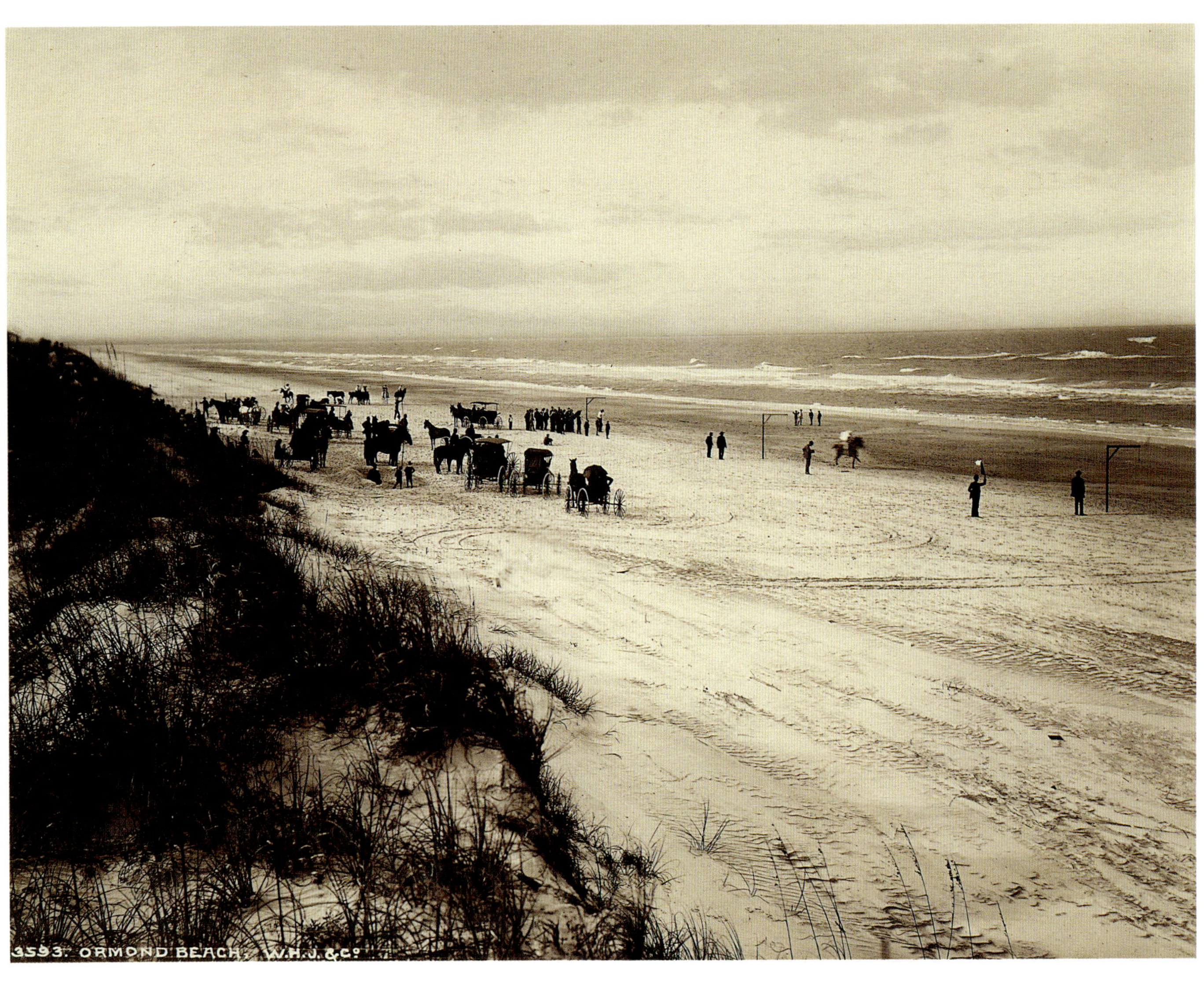

WILLIAM HENRY JACKSON

Horse Races on Ormond Beach

ca. 1900

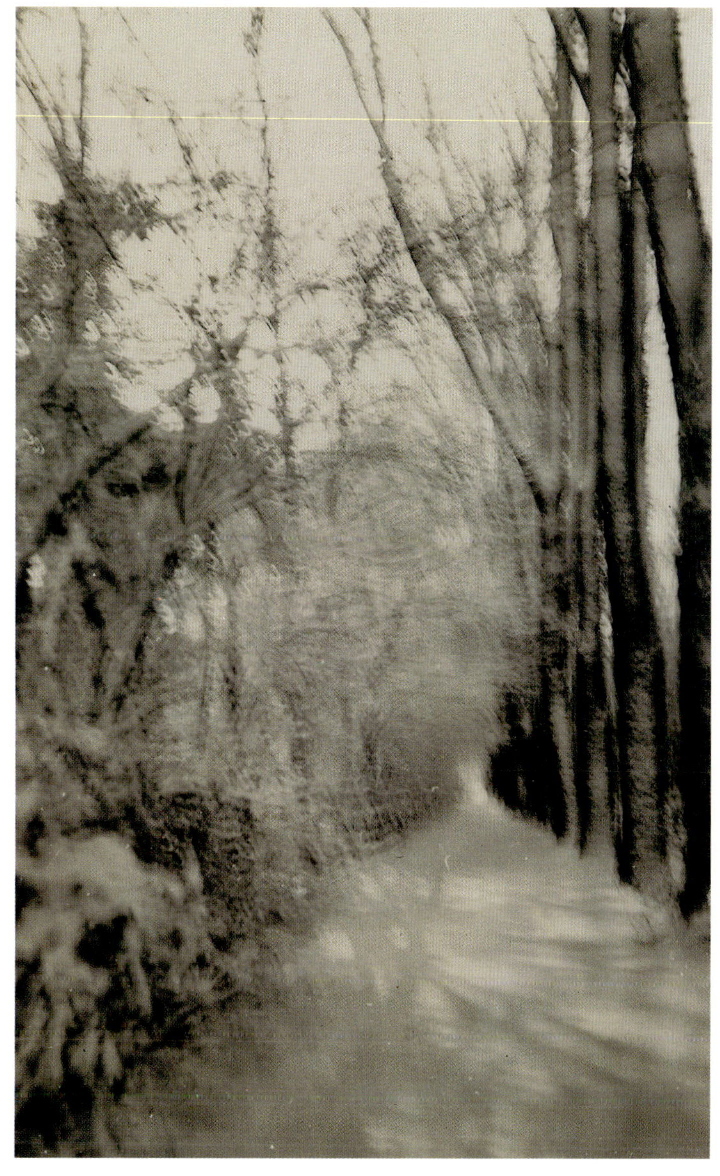

KATE MATTHEWS

A Snowy Morning, Ashwood Avenue, Pewee Valley, Kentucky
from the "Kate Matthews Family Album"
ca. 1900

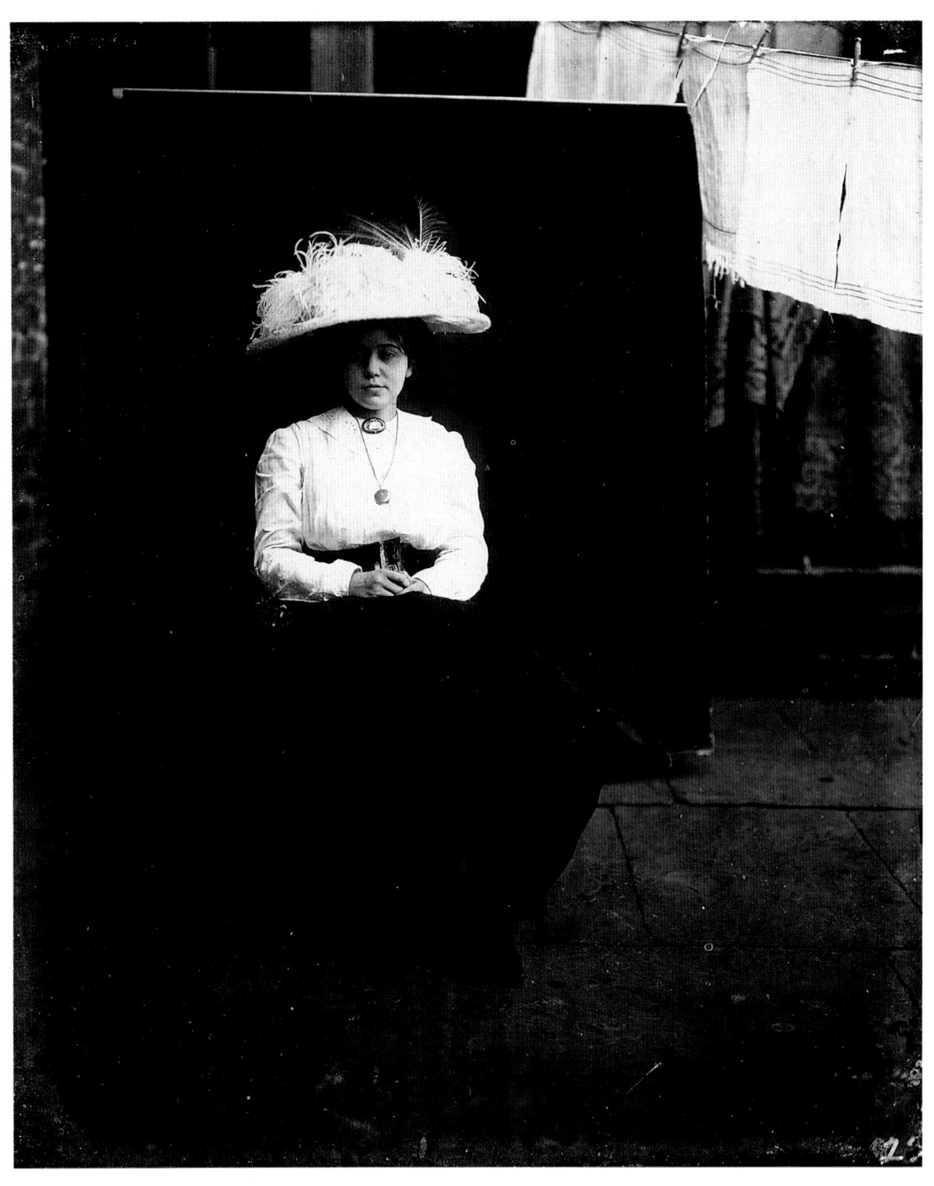

ERNEST J. BELLOCQ
Woman in a White Hat
ca. 1911–13

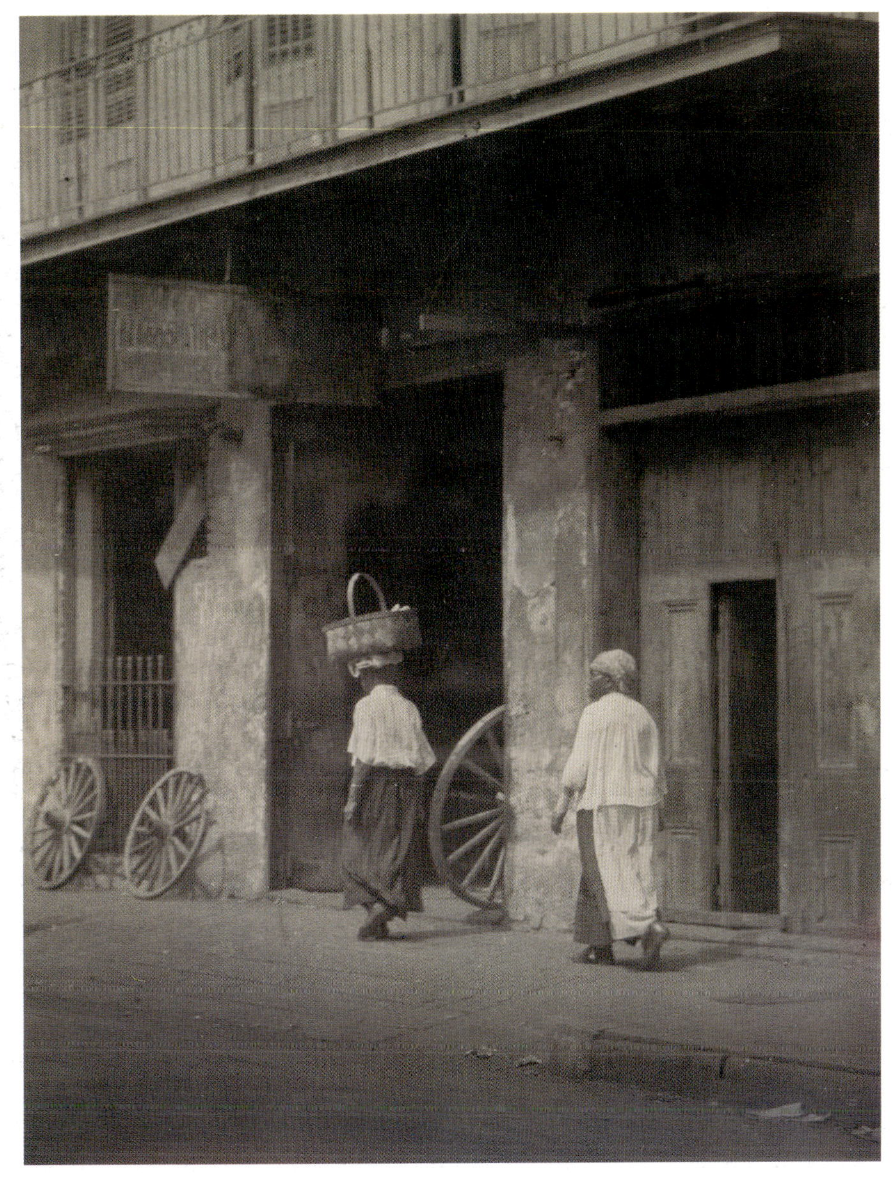

ARNOLD GENTHE

Chartres Street, Formerly the Main Shopping Thoroughfare, New Orleans, Louisiana from the book *Impressions of Old New Orleans*

1925 or 1926

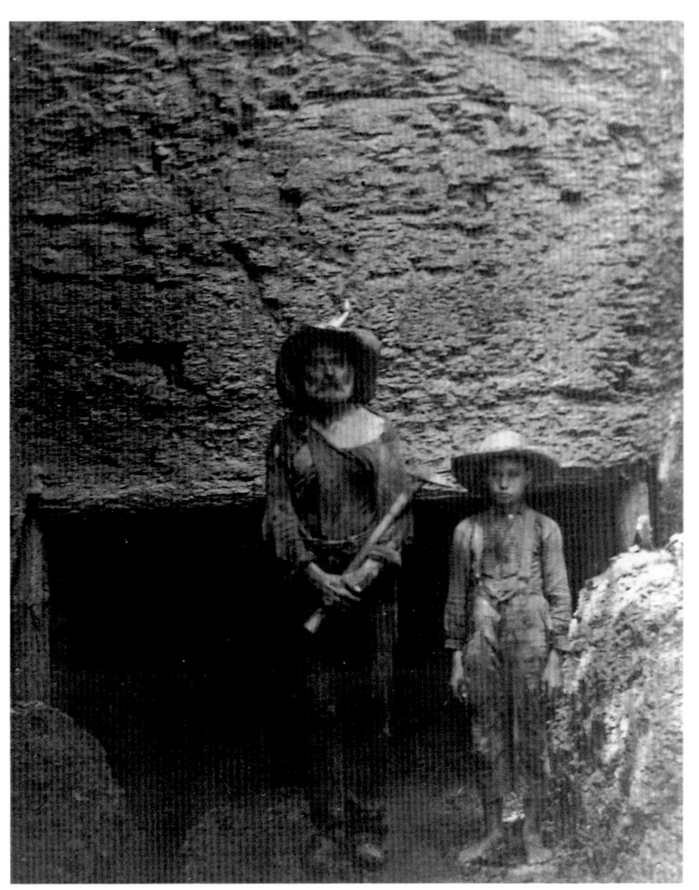

GEORGE H. DABBS

Coal Opening on the Lurn Drake Farm, Butler County, Kentucky from the "Arthur Y. Ford Album"
ca. 1900–1904

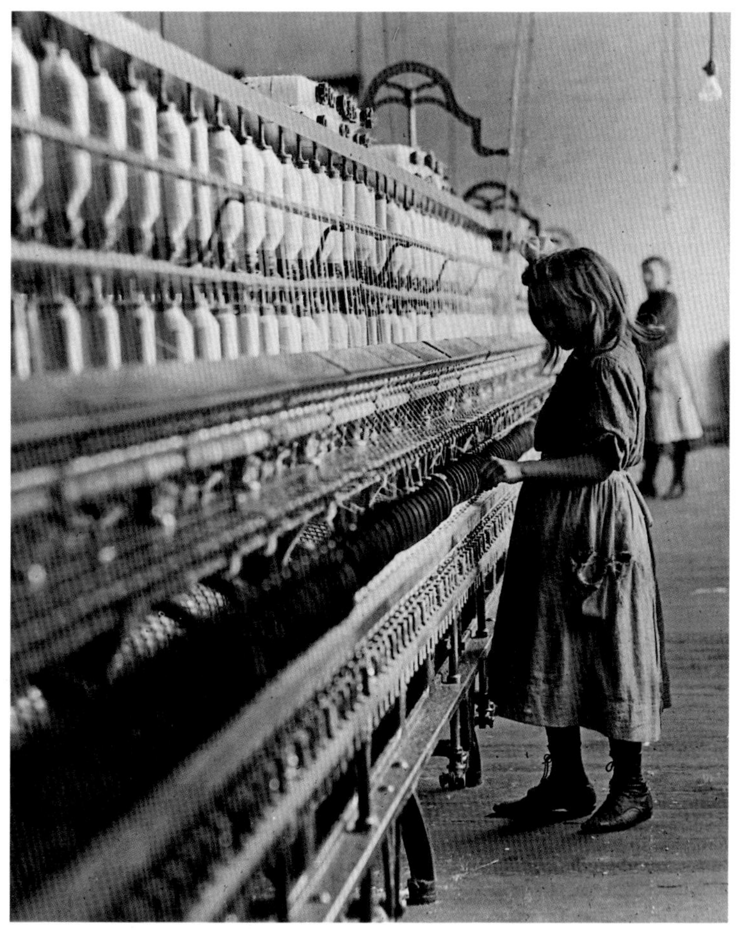

LEWIS W. HINE

Sadie Pfeifer, 48 Inches High. One of Many Small Children at Work from the series "Child Labor"
1908

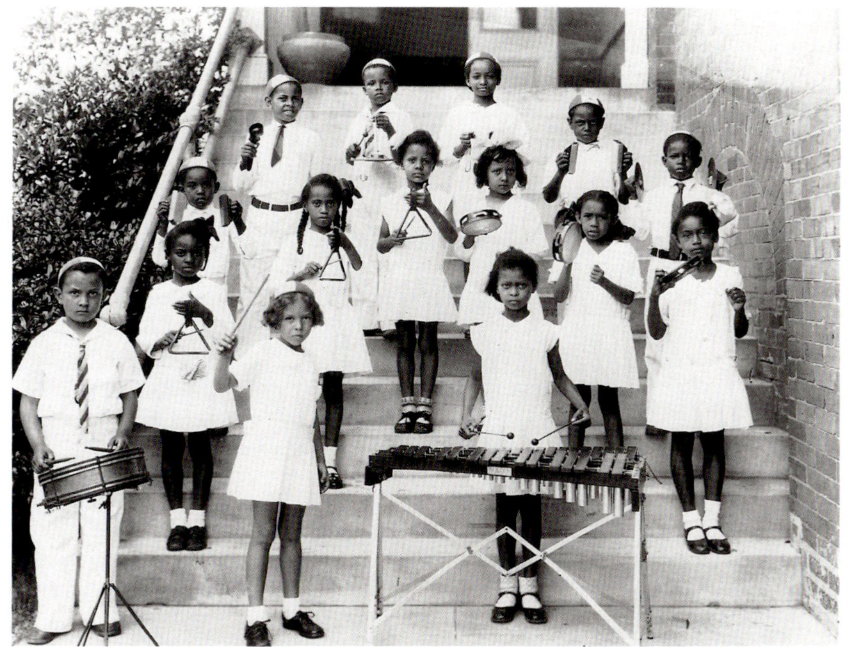

ARTHUR P. BEDOU

Craig School Kinder Band, New Orleans, Louisiana

ca. 1930s

MOTHER ST. CROIX

Girls around the Statue of the Sacred Heart of Jesus, Ursuline Convent Academy, New Orleans, Louisiana

ca. 1905

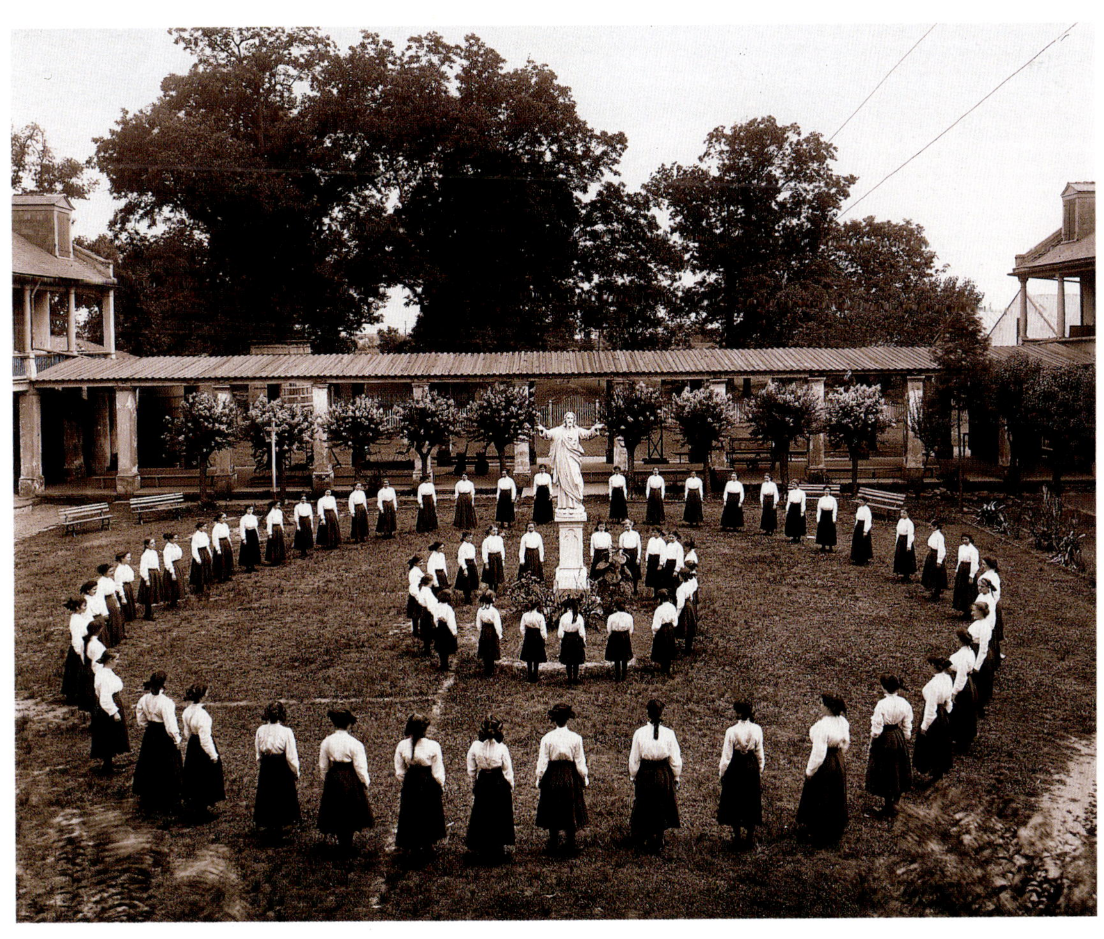

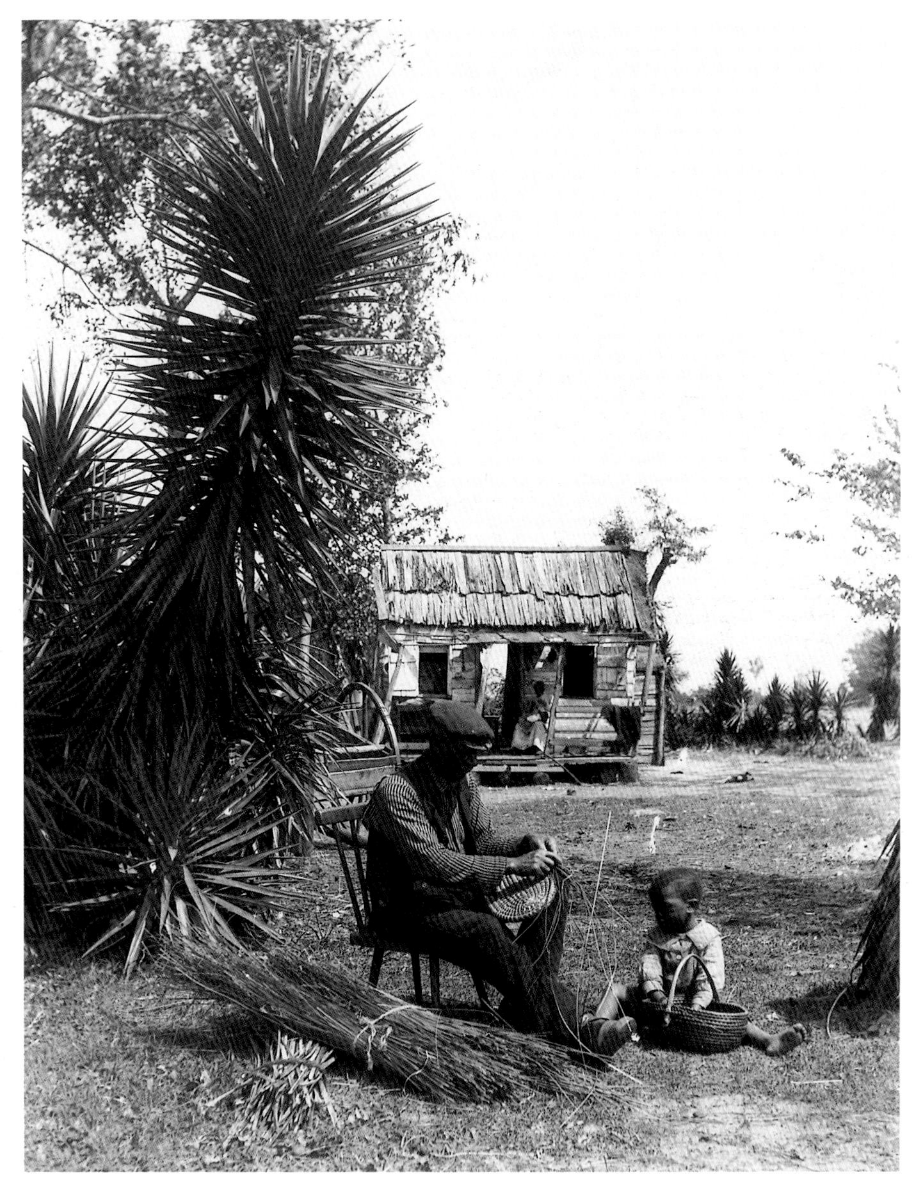

LEIGH RICHMOND MINER

Alfred Graham, The First Teacher of Basketry at Penn, Brought the Craft from Africa as a Boy

1909

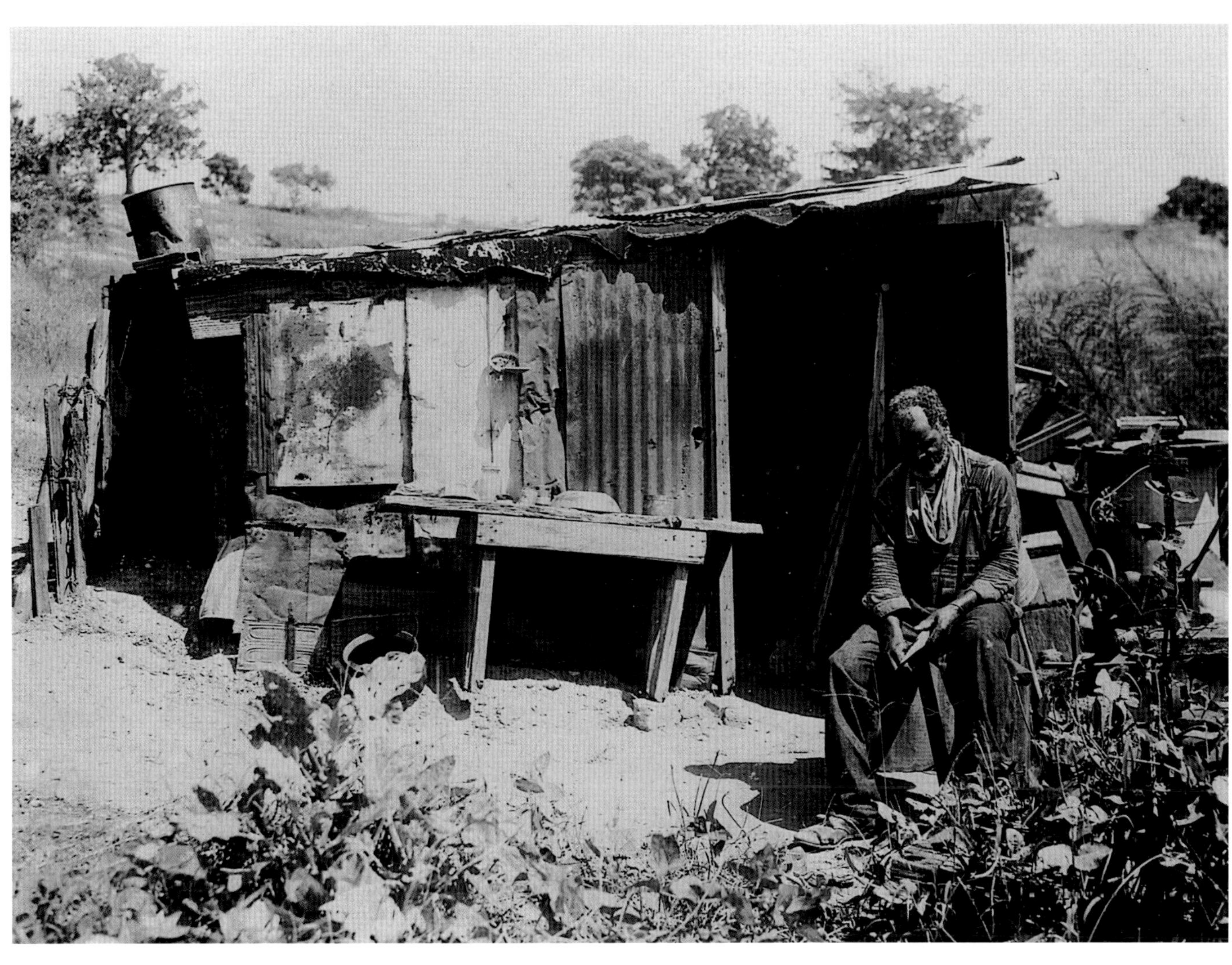

PRENTICE H. POLK
Charles Turner at His Cabin
1930

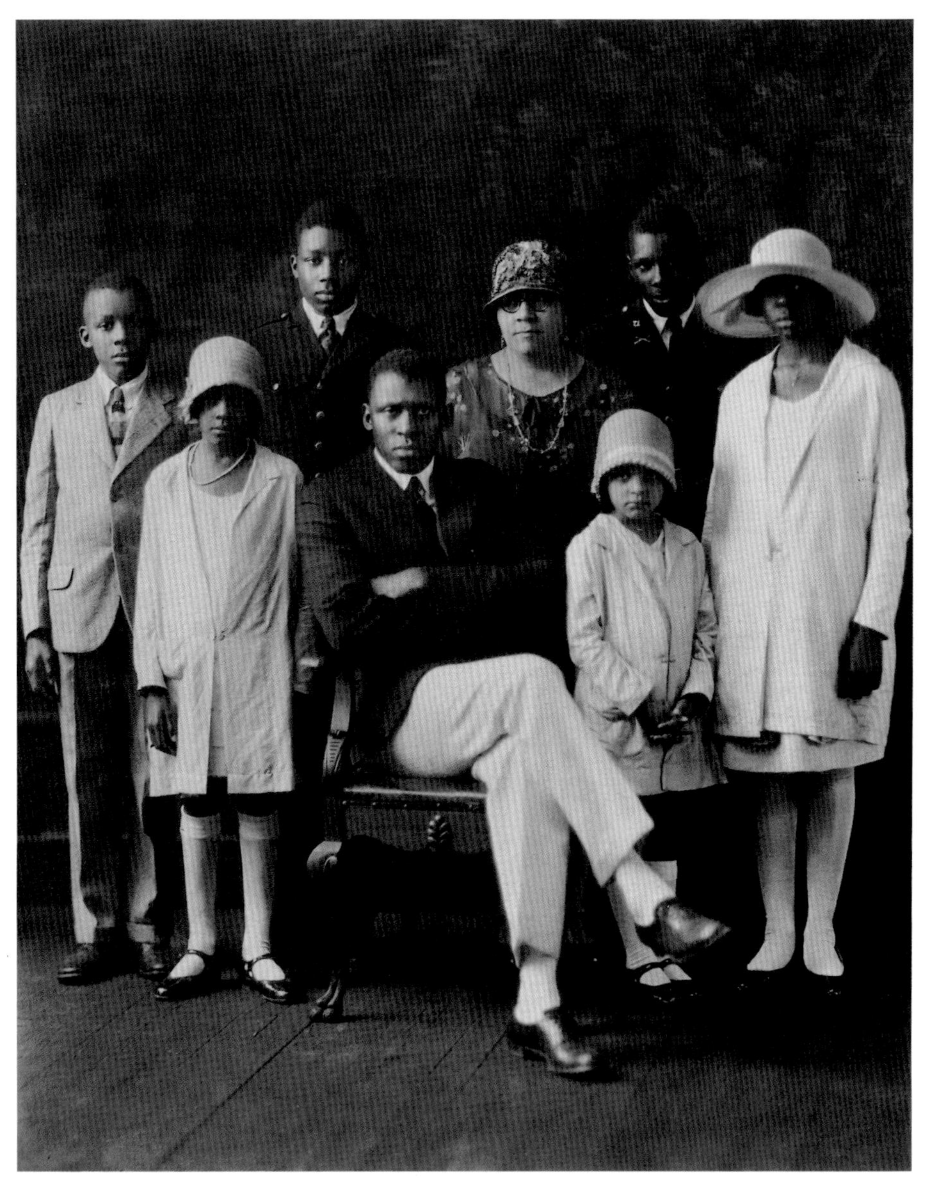

PRENTICE H. POLK

Portrait of Mr. and Mrs. T. M. Campbell and Their Children

ca. 1932

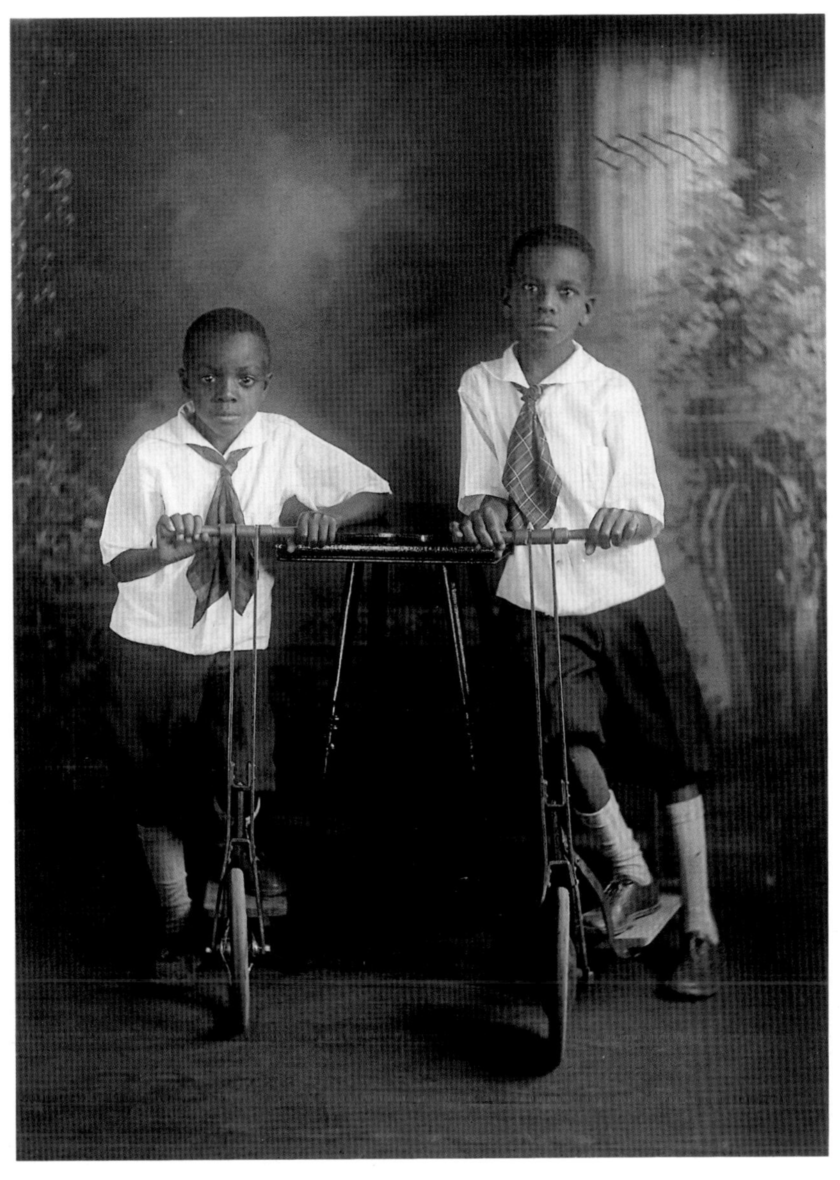

RICHARD SAMUEL ROBERTS
Portrait of Hilliard and James Hopkins
ca. 1920s

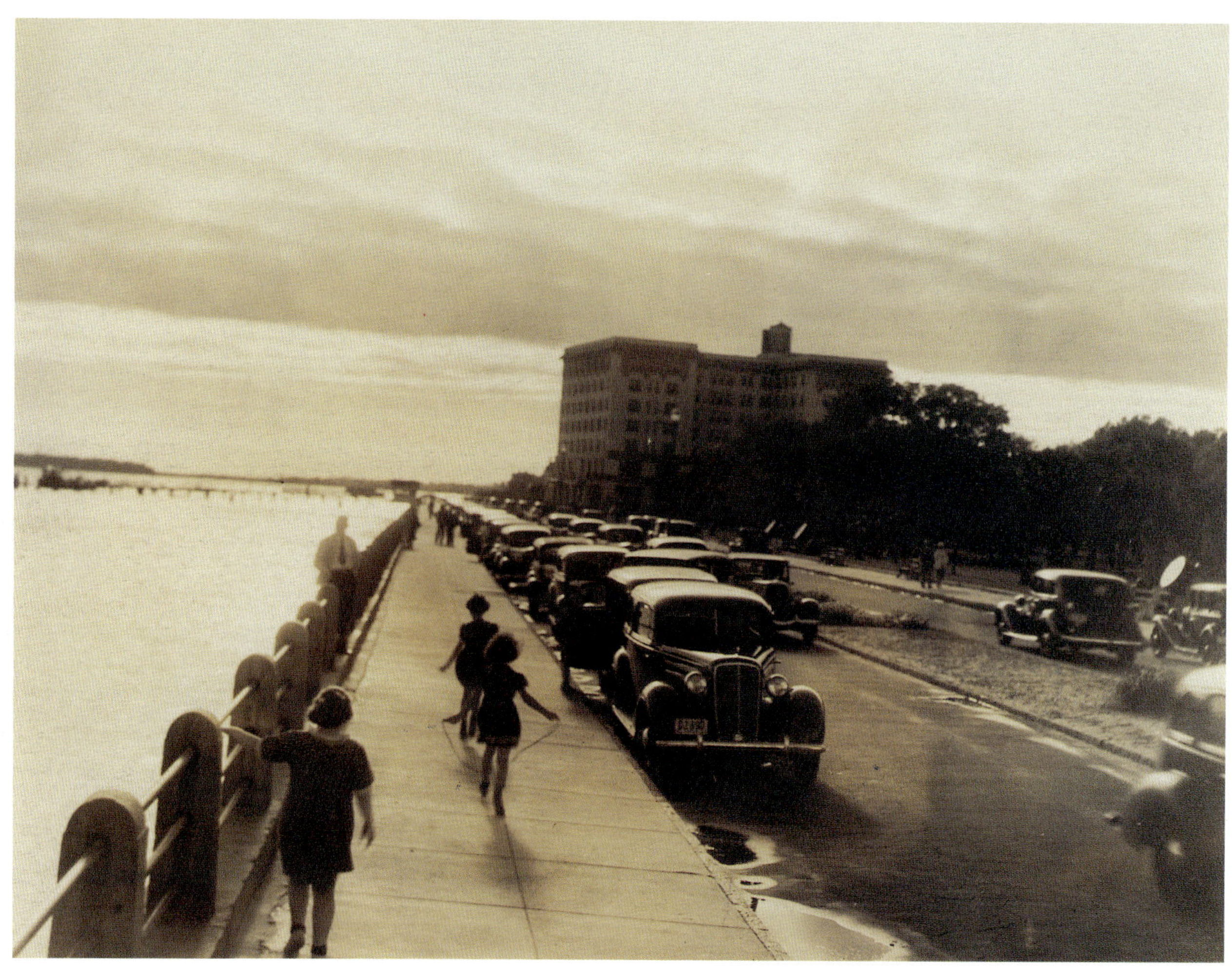

BAYARD WOOTTEN

Sunset across the Ashley from the Battery, Charleston, South Carolina
ca. 1935

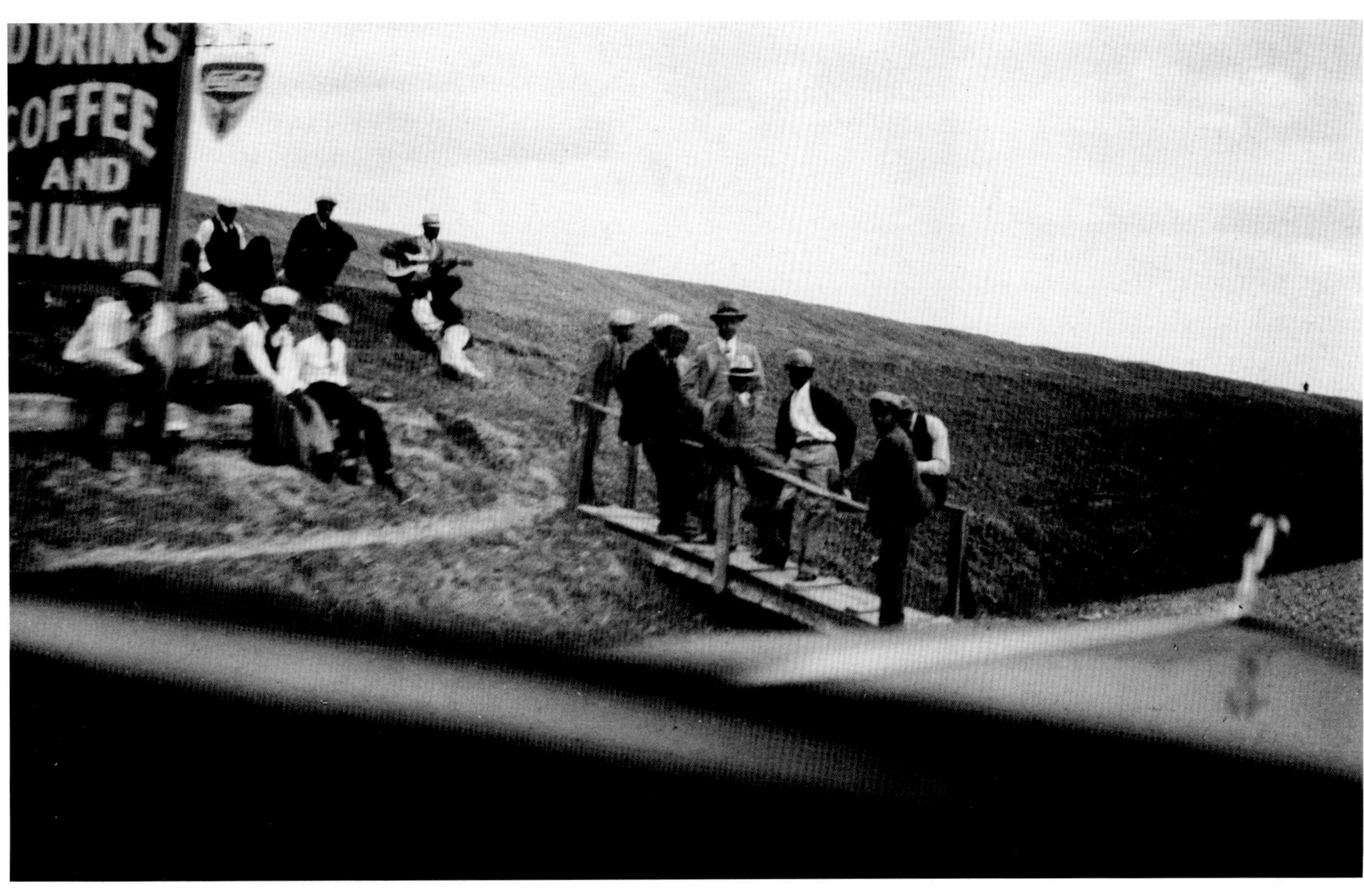

WALKER EVANS

Levee Seen from Car Window, Vicinity New Orleans

1935

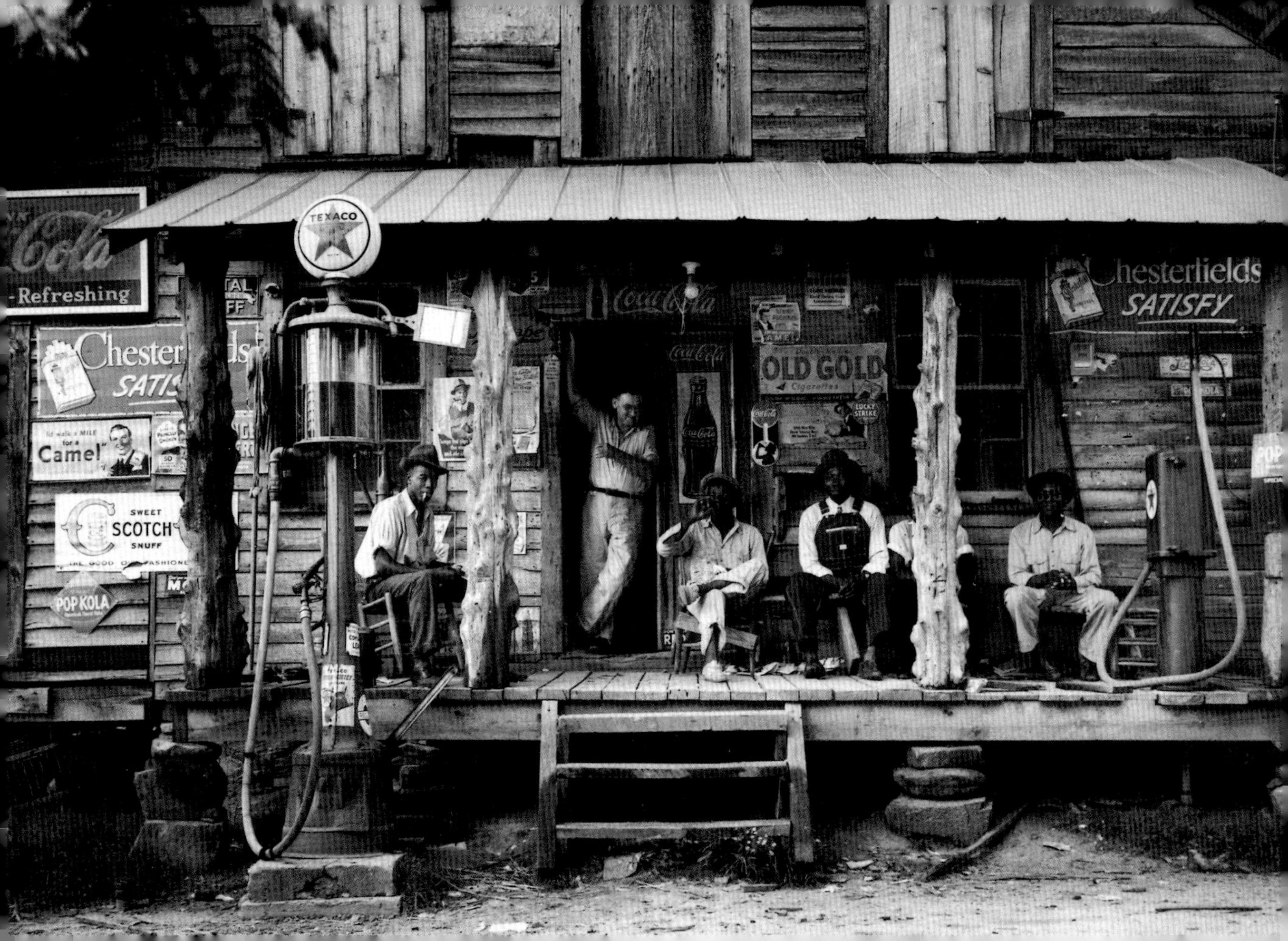
Cola
-Refreshing
TEXACO
Chesterfields
SATISFY
Camel"
SWEET
SCOTCH
SNUFF
POP KOLA
Coca-Cola
OLD GOLD
Cigarettes
LUCKY STRIKE

WILLIE MORRIS

BLESSED THAT WE WERE

The mid-1930s to the 1950s coincide with my own birth and growing up in a little village in the Mississippi Delta. Indeed, a number of these pictures were taken in places not far from my hometown. For that reason among many, these photographs resonate for me in reality and remembrance. They are my own *deja-vus*.

We seemed so isolated in the small-town South then. My childhood and teenage years were poised, fragilely and inevitably, before *Brown v. Board of Education.* In the vast alluvial fields of the Delta we saw the Negroes chopping the cotton with their hoes. In an adjacent field would be the Angus cattle. The vista was forever of black earth, black people, black beasts, and we could hear the muffled song:

I ain't got too long now, I ain't got too long . . .
I ain't got too long now, I ain't got too long . . .
The man he comin' for me soon.

These were the years in the South of grueling rural poverty, of the malignant tenant system, of the black exodus to the North—surely one of the largest migrations in human history—and then the burgeoning urbanization undergirded by the mechanization of agriculture, a mechanization so sweeping that on a trip through the Delta the writer Brother Will Campbell looked across the land and claimed he saw a monstrous tractor cultivating the rows, empty and without a driver.

Whether taken in the thirties, forties, or fifties, these photographs share an ineluctable thread: people gathered in clusters in towns and stores, by creeks and levees, the very façades of buildings with their signs and posters inviting the native human species: *community*. All these evoke the words of my friend Eudora Welty, two of whose photographs grace this exhibition, about the South's profound sense of place, not simply in the historical or philosophical way, "but in the worlds of sight and sound and smell, in its earth and water and sky and in its seasons, and in its sense of generations and continuity." Miss Welty took her Mississippi photographs while working for the WPA during the Depression, and of course strikingly represented here are the works of her distinguished associates involved with the Farm Security Administration in these years: Walker Evans, Dorothea Lange, Ben Shahn, Marion Post Wolcott.

In these photographs, I note for my own personal discernment several indelible categories, or characteristics, of those years, the images of which resuscitate for me and help keep afresh in the heart's core the indwelling memories.

Southerners Passing Time (as only they can in the South, then and now): A Tennessee medicine show, a Georgia boy reading a comic book in a car, men examining a watermelon on a courthouse lawn. Margaret Bourke-White's image of Louisville flood victims under a garish billboard shows them waiting, waiting. Lange's picture of men loitering on the front porch of a crossroads store in Alabama in 1937 is as familiar to me, almost spookily so, as anything I ever knew in my childhood.

Southerners Working: A woman making biscuits, picketing copper miners waiting for the scabs, people arranging tobacco in a North Carolina warehouse. Reverend Lonzie Odie Taylor's depiction of four black bank owners proudly standing in front of the Tri-State Bank in Memphis in 1946 presages a much newer day. W. Eugene Smith poignantly captures a black midwife and her apprentice easing the pain of birth.

Civil War Vestiges: Bayard Wootten's camera appropriates the Battery and the old Fort Sumter Hotel in Charleston. Walker Evans photographs a monument in the battlefield at Vicksburg—a particular one I well remember from my earliest days when my grandparents took me there and I wondered what on earth had *happened* here to explain these sober, steadfast monuments.

Exteriors of Buildings: My personal favorites among the many here are Stern J. Bramson's neoned Louisville scene in 1946, and three of Walker Evans's, vintage 1936—the summer of the Berlin Olympics—the stunning juxtapositions of a Negro shack and the county courthouse in Tupelo, Mississippi, and of Atlanta frame houses and a billboard proclaiming Carole Lombard's *Love Before Breakfast;* and the roadside stand in Birmingham with the boys out front hoisting the big watermelons. This latter photograph is worth tarrying before for the signs alone; the only time I met Evans I told him I admired him for his signs, among other things.

How We Lived at Home: Jack Delano's picture of the elderly couple sitting in the parlor of their mansion suggests the sumptuous and sedate style in the midst of the Depression, and Fonville Winans's of Cajuns at dinner makes me wish I had been with them at that jolly long-ago repast.

Symbolic Representations of Southerners: Clarence John Laughlin's *Insect-Headed Tombstone* and his *Mirror of Long Ago*, both set in Louisiana, display this bizarre master's high gothic romanticism; the young woman in the plantation mirror is as mystical as the most evanescent dream.

Black and White: Lange's *Plantation Overseer and His Field Hands* in Mississippi in 1936, Wolcott's white cashiers paying off cotton pickers in Mississippi in 1939, Marion Palfi's *To the Colored Waiting Room, Florida* in the 1940s, John Vachon's courtroom scene in Virginia in 1941, W. Eugene Smith's burning cross at a North Carolina Klan rally in 1951, Dan Weiner's solitary white passenger on an empty bus during the Montgomery boycott of 1956, and Wolcott's arresting image of a Negro man using the "colored" entrance to a movie theatre in Belzoni, Mississippi, in 1939—each of these reminds us where we as Southerners have been in the long inexorable journey. Wolcott's photograph is especially significant to me, for Belzoni was an adjoining town, and I went to picture shows at that very theatre. I remember as yesterday the "colored stairway," the ten cents admission, and the Dr. Pepper sign.

And, finally, *Portraits:* Two couples in a booth of a juke joint in Florida in 1939, a family on the road in Oklahoma in 1938, a Georgia sharecropper couple, a window display at a photo studio in Birmingham in 1936, a little black girl behind vines on a Tennessee porch in 1938, a black mother and child in Florida, a white mother and son in Arkansas in the 1940s—and Evans's abiding Allie Mae Burroughs, wife of an Alabama cotton tenant farmer, 1936. "These Southern ancestors, black and white," Alex Haley once wrote about old story-telling men, and women with hands deeply wrinkled from work, "have always struck me as the Foundation Timbers of our South, and I think that we who were reared and raised by them, and amongst them, are blessed that we were."

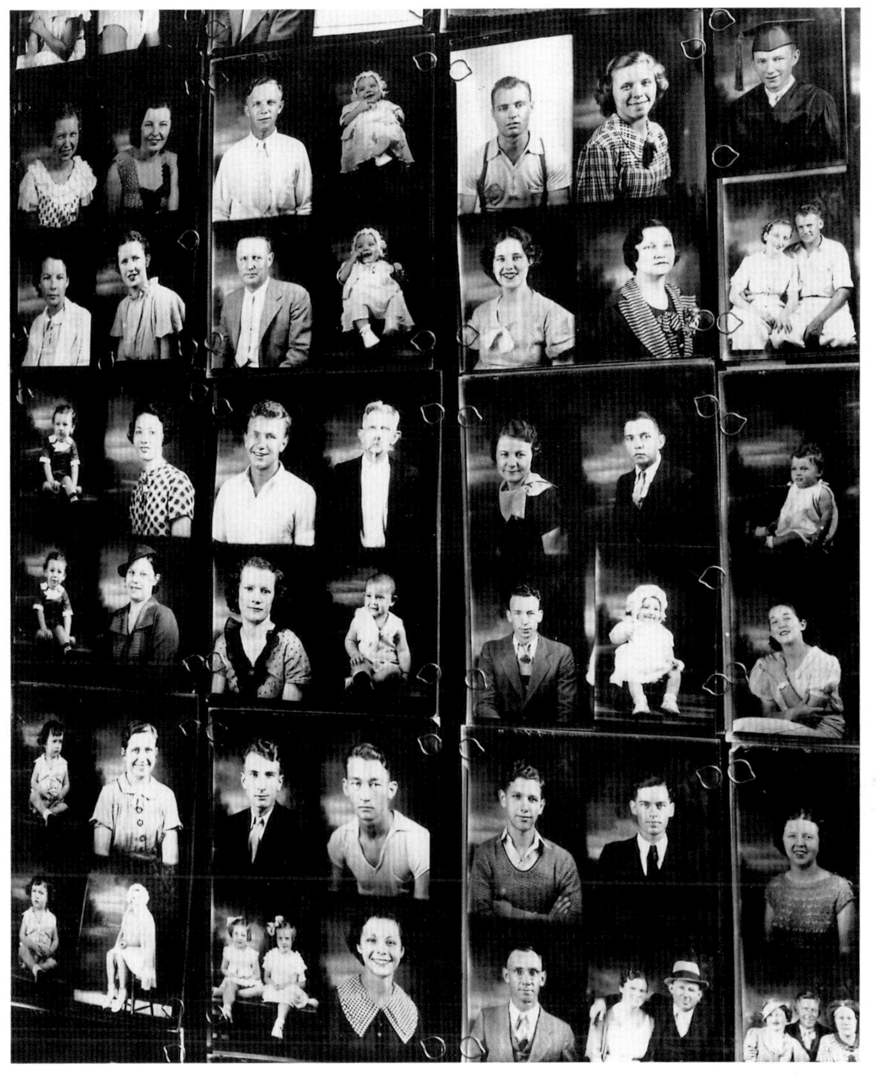

WALKER EVANS
Photographer's Display Window, Birmingham, Alabama
ca. 1936

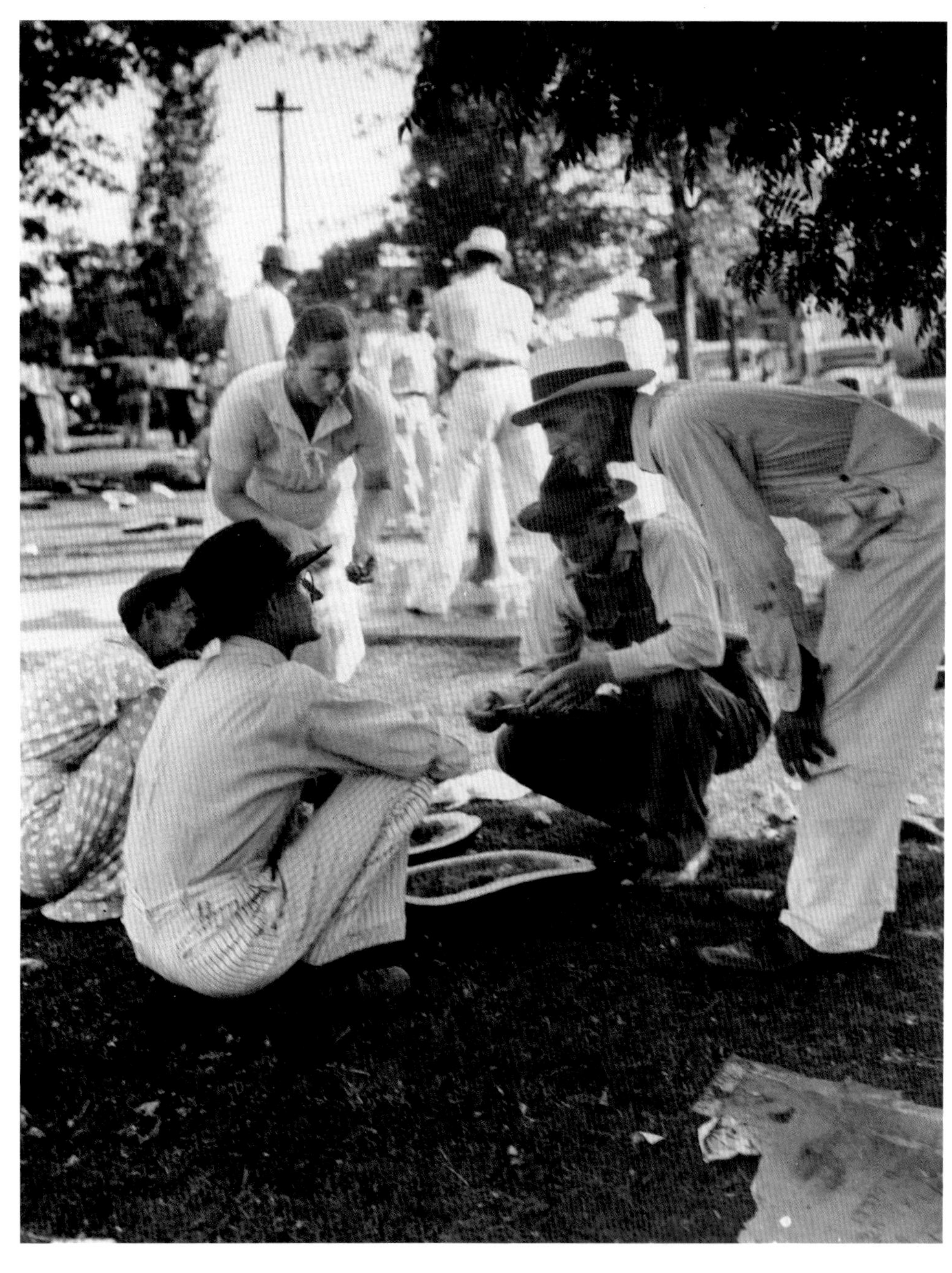

EUDORA WELTY

Political Rally on the Courthouse Grounds, Pontotoc, Mississippi

1930s

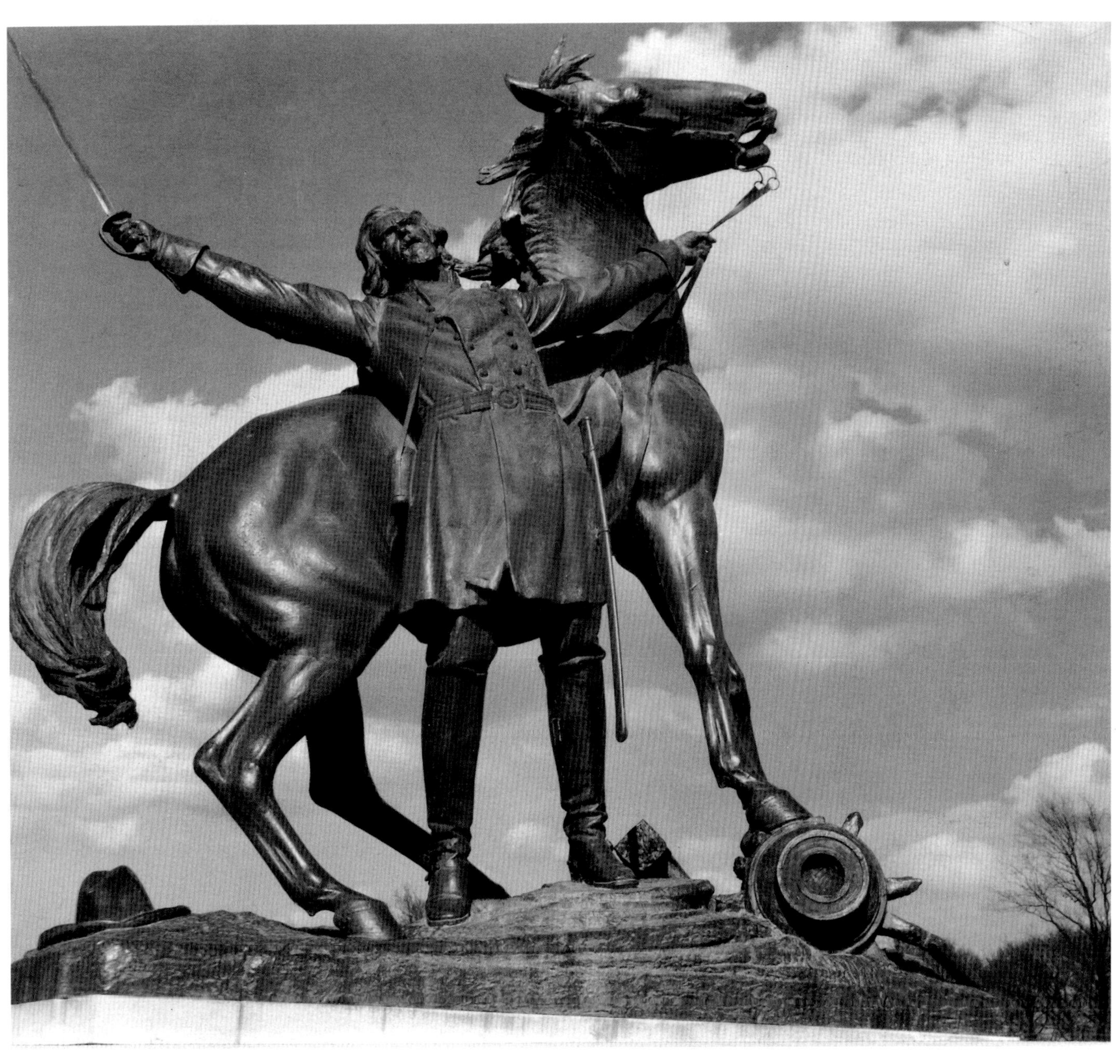

WALKER EVANS
Battlefield Monument, Vicksburg, Mississippi
1936

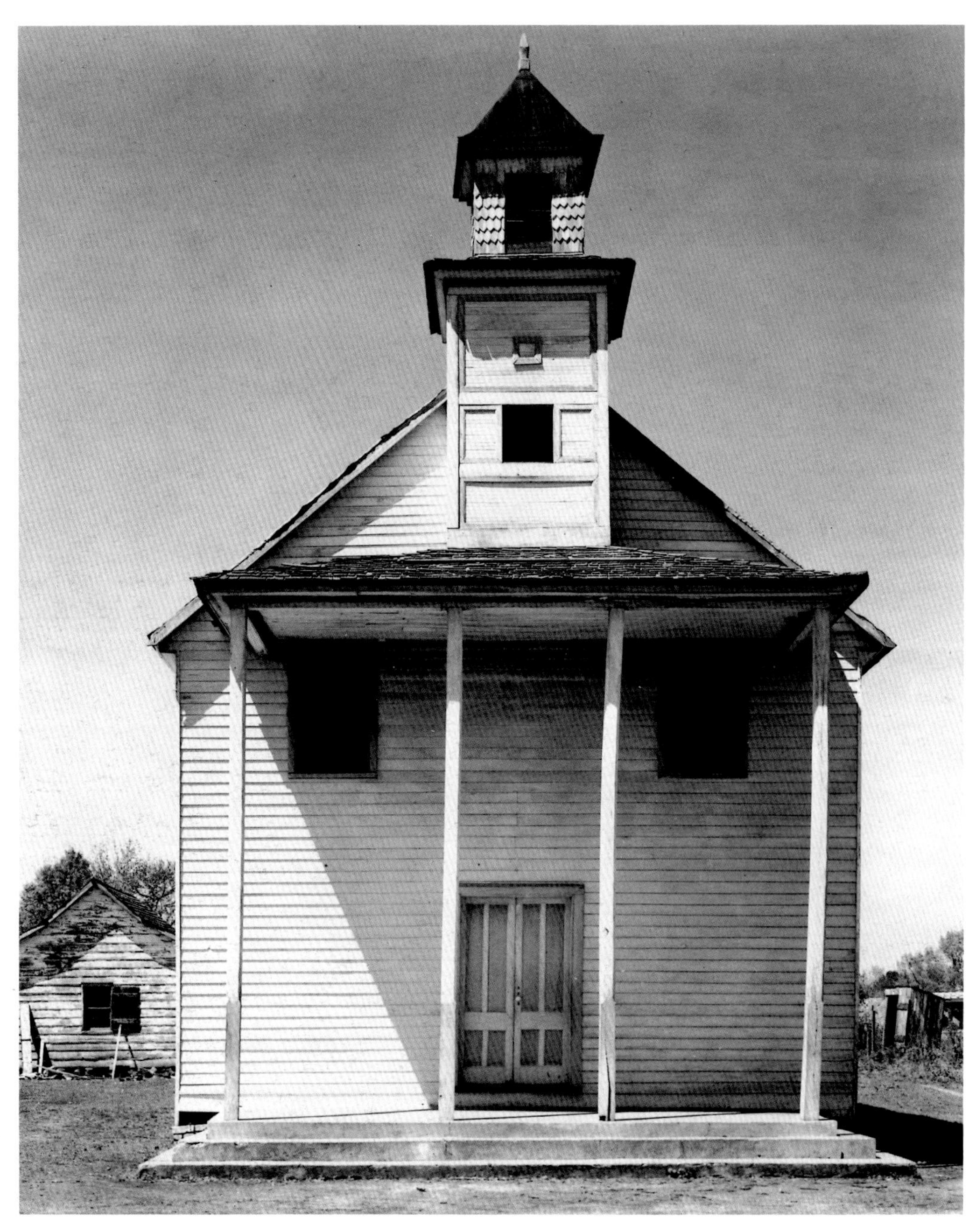

WALKER EVANS
Negro Church, South Carolina
1936

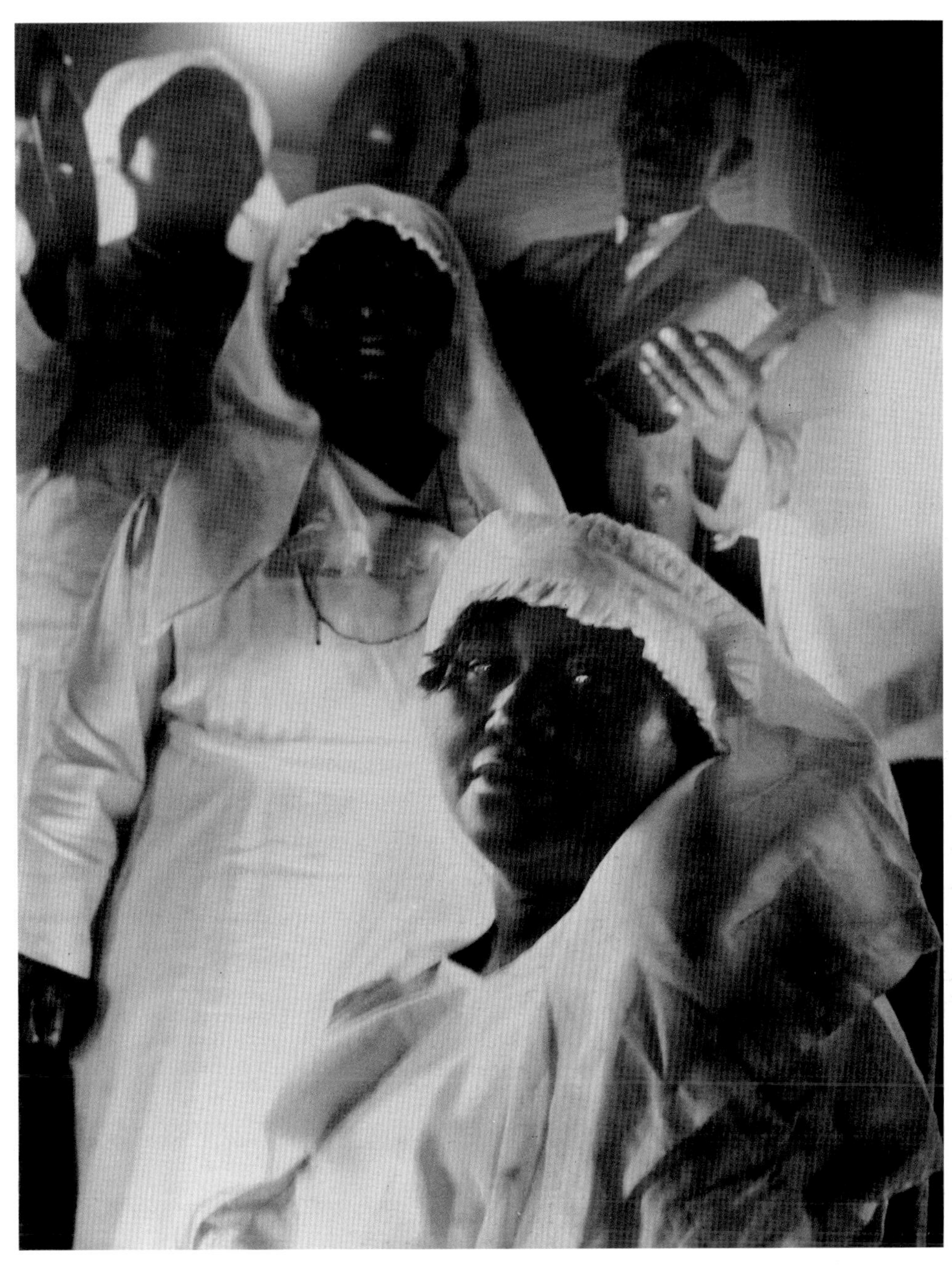

EUDORA WELTY

Preacher and Leaders of Holiness Church, Jackson, Mississippi

1939

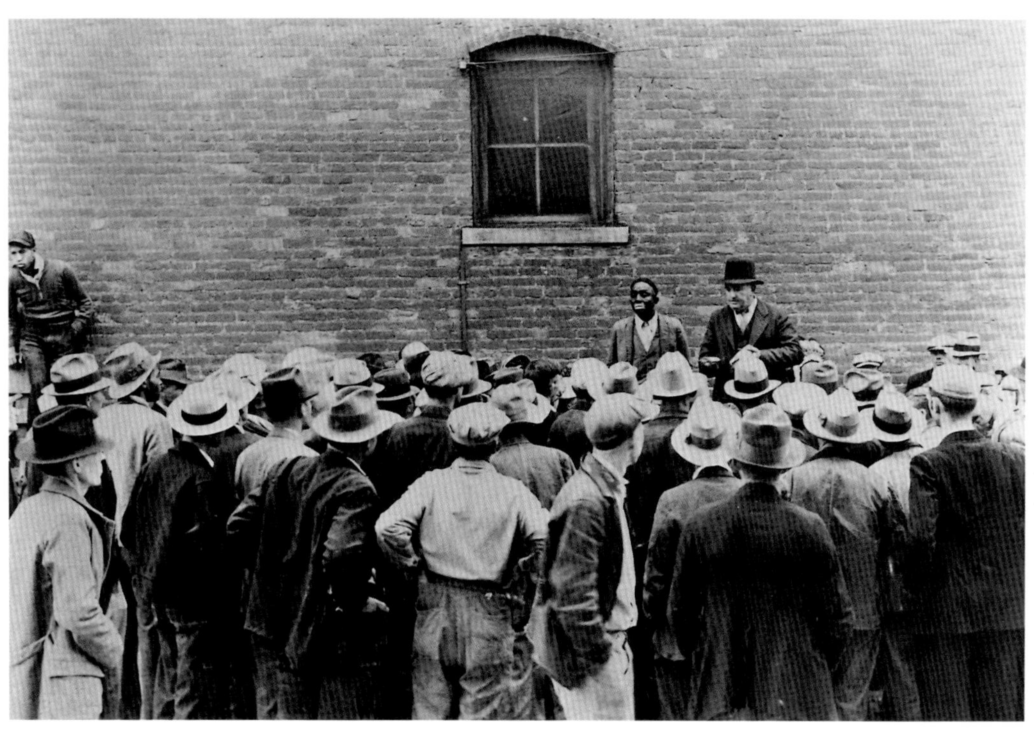

BEN SHAHN

Watching a Medicine Show, Huntingdon, Tennessee

1935

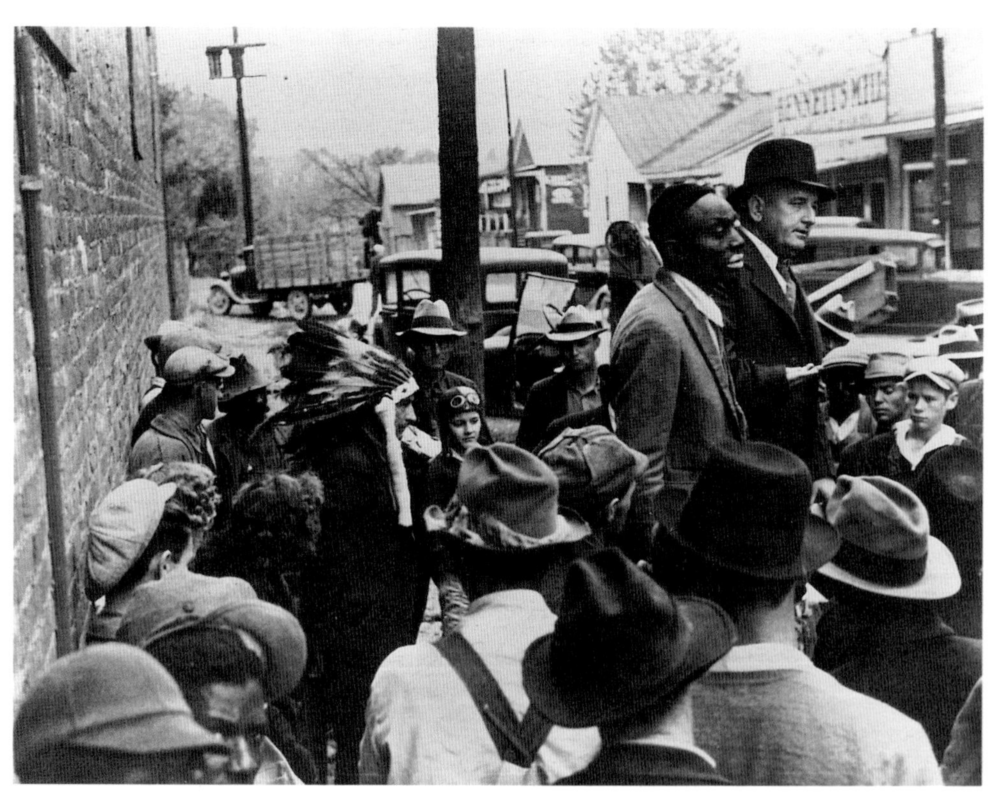

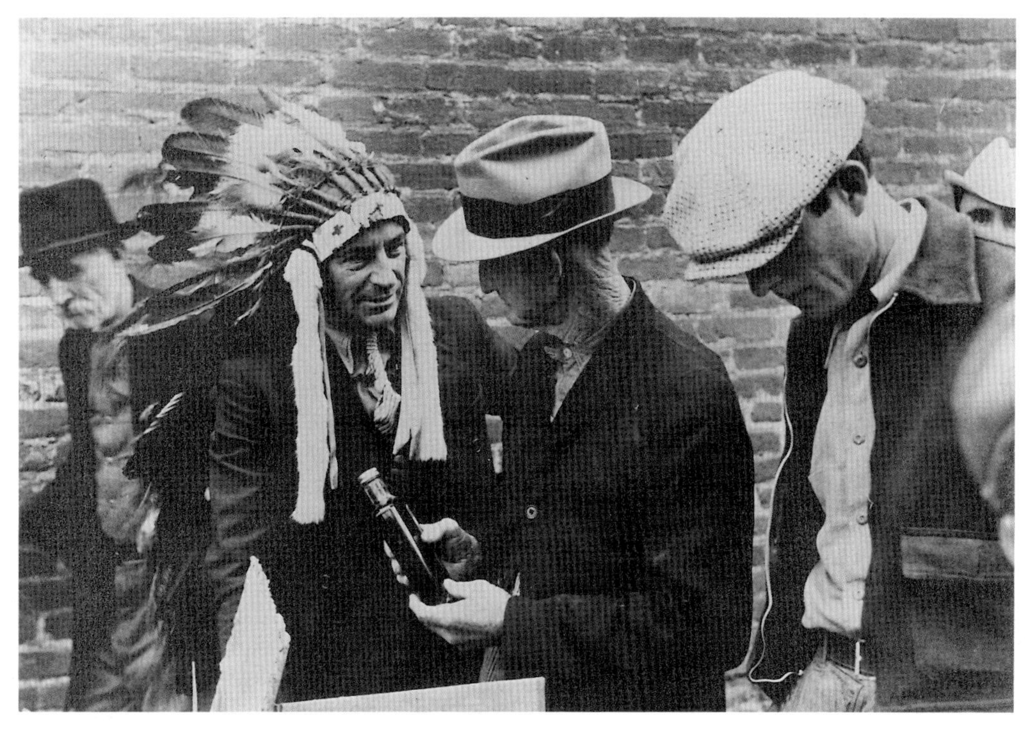

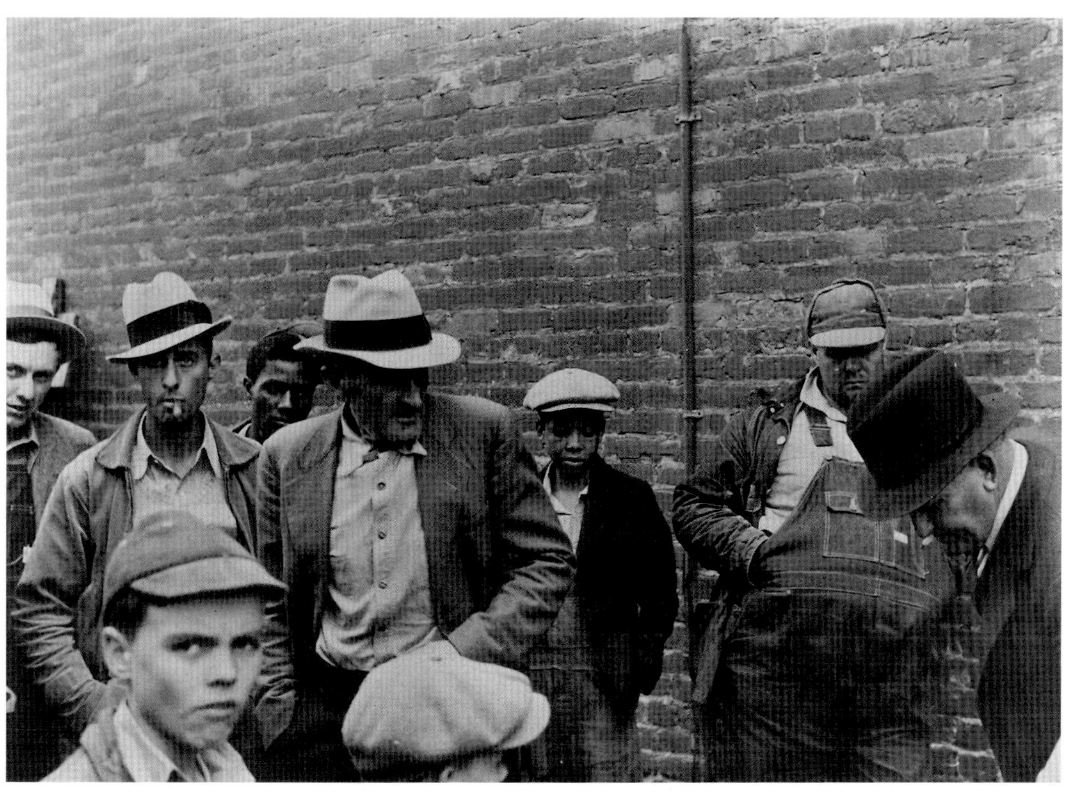

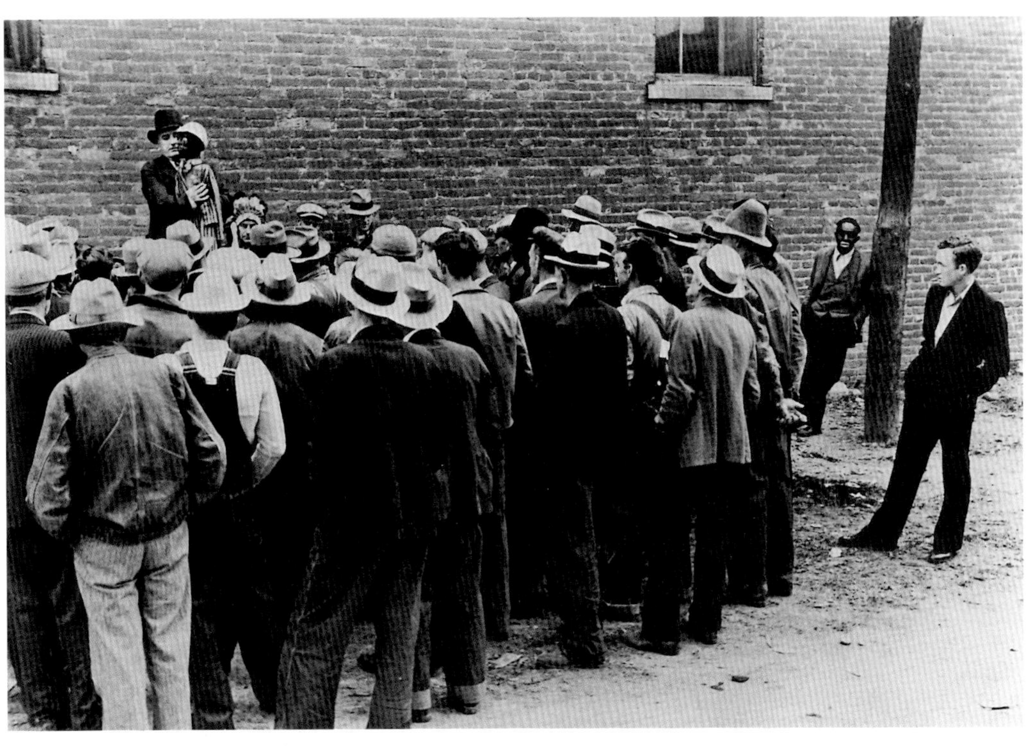

BEN SHAHN

Watching a Medicine Show, Huntingdon, Tennessee

1935

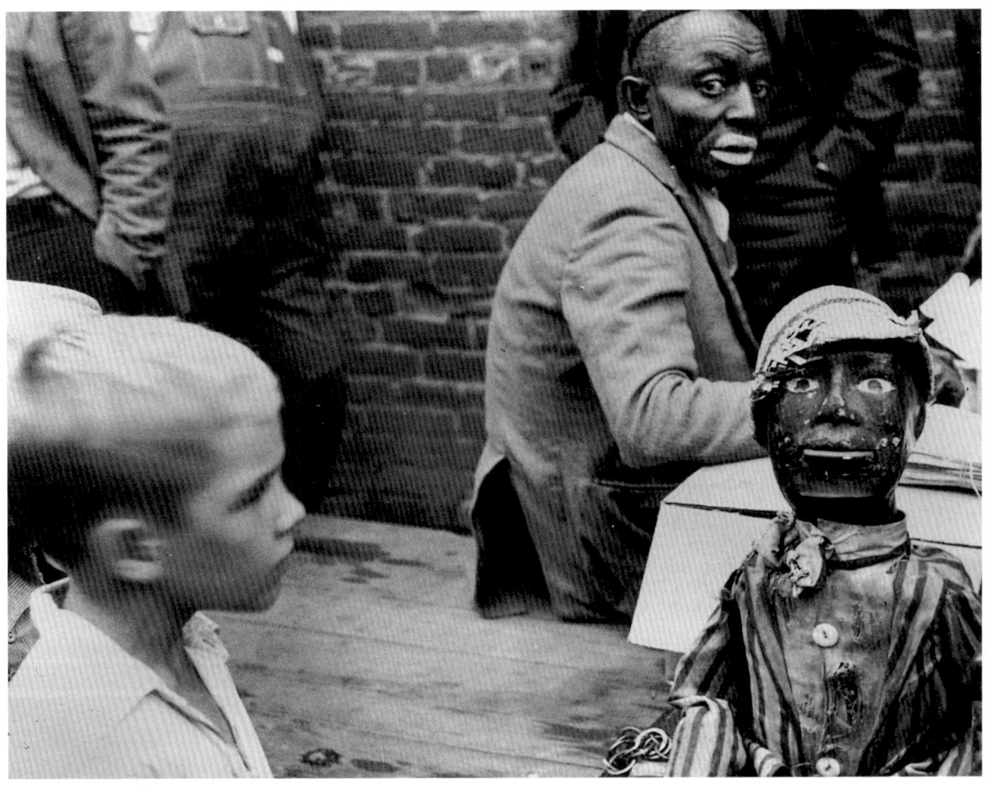

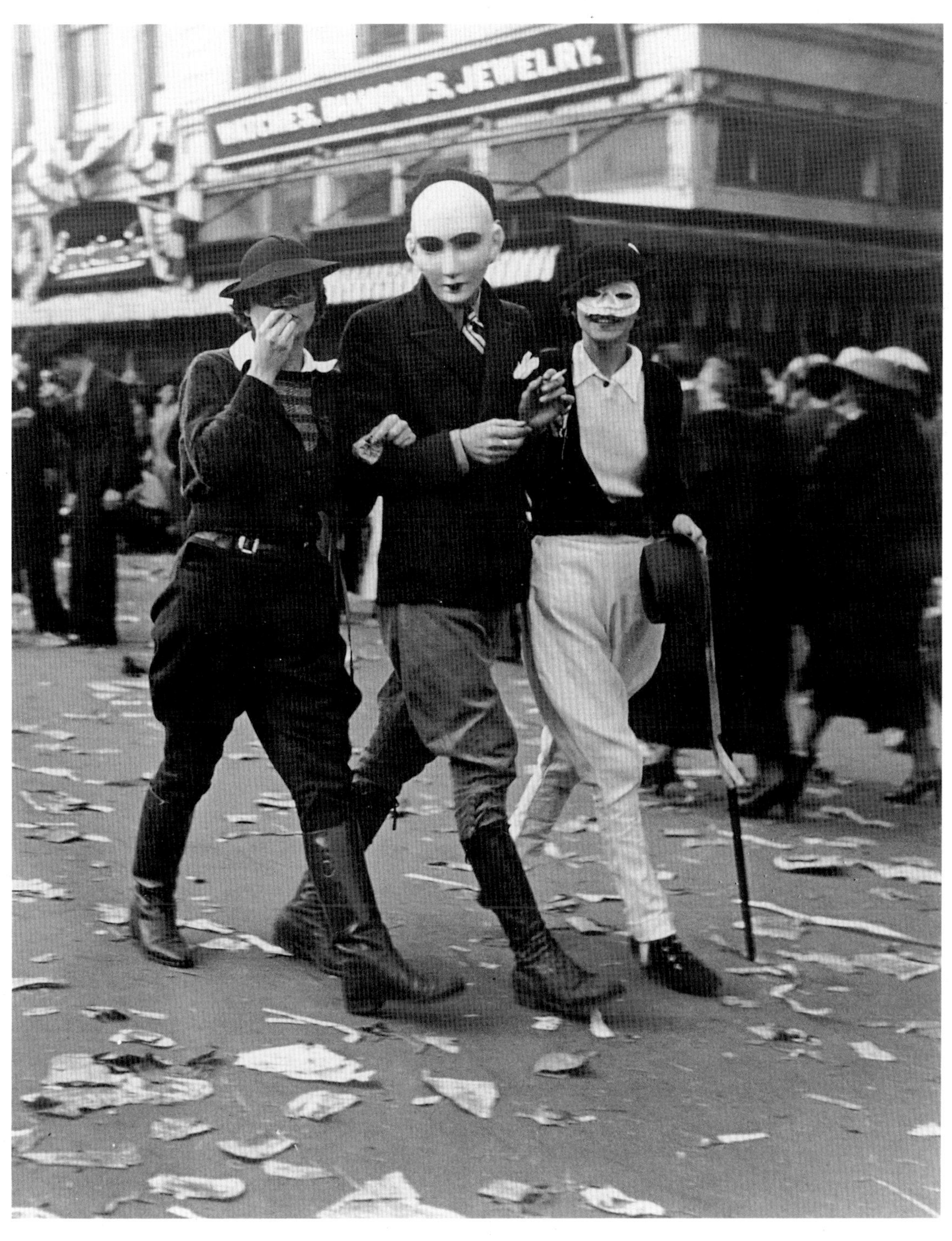

JOHN GUTMANN

The Game, New Orleans, Louisiana

1937

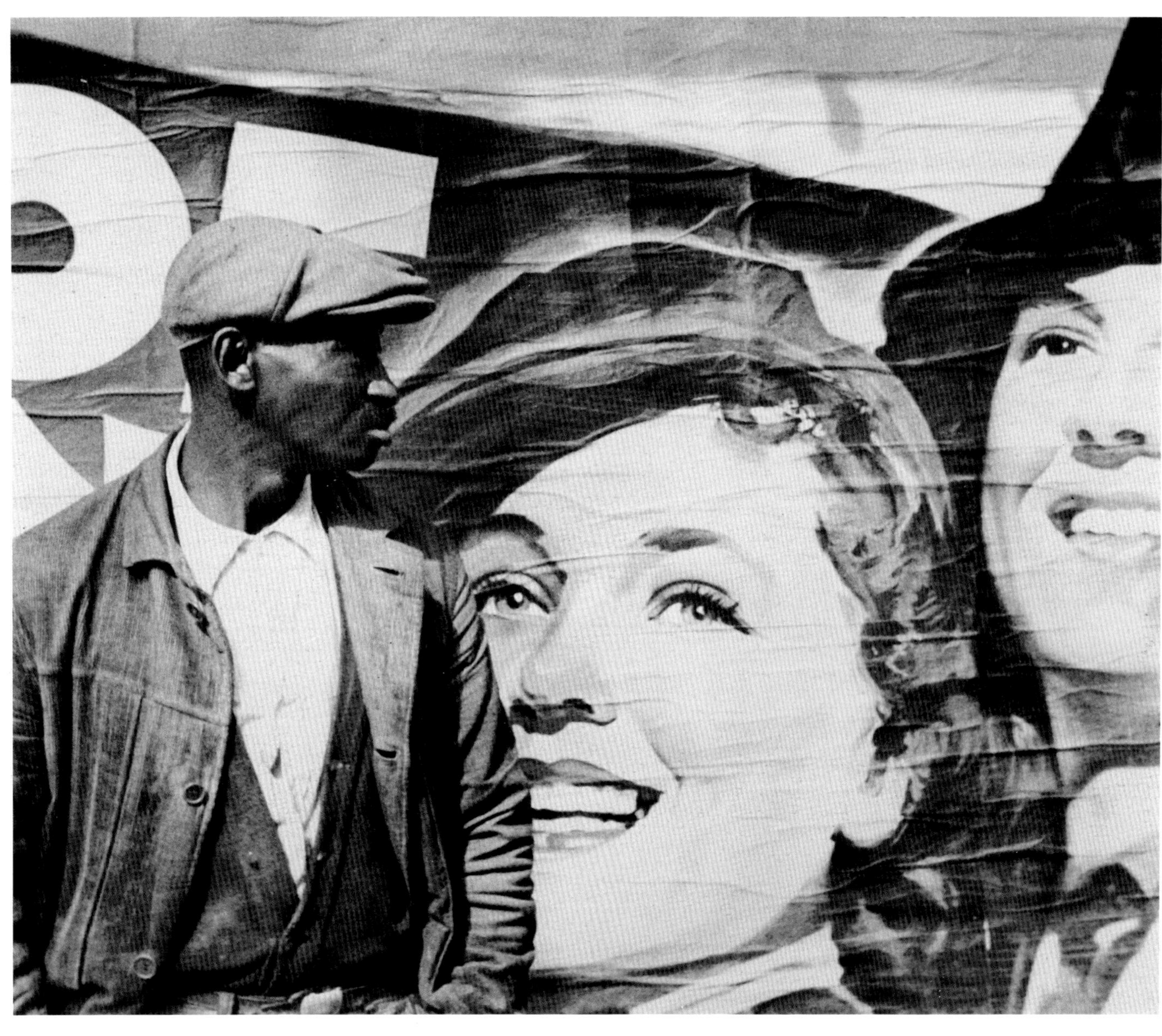

WALKER EVANS
Street Scene, Southern City
ca. 1936

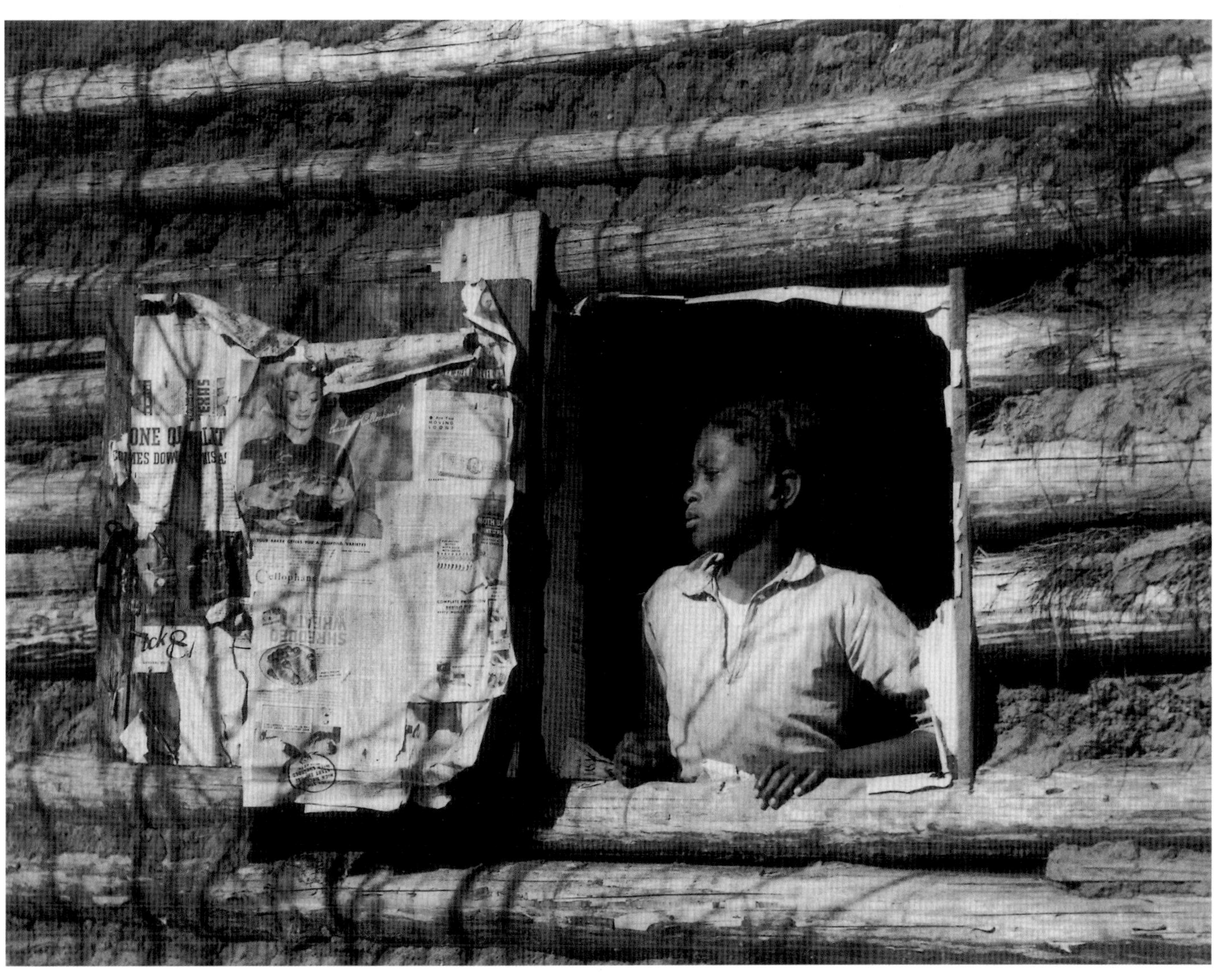

ARTHUR ROTHSTEIN

Aletta Bendolph in Log Cabin, Gee's Bend, Alabama

1937

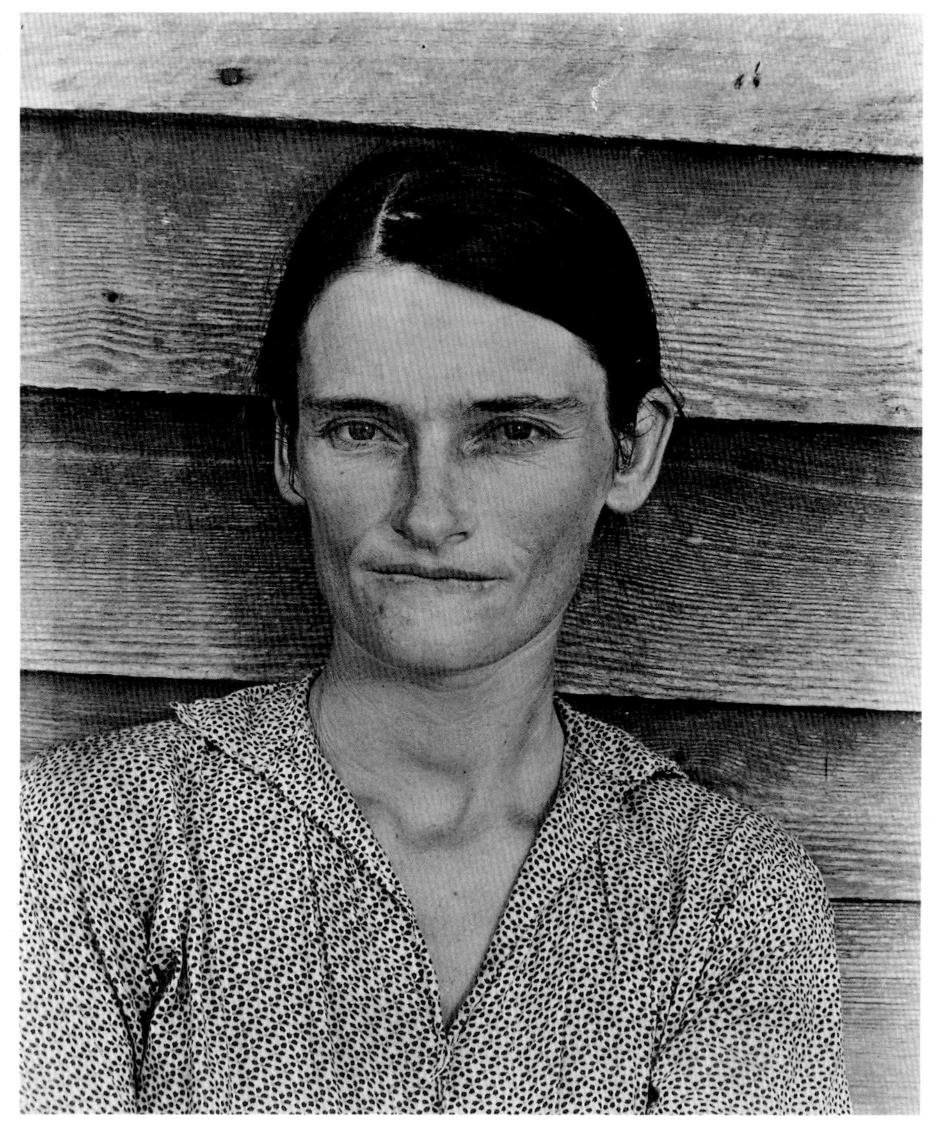

WALKER EVANS

Allie Mae Burroughs, Wife of a Cotton Sharecropper, Hale County, Alabama

1936

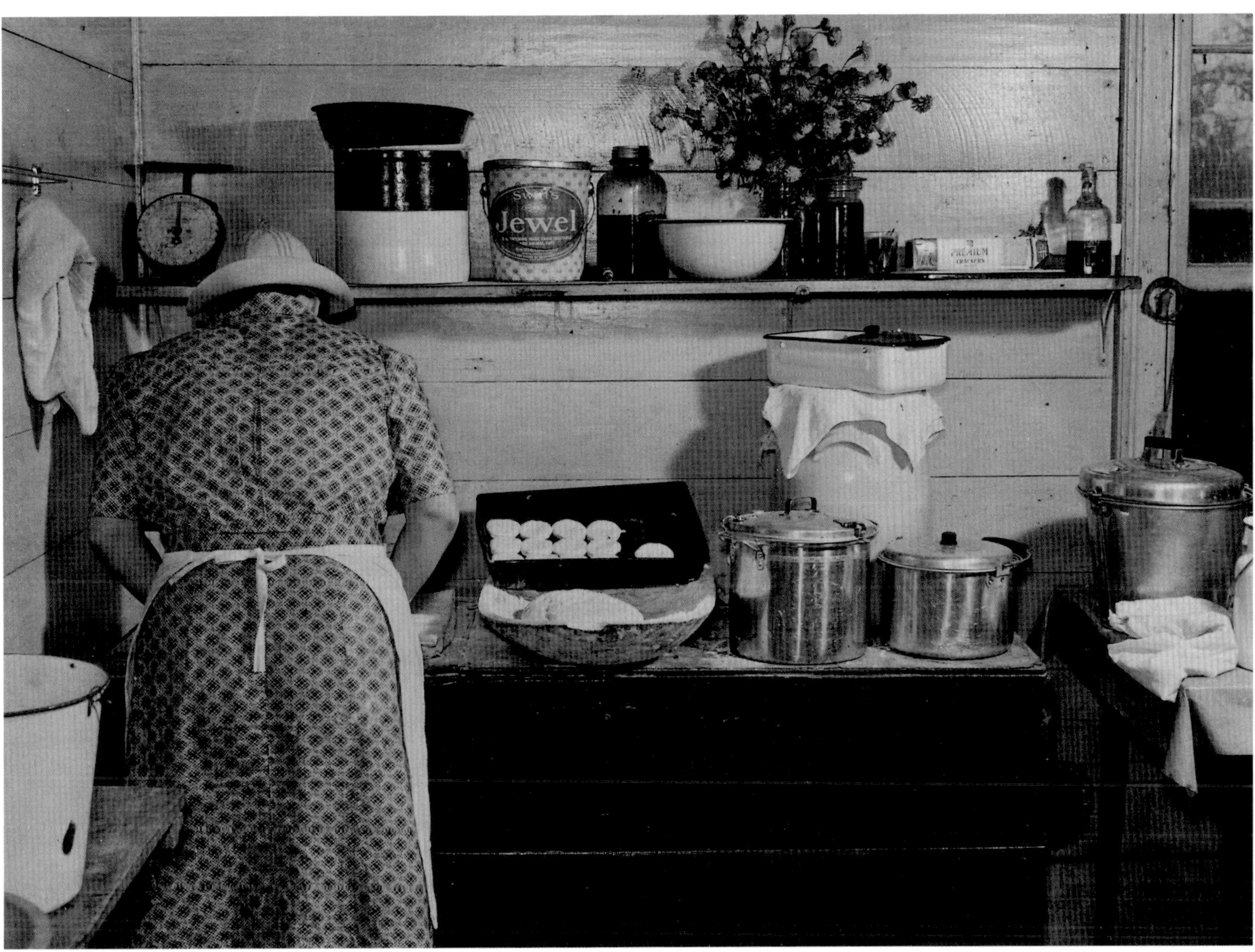

MARION POST WOLCOTT

Making Biscuits for Dinner on Corn Husking Day.
The Fred Wilkens Farm near Tallyho, North Carolina
1939

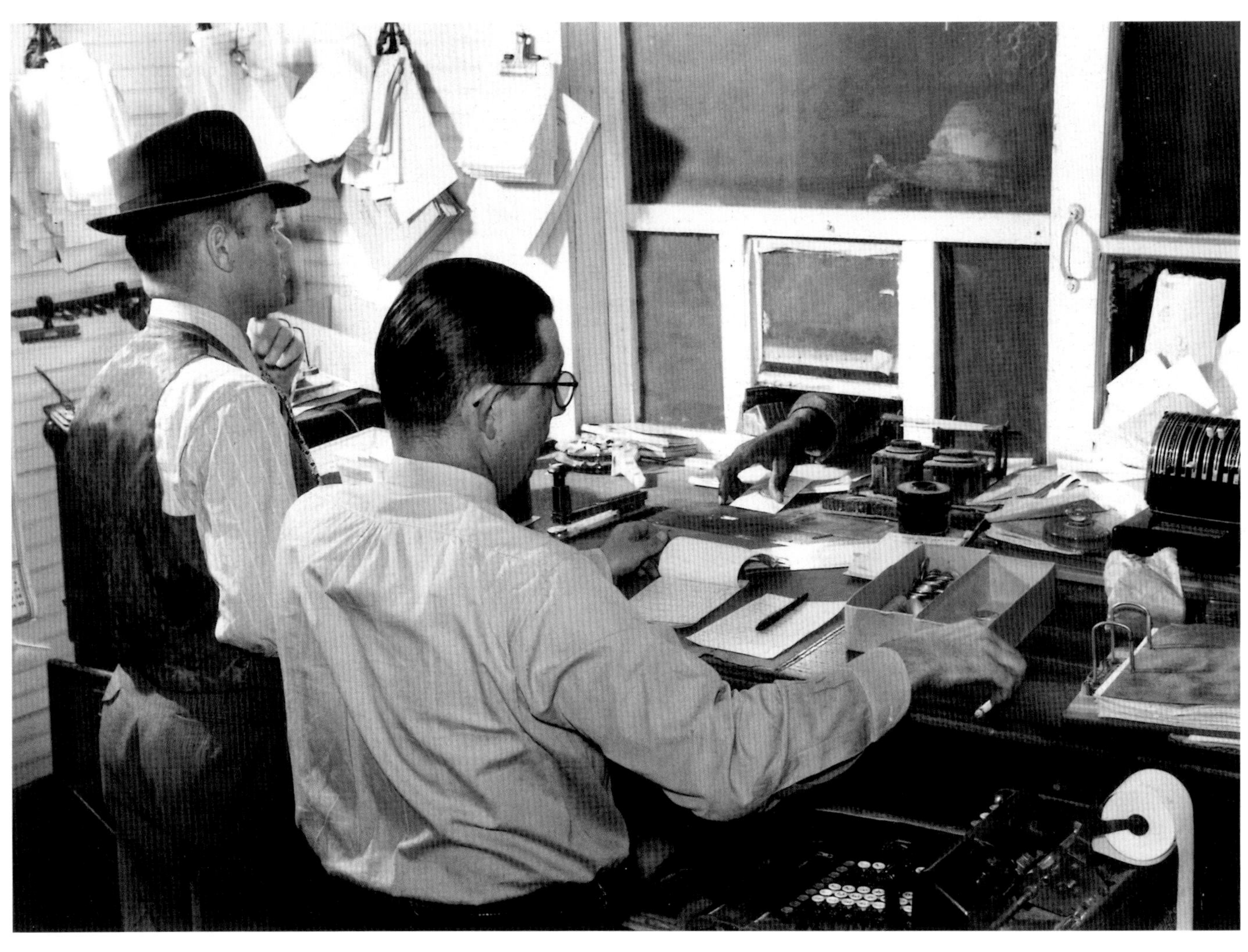

MARION POST WOLCOTT

Cashiers Paying Off Cotton Pickers in Marcella Plantation Store, Mileston, Mississippi

1939

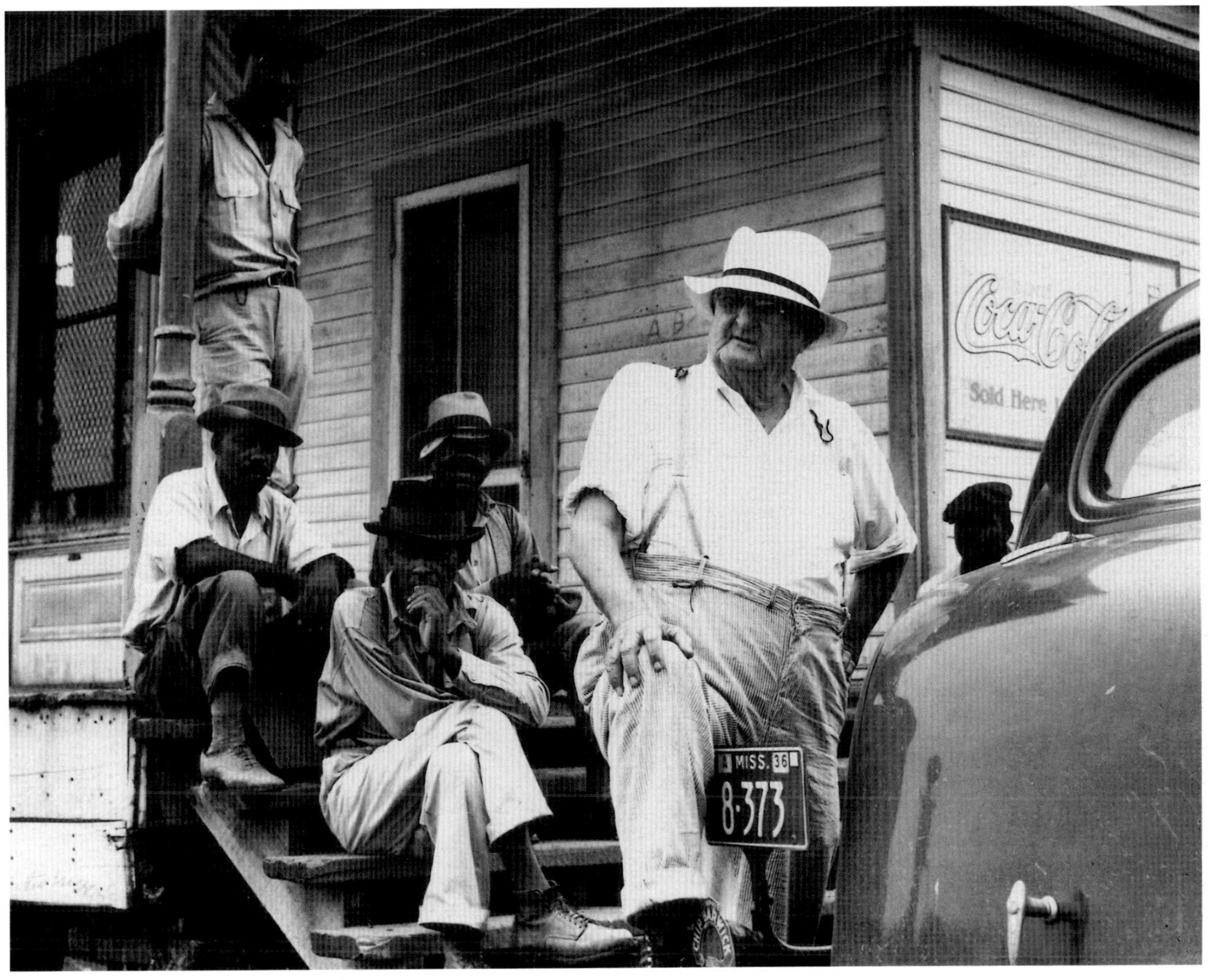

DOROTHEA LANGE

Plantation Overseer and His Field Hands, near Clarksdale, Mississippi

1936

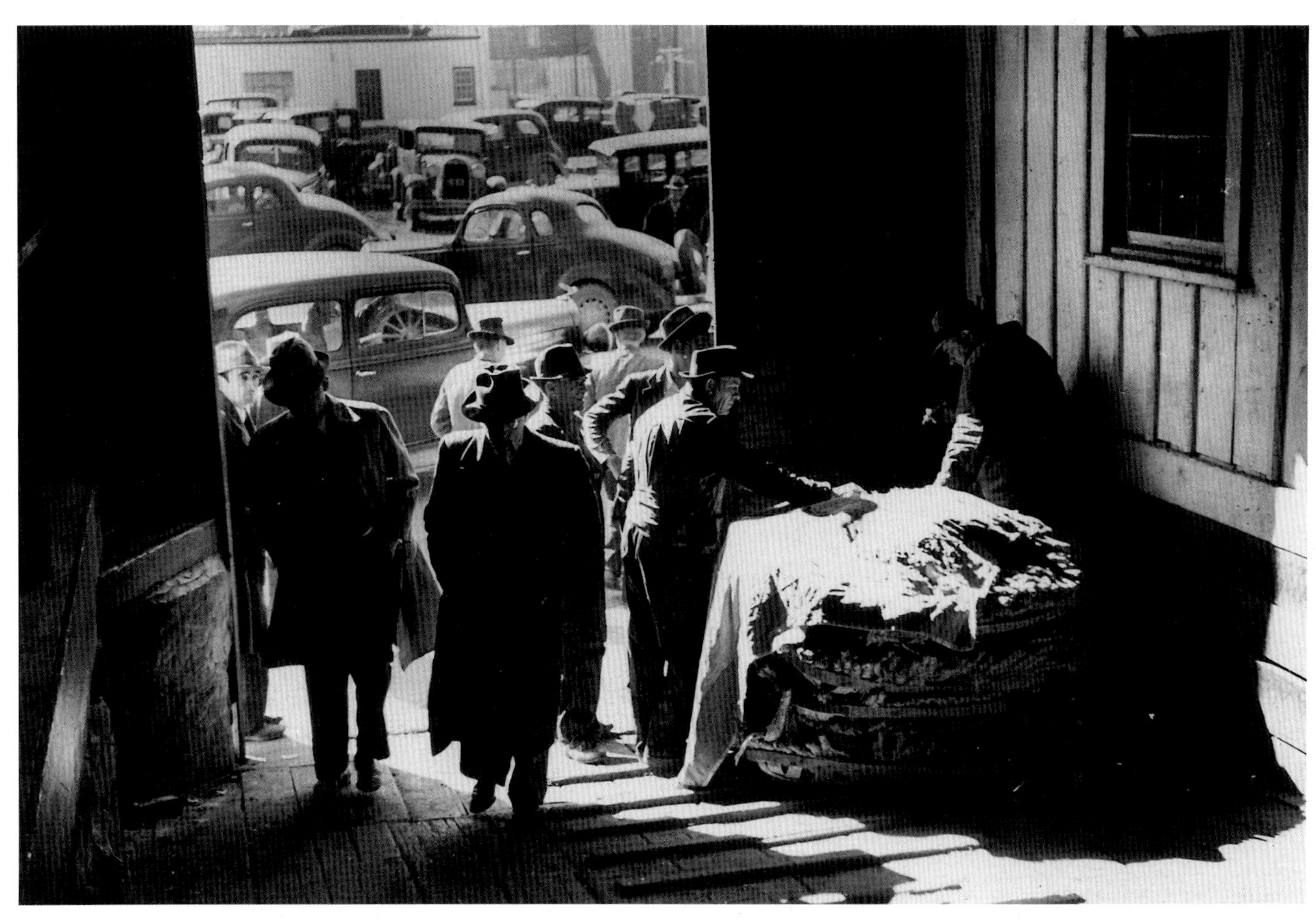

MARION POST WOLCOTT

Arranging Tobacco in Baskets Before Auction in Warehouse, Mebane, North Carolina

1939

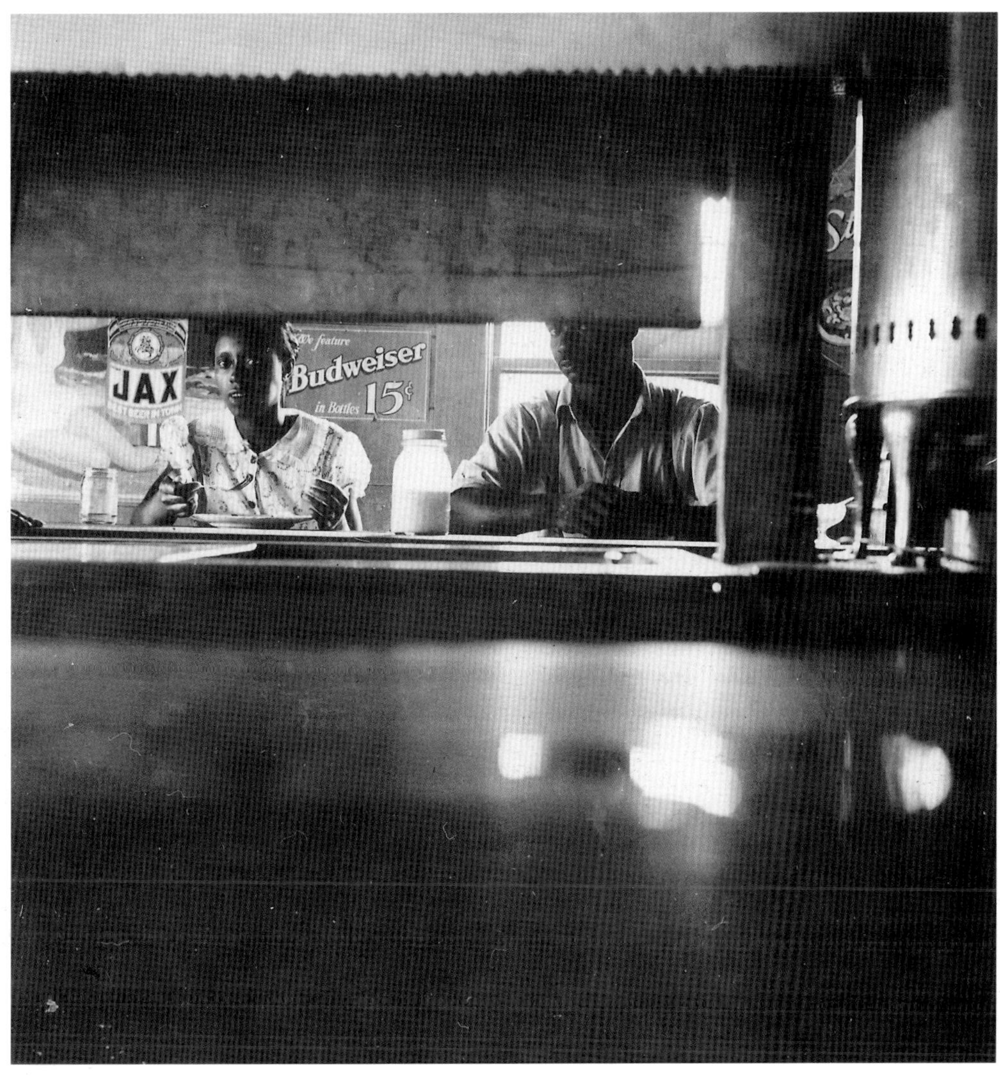

DOROTHEA LANGE
Killing Time, Mississippi. The Board that Divides Service to Whites and Blacks
1938

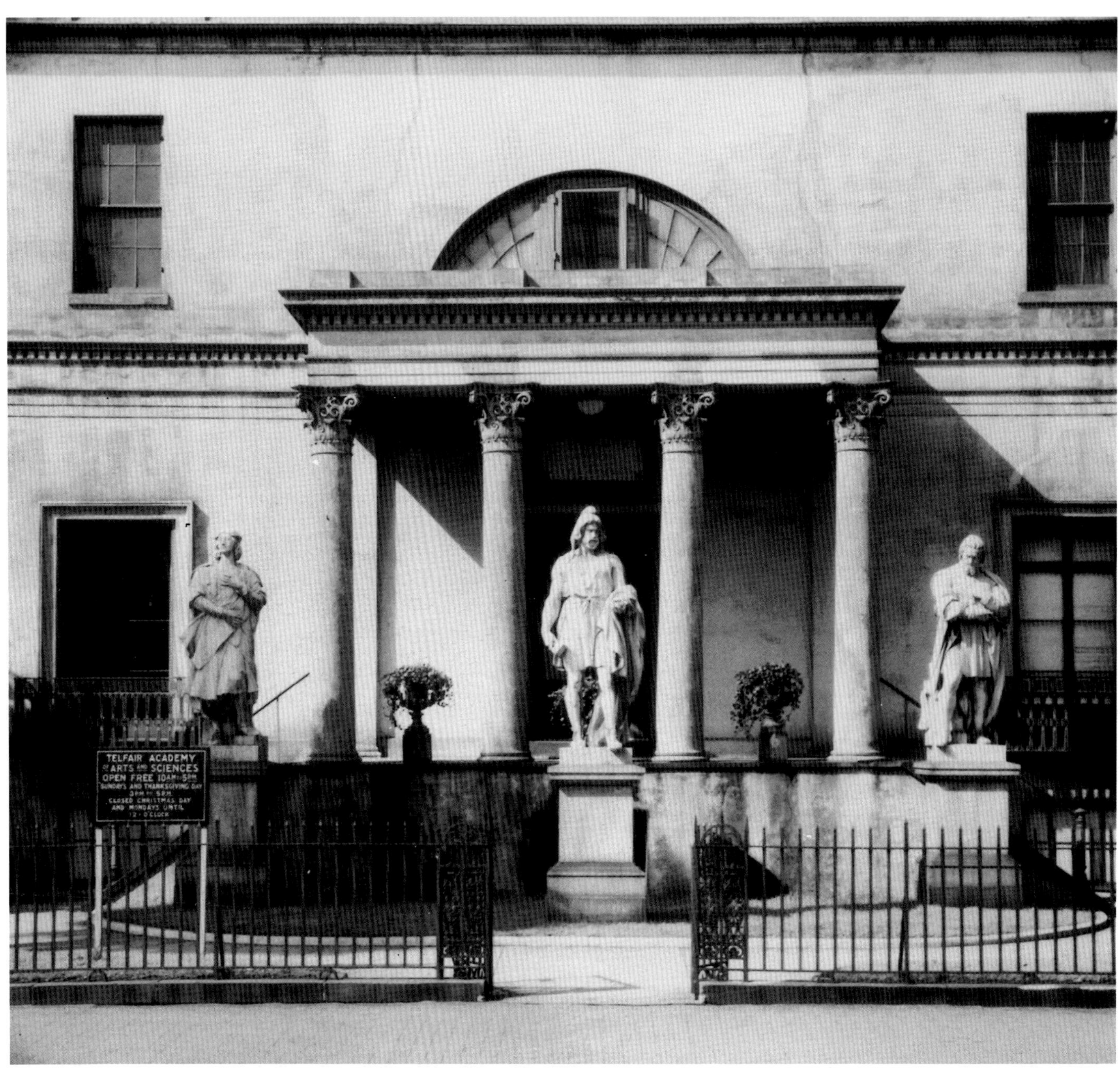

WALKER EVANS

Telfair Academy of Arts and Sciences, Savannah, Georgia

1935

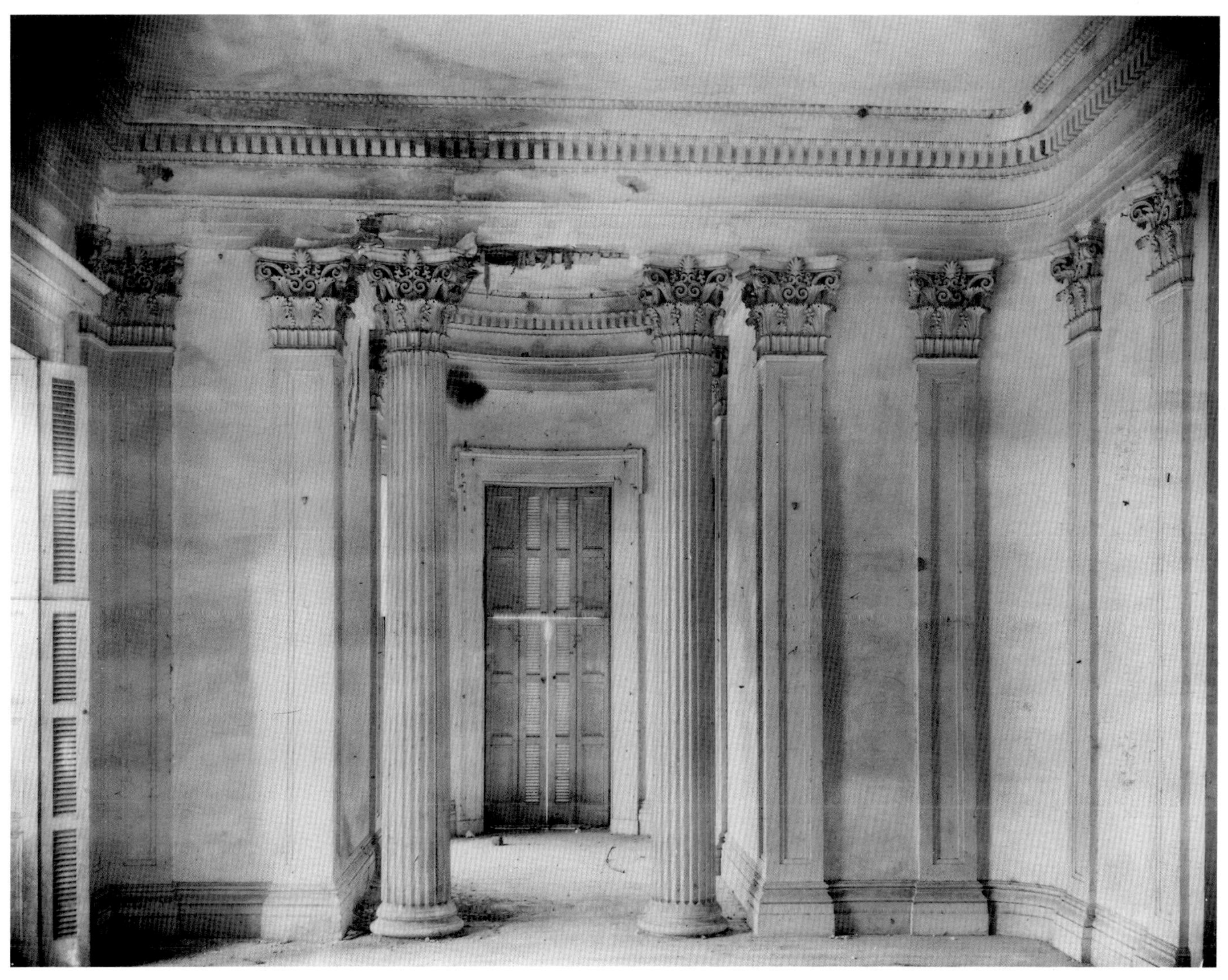

WALKER EVANS
Breakfast Room at Belle Grove Plantation, White Chapel, Louisiana
1935

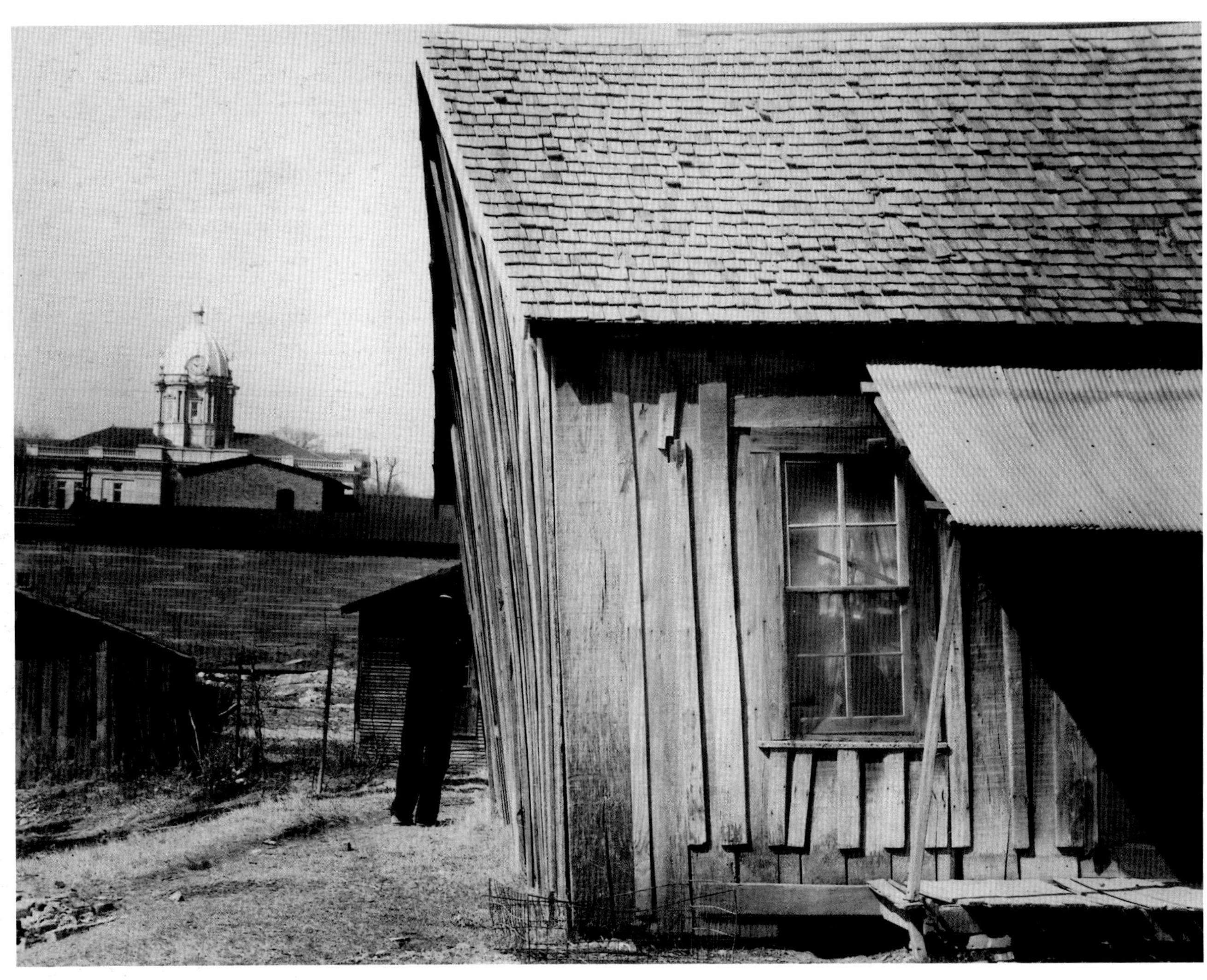

WALKER EVANS
Tupelo, Mississippi
1936

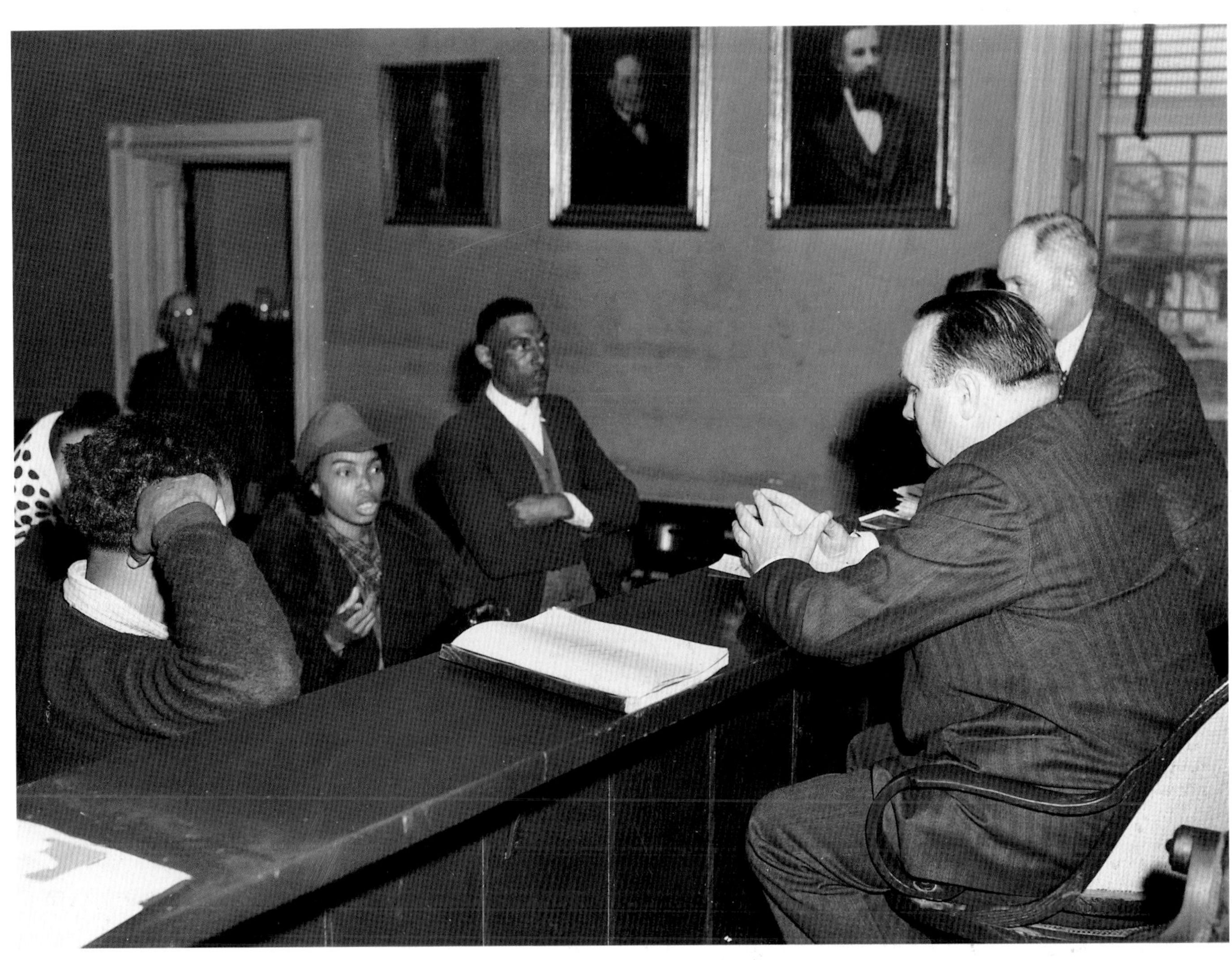

JOHN VACHON
A Day in Court, Rustburg, Virginia
1941

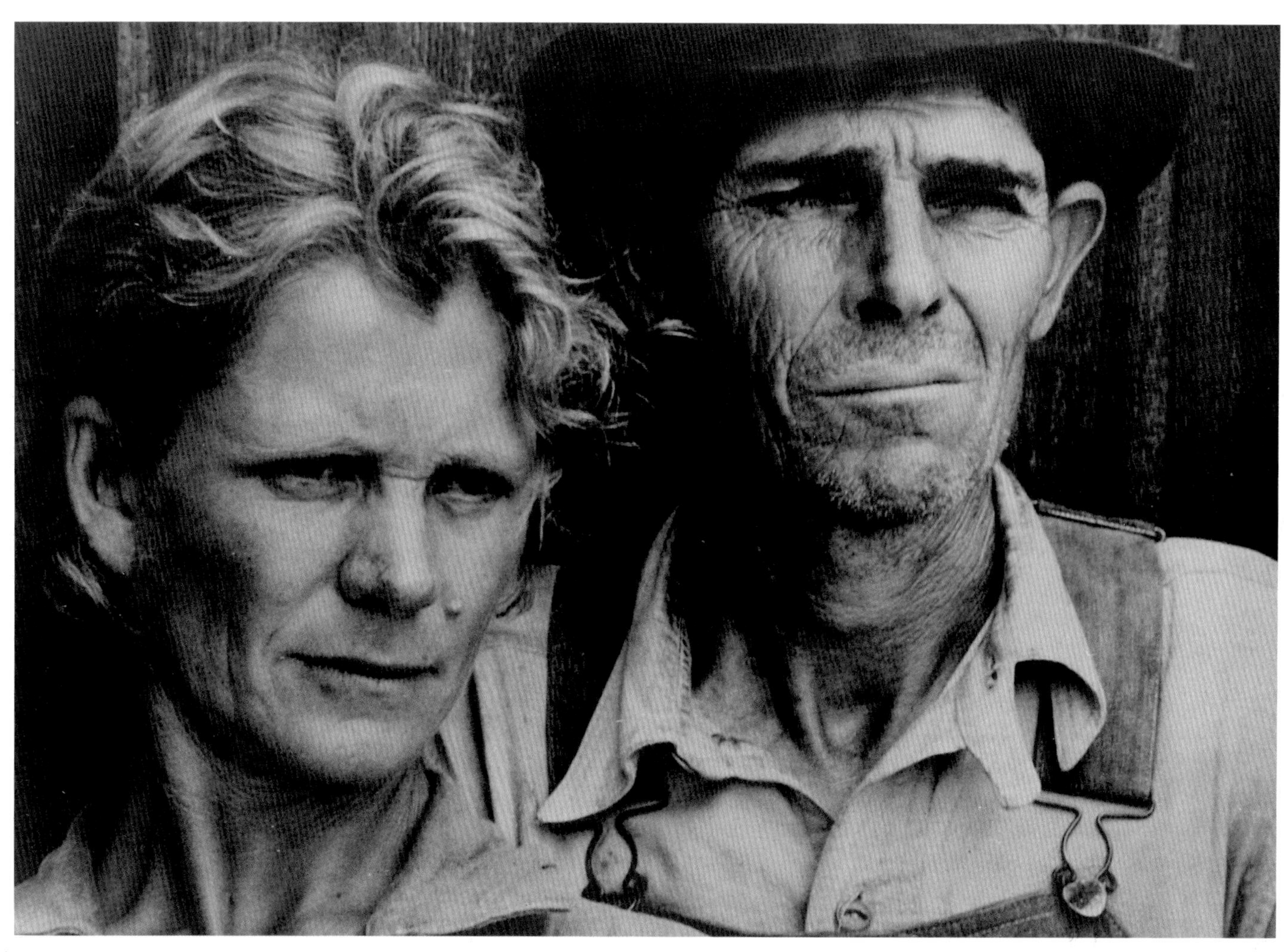

MARGARET BOURKE-WHITE

Maiden Lane, Georgia from the series "You Have Seen Their Faces"
1936–37

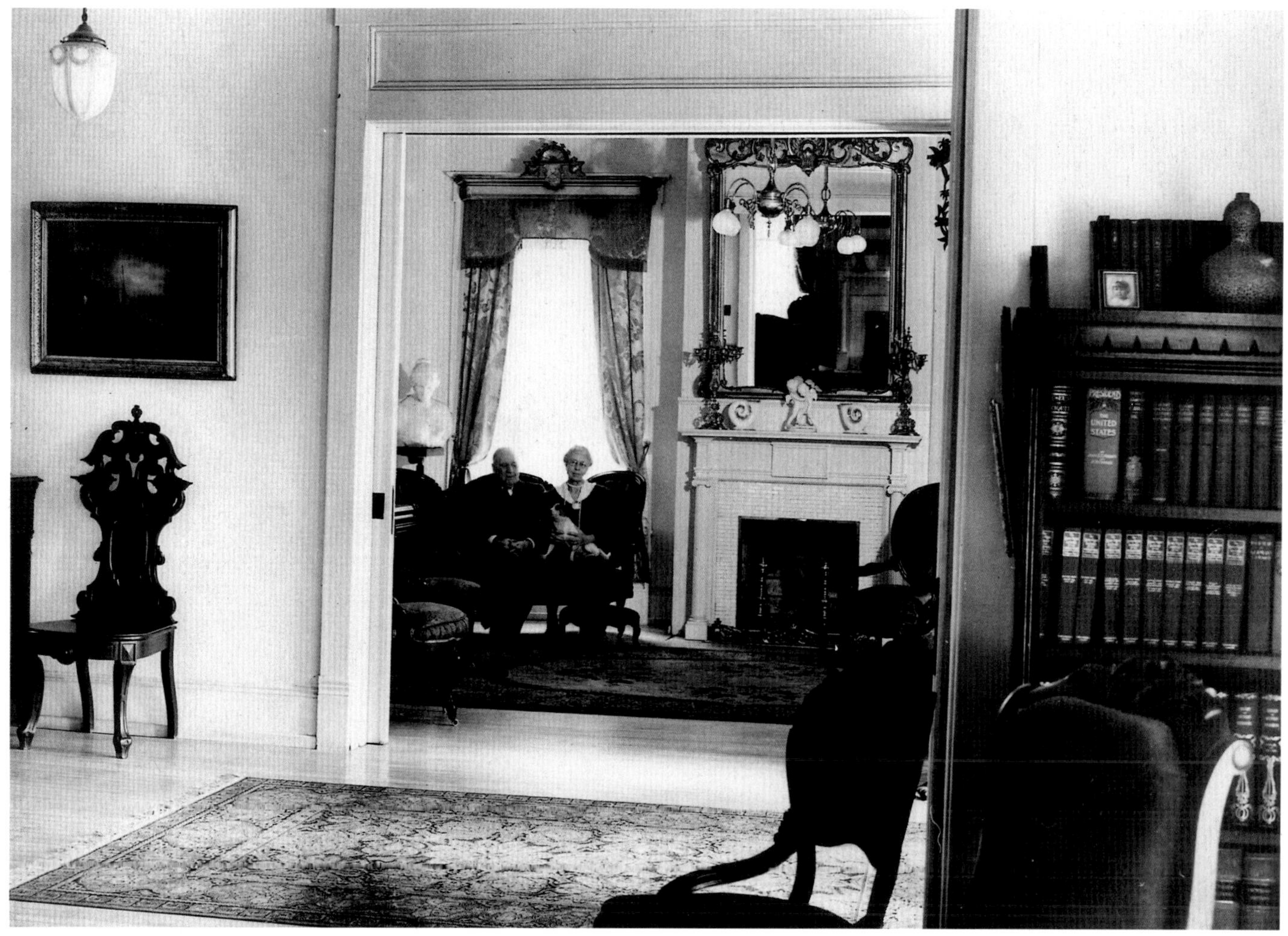

JACK DELANO

Portrait of a Couple, Greene County, Georgia

1940

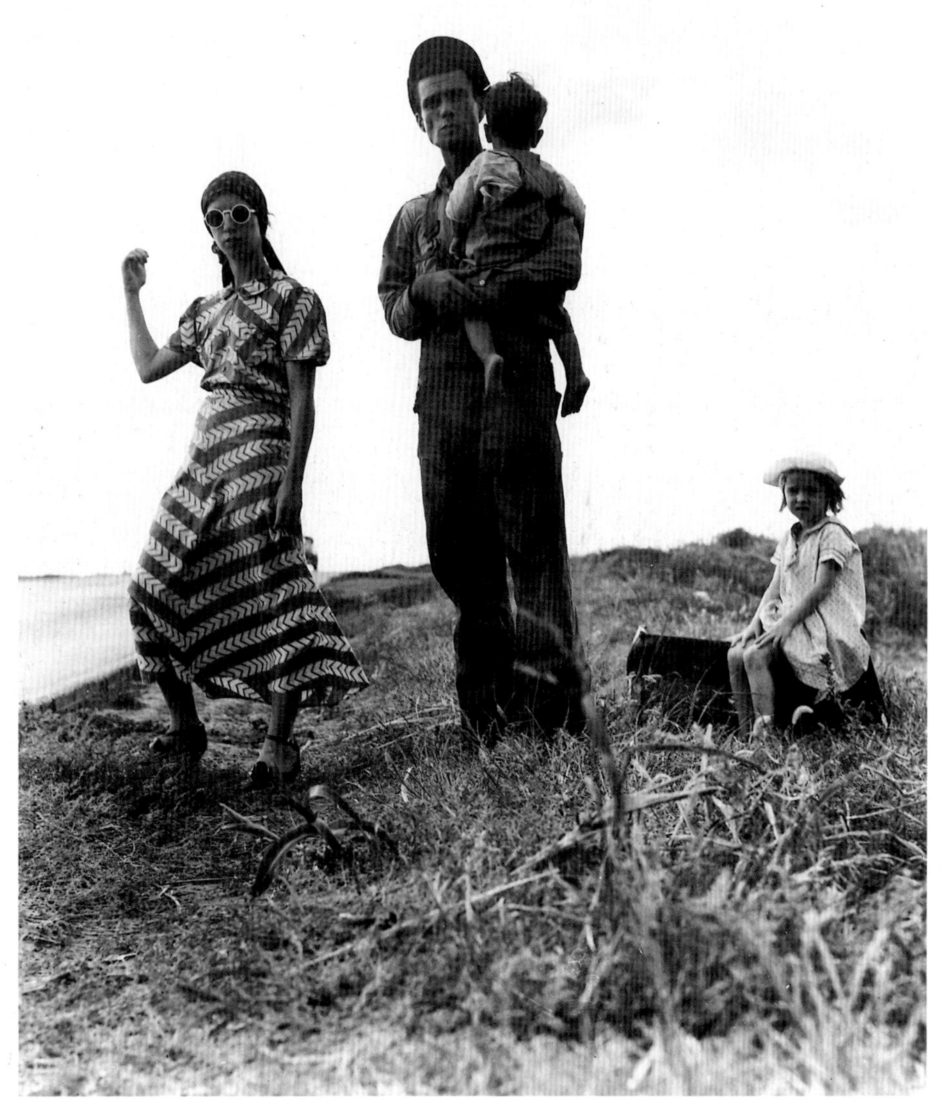

DOROTHEA LANGE

Family on the Road, Oklahoma

1938

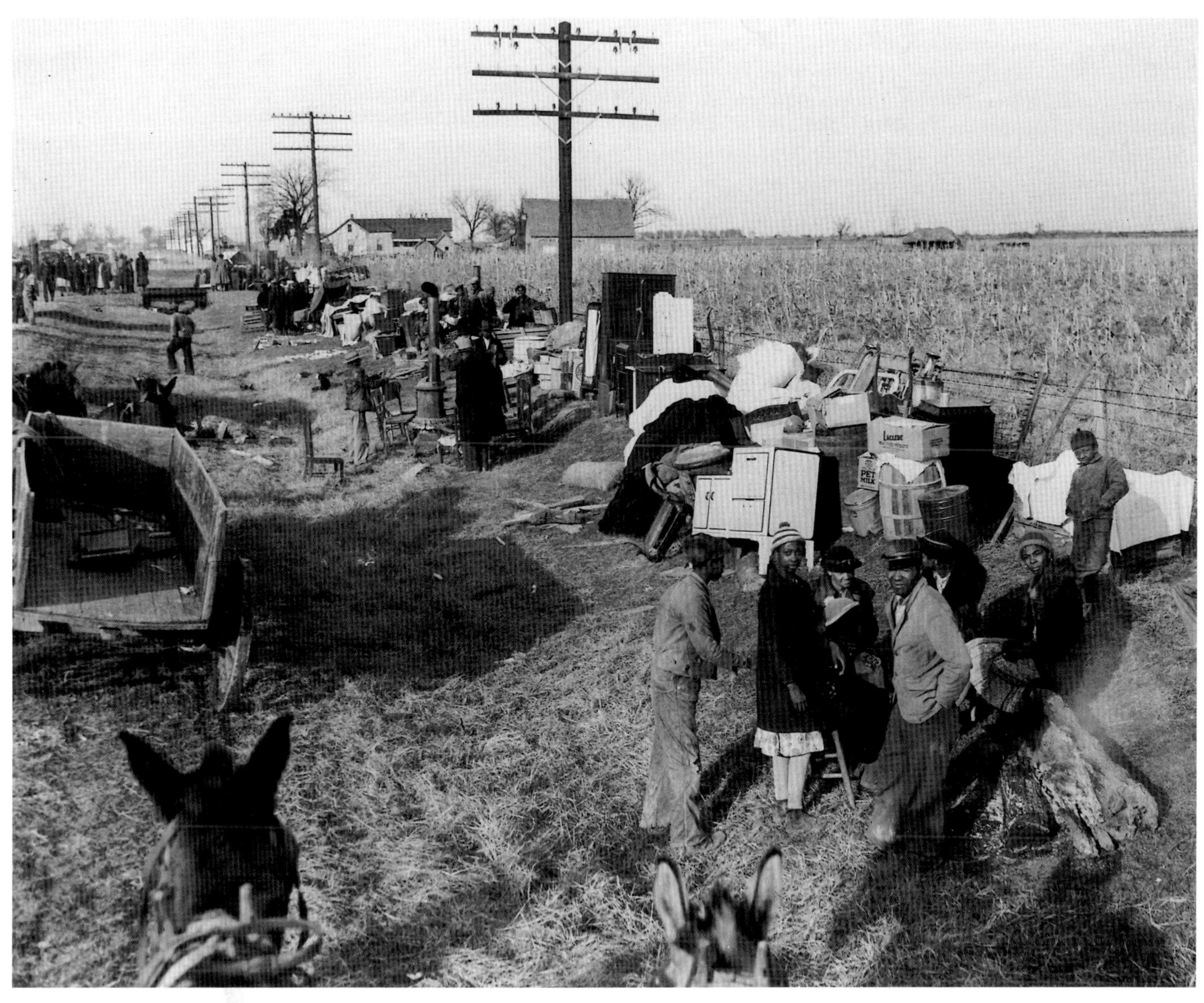

DOROTHEA LANGE

The Families of Evicted Sharecroppers of the Dibble Plantation, near Parkin, Cross County, Arkansas

1936

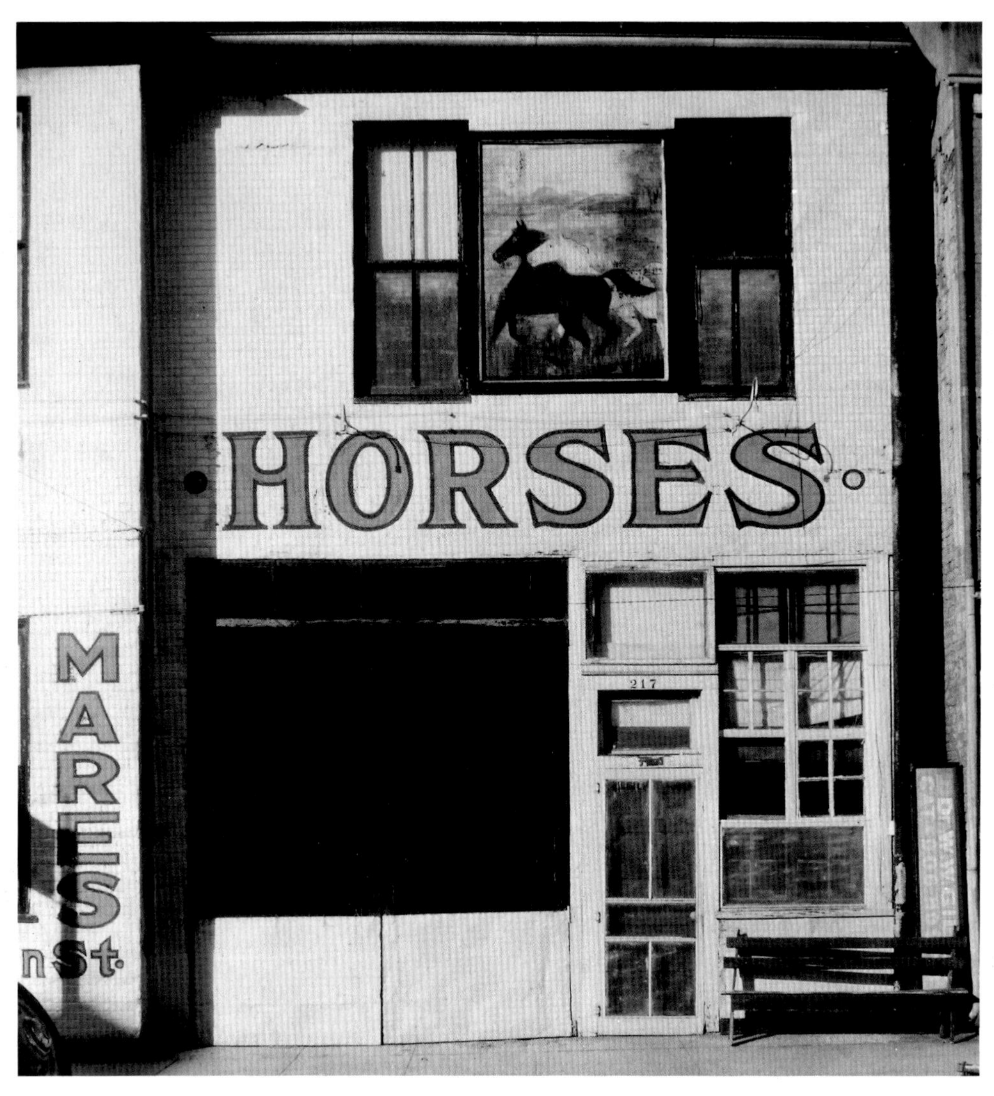

WALKER EVANS
Stables, Natchez, Mississippi
1935

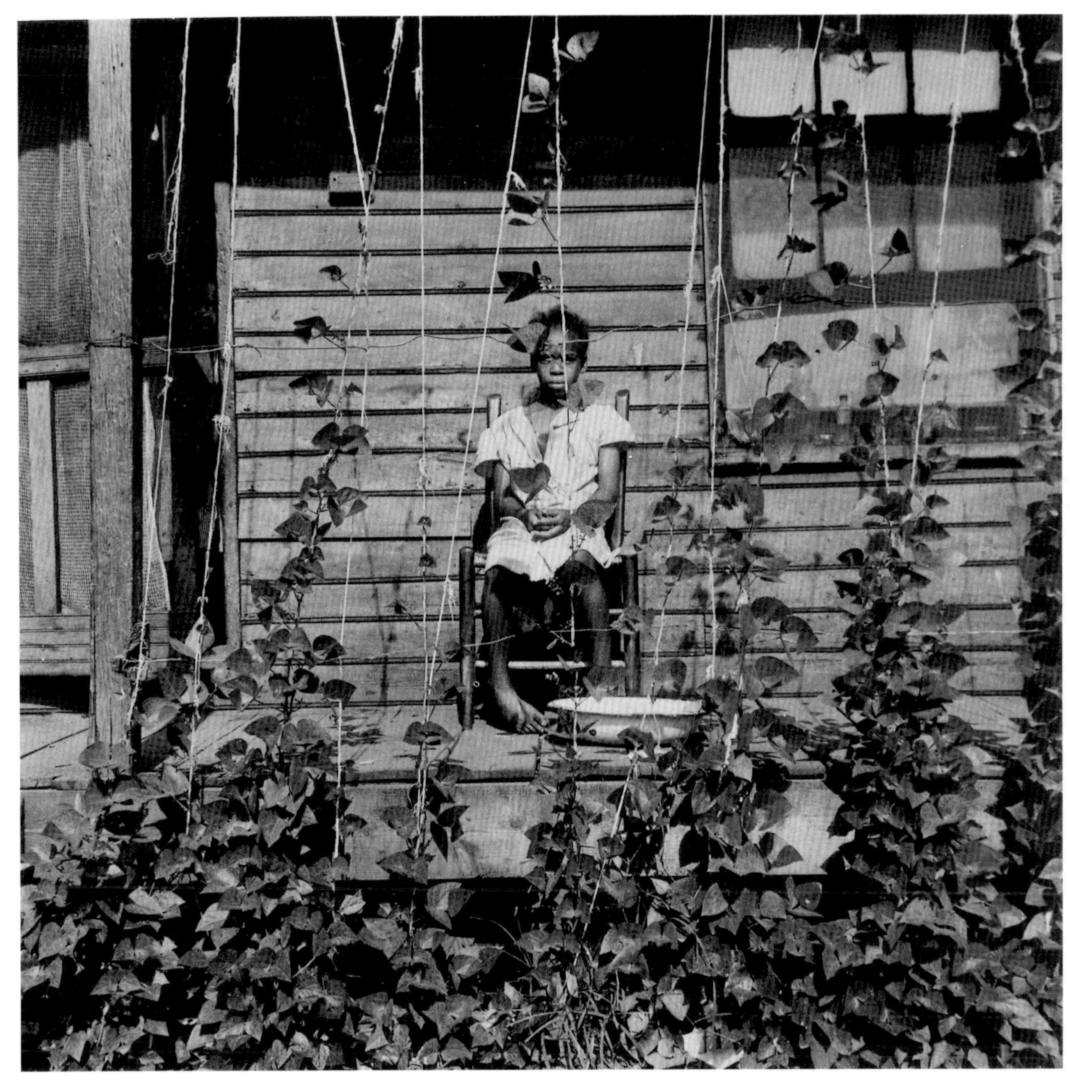

DORROTHEA LANGE

Tennessee

1938

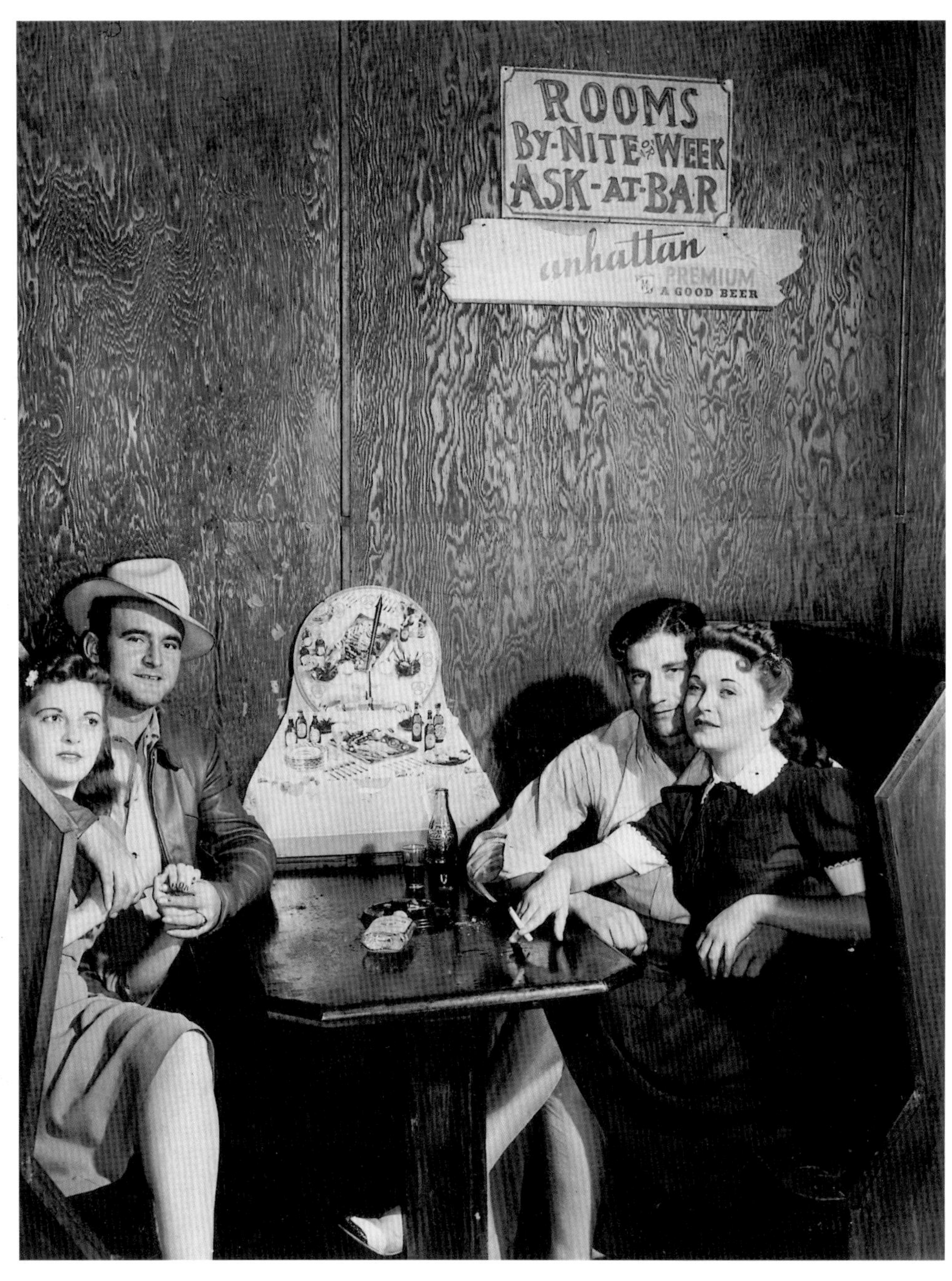

MARION POST WOLCOTT

Two Couples in Booth at Juke Joint, Moorehaven, Florida

1939

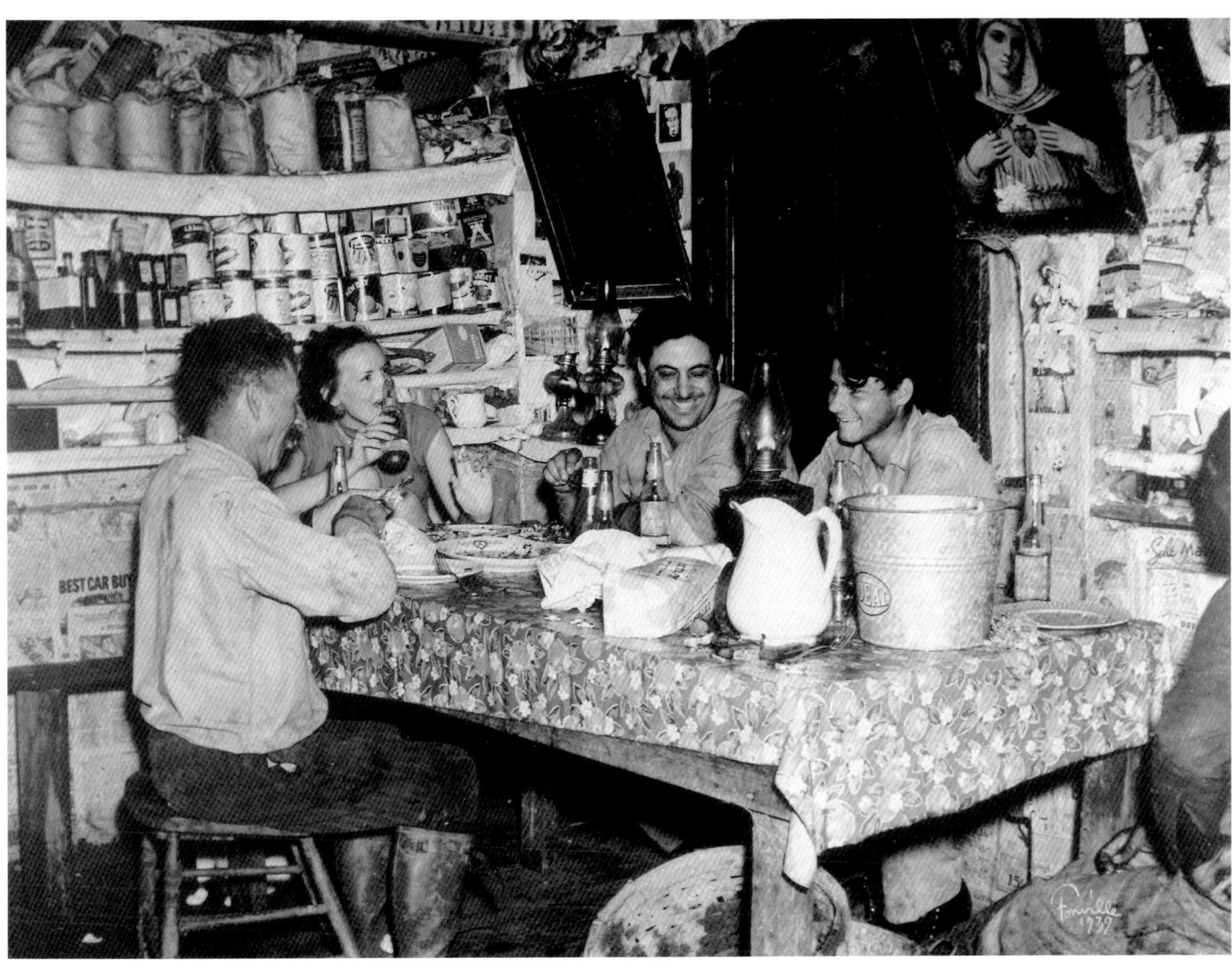

FONVILLE WINANS

Cajun Fare (Fat of the Land, Morgan City, Louisiana)

1939

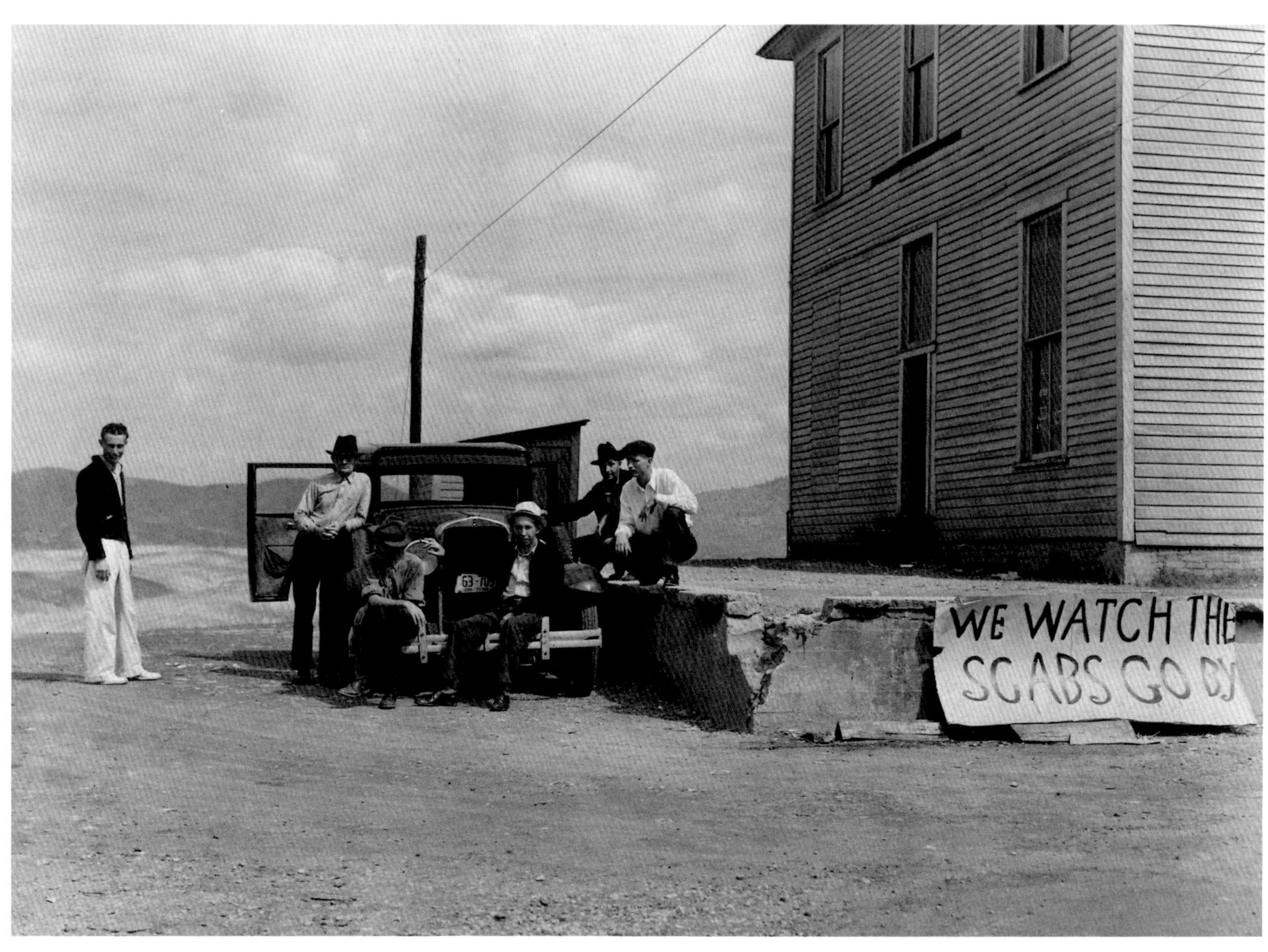

MARION POST WOLCOTT

Union Members Waiting for the Strike-Breaking Scabs to Come Out of the Copper Mines, Ducktown, Tennessee

1939

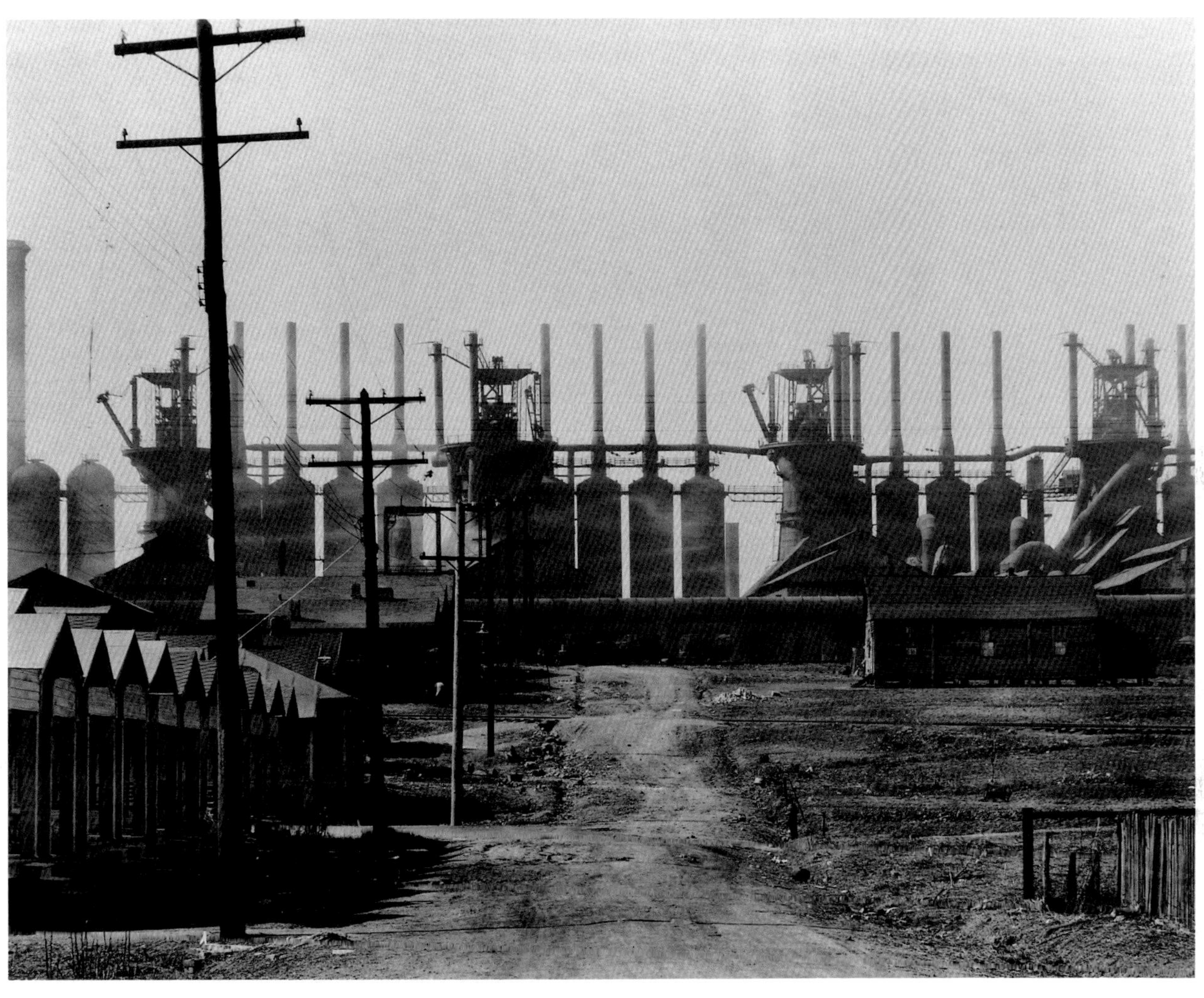

WALKER EVANS

Steel Mill and Workers' Houses, Birmingham, Alabama

1936

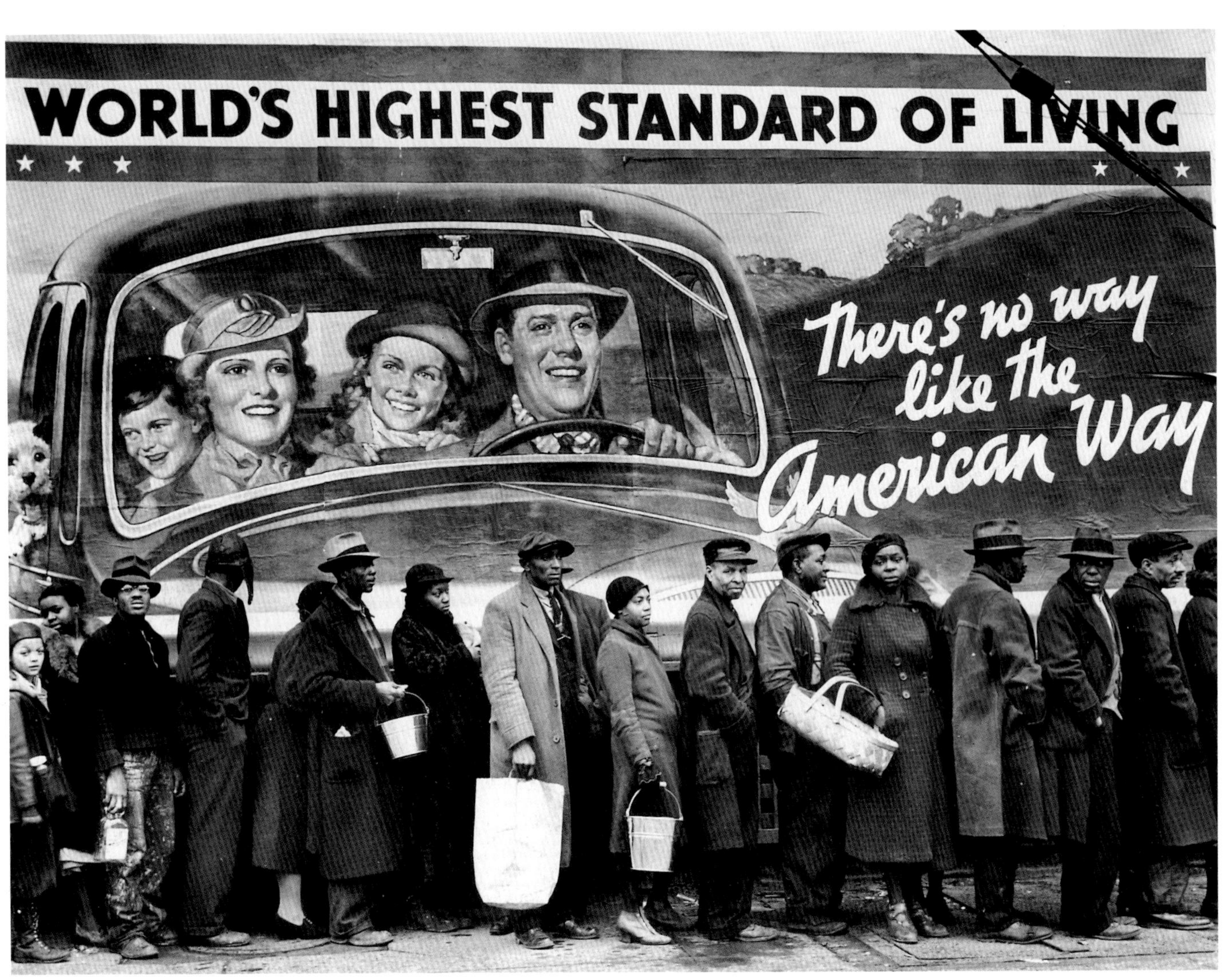

MARGARET BOURKE-WHITE

At the Time of the Louisville Flood, Louisville, Kentucky

1936–37

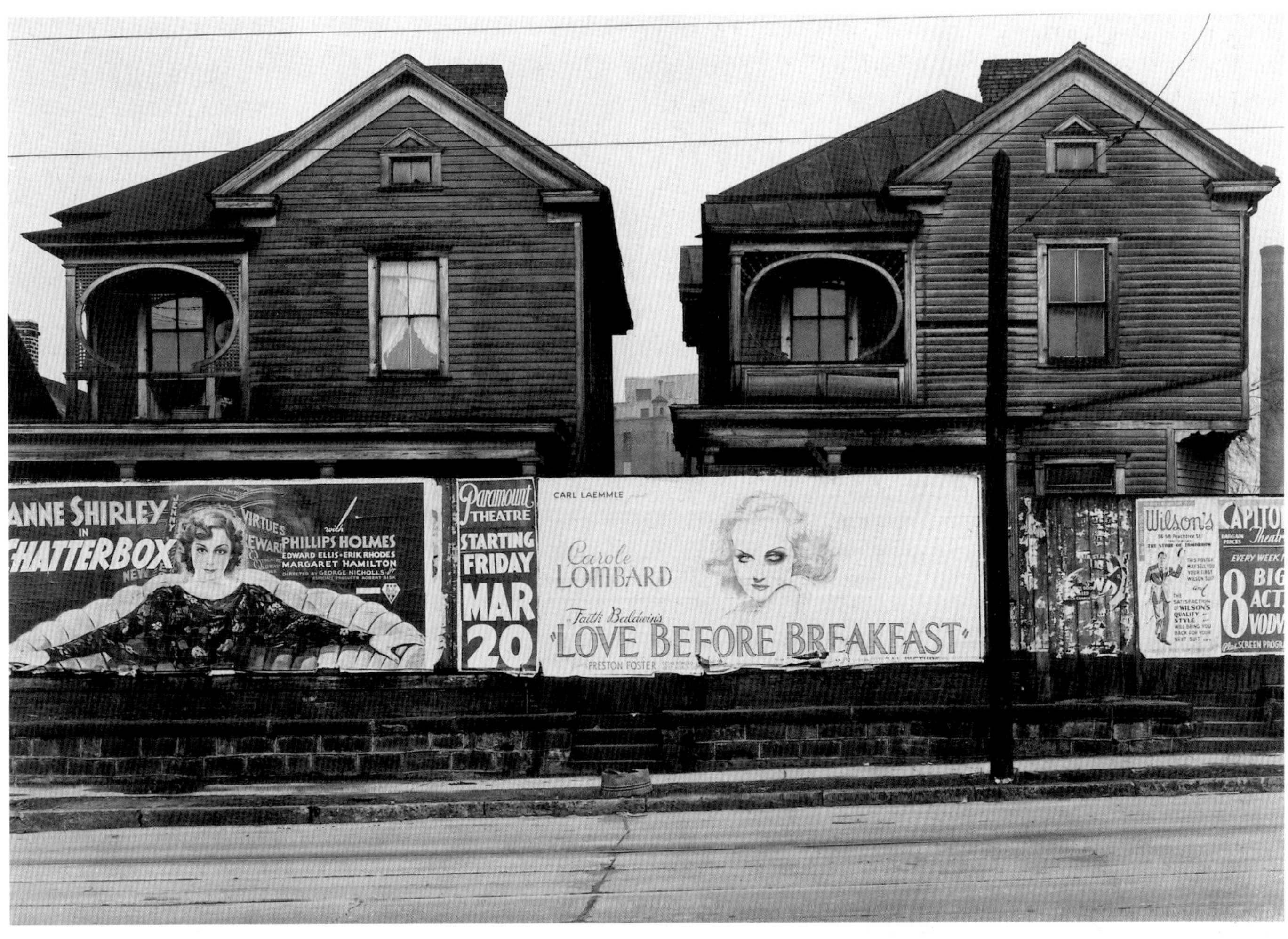

WALKER EVANS

Houses and Billboards in Atlanta, Georgia

1936

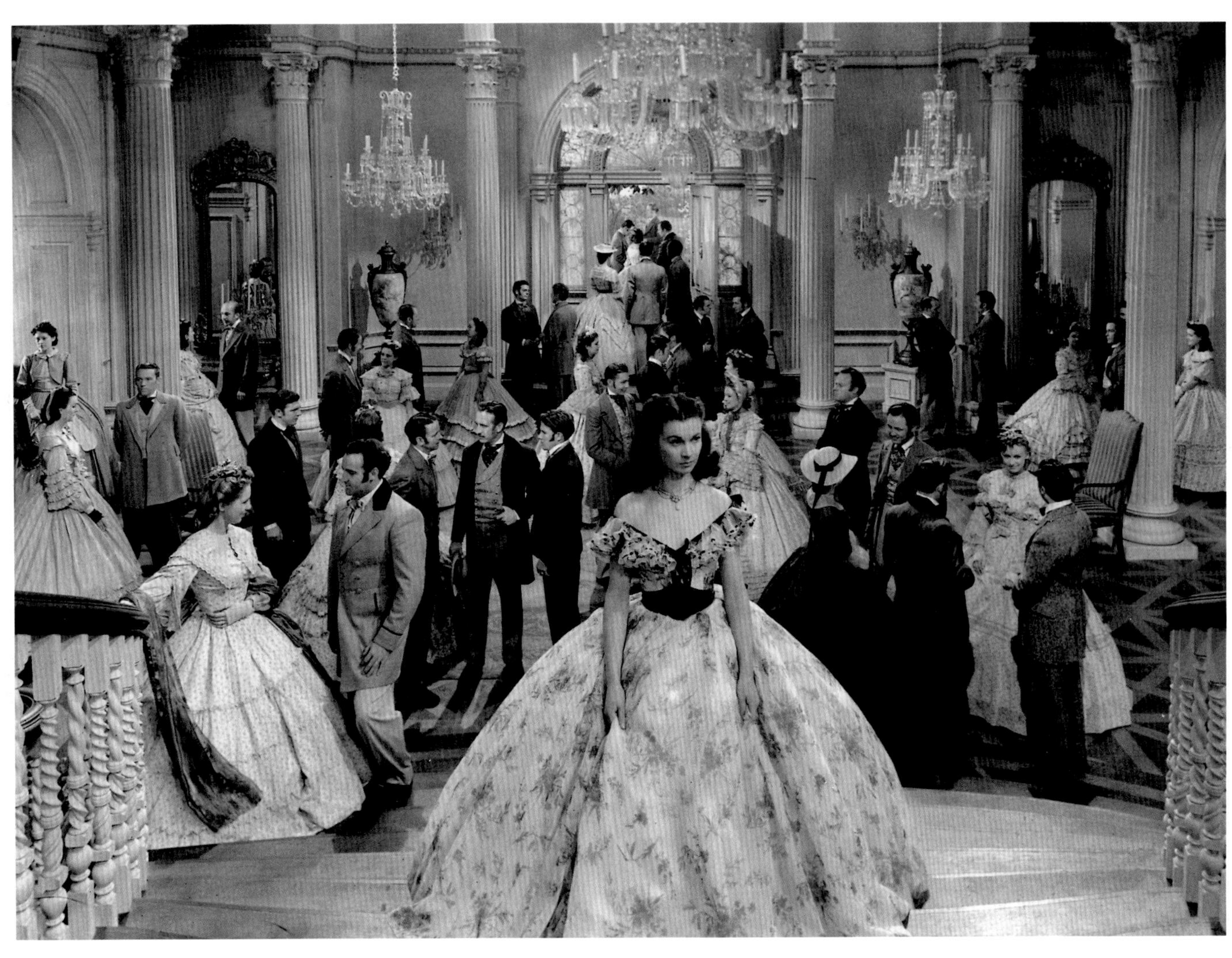

FRED A. PARRISH

Vivien Leigh as Scarlett O'Hara Ascending the Staircase at Twelve Oaks in "Gone With the Wind"

1939

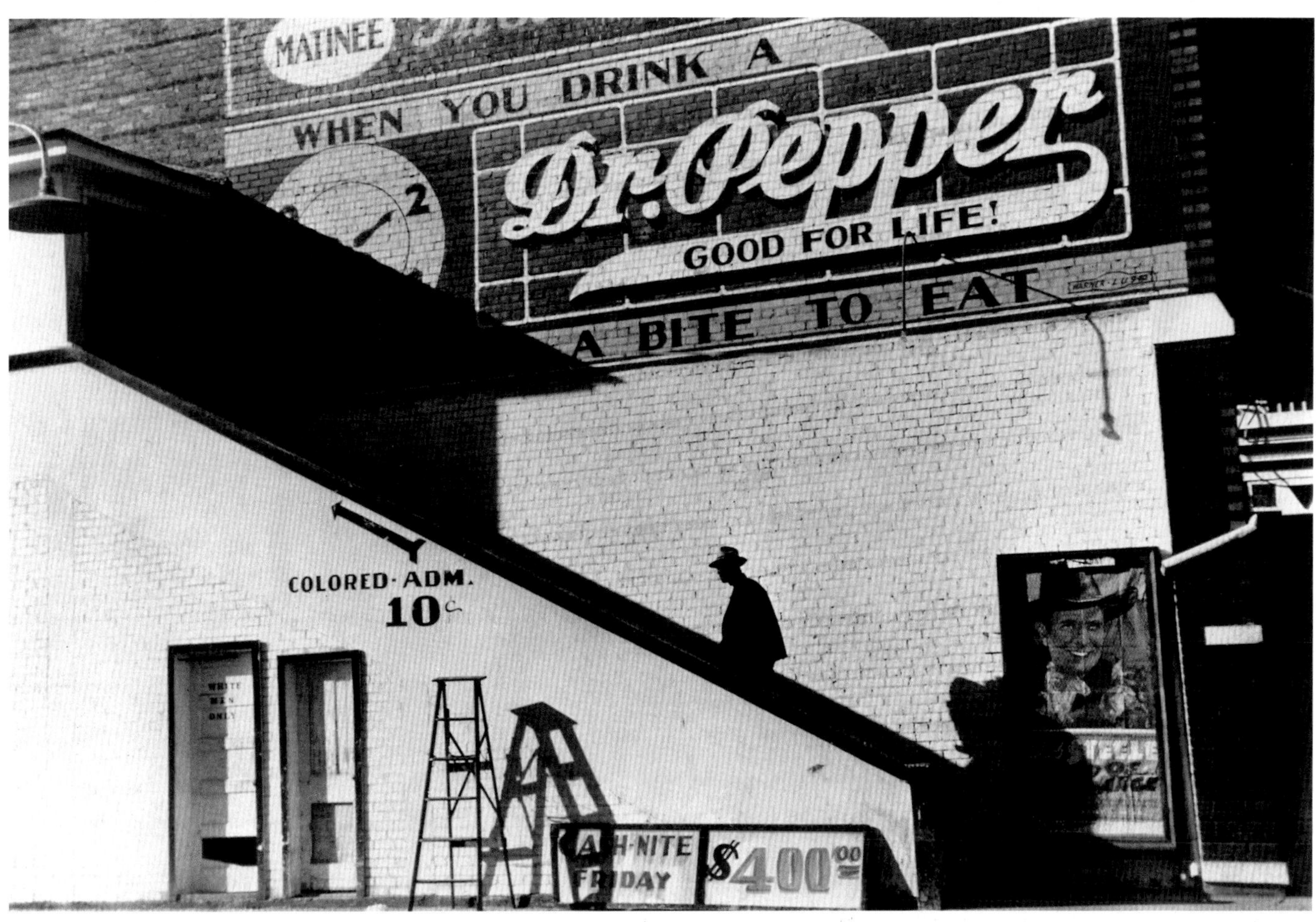

MARION POST WOLCOTT

Negro Man Entering a Movie Theatre by "Colored" Entrance, Belzoni, Mississippi

1939

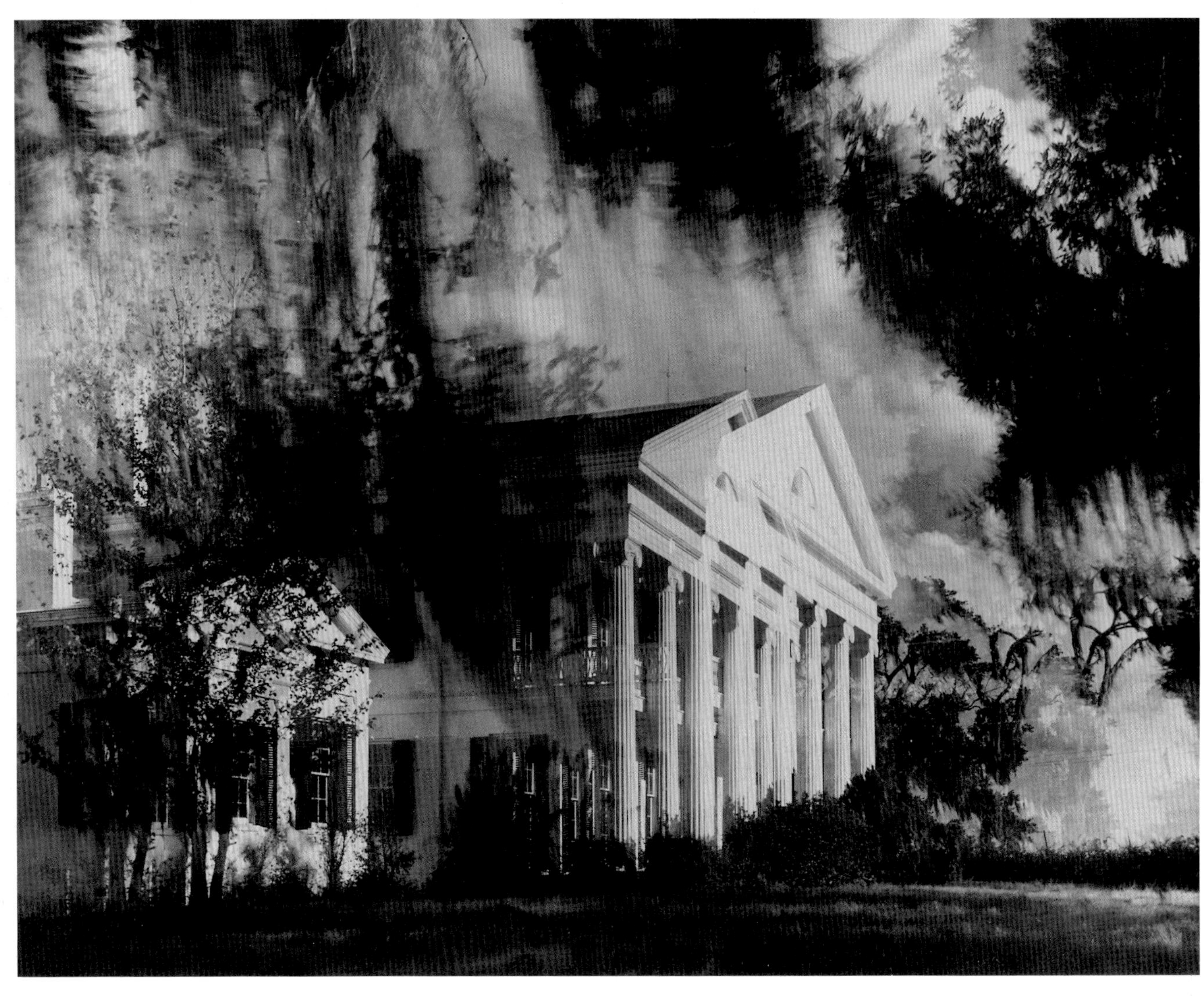

CLARENCE JOHN LAUGHLIN
The Waters of Memory
1946

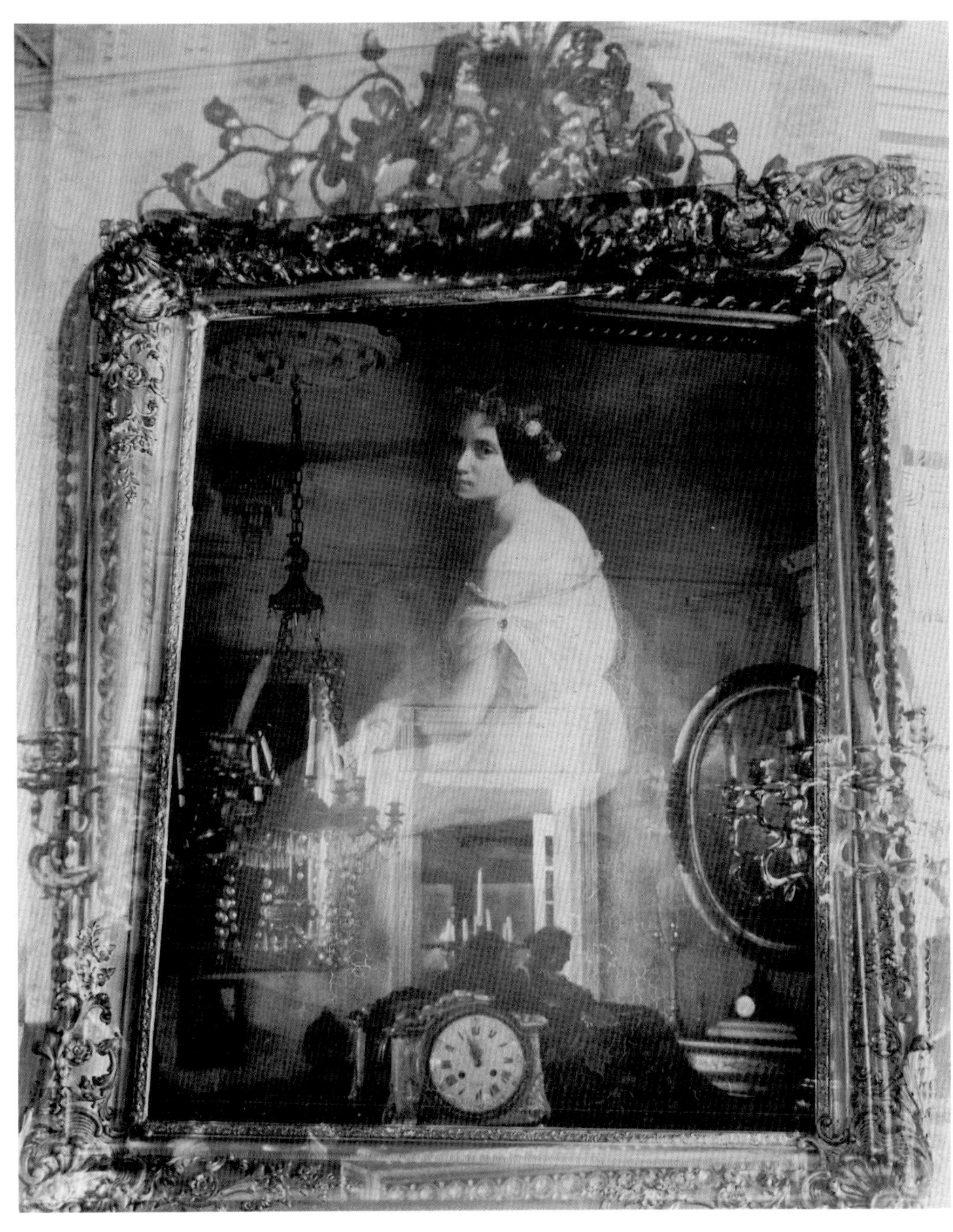

CLARENCE JOHN LAUGHLIN
The Mirror of Long Ago
1946

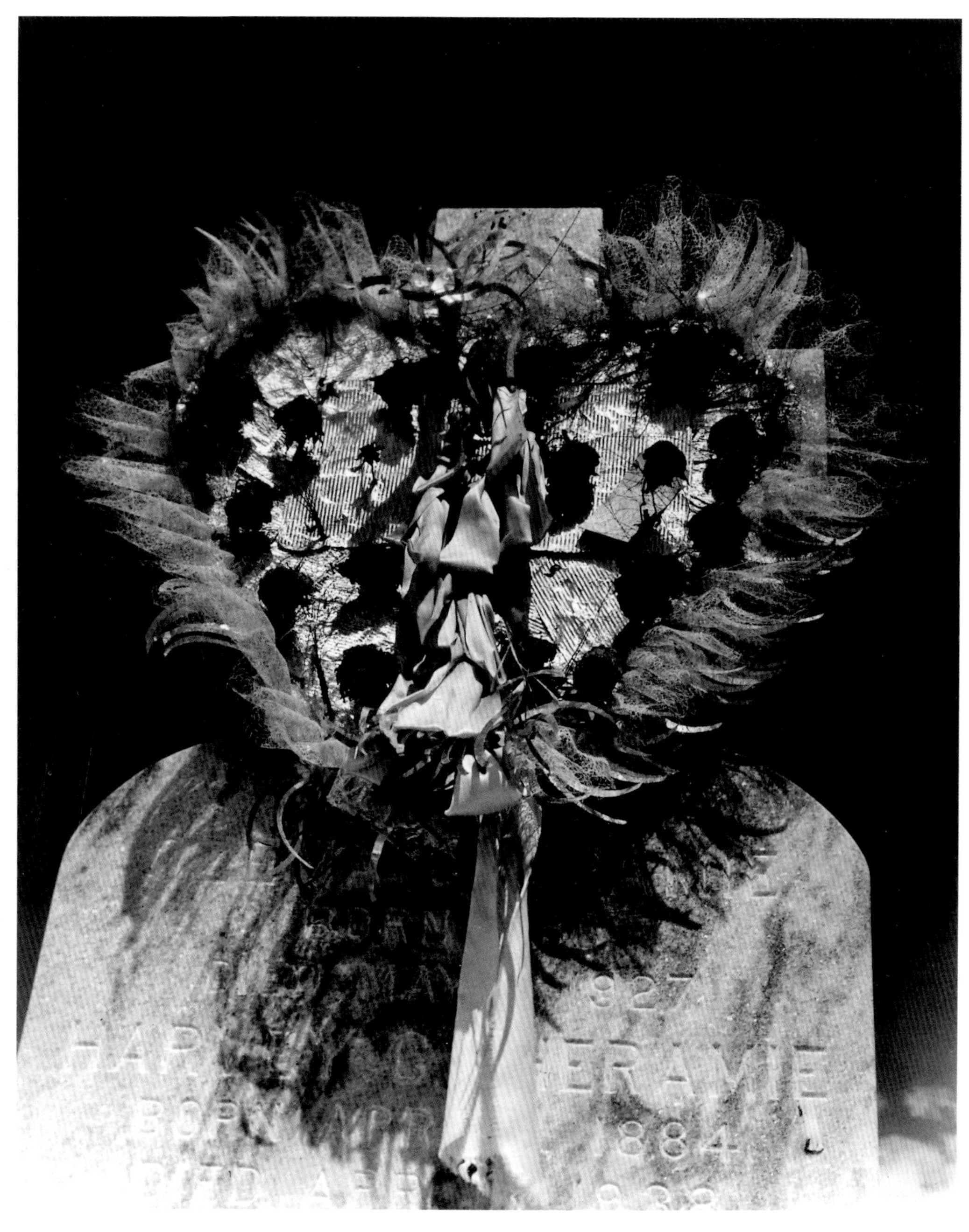

CLARENCE JOHN LAUGHLIN

The Insect-Headed Tombstone

1953

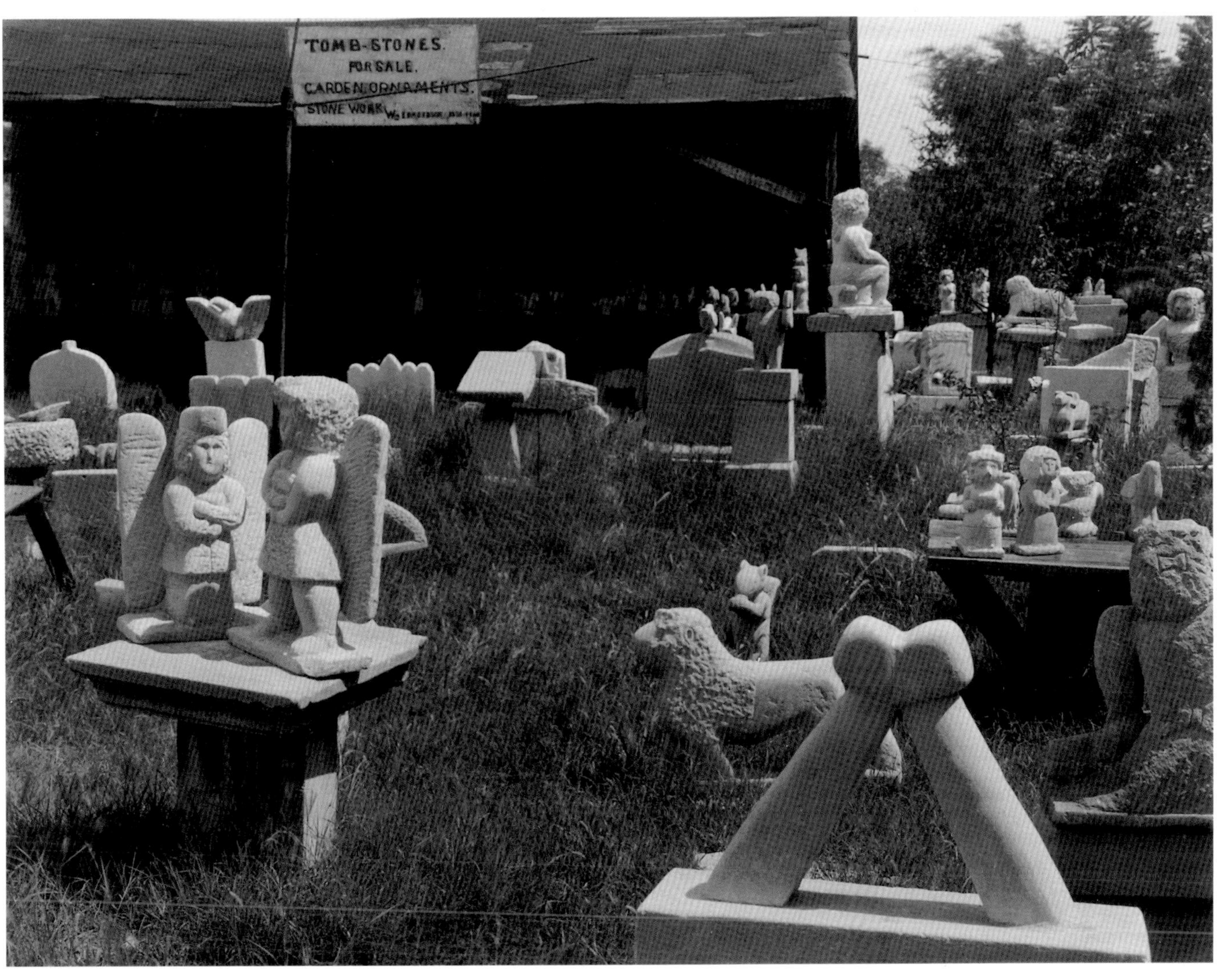

EDWARD WESTON

William Edmondson's Sculpture, Nashville, Tennessee

1941

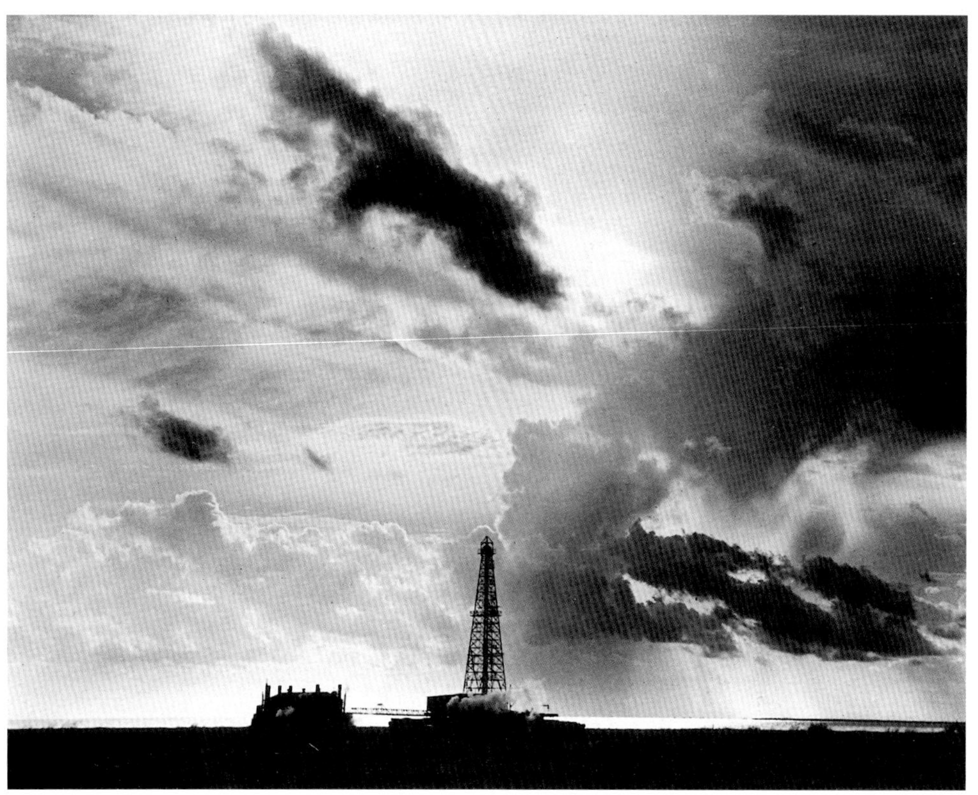

TODD WEBB

Louisiana Oil Field

1947 or 1948

EDWARD WESTON

Union Station, Nashville, Tennessee

1941

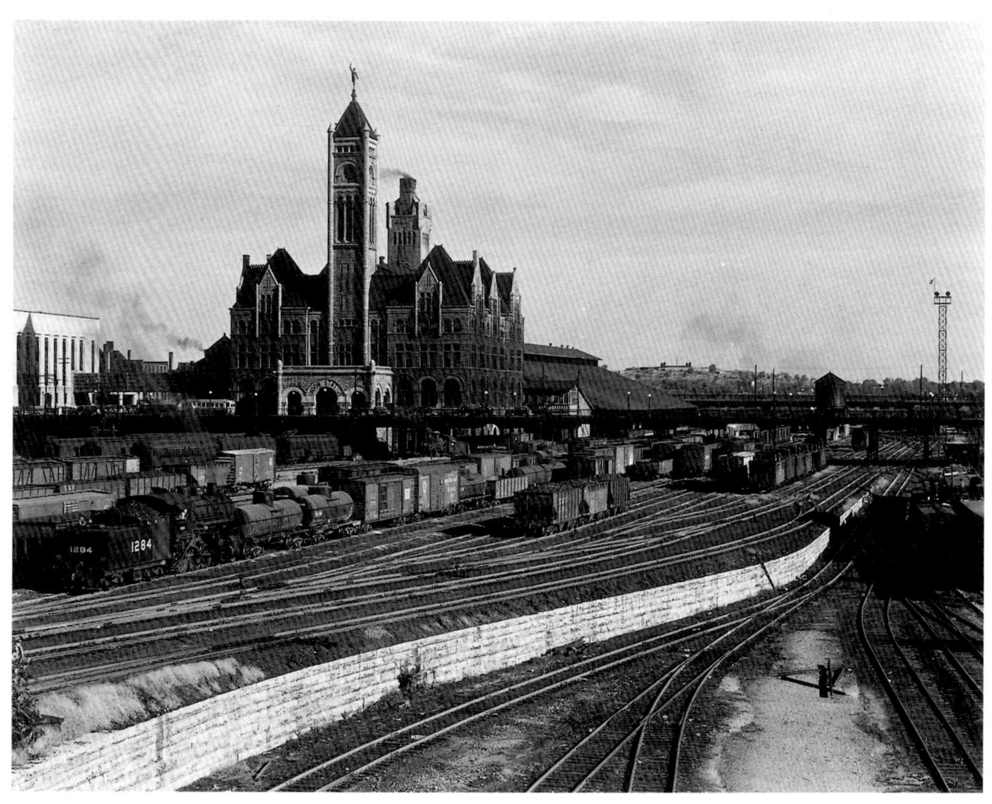

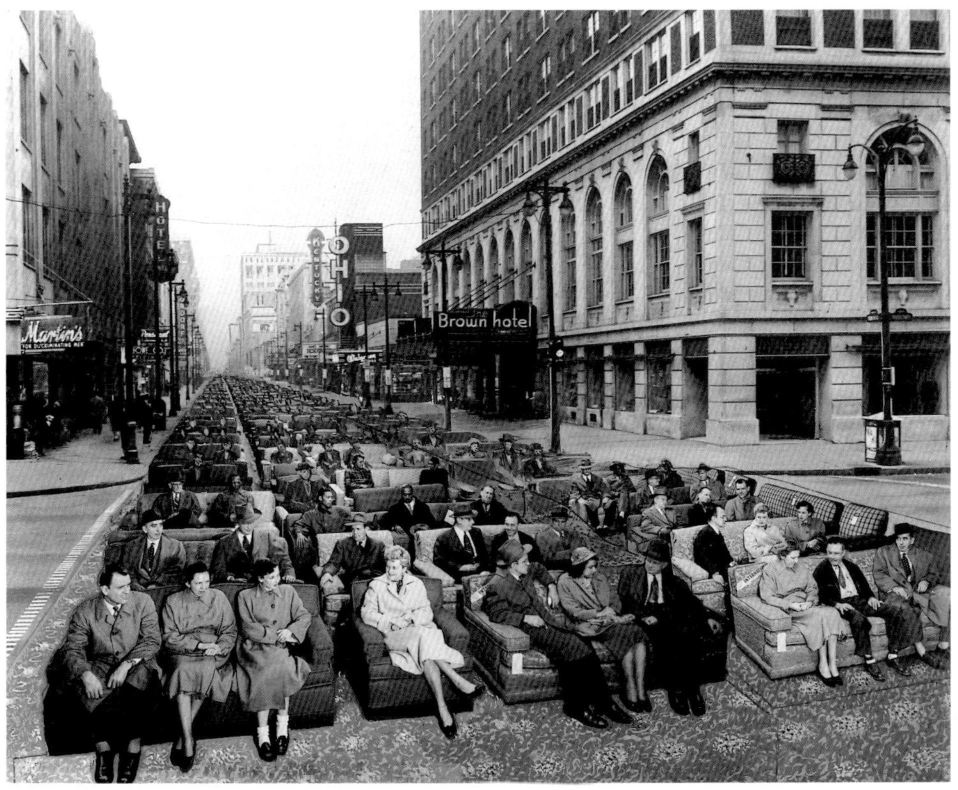

STERN J. BRAMSON

Composite Photo for Newspaper Advertisement, Fourth and Broadway.
Client: Howell Furniture Company, Louisville, Kentucky
1952

O. WINSTON LINK

Main Line on Main Street, Northfork, West Virginia
August 29, 1958

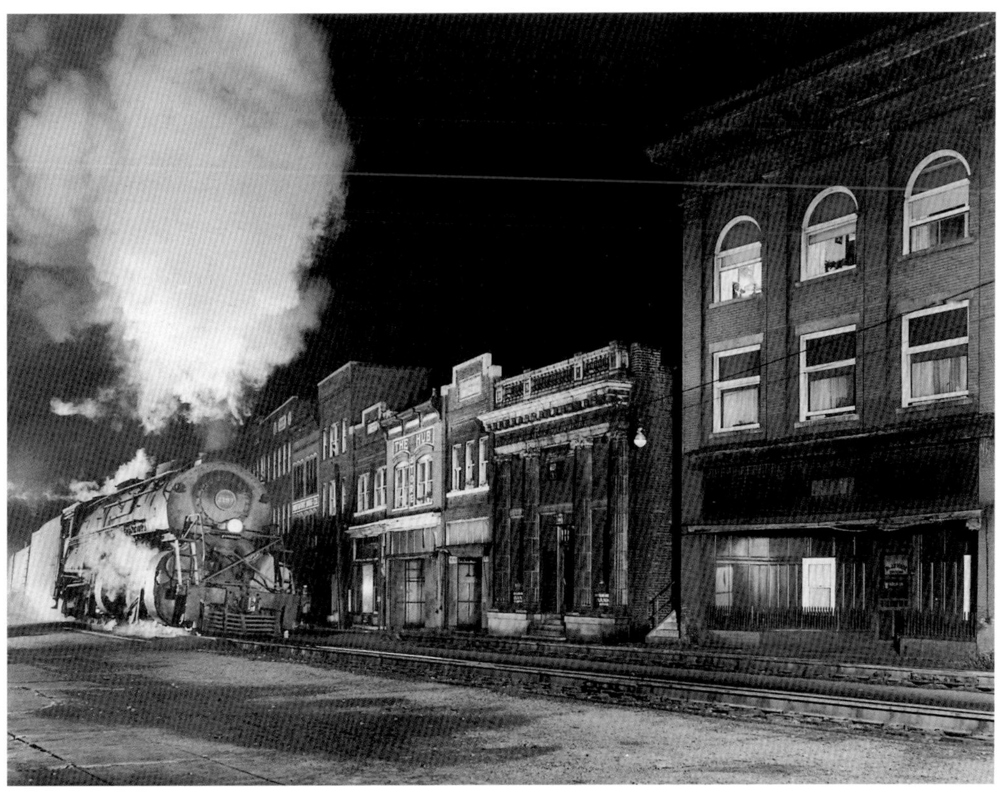

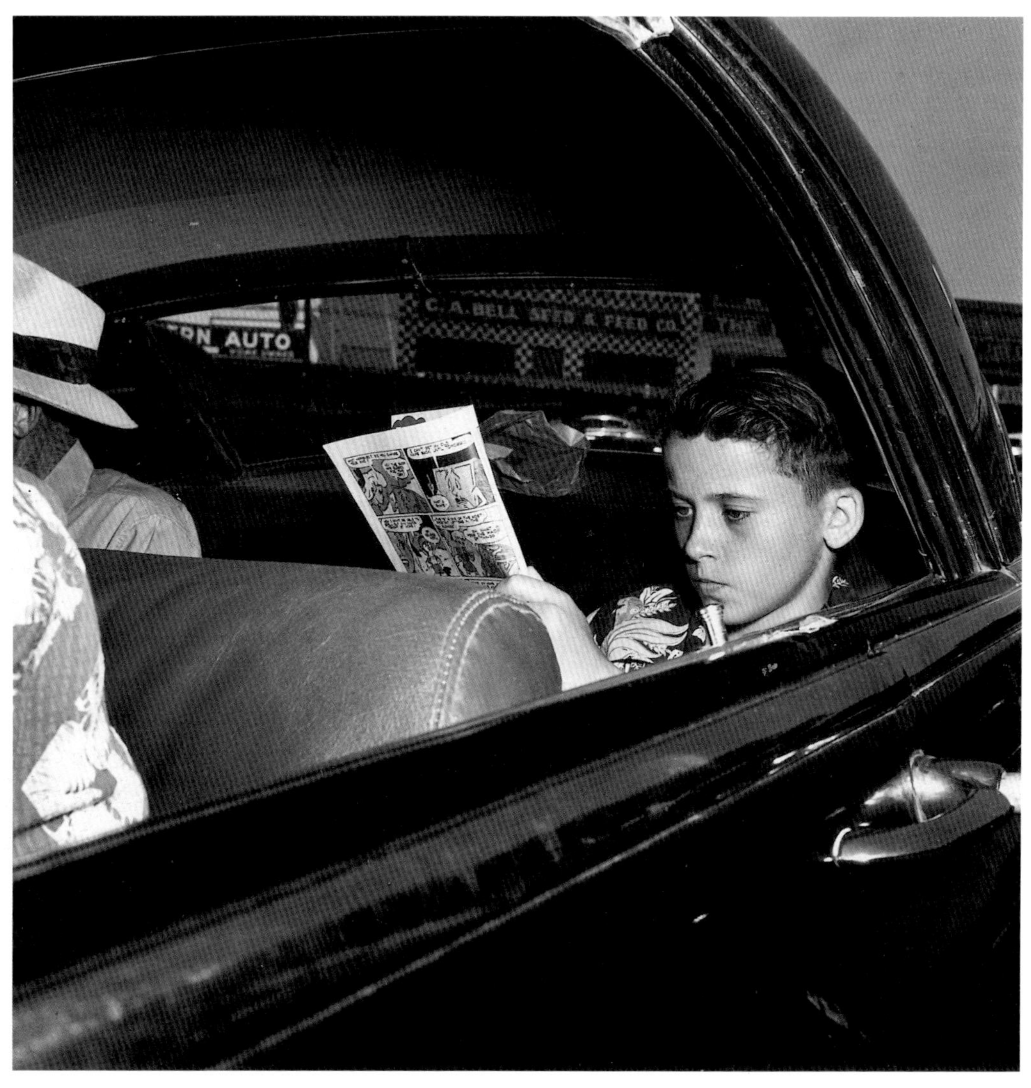

FERNE KOCH

"Plutocrat," Blakely, Georgia from the "Comic Series"

1950

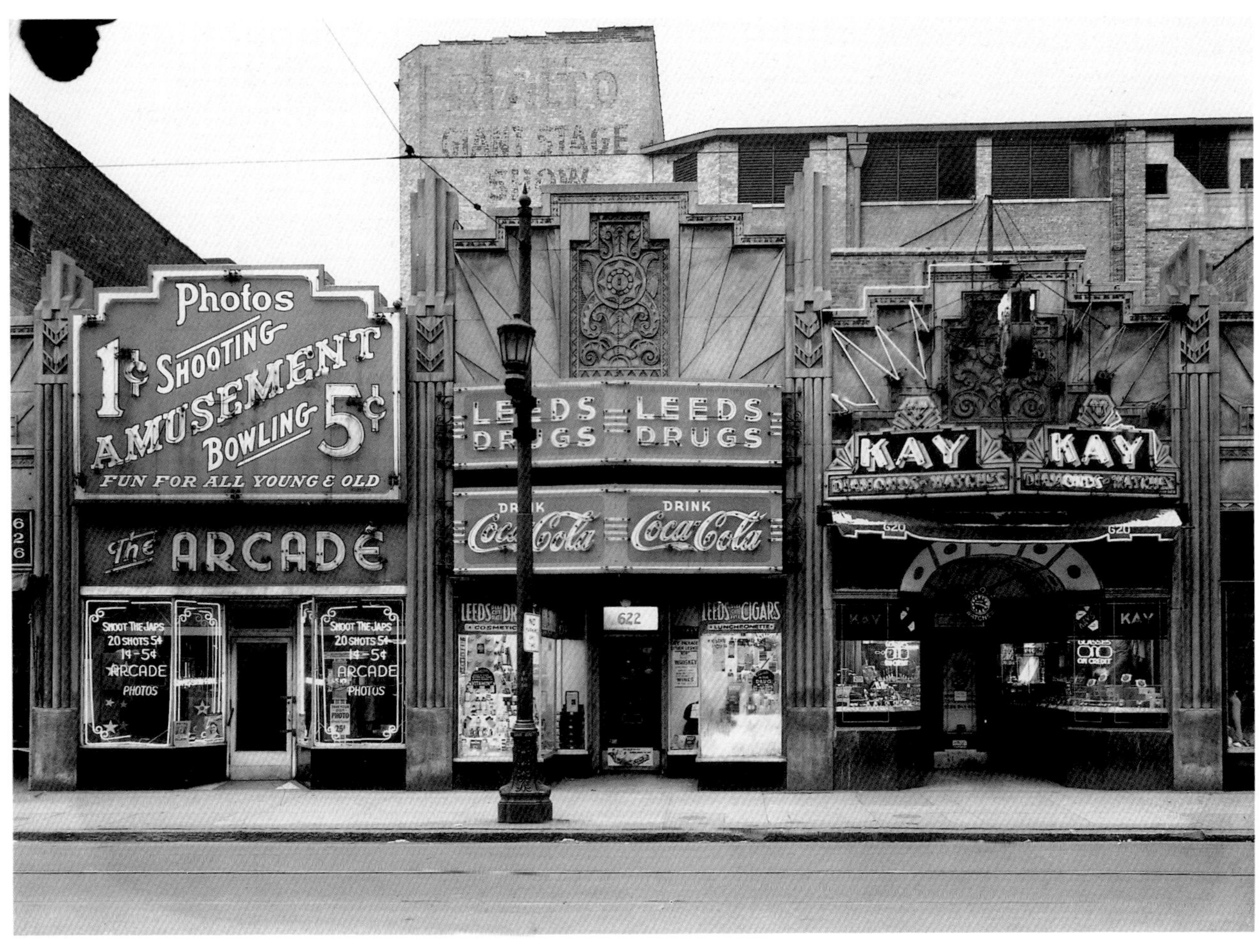

STERN J. BRAMSON

Rialto Block, 600 S. Fourth Street, Louisville, Kentucky

1946

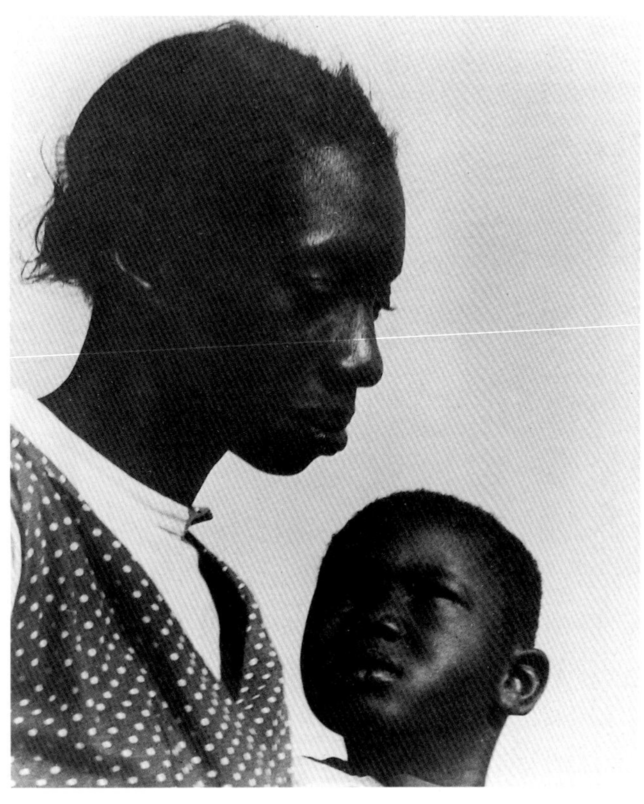

CONSUELO KANAGA

Mother and Son or The Question (Florida)
1950

MICHAEL DISFARMER

Woman in Print Dress and Young Boy with Ice Cream Cone
1939–46

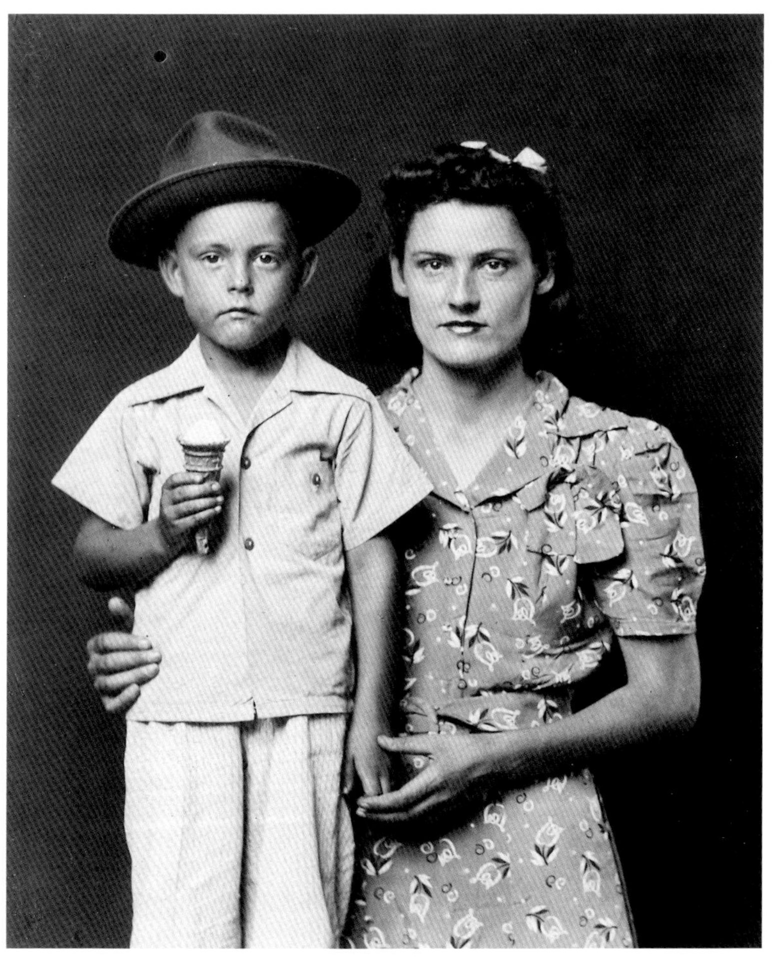

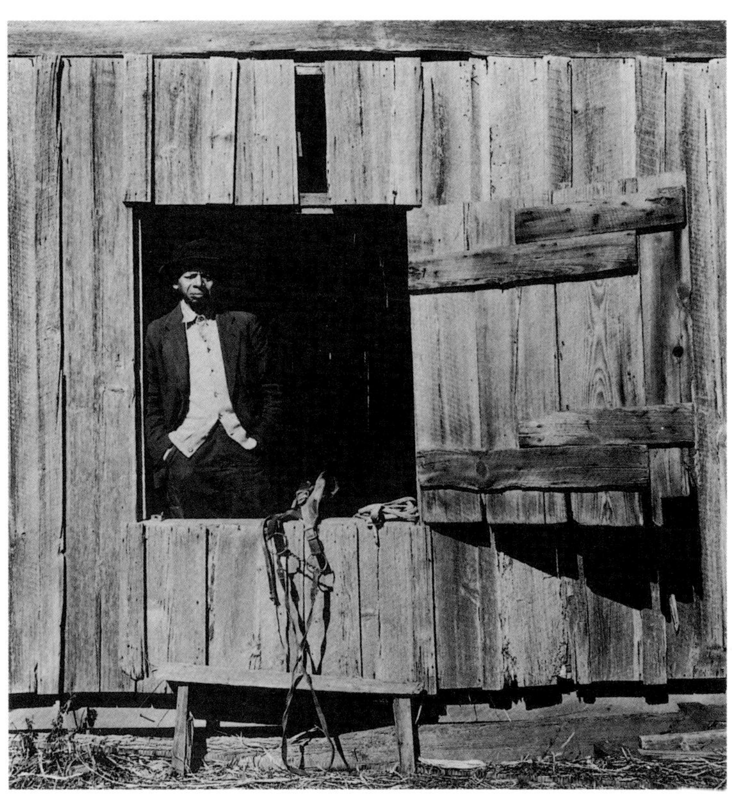

MARTHA MCMILLAN ROBERTS
Farmer Jack Wade, Quebie Town, South Carolina
1948

REVEREND LONZIE ODIE TAYLOR
Tri-State Bank Opening, Memphis
ca. 1946

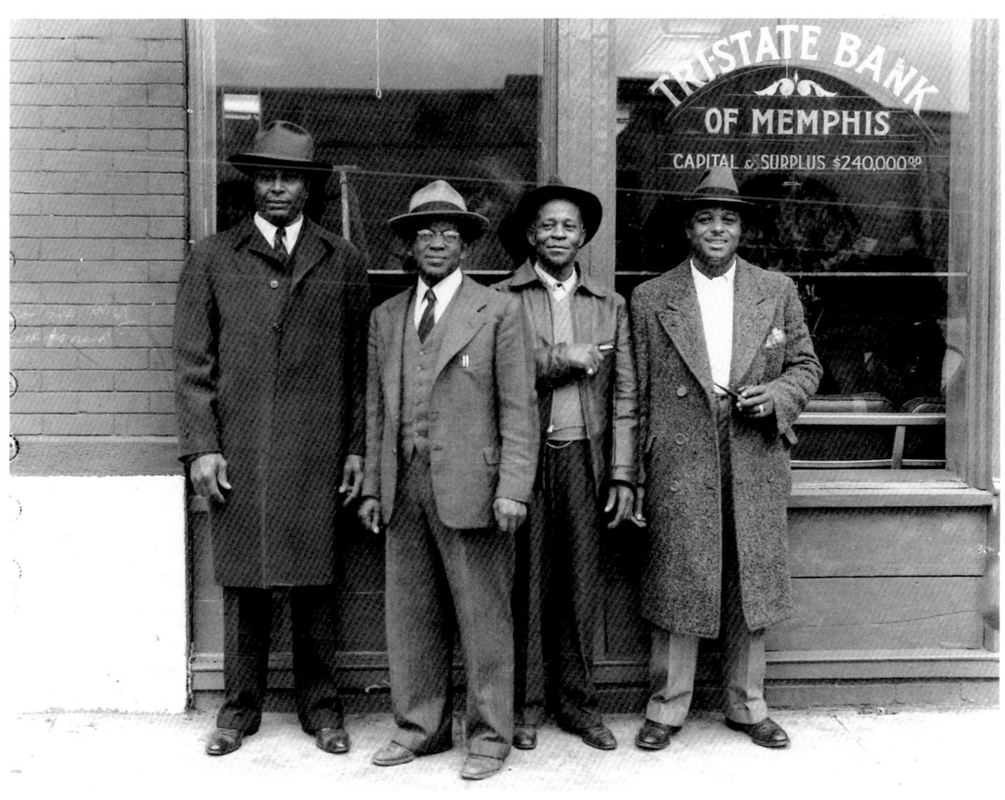

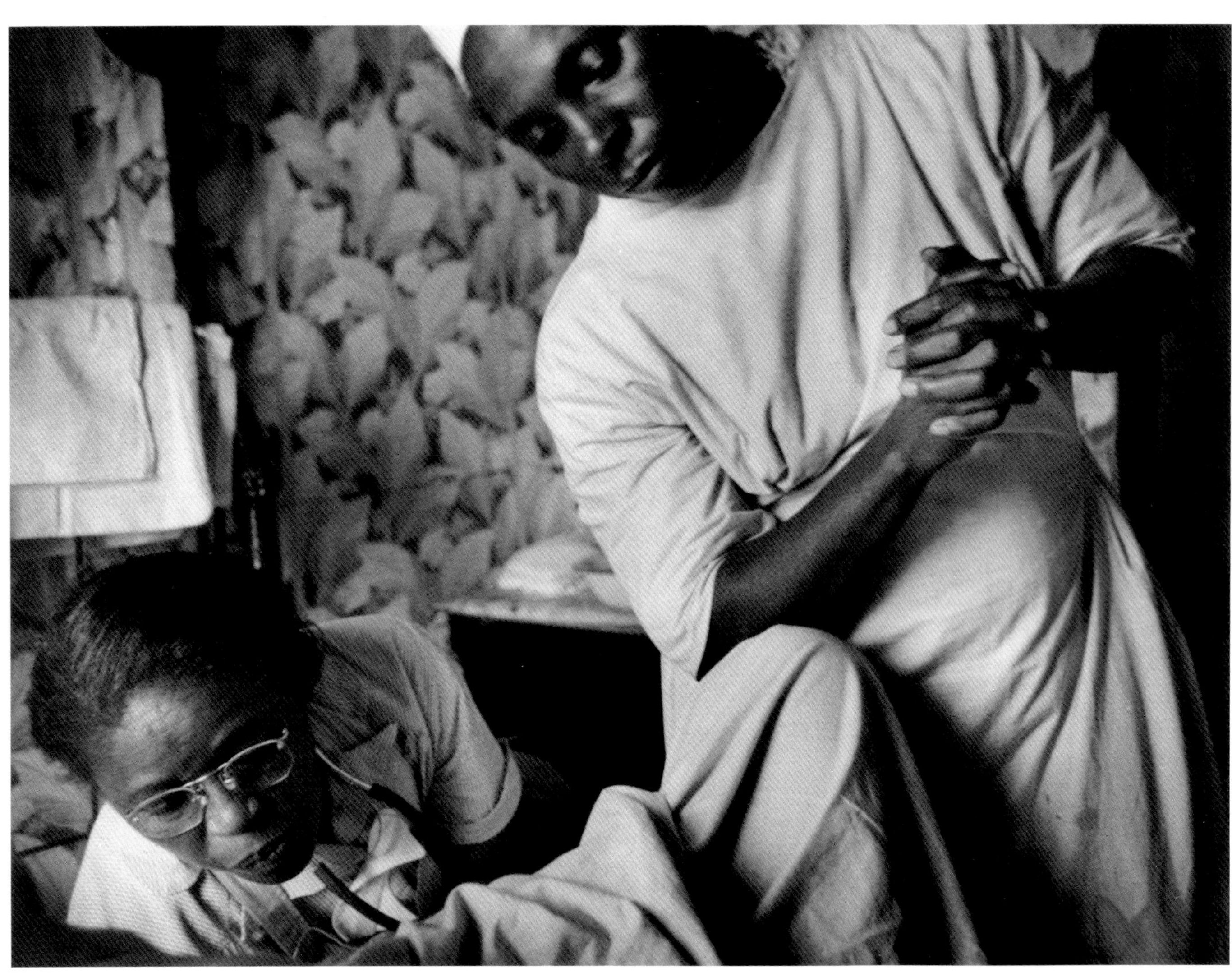

W. EUGENE SMITH

Untitled [Maude attending patient, assistant looking on with clasped hands]
from the series "Nurse Midwife. Maude Callen Eases Pain of Birth, Life and Death"
1951

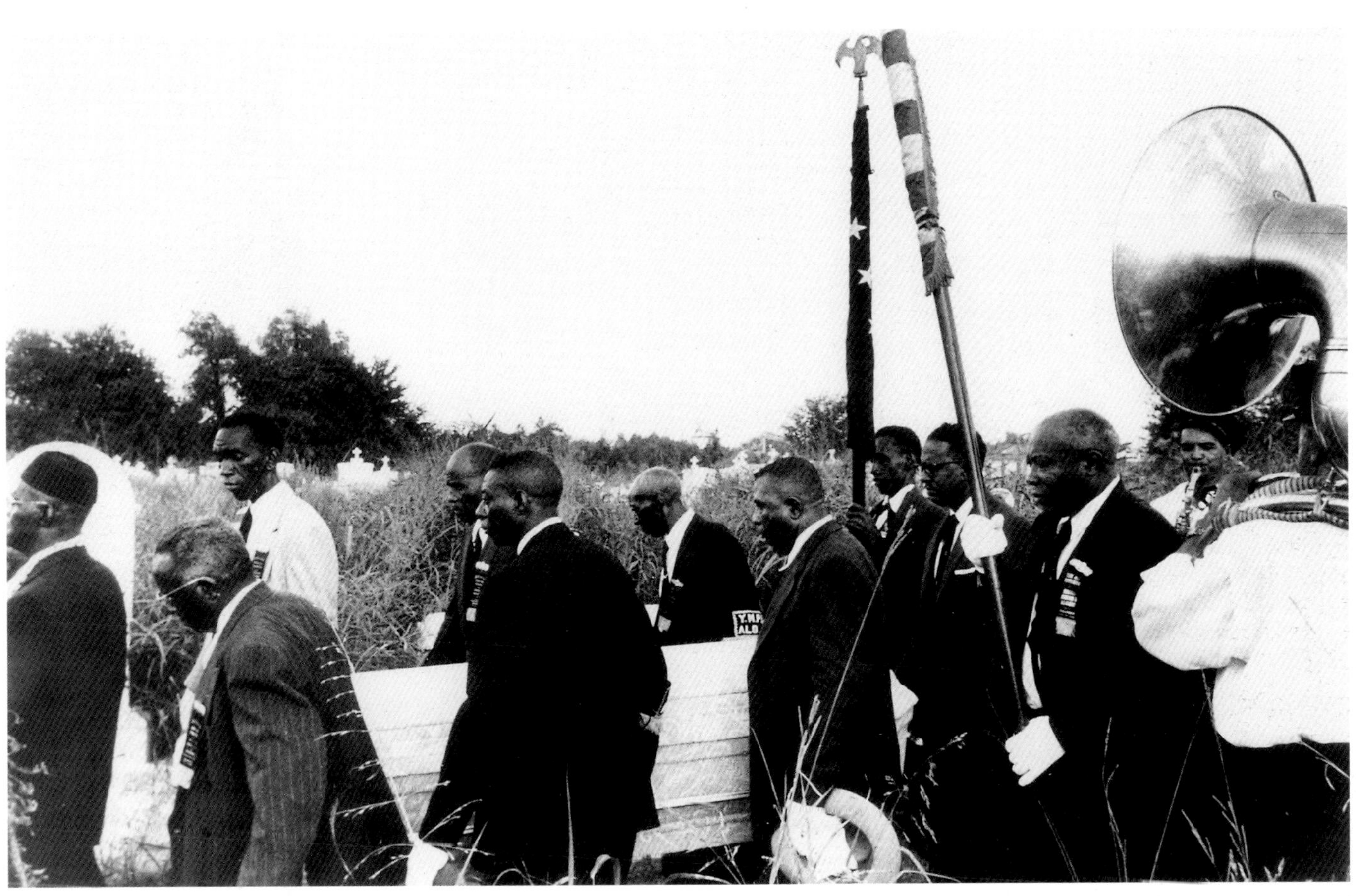

RALSTON CRAWFORD

Eureka Brass Band at McDonoghville Cemetery, New Orleans, Louisiana

1956

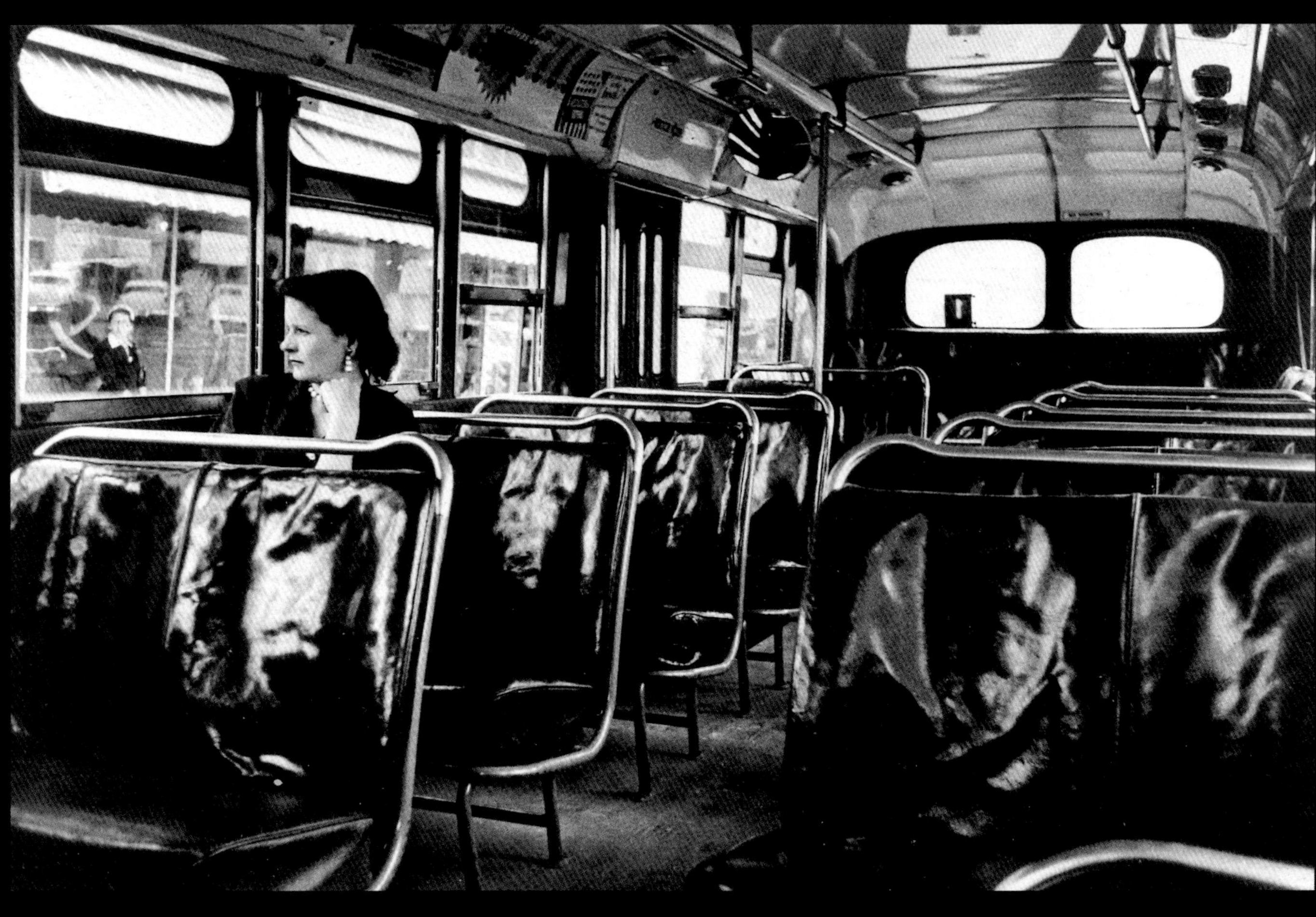

DAN WEINER

White Rider during Bus Boycott, Montgomery, Alabama

1956

BOBBIE ANN MASON

ACROSS THE DIVIDE

When I was growing up, I had little opportunity to learn about a culture that existed right in my town. Blacks made up only a small percentage of the overall population in Western Kentucky, but the glimpses I got of them were enough to stir my curiosity and make me feel something was missing from my education. At that time Southern whites were a defeated people, still to some degree outcasts within America: backward-looking descendants of the Rebels. Grotesque racism grew out of our low self-esteem, further alienating us from America as a whole and from our own humanity.

In this collection of photographs from the South, so many of the scenes show whites in isolation: Beauty Queen. Lone Bus Rider. The Football Player. Even the white-spired Church in the Cotton Field and the lonely Rebel Gas Station. In another picture, two black men sit on an RC-Cola bench, arms crossed protectively, while a white man sits on an adjacent bench, legs crossed casually, arms outstretched expansively. The blacks are vulnerable, so they huddle, while the white man relaxes in his privileged arrogance.

Yet among a good many white people, there was a powerful attraction to the taboo black culture. When I was about ten years old, my father and I listened to late-night radio on WLAC, Nashville. White DJs John R and Gene Nobles played black music—what were then called "race records." The music came up from the Mississippi Delta and branched off to Chicago and Kansas City. It was music you didn't hear on Patti Page–Perry Como daytime radio. It was rhythm-and-blues, surging and powerful and painful and exhilarating. My father and I listened to it, sharing something I didn't understand. I was only a child, but somehow I knew there was something essential in the songs of Big Bill Broonzy and Memphis Slim and Little Walter. The music was alien and yet somehow closer to my own experience than were the tea parties of more privileged little girls. I sensed that in encouraging me to love this music as he did, my father was teaching me something important.

Along came Elvis. I was ready. He emerged at the moment of a great shift, the year of the *Brown v. Board of Education* decision. Across the nation, white kids' parents thought Elvis sounded black and therefore primitive and dangerous. But Elvis was less a problem for white parents in the South. He wasn't that strange here. In fact, he seemed very familiar. When he wiggled his way through the Ed Sullivan Show, my parents and I were captivated. And he won over the children of white people all over the country, because the kids instinctively understood how vapid white culture was becoming. If Elvis was somehow bringing us the creative energy he had found in black music, we whites soon wanted it and needed it. White people, alienated from the black race by our inhumane beliefs and practices, were a vitiated, sorry bunch of folks—white bread, and stale at that.

Rhythm-and-blues and rock-and-roll couldn't be contained behind the fence or in the back of the bus. Sound travels. We heard it. For a long time, white people had been enthralled (partly in secret) by black music. And by the mid-fifties we loved it so much we wanted to possess it, to appropriate it, to *feel* it. We apparently thought it was our privilege to borrow it, but we also wanted it bad enough to steal it. What Pat Boone did with "Tutti Frutti" remains an embarrassment, but Elvis could "Tutti Frutti" rings around Pat. Elvis wasn't Little Richard, but he was something of a translator.

Today what we think of as American music, our export to the world, comes mainly from African-American culture. The blues is bigger and deeper than white people's sorrows; we can be engulfed in it, it's so deep and wide. Mark Twain, whose well-known despair and cynicism were intensified by his futile battle against the racial injustice of the society of his time, often said he found blacks to be superior to whites. He embraced black culture, and he loved spirituals so deeply he would sing them at dinner parties. For him, the music of the black race reached across the racial divide.

In the fifties and sixties, rock-and-roll helped bridge that divide for many Americans, but of course the divide, though it may be narrower, remains. White people can't truly sing out of the suffering that gave rise to black music. Whites can't know black suffering or anger from the inside. But the legacy of slavery and segregation is something that all Americans share, in differing ways. Historically, whites were responsible for the cruelty and injustice that caused the blacks' travail. We're implicated, so the music fueled by black pain haunts us and draws us in. To some degree, it's our music, too.

Maybe someday the divide will finally close. But in the years of segregation, it was a chasm. As a result, people on both sides were often trapped in isolation. The photographs here show various lone, lonely-looking whites. Some of the black persons shown in these photographs are also alone—isolated by the shame of indignity, or on the other hand by the power of affirmation. Whether alone or in groups, black Americans in these pictures are singing, demonstrating, resisting. Most shocking, perhaps, of all the photographs is the group of sanitation workers who had to hold up signs declaring I AM A MAN, a message to a society that was almost inconceivably blind. The faces in the photos show the truth of the people's rage, their sorrow. Look at the faces of Fannie Lou Hamer and Martin Luther King. You can almost hear the power and urgency of their voices. Martin Luther King uttered the American dream most deeply and made us suspect that African Americans are the truest Americans, the ones who have fought longest for what we claim to champion: freedom, independence, self-determination. Their music filled the silence of segregation.

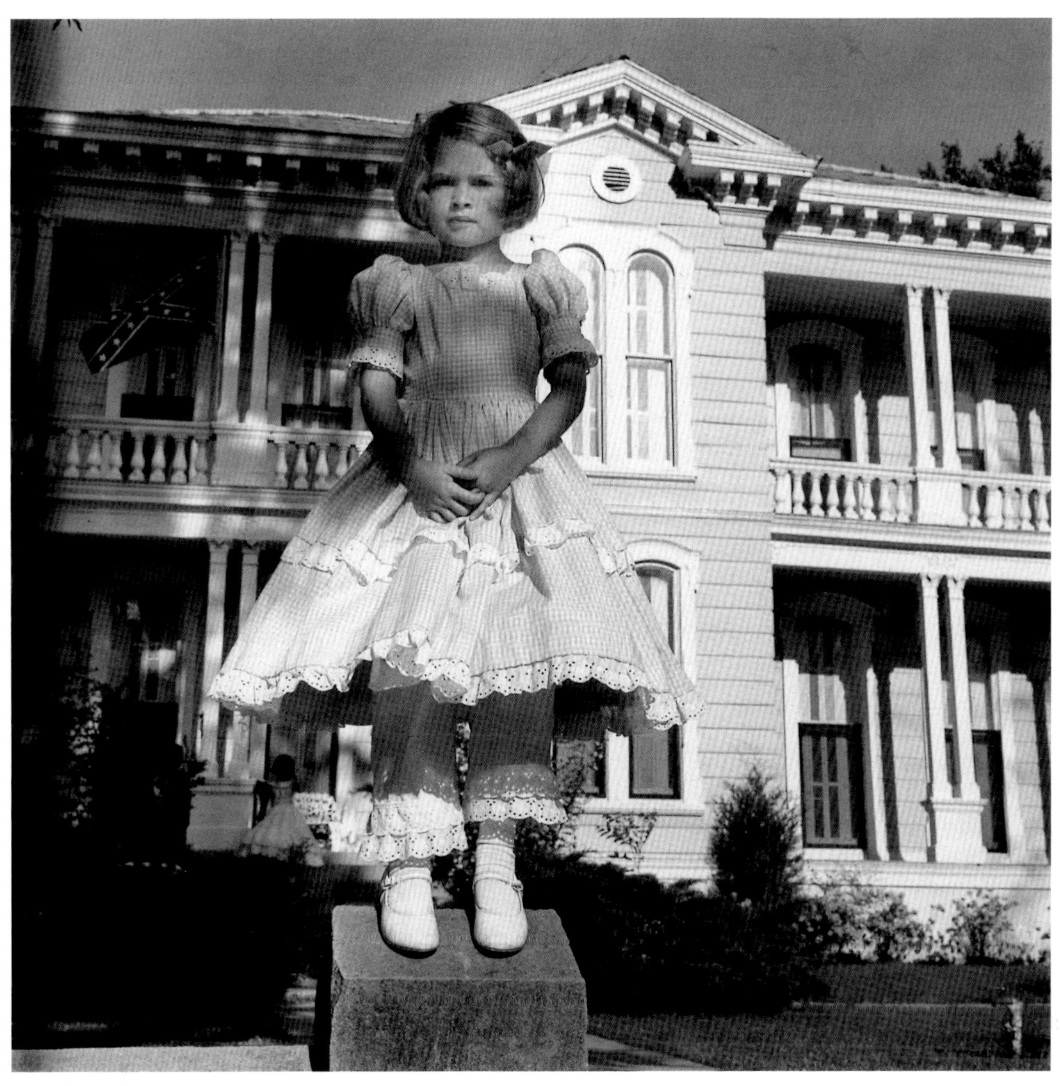

ALAIN DESVERGNES
Yoknapatawpha, Oxford, Mississippi
1963

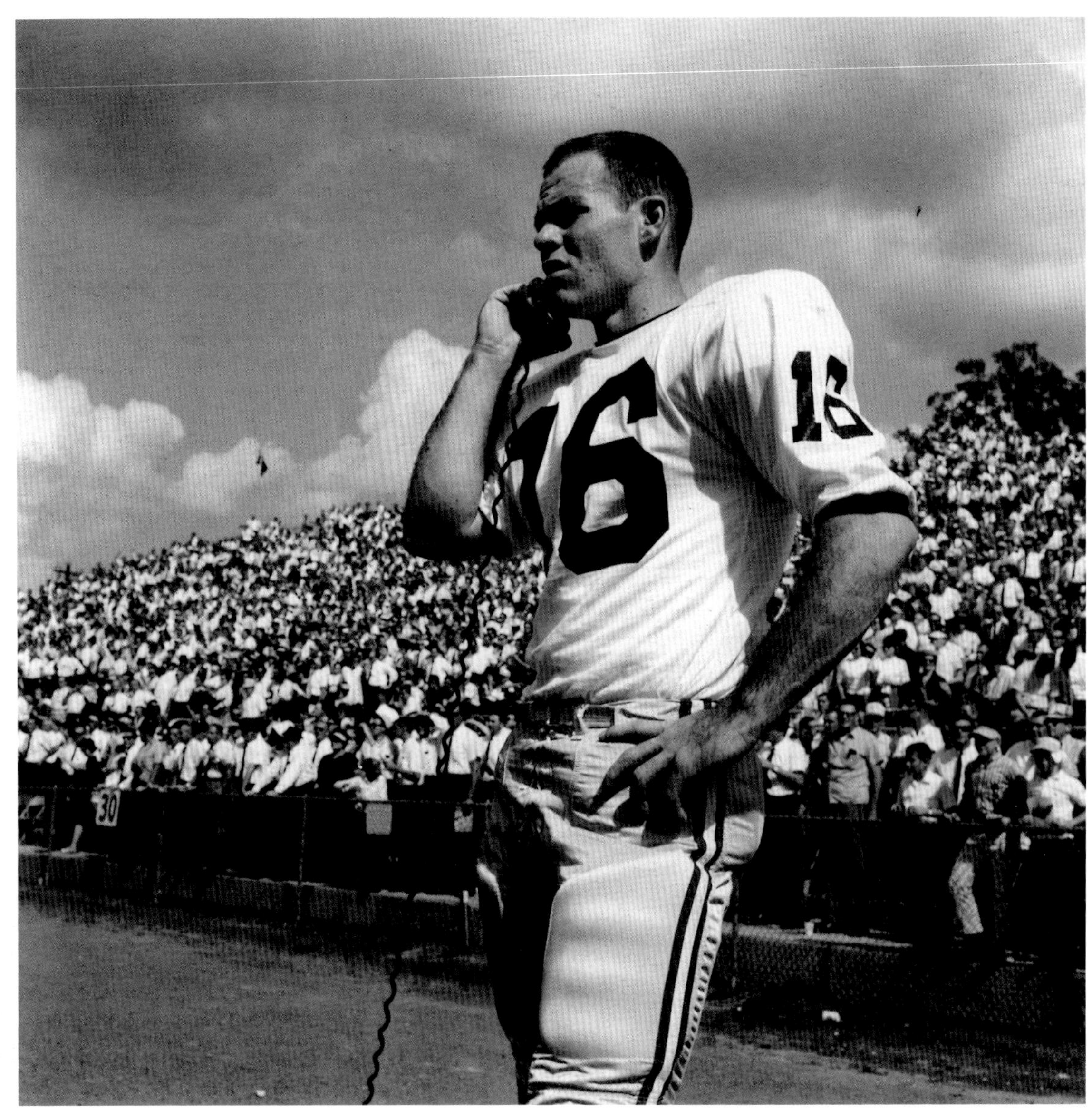

ALAIN DESVERGNES

Yoknapatawpha, Oxford, Mississippi

1963

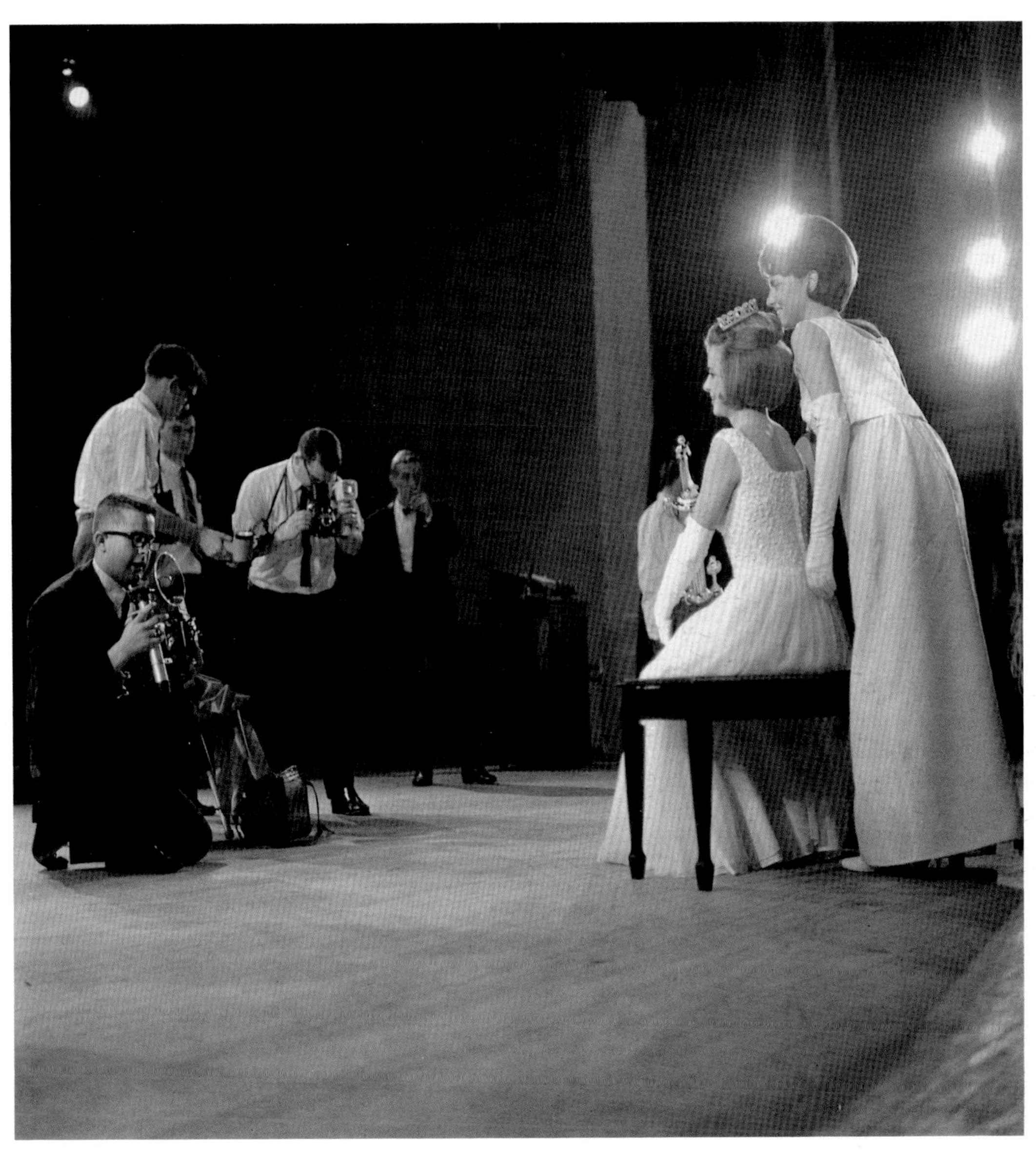

ALAIN DESVERGNES
Yoknapatawpha, Oxford, Mississippi
1963

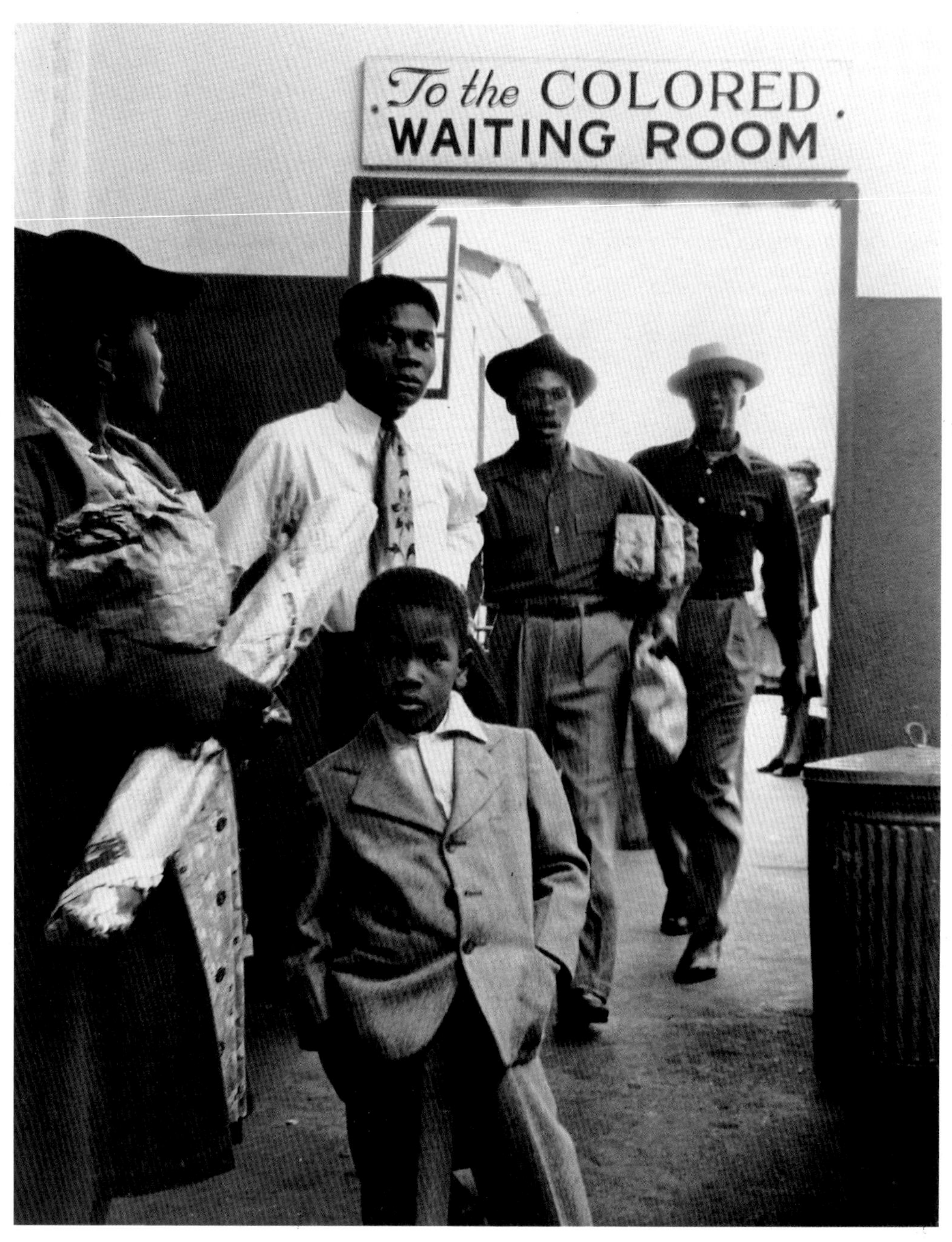

MARION PALFI

To the Colored Waiting Room, Florida

1945–49

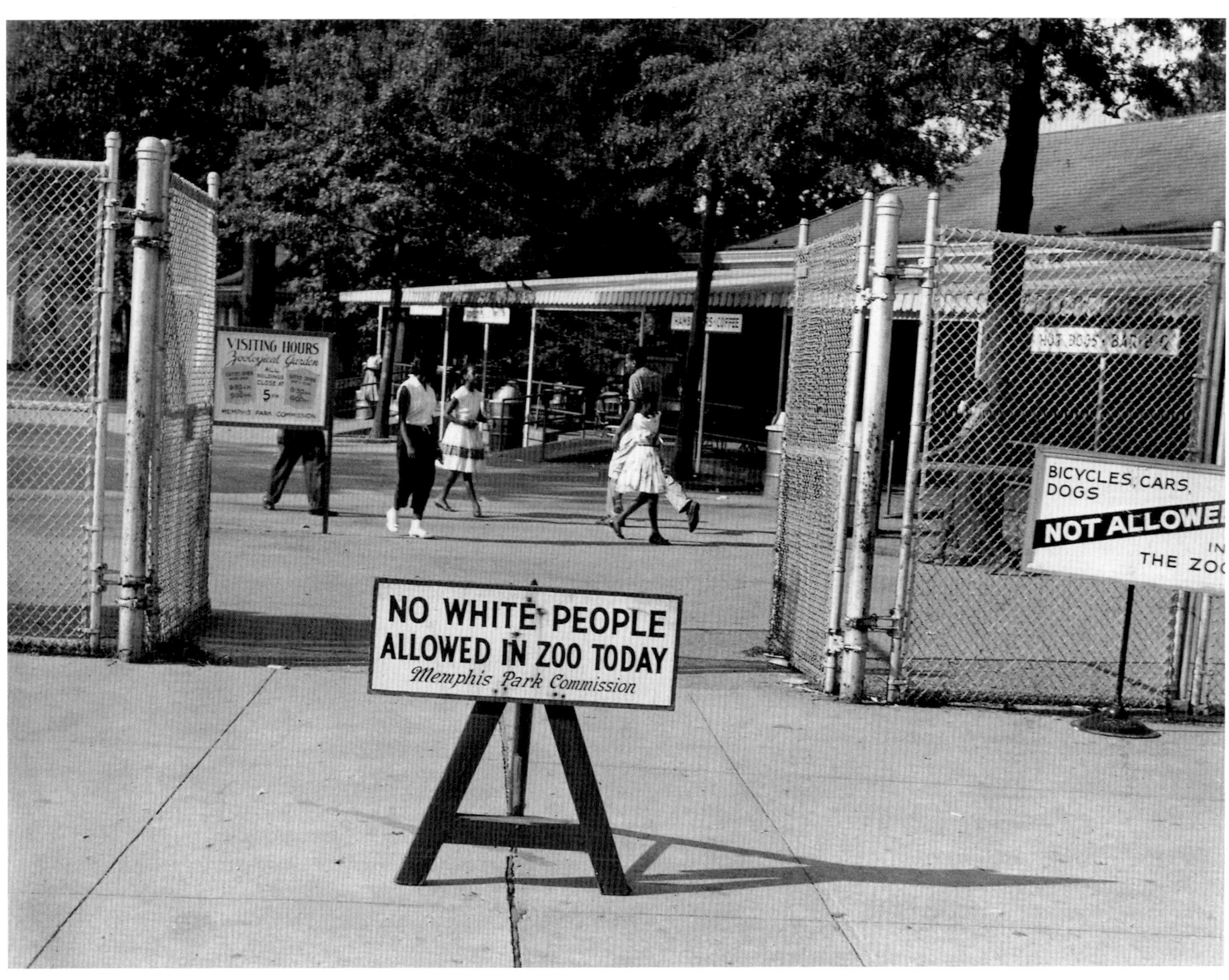

ERNEST C. WITHERS

"No White People Allowed in Zoo Today"

1950s

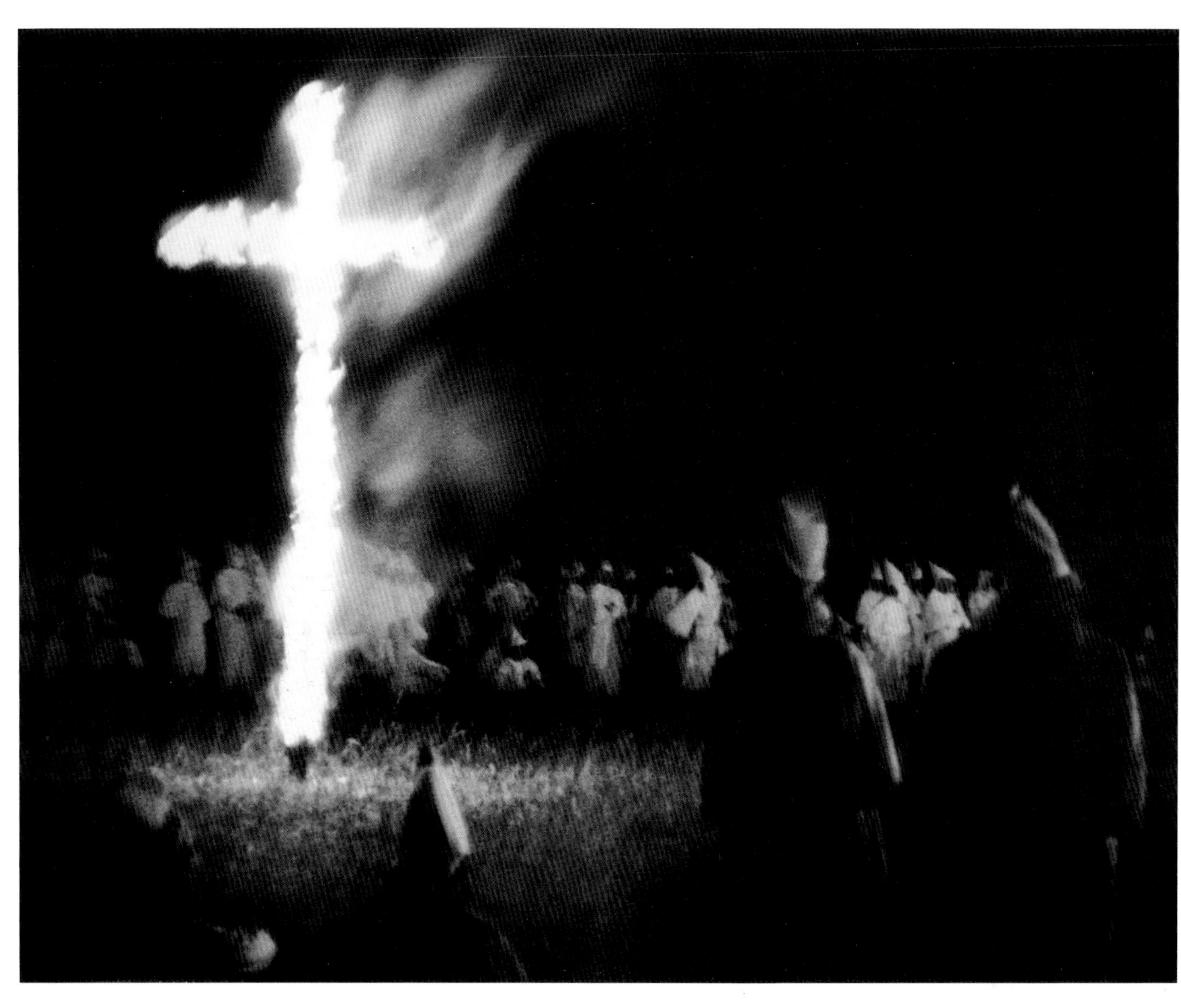

W. EUGENE SMITH
Ku Klux Klan Meeting, North Carolina
1951

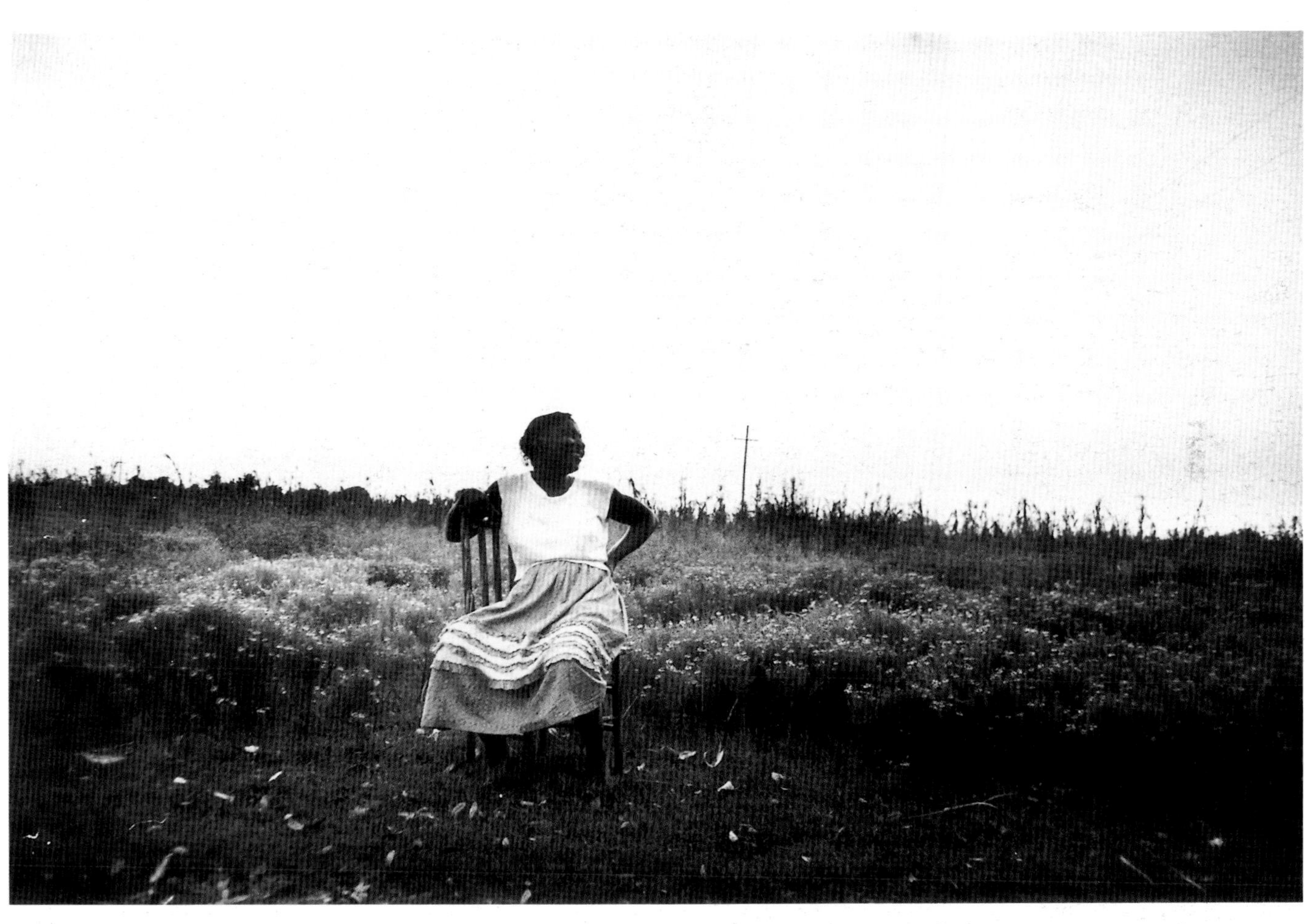

ROBERT FRANK

Beaufort, South Carolina from the series "The Americans"

1955–56

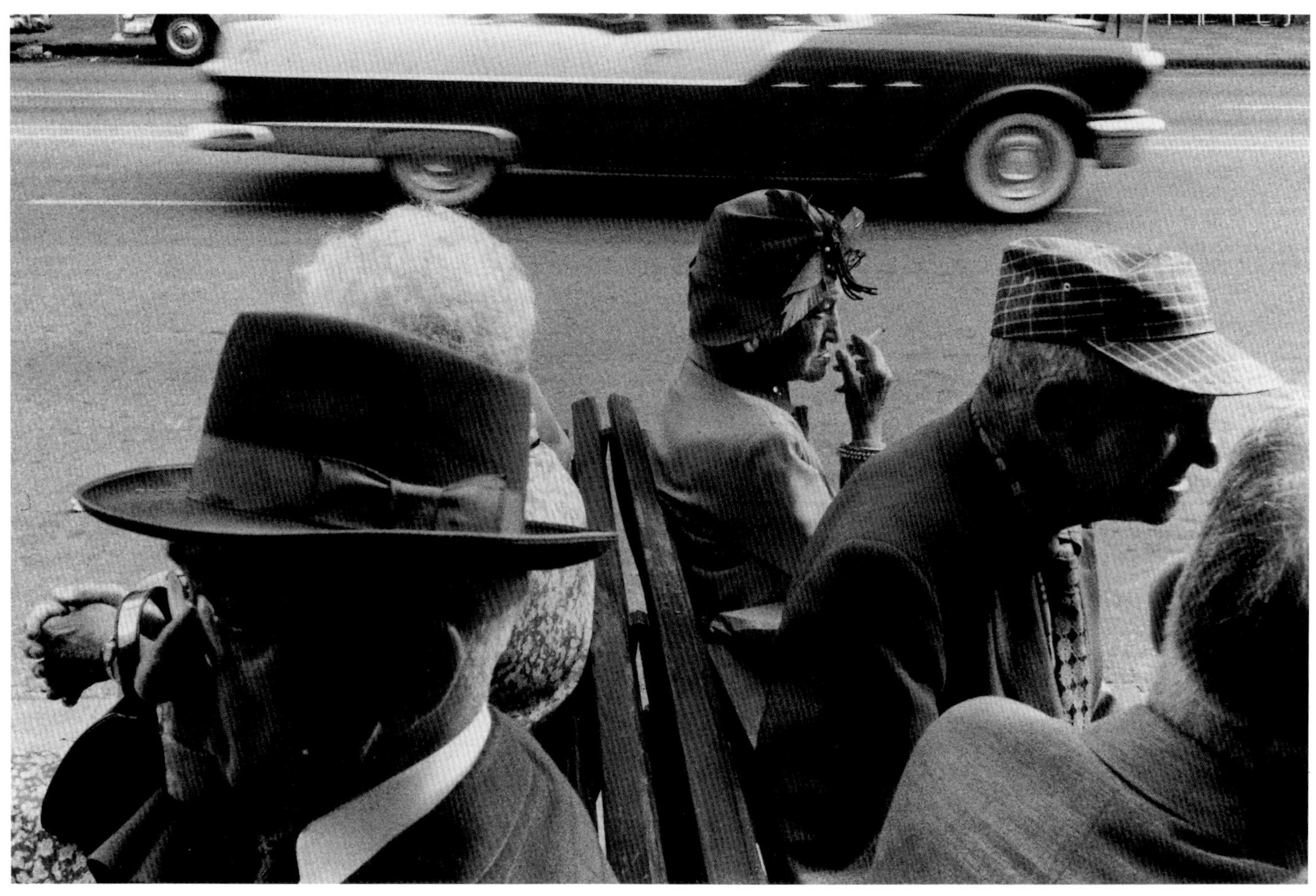

ROBERT FRANK

St. Petersburg, Florida from the series "The Americans"
1955–56

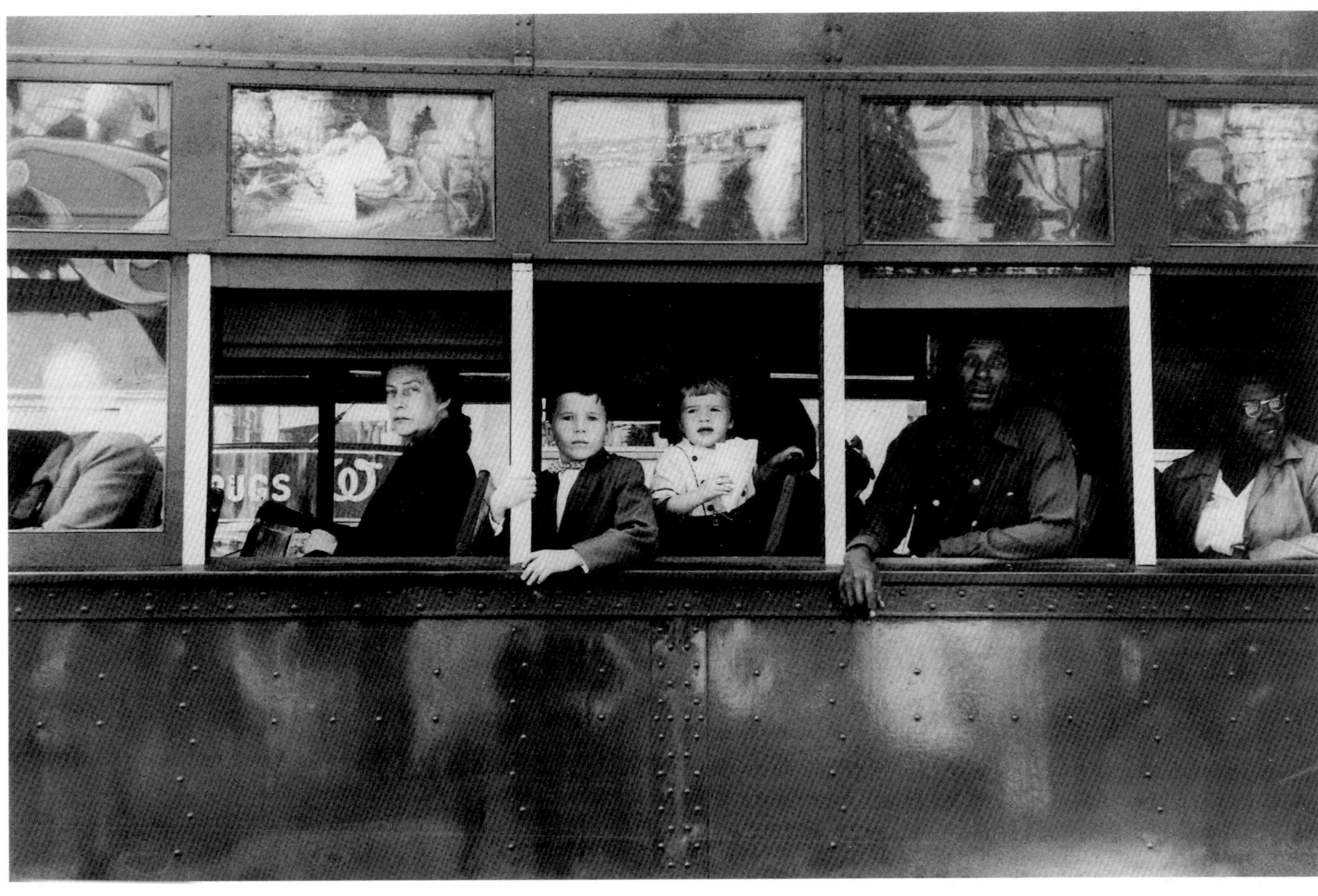

ROBERT FRANK

Trolley, New Orleans from the series "The Americans"

1955–56

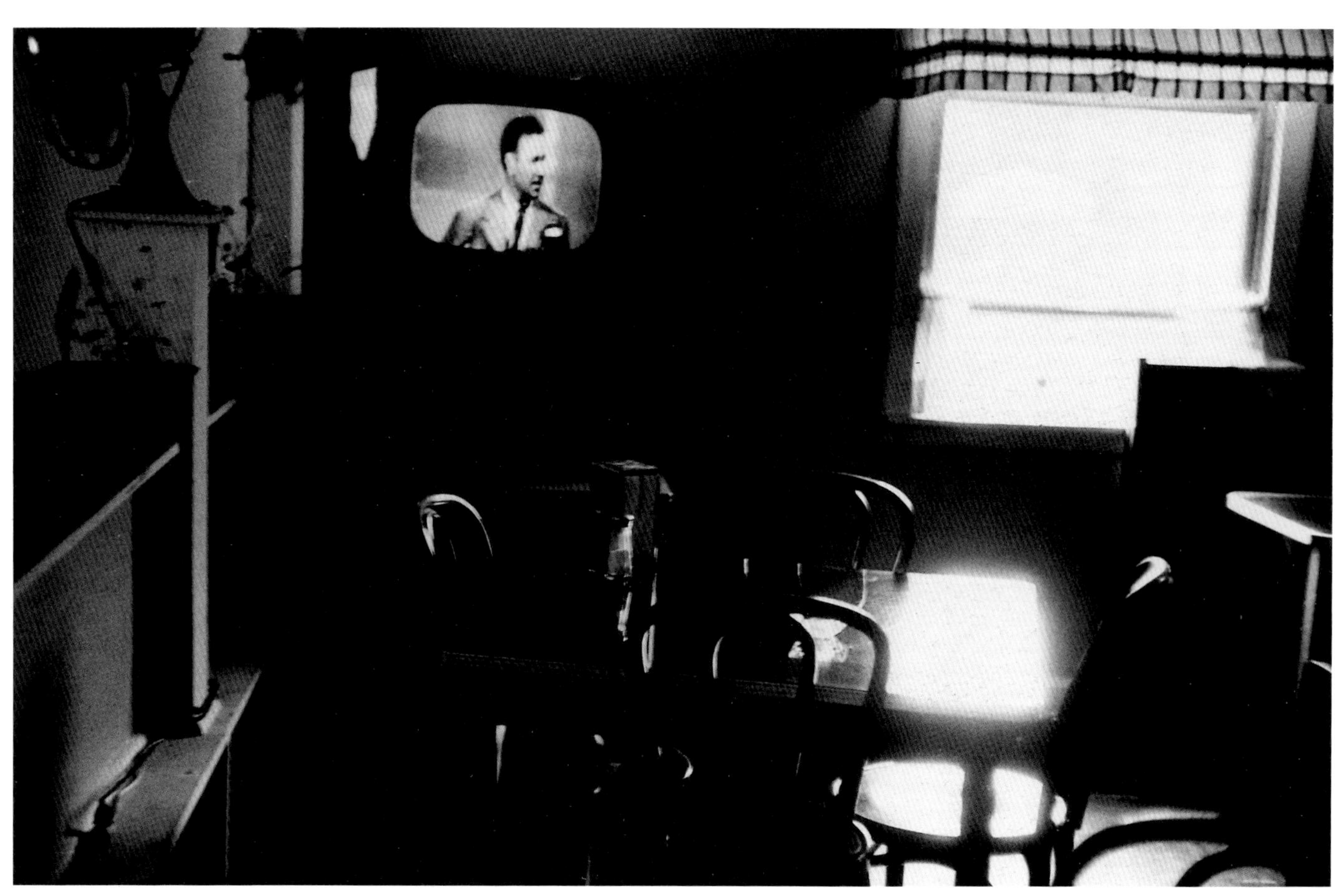

ROBERT FRANK

Restaurant, U.S. 1, Leaving Columbia, South Carolina
from the series "The Americans"
1955–56

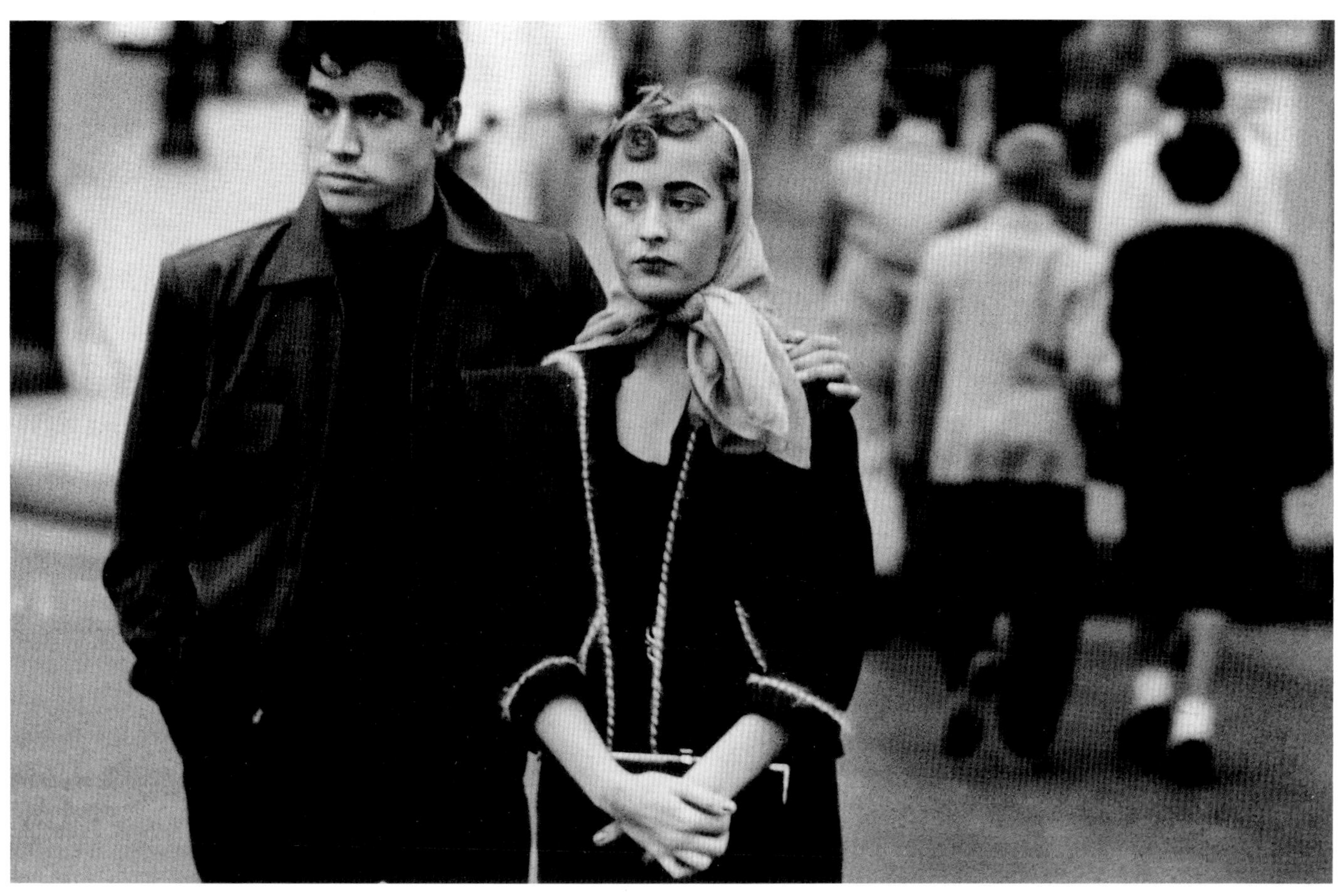

ROBERT FRANK

Chattanooga, Tennessee from the series "The Americans"

1955–56

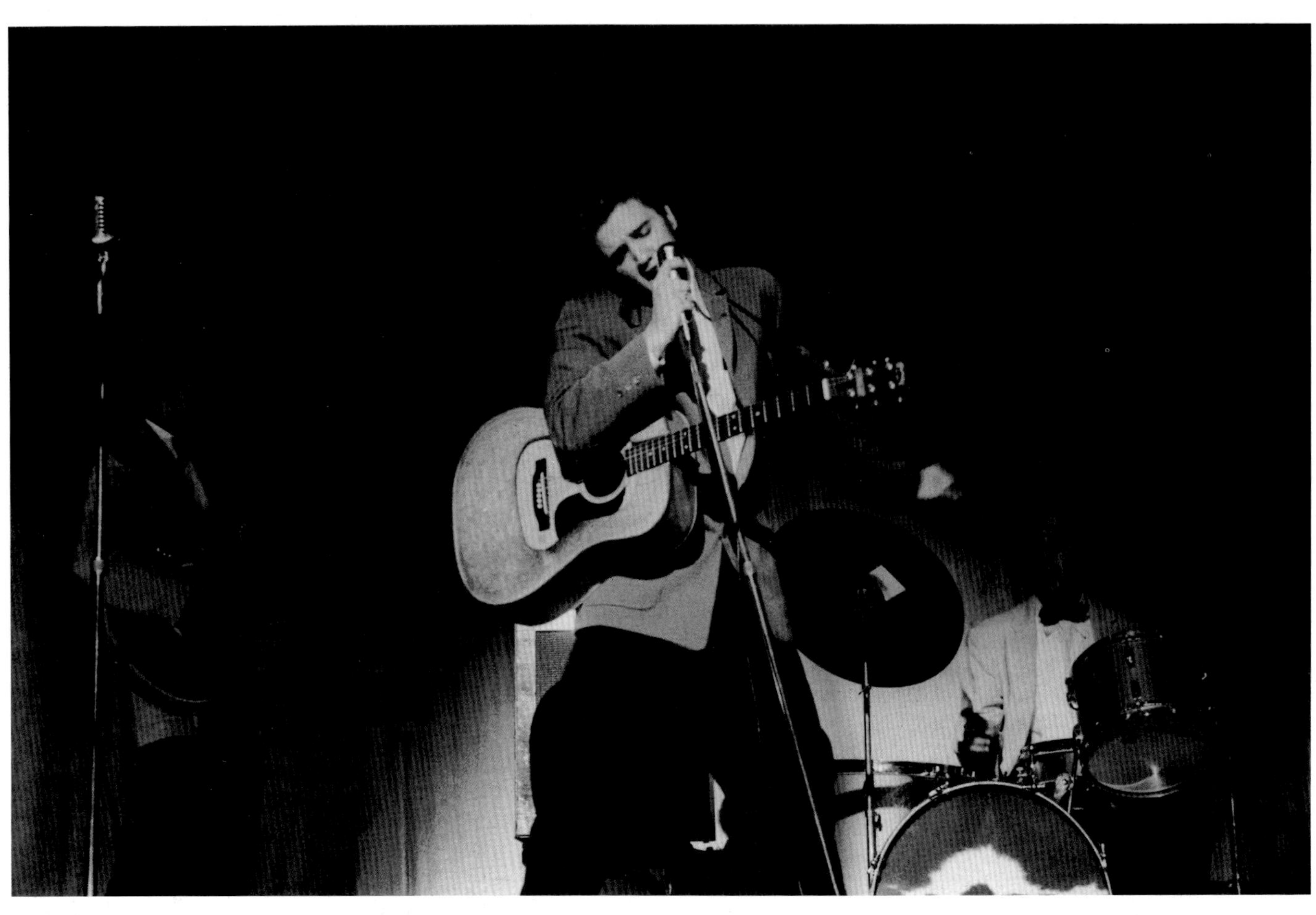

JAY B. LEVITON
Elvis Presley, Jacksonville, Florida
August 10, 1956

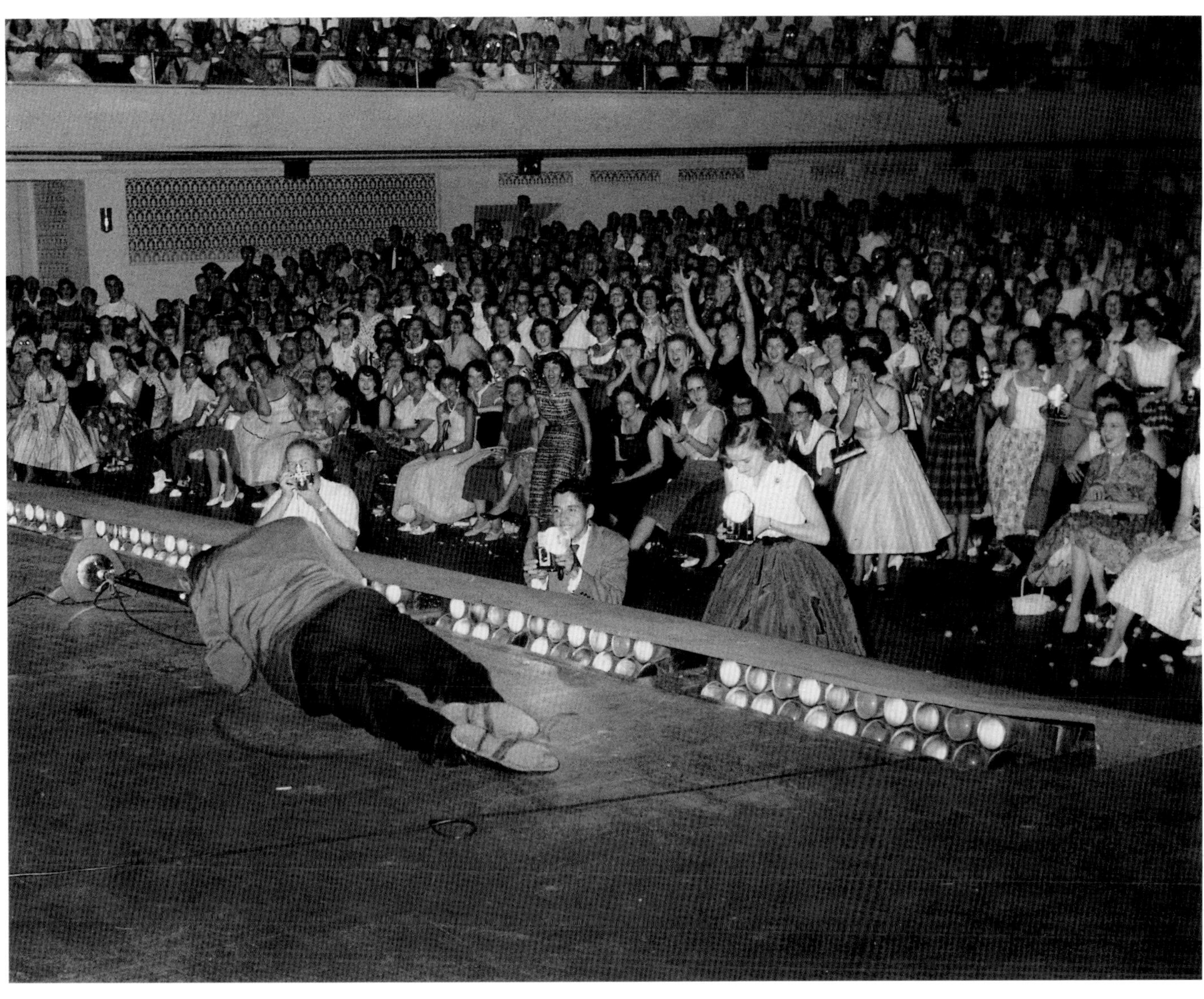

JAY B. LEVITON

Elvis Presley, New Orleans, Louisiana

August 12, 1956

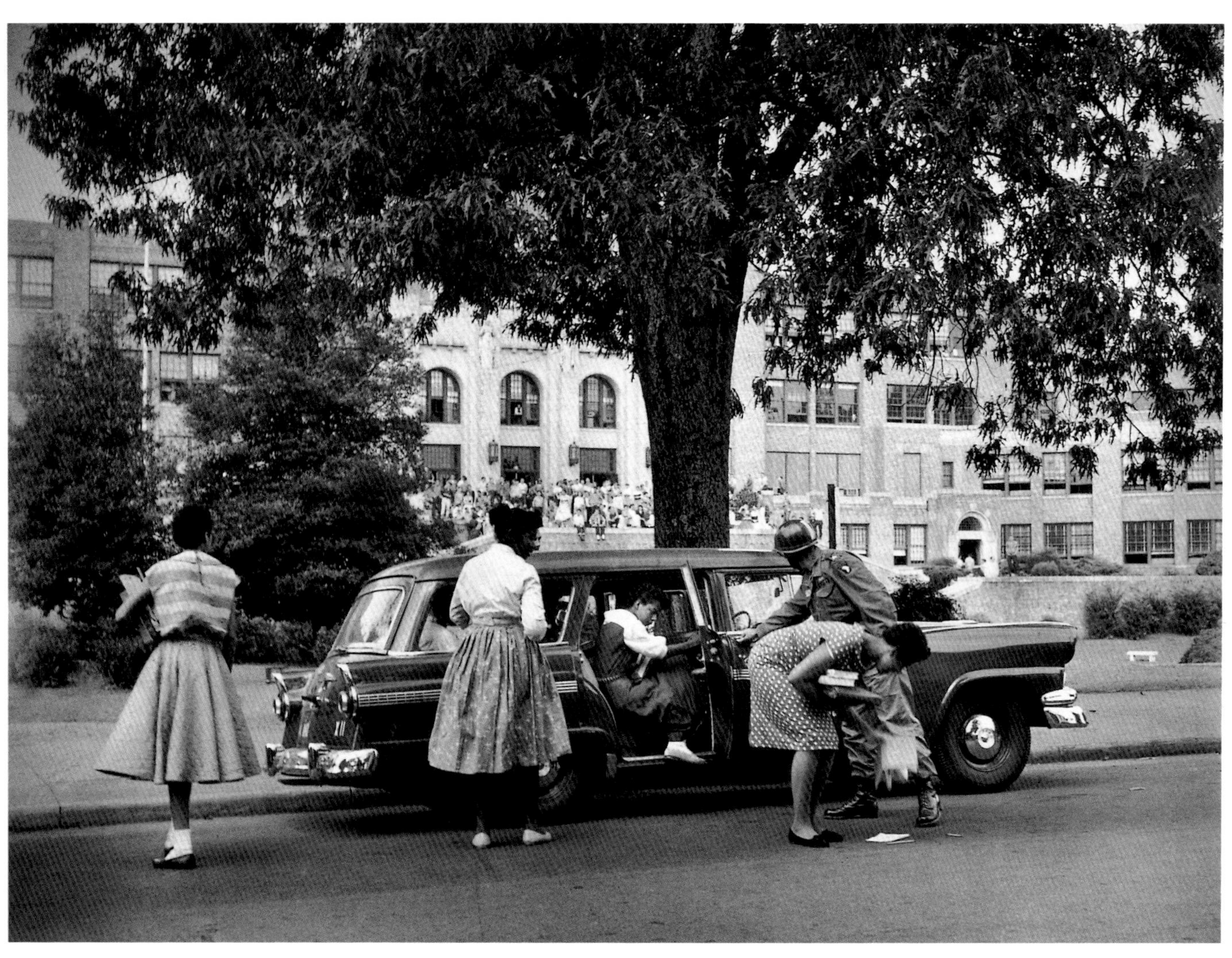

ERNEST C. WITHERS

Desegregation of Central High School by "Little Rock Nine,"
Little Rock, Arkansas
1957

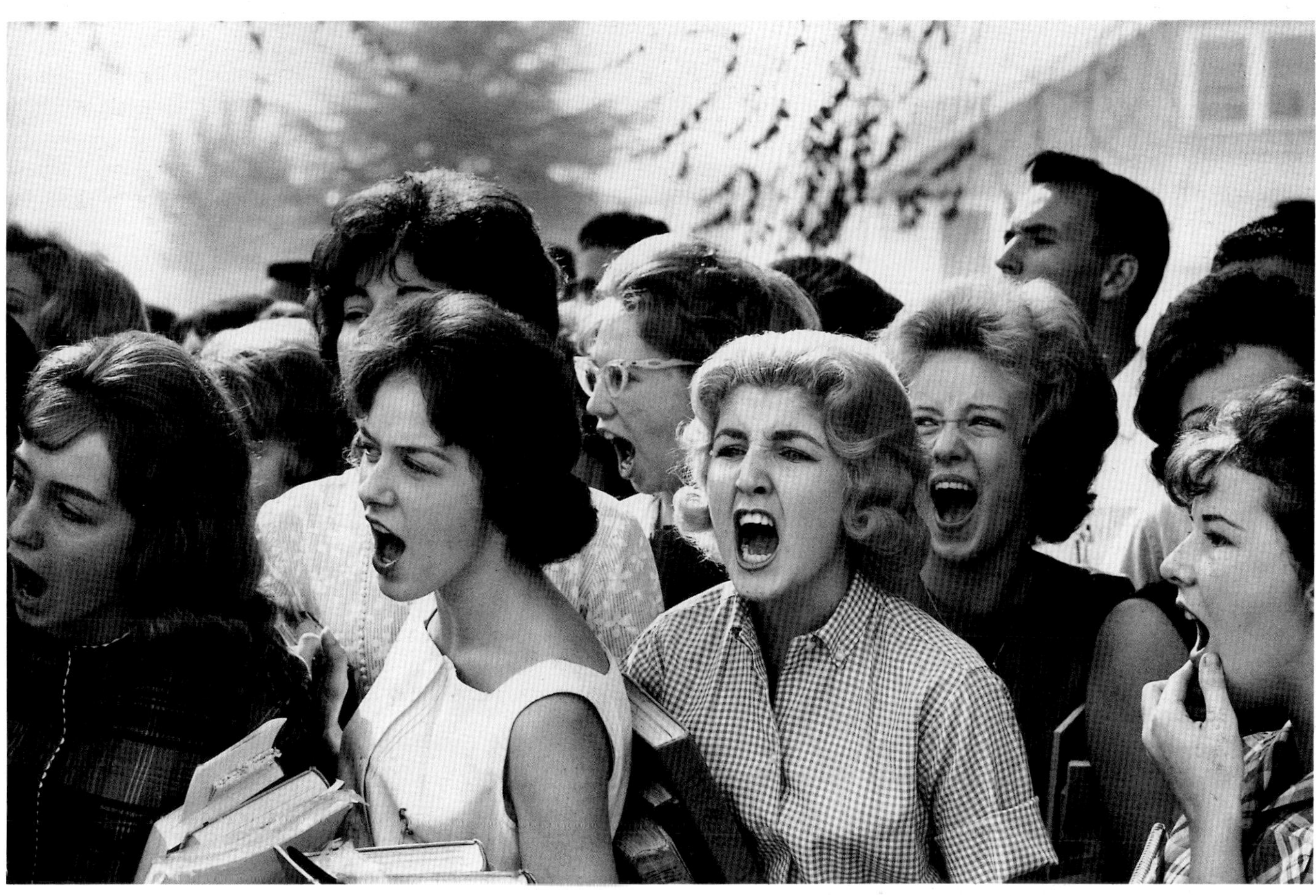

FLIP SCHULKE

White Students in Montgomery Demonstrate against Integration in Their High School, Montgomery, Alabama

September 1963

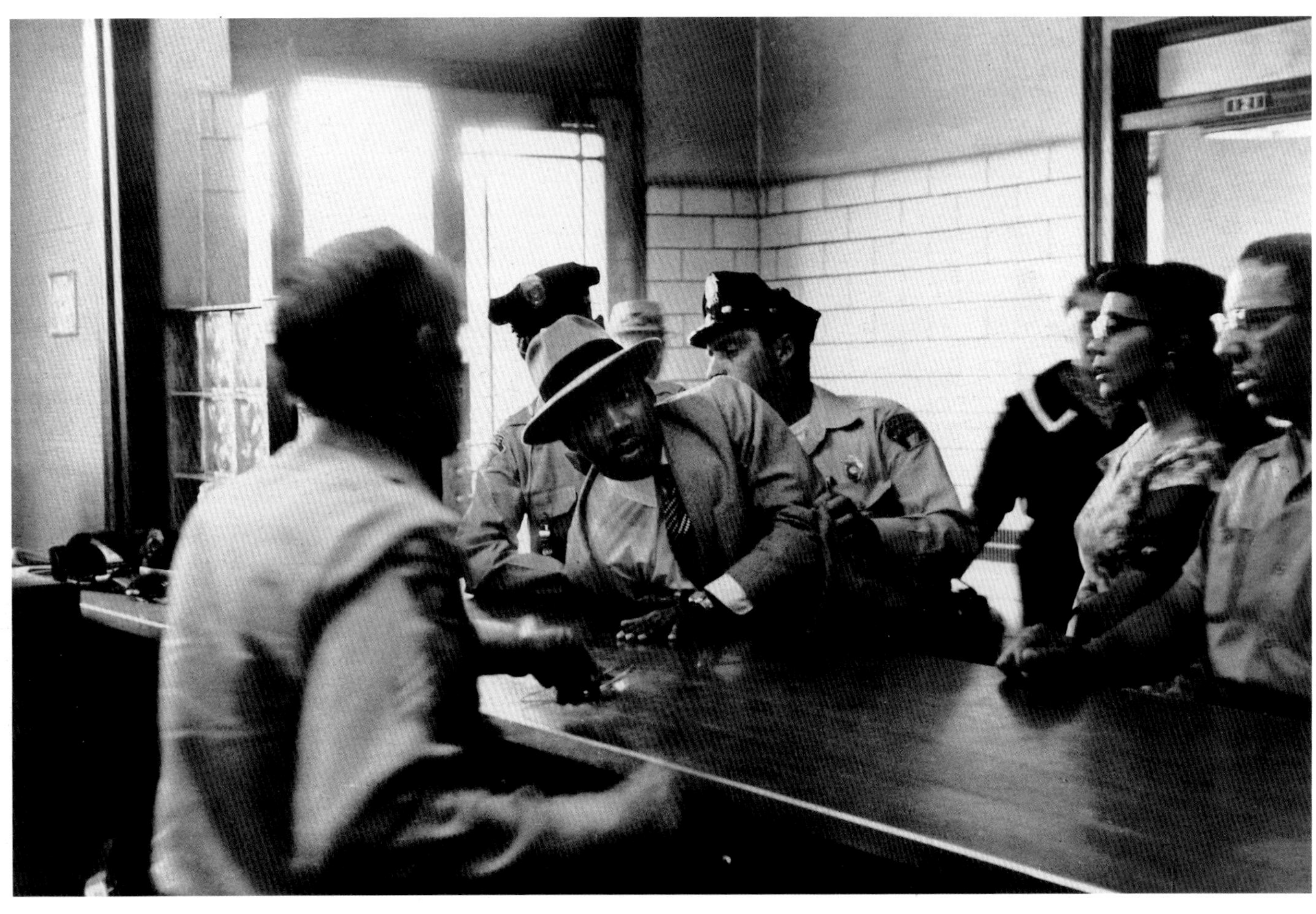

CHARLES MOORE

Martin Luther King, Jr., Arrested, Montgomery, Alabama

1958

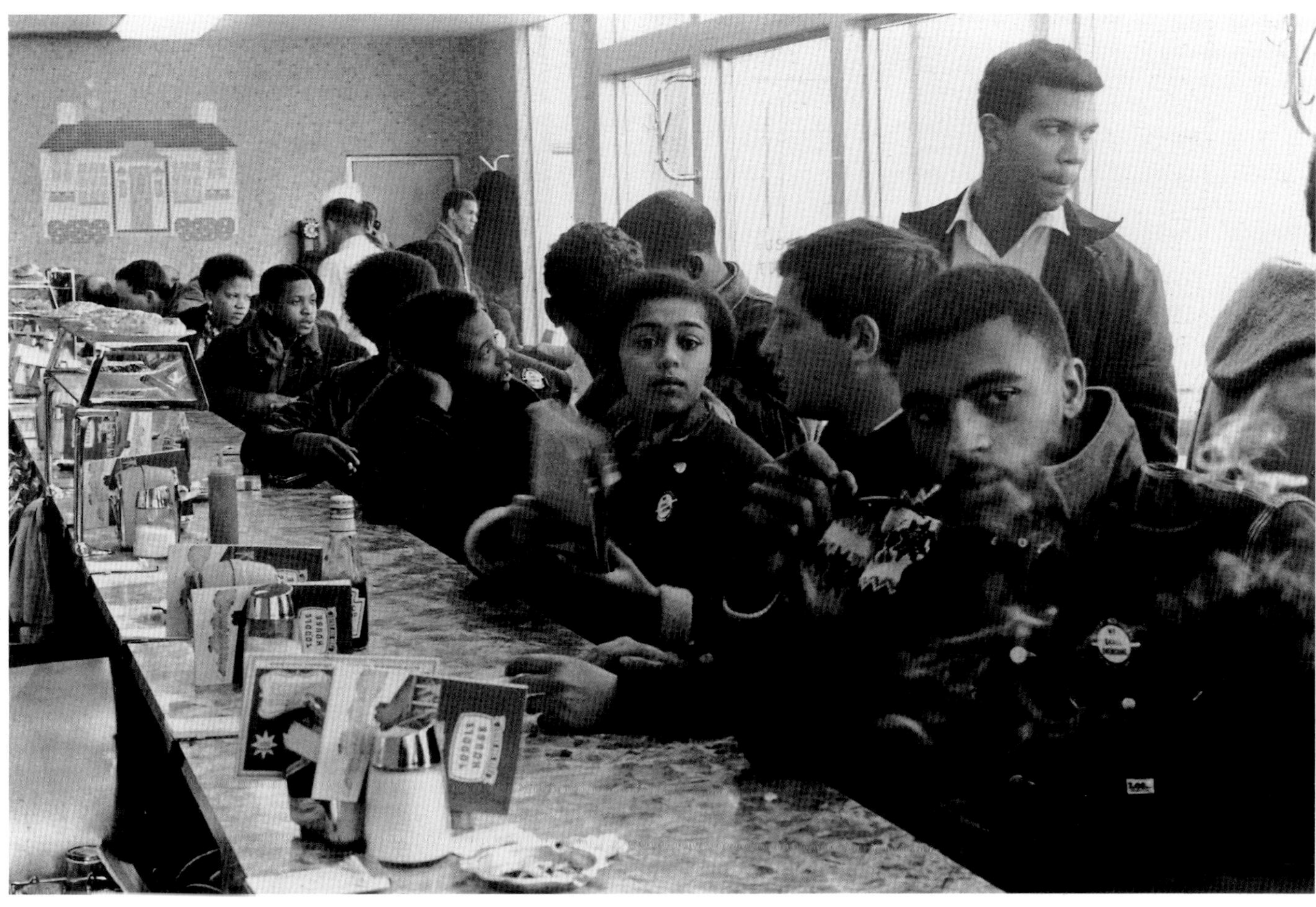

DANNY LYON

SNCC Activists Sitting at a Lunch Counter, Atlanta, Georgia
Winter 1963–64

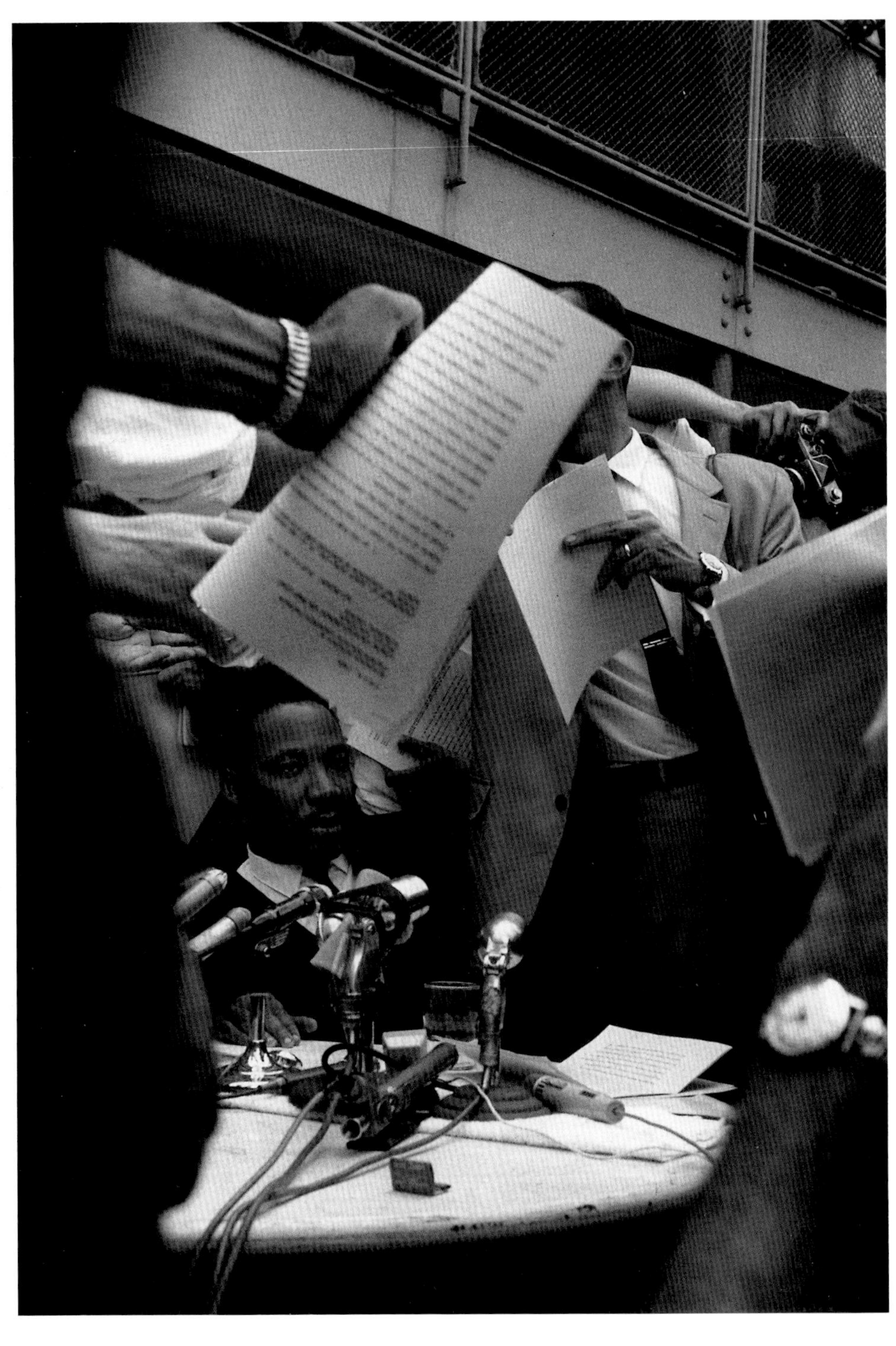

ERNST HAAS

Martin Luther King, Jr., at Press Conference, Birmingham, Alabama
May 1963

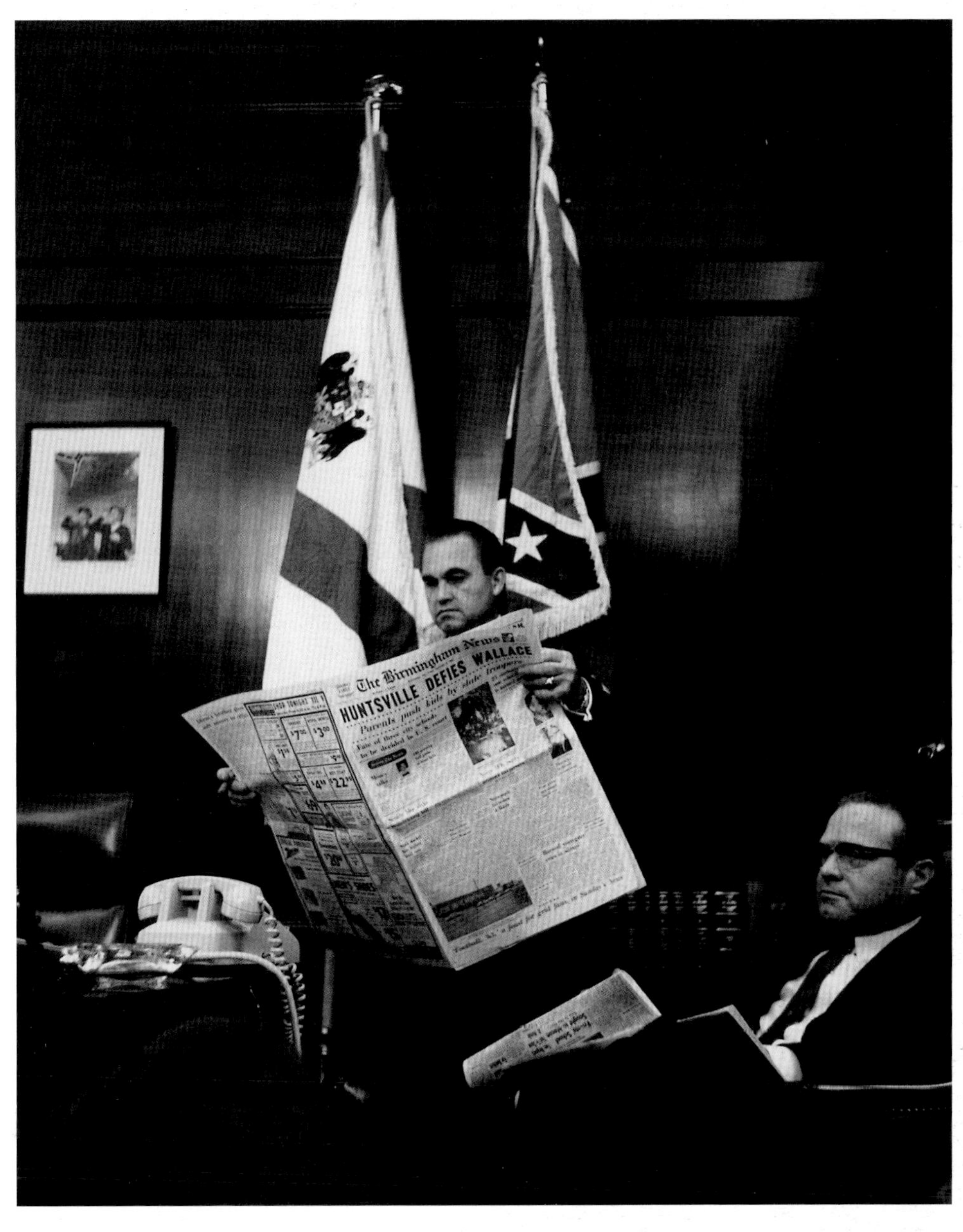

FLIP SCHULKE

Governor George Wallace Reading The Birmingham News

1963

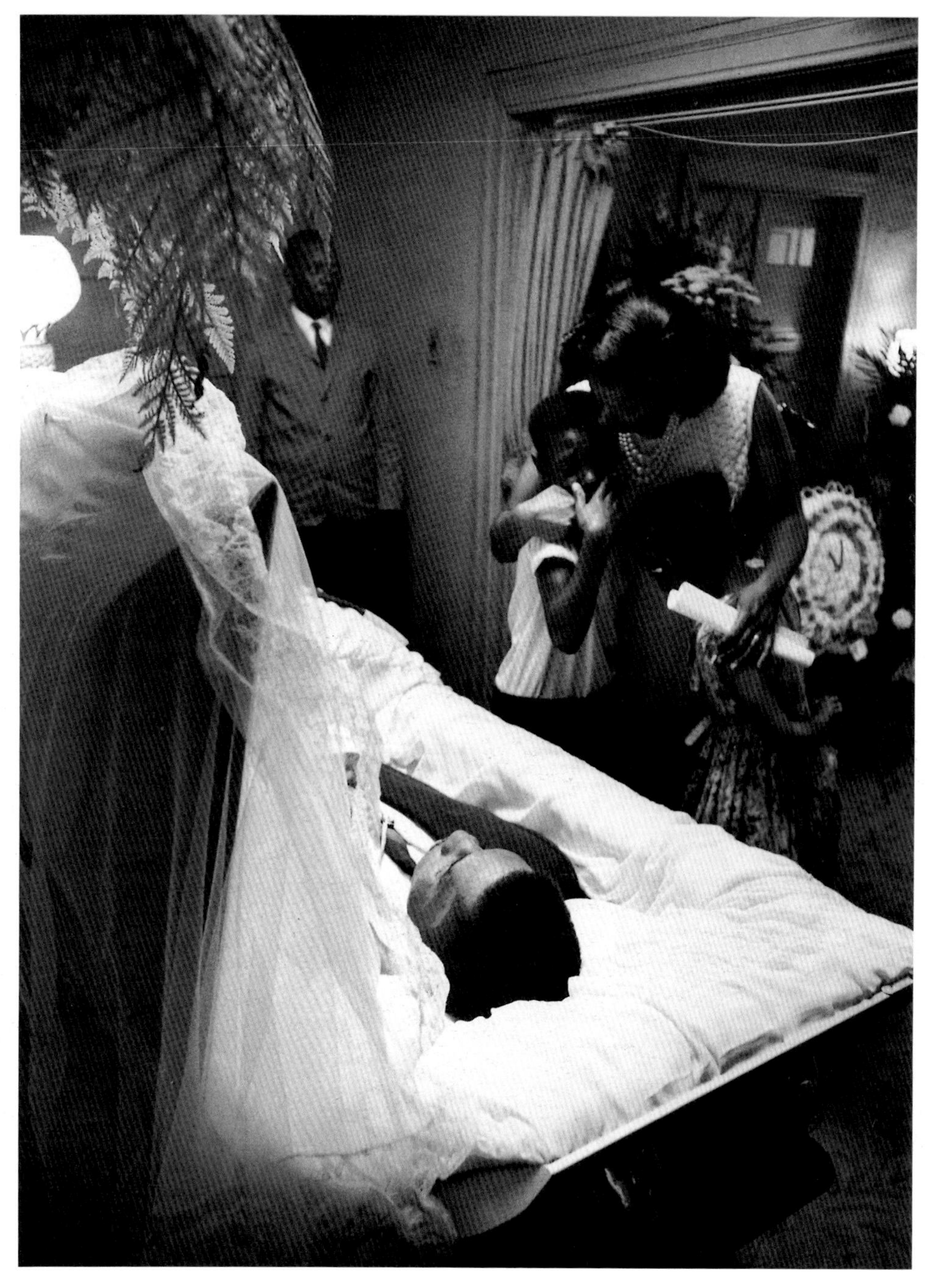

FLIP SCHULKE

Myrlie Evers and Her Children at the Casket of Medgar Evers, Jackson, Mississippi

June 1963

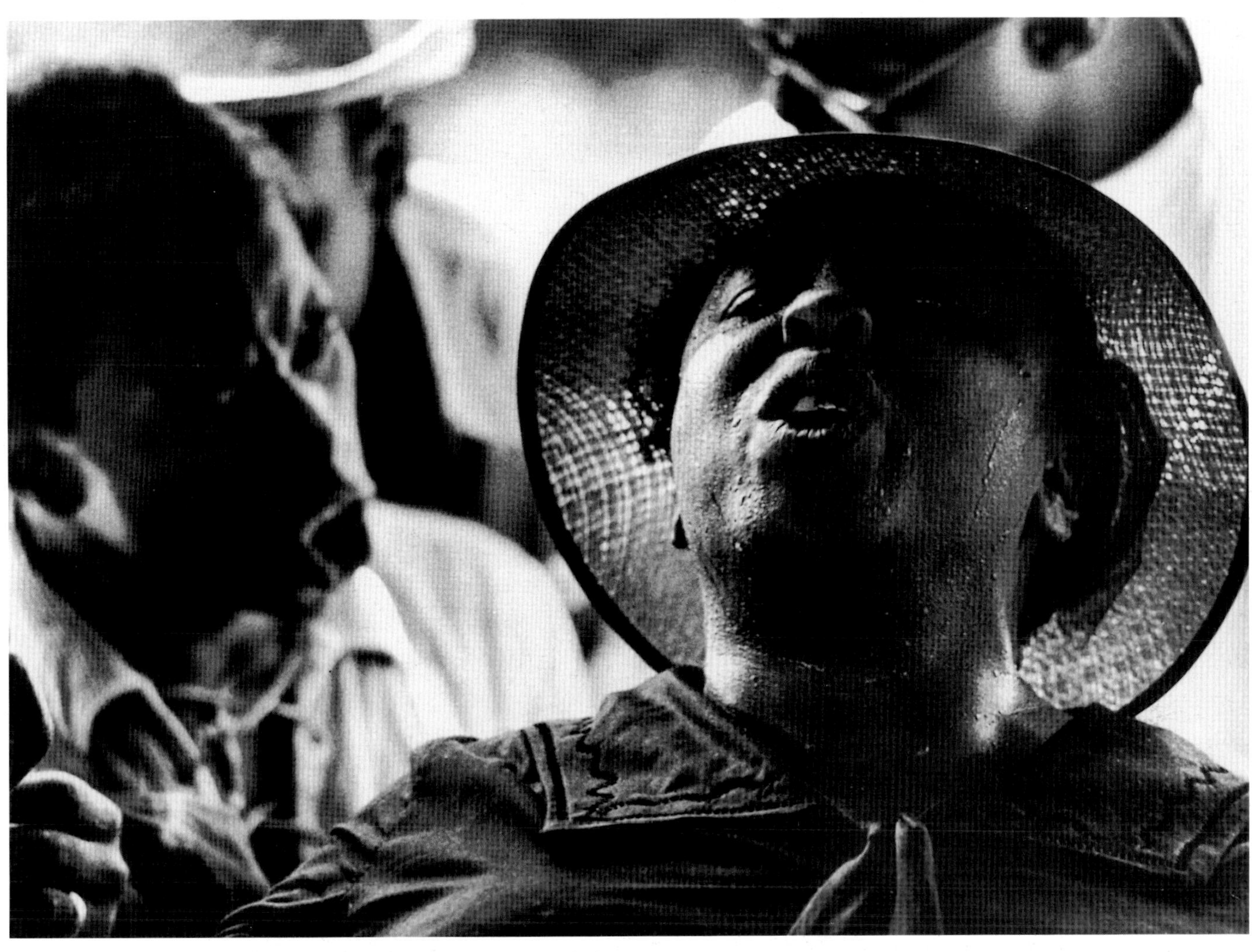

CHARMIAN READING
Fannie Lou Hamer Singing, March Against Fear, Mississippi
1966

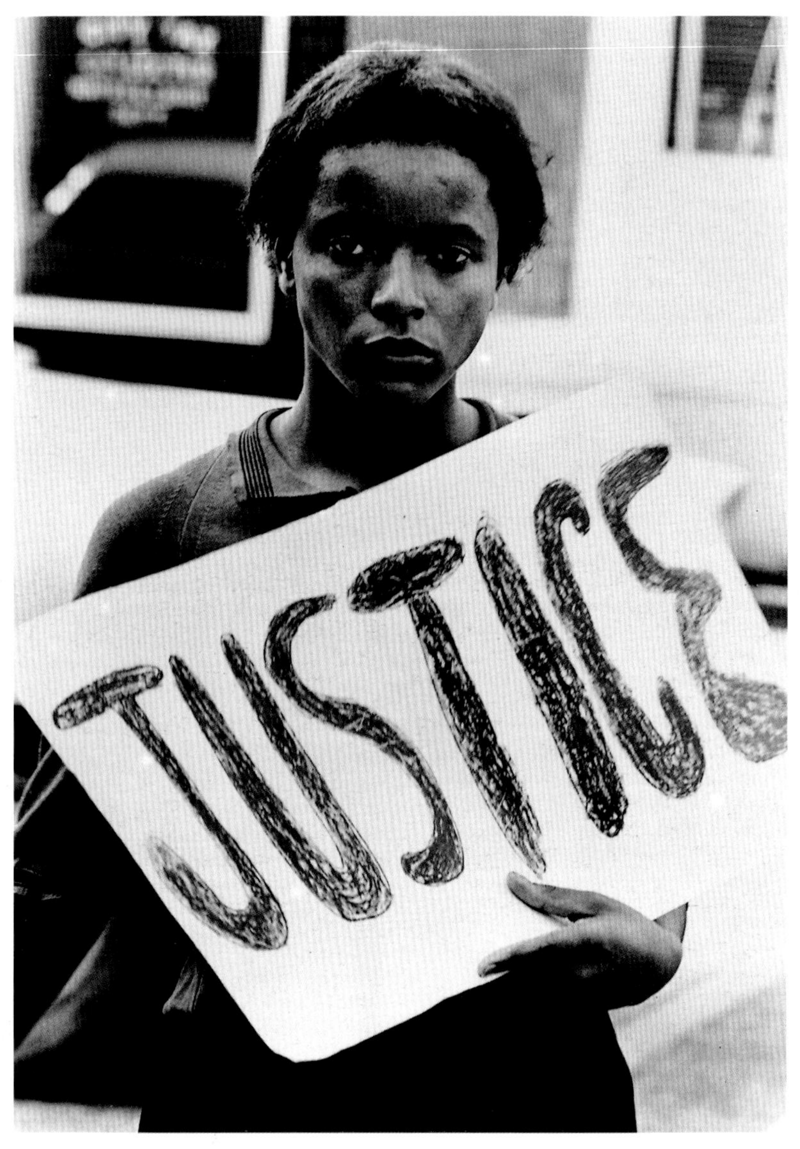

DECLAN HAUN
Integration Protest, Monroe, North Carolina
August 1961

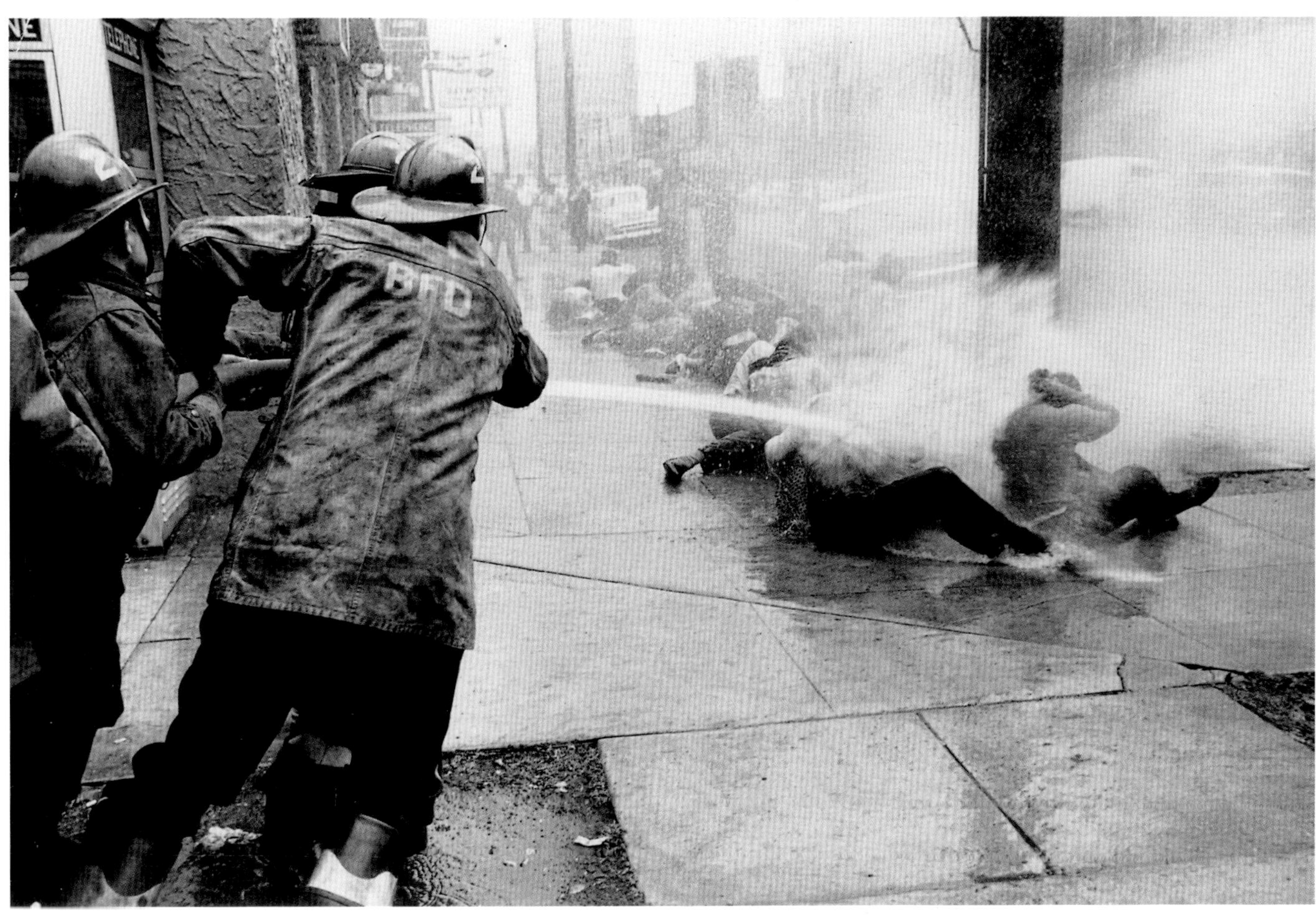

CHARLES MOORE

Firemen Blasting Demonstrators, Birmingham, Alabama

May 3, 1963

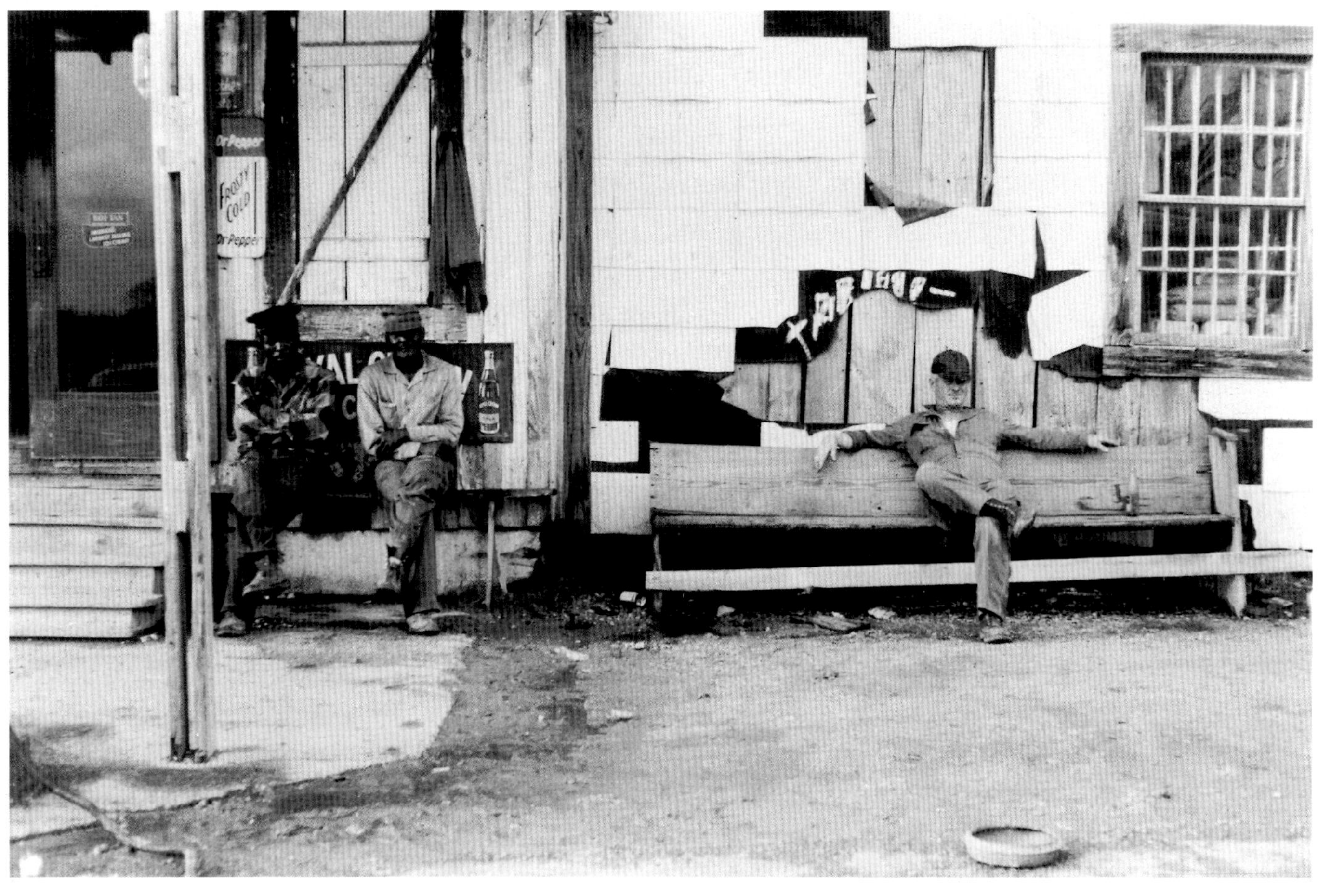

HENRI CARTIER-BRESSON

Hinds County, Mississippi

1962

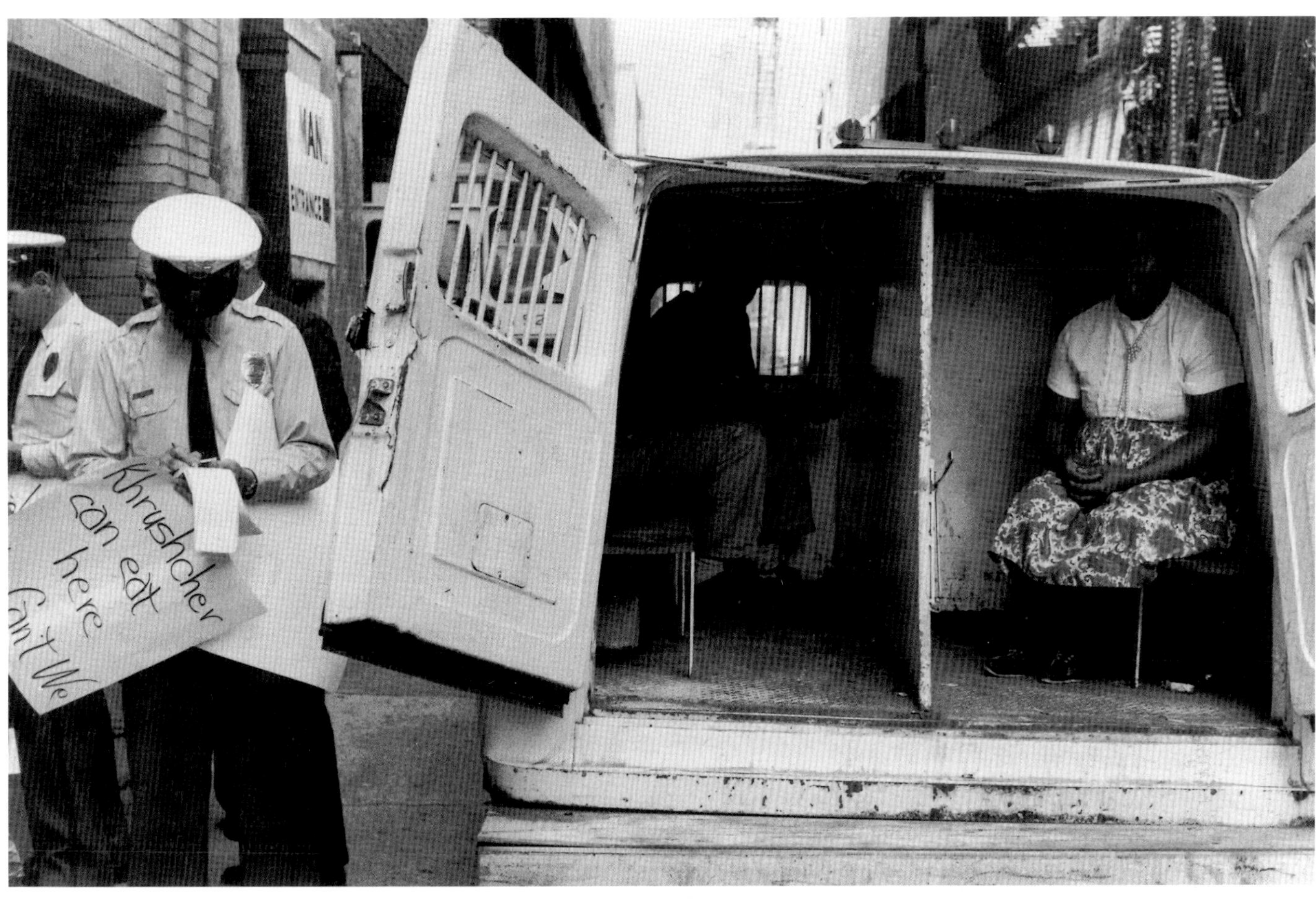

BRUCE DAVIDSON

Arresting Demonstrators, Birmingham, Alabama

1963

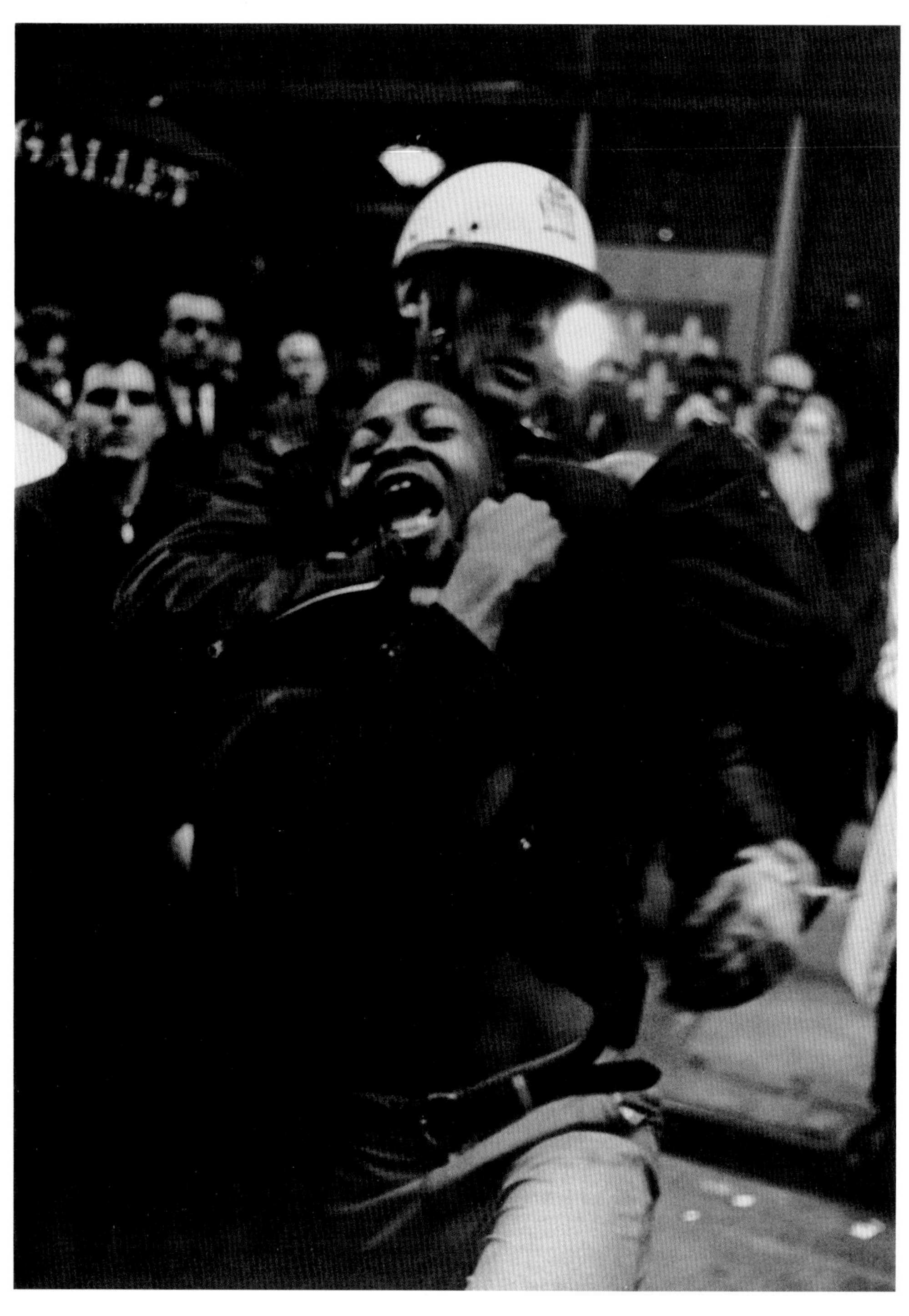

DANNY LYON

Taylor Washington Arrested at Leb's Delicatessen, Atlanta, Georgia

1964

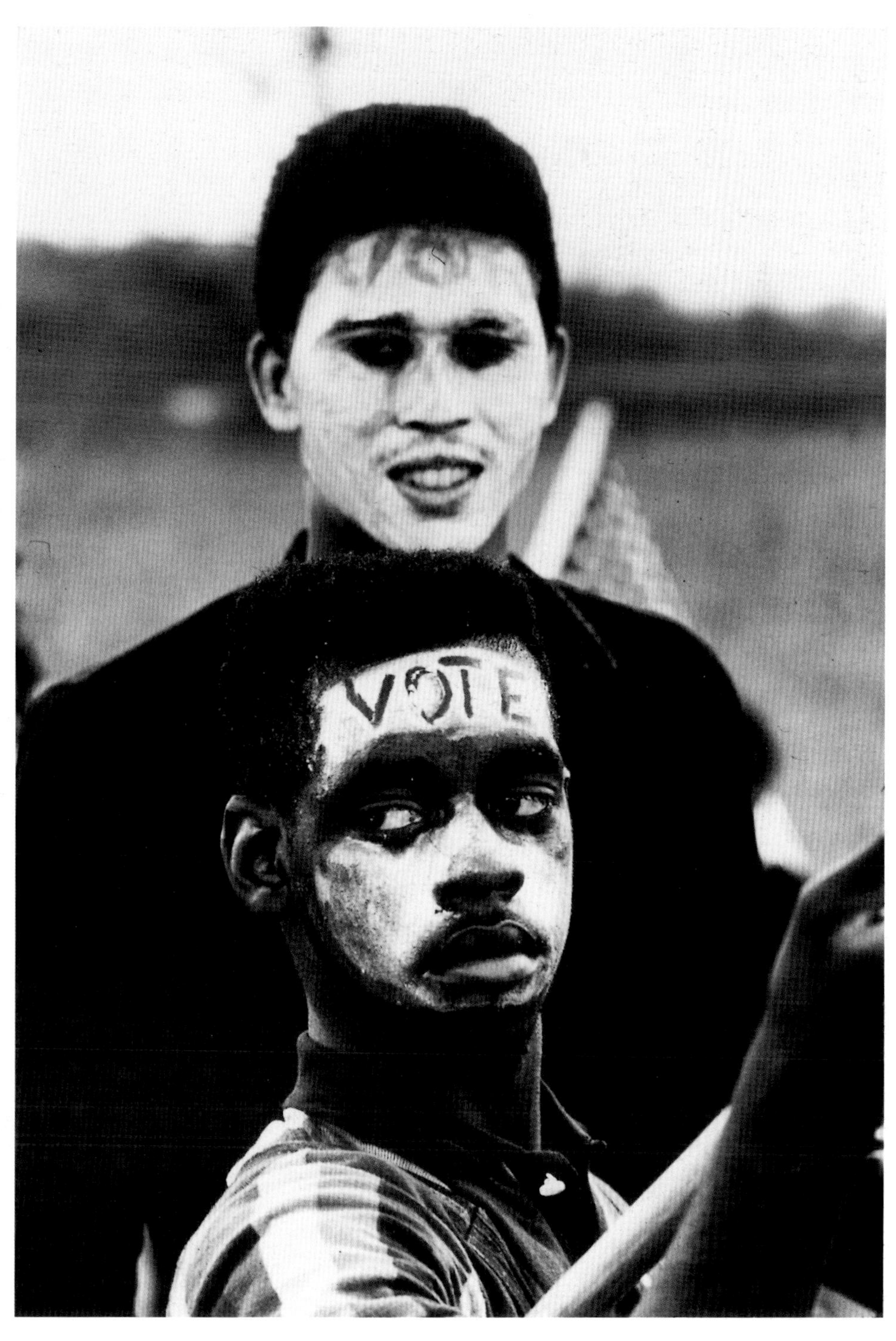

MONETA SLEET, JR.

Two Teenaged Supporters of the Selma March
March 1965

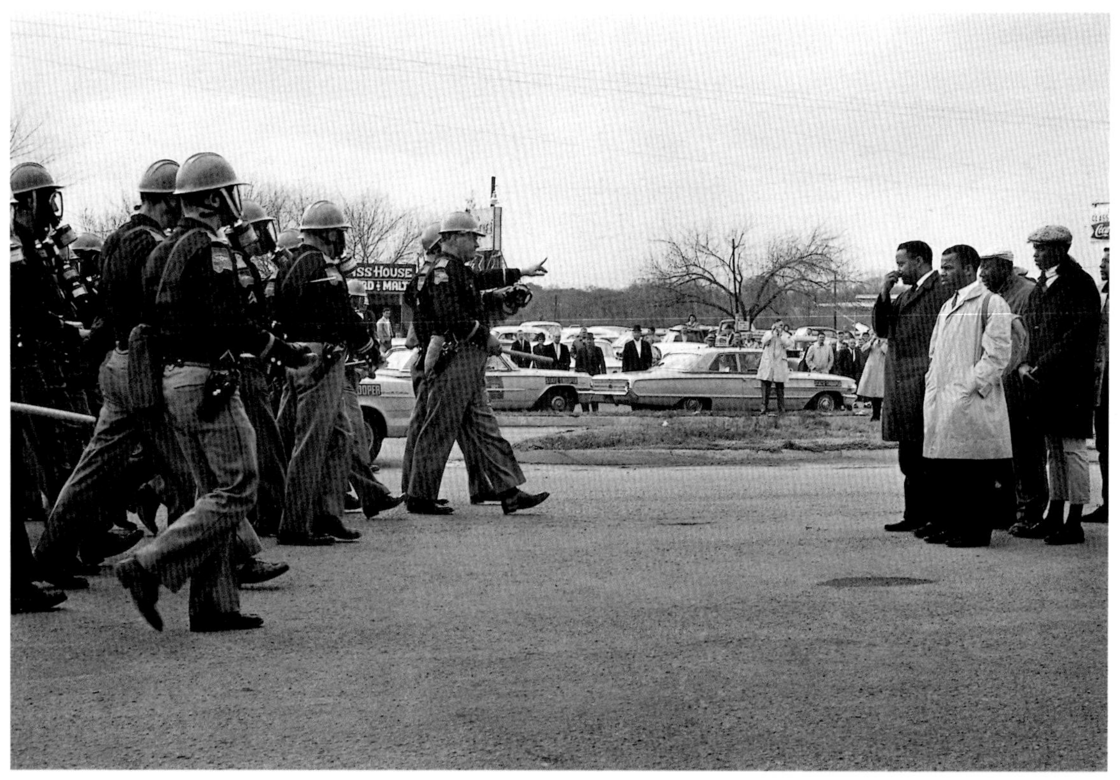

JAMES "SPIDER" MARTIN

State Trooper Gives Marchers Two-Minute Warning, Selma, Alabama
March 7, 1965

JAMES "SPIDER" MARTIN

Barricade at Selma after "Bloody Sunday"
March 7, 1965

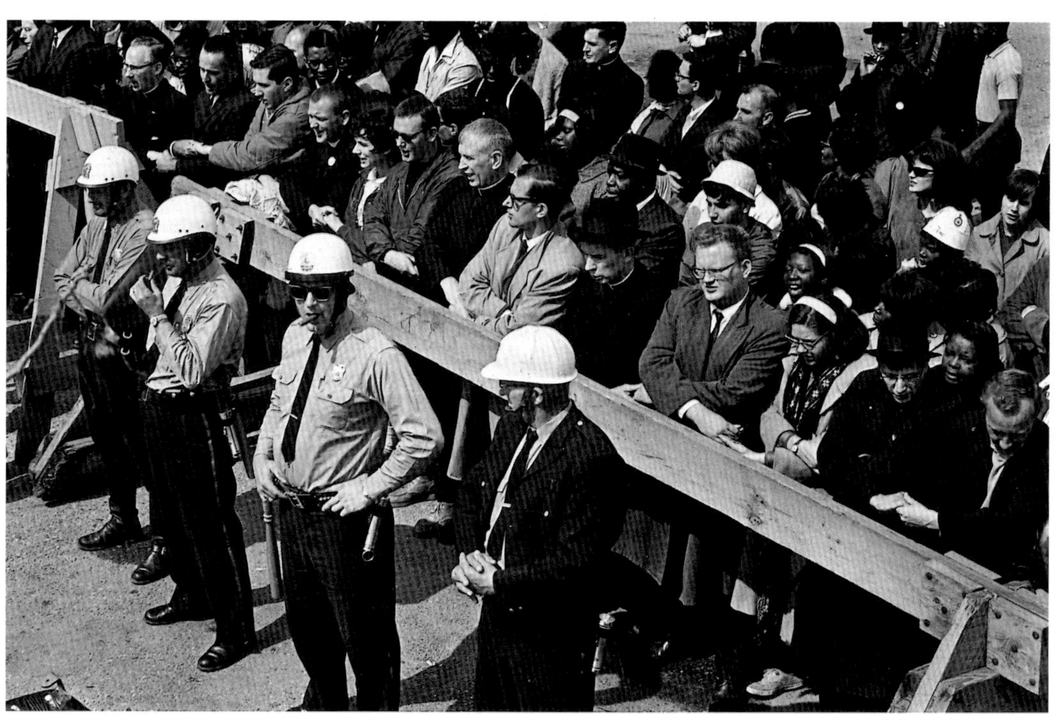

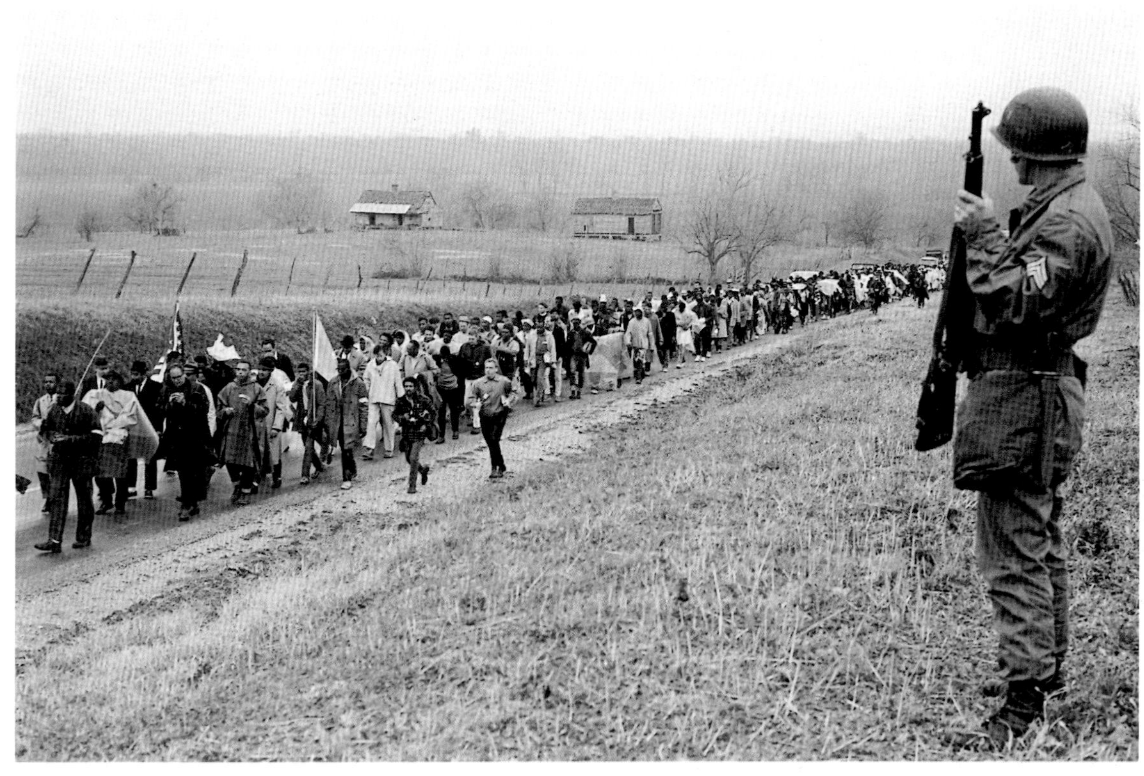

JAMES "SPIDER" MARTIN
Selma-to-Montgomery March Makes Its Way Through Lowndes County Under Armed Guard
March 1965

JAMES H. KARALES
Selma-to-Montgomery March, Alabama
March 1965

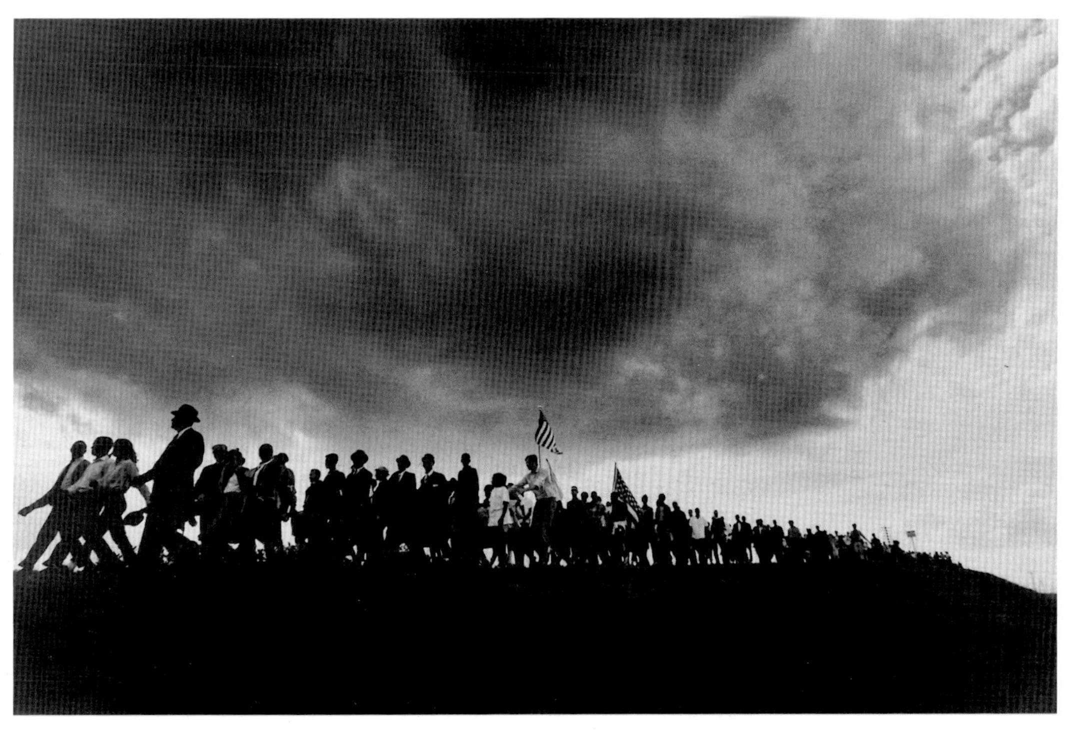

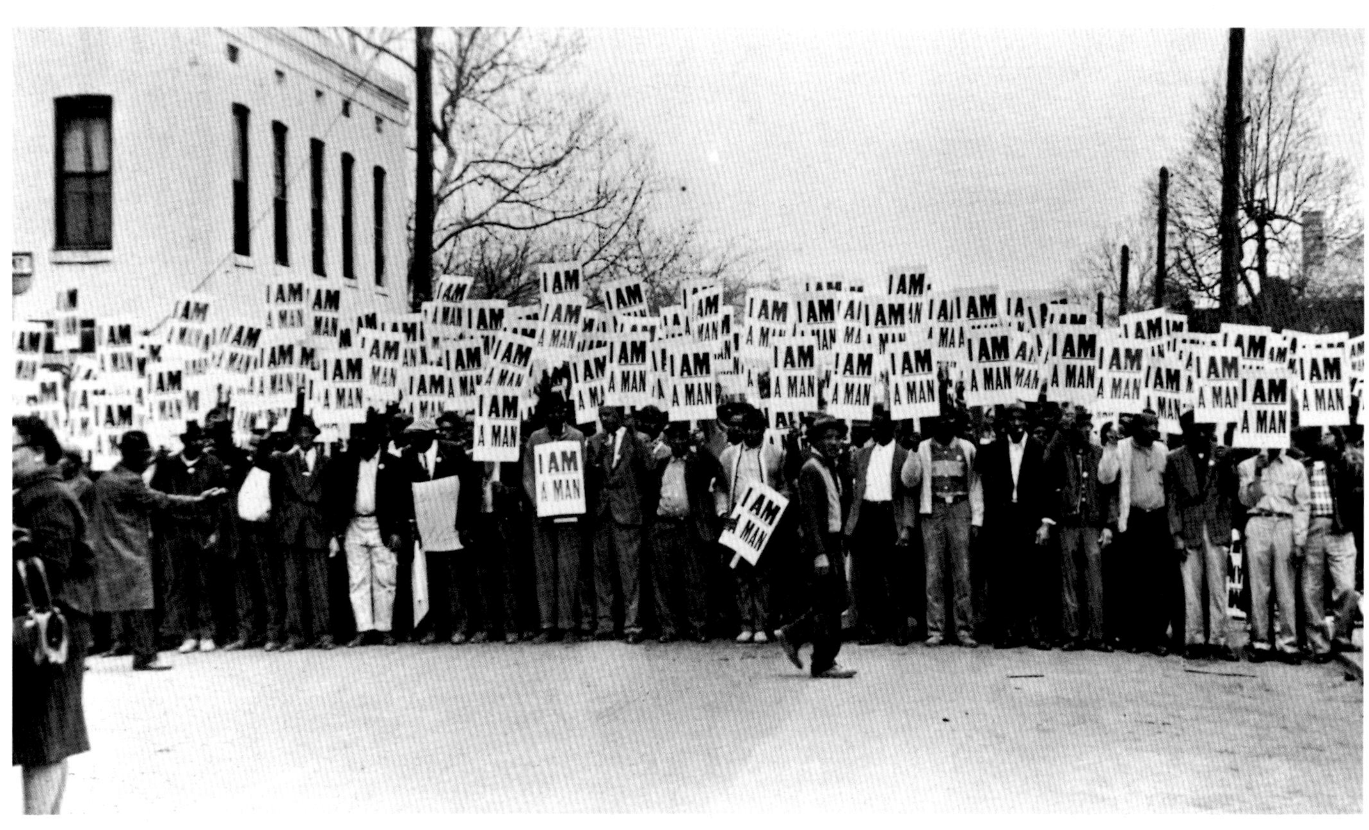

ERNEST C. WITHERS

I Am A Man (Sanitation Workers Assemble in Front of Clayborn Temple for a Solidarity March, Memphis, Tennessee)
March 28, 1968

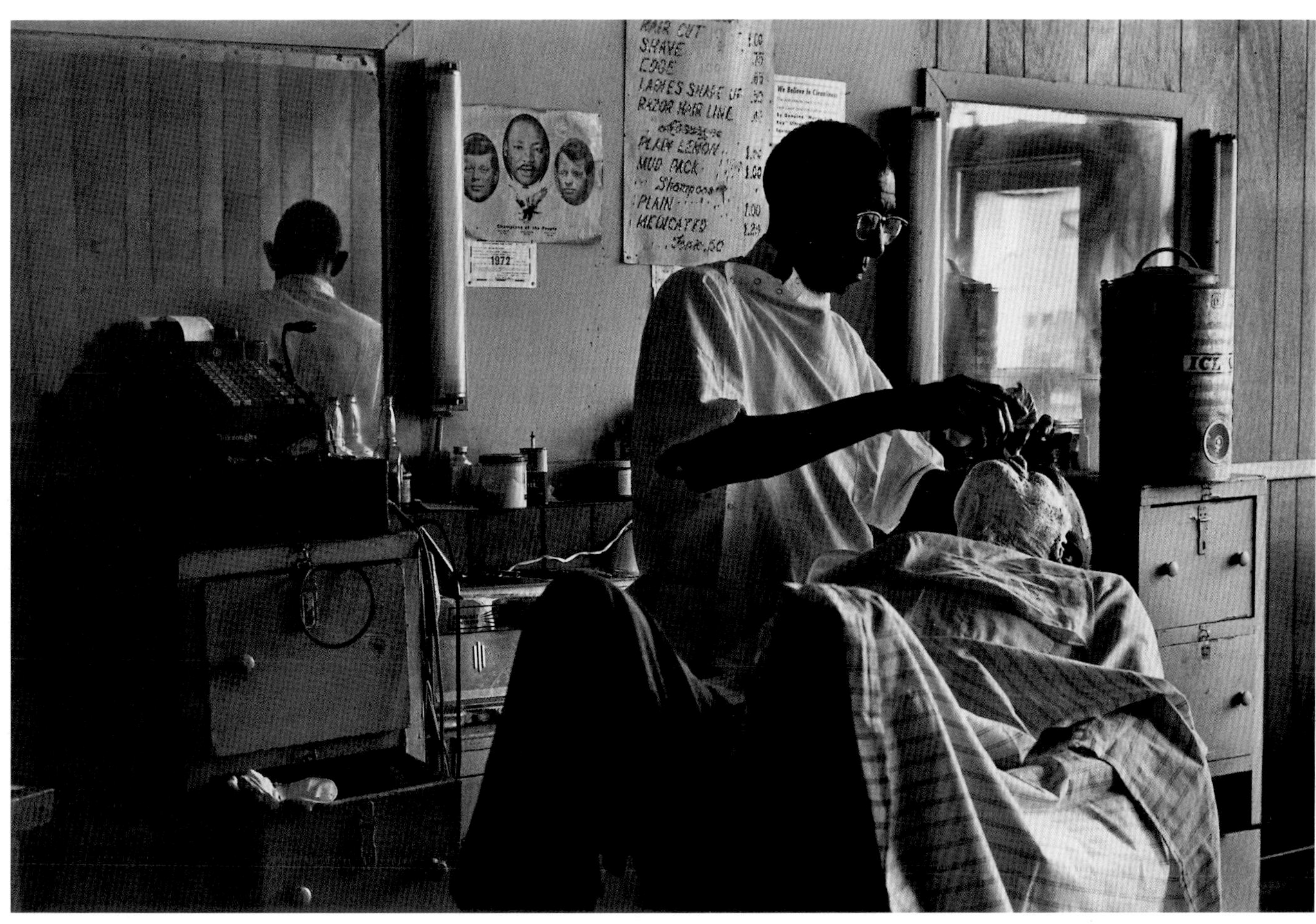

CHESTER HIGGINS JR.

Tuskegee Barber Shop, Tuskegee, Alabama

1972

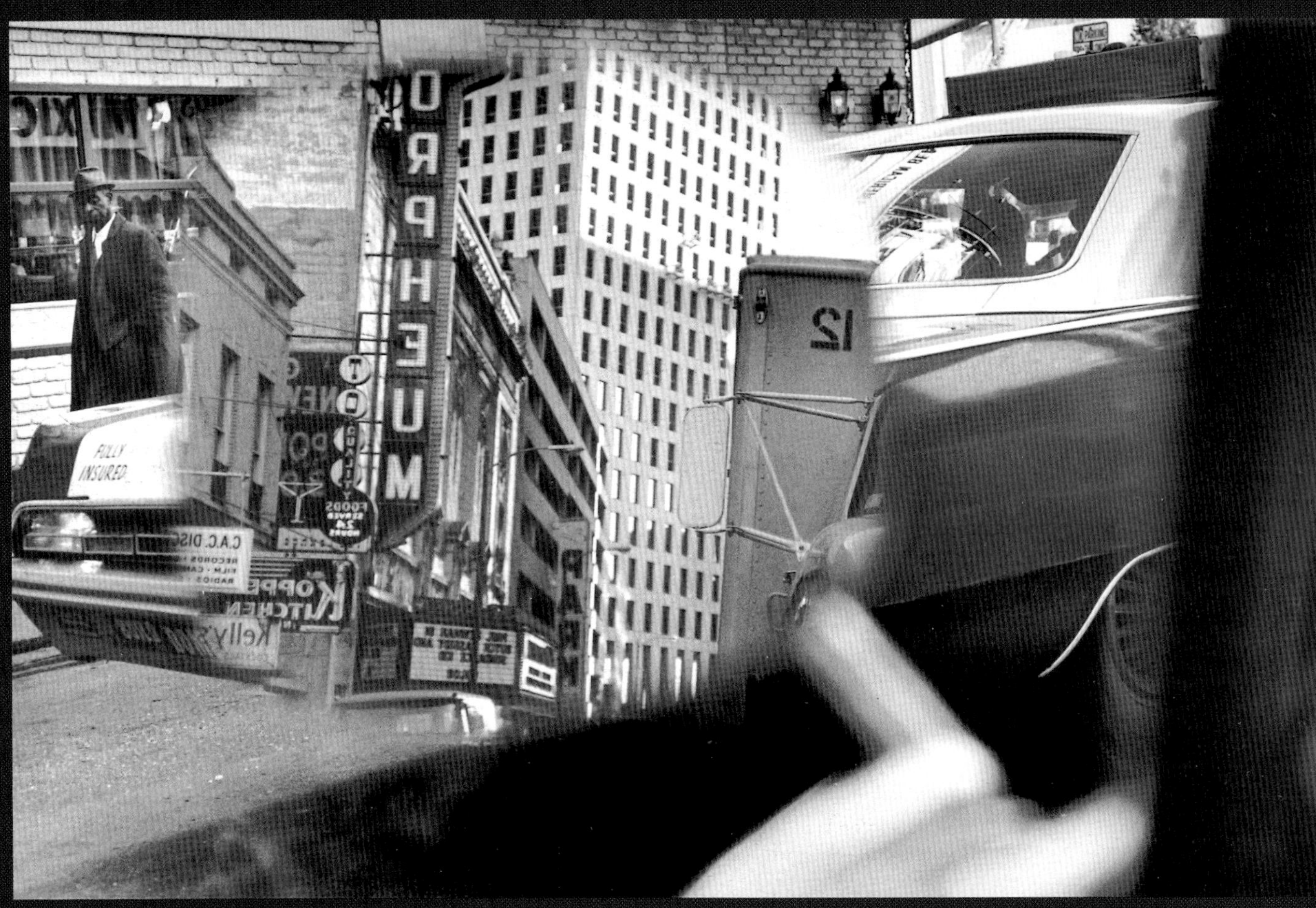

LEE FRIEDLANDER
New Orleans, Louisiana
1969

JOSEPHINE HUMPHREYS

I WILL TELL YOU A PLACE

Sometimes the South is hard to see because it's so full of images of itself. Southerners love Southern stories and pictures, an obsession that feeds art but keeps you guessing about truth. So in the spring of 1987 I drove six weeks through all the Southern states, just to look, and I believe the South I saw was the true one: beautiful, trashy, desolate, busy at business, still haunted, deeply self-conscious in oddly shallow ways, innocent and sinful. I wrote while I drove, or later at night in the sweet-smelling rooms of unchained motels.

Cheaha, Alabama, from a Chevy van: Drenched in radio gospel, the landscape of northern Alabama takes on mystery, like a Cana or Delphi, where all believe a god resides, controls lives, can conquer death and evil. In thick forest of the Cheaha Wilderness, no houses, no people, but these hand-lettered signs, nailed on pines: "Jesus is alive and he lives *here.*" Christ as a woodland deity? The South wants, so bad, to be a sanctified place.

Birmingham: City of Martin Luther King's great letter from jail and I'm following a school bus full of children, all black . . . Morning spent sitting outside the once-bombed Sixteenth Street Baptist

Church. Couldn't work up courage to go in. Afternoon, with rain falling from a sunny sky, wandered an obsolete ironworks, machinery dripping and glistening.

Tupelo, Mississippi: Passed up Graceland. The name tempted—am I not in search of the sacred places?—but afraid it wouldn't be one. Instead sped down Highway 78 into the green Delta to the Tupelo exit, Elvis Presley Street, and a tiny white house on a grassy rise. "The Birthplace." Porch no bigger than the swing it holds. Inside: two rooms, the front one filled by an iron bed, where Miss Essie Clayton, white-haired, sat to answer questions. Mine was about the photo on the wall. "That's Elvis and his mama and daddy," Miss Clayton said. In other pictures I'd seen, Vernon and Gladys never looked too good (putting it mildly)—all hollow-eyed and haggard. In this, Vernon is blond with a Robert-Redford face. Gladys is dark—bigger eyes, luscious mouth—and heartbreakingly beautiful. "They look like movie stars!" "Well," Miss Clayton said, "they were real young, then." Between them, combining their looks, is their boy. "Did you like his music?" I asked, not expecting that she had. "I loved his music," she said quietly. "I loved Elvis."

Tchula: Blues town, black town, seems built of auto parts and scrap lumber. Here is where I would want to stay if I were looking for a home. But no white people in sight.

Jefferson, Texas: Bayou town, tourist town. Postal workers' convention under way, filling two good old hotels and twenty-five bed-and-breakfast houses. Five P.M., an electronic carillon plays what sounds like Presbyterian hymns, sad and pretty. At night a fish fry, men in plaid shirts, women with big pocketbooks. People both black and white eating catfish.

Beaumont: Late Saturday afternoon, sudden fear. Town looks bad, an end-of-the-road place with an air of desperation. Too many pickups, rebel-flagged rear windows; hitchhikers; men sitting on sidewalk. Searching for the heart, the downtown, I find a civic center and a convention hall, but not a living soul.

Oxford, Mississippi: To Faulkner's house this morning, early. Cedars along the walk thick with noisy grackles; the house wide, low, plain. On the roof a black man in overalls cleans leaves from the gutters with a broomstick. Inside, heavy dark furniture in musty rooms. Joyless-looking kitchen. He lived here thirty-two years. Tattooed young man, the guide, says neither Mr. nor Mrs. F. was easy to get along with. They came from good families, he says, but "something went bad" with the generation of William and Estelle, producing much misery. "Producing also some great writing," I remind. "Yes, but I'm not sure I'd want to pay the price, to become a great writer, that Mr. Faulkner had to pay. I'd rather be—an ordinary fellow." Outside, the grackles have gone.

Mobile, Alabama: Noon at Bienville Square, corner of Dauphin and Conception—my favorite place so far. Maybe not sacred but, for the moment, celebrative. Band in a bandstand (Sam Cooke's "Trouble Don't Last Always"), vendor with chicken and biscuits, people on blankets in the grass, guy on a bench reading *The Sociology of Islam,* and all around the square are square old stores: Lerner's, Eckerd's,

Woolworth's. But at the matinee race at Mobile Greyhound Park, men in the grandstand are lone and skinny as the hounds.

Florida Highway 98 East to Perry: Swamp. Blue flowers, yellow flowers. Old concrete bridges across black rivers. Nina Bowdin's independently operated service station and taxidermist. White-tailed deer, black squirrel, red squirrel, big fish all mounted on the wall. Selling (to me) barbecue with extra hot sauce, pickled eggs. I don't ask barbecued what. Lu's place south of Perry: smoked mullet and boiled peanuts. Churches along this road: Pentecostal Holiness, Church of Christ, Church of God, Assembly of God, Foursquare, Nazarene, Seventh Day Adventist. Road west to Suwannee, straight white dirt; pines, scrub palmetto. "Trucking for Jesus" on a bumper.

Wakulla Springs: 600,000 gallons of water a minute, origin unknown. Experts say maybe from Florida rain collecting in the limestone and seeping down to a single flow, or maybe from all over the South, mountain waters diving to an underground river, rushing lightless to this sudden outspring. In the old hotel, a stuffed fourteen-foot alligator.

Clewiston: Sugar town, picture perfect, touted as peaceful despite mixed population of white, black, Seminole, Cuban, Haitian. But something's wrong. People are afraid, won't talk. Secretary gave hints but only outside (no eavesdroppers): "Parents lose their jobs if kids cause trouble in school." Haitian cane-cutter asks, "What kind of writer are you?" I say fiction. "Not truth?" No. "If I were a writer," he says, "I would write the truth." I'm shamed to silence. He studies me, then says, "I will tell you a place. Go to Belle Glade. Six blocks on Avenue E, then right on Avenue Six. Look at this place. Describe it with your writing."

Belle Glade: Avenue Six. I thought it was a prison. Multistoried concrete blockhouses, grim, railed like cheap hotels . . . dusty field, dozens of buses loading work gangs. Some Haitian, some American, but the scene like nothing I've ever witnessed—or heard, or read—in America. And I watched, sinking, knowing that what I saw I could not describe. Evils I'd thought long buried, beyond my powers to tell outright.

Radio, coming home: The Soul Stirrers: "There's a story in every song that we sing."

Nothing else in my journey so changed my notion of the South as those tenements, and what I learned about the sugar towns. But I never described them with my writing. When I got home, it was Easter. I wanted to forget what I saw in Belle Glade; I wanted to start a new novel.

One year in my life, I lived outside the South—1968, the year of Martin Luther King's death. I was twenty-three. I remember thinking, maybe I won't go back. But I did. Now almost three decades later I'm glad and here's why: because all of our past here—the old imagery, ghosts, evil, mysteries—lasts, and must be reckoned with. If you're a Southerner in the South with your eyes and ears open, you're never in danger of complacency. If you're a novelist you'll always have a story, and underneath the story, truth will run.

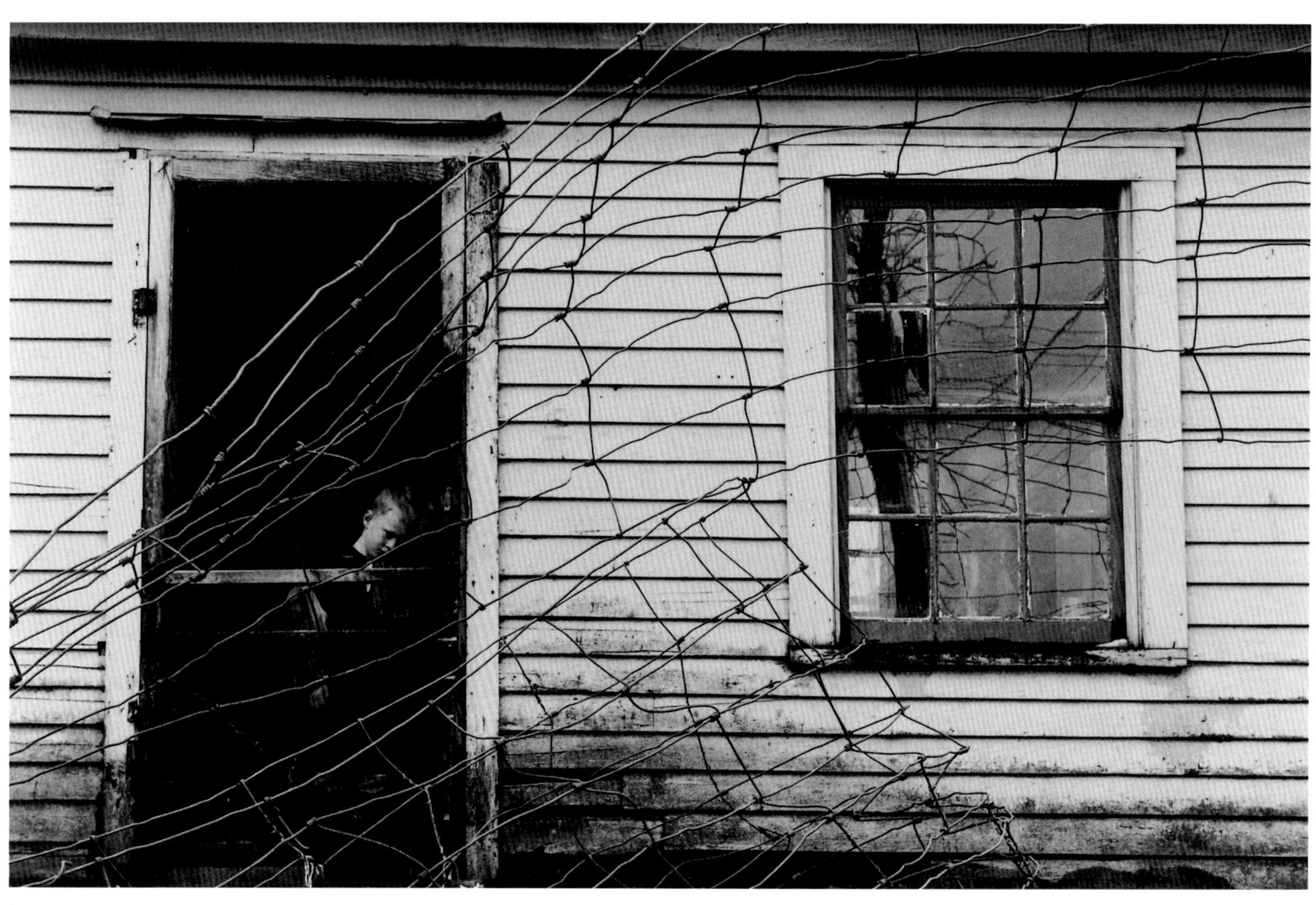

RALPH EUGENE MEATYARD
Untitled
1954–56

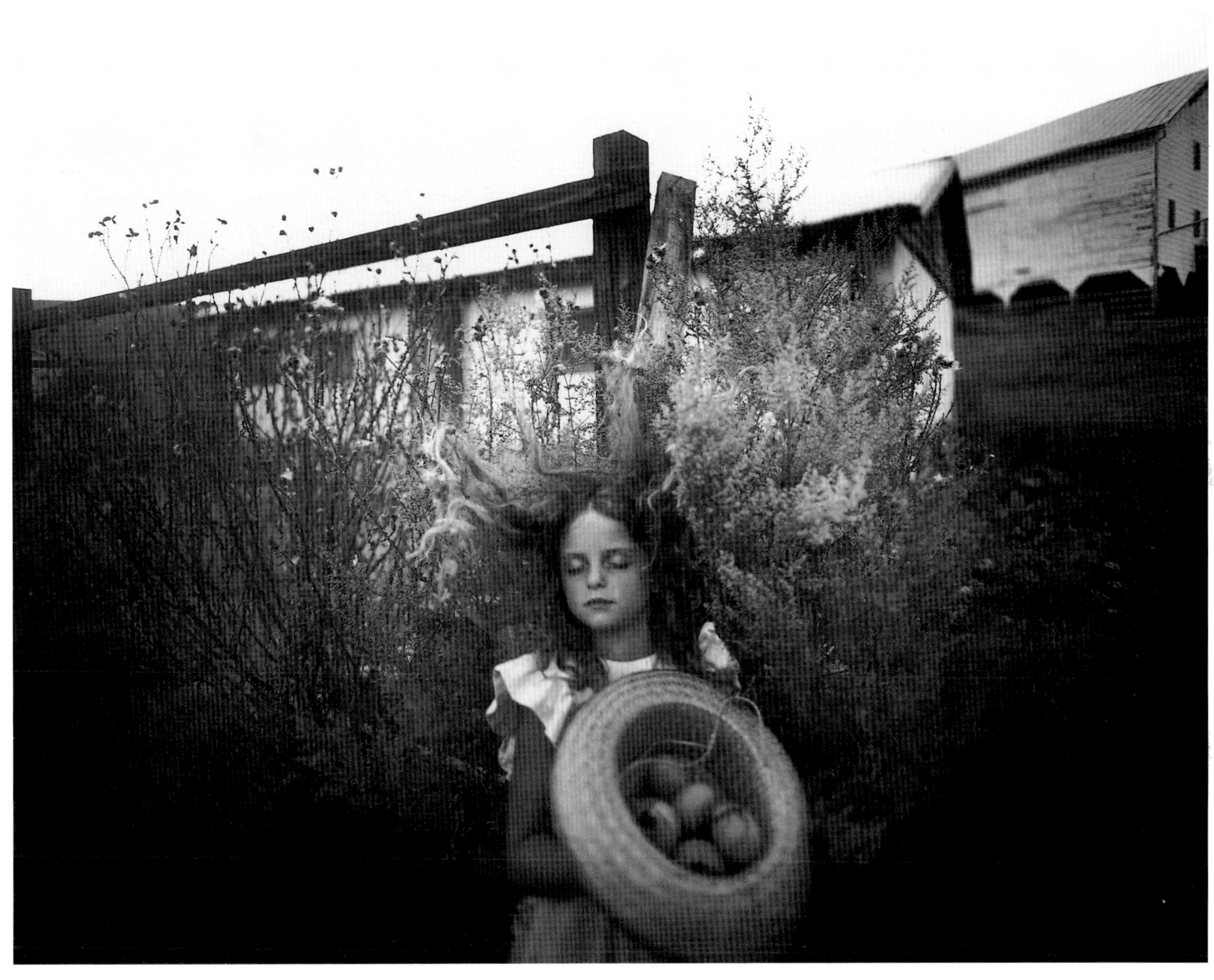

SALLY MANN
Yard Eggs
1991

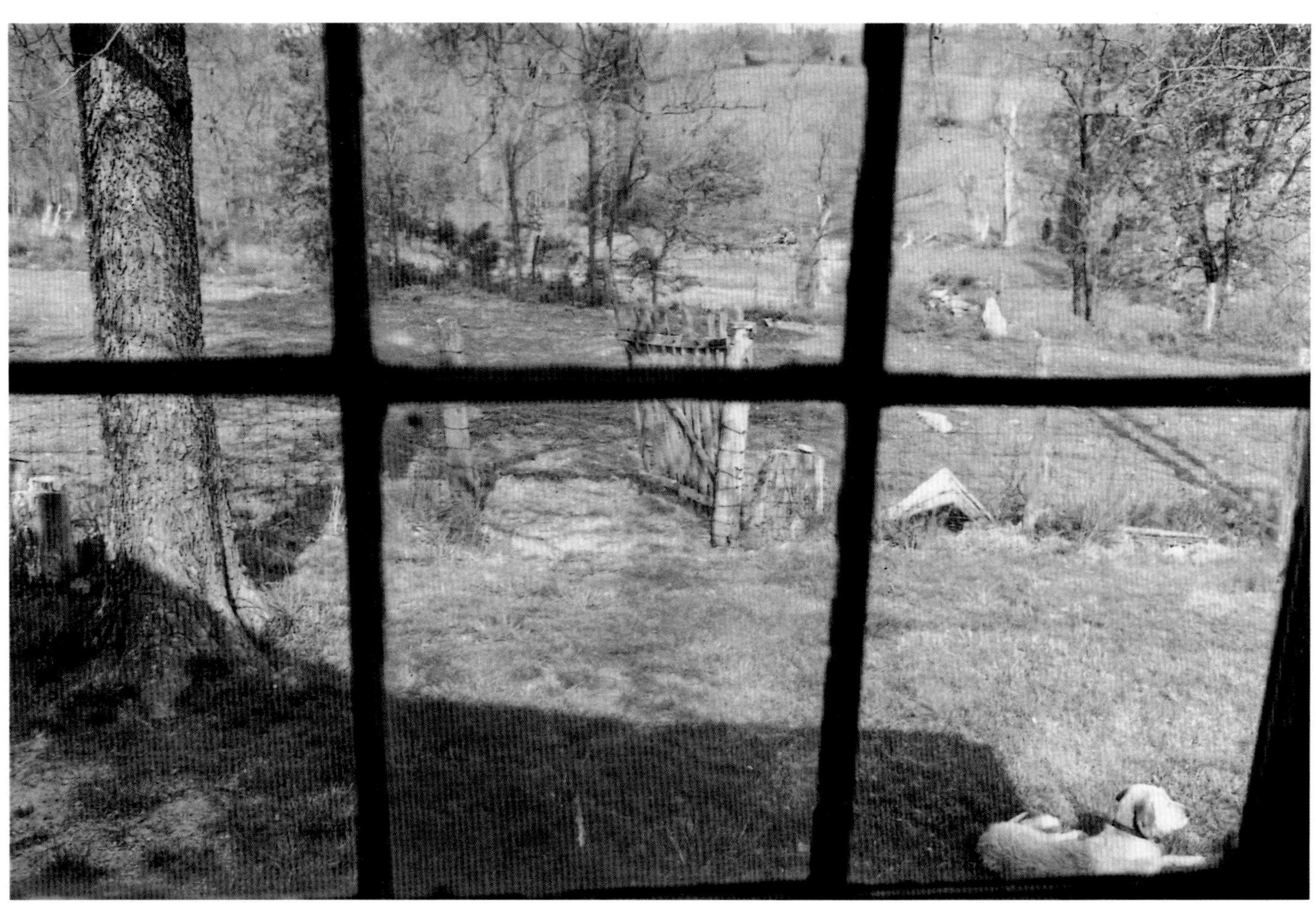

LEE FRIEDLANDER
Versailles, Kentucky
1976

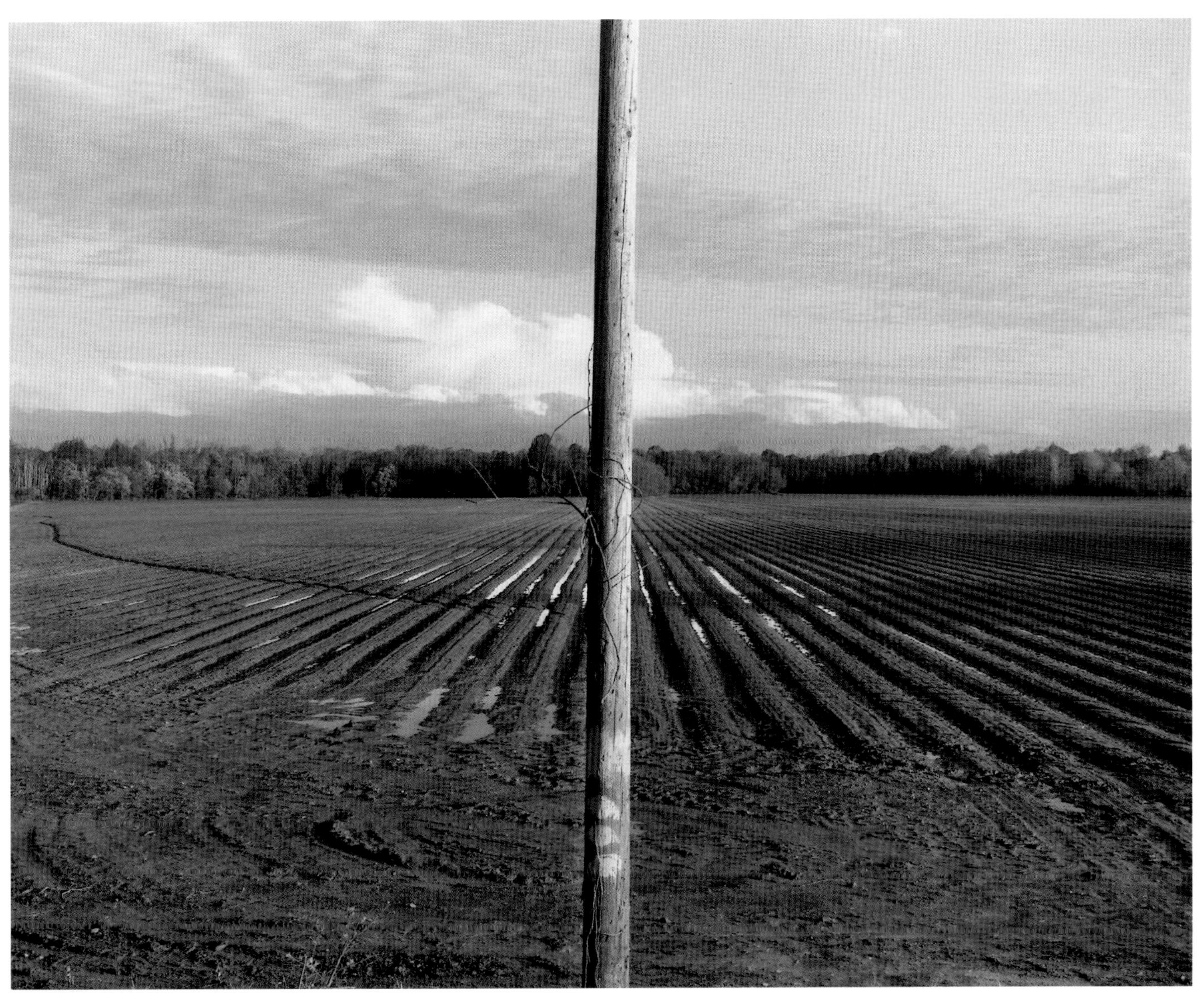

GREGORY CONNIFF

Cotton Field, Lafayette County, Mississippi

1993

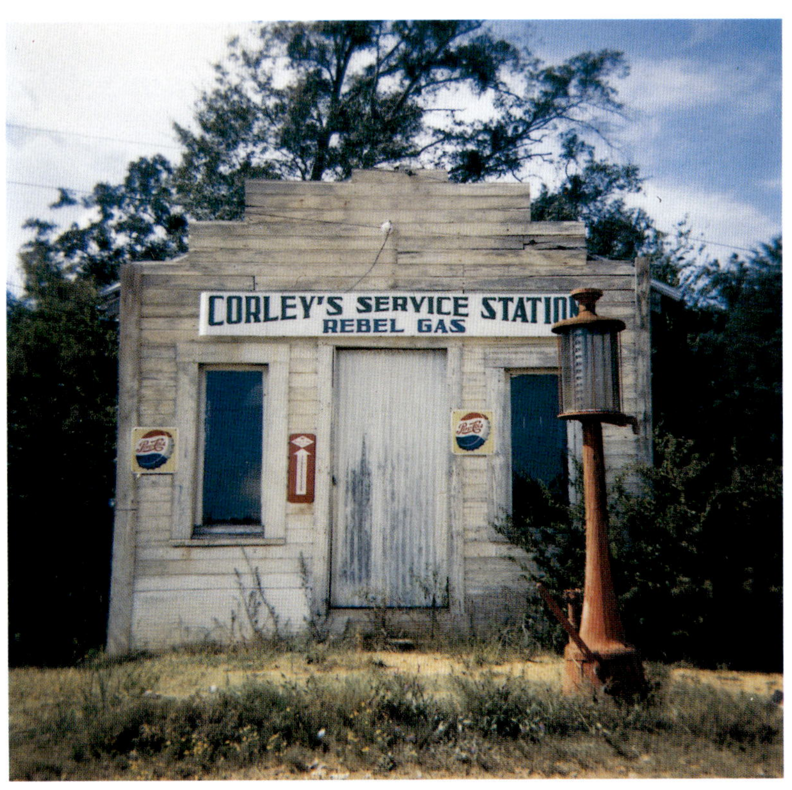

WILLIAM CHRISTENBERRY

Rebel Gasoline Station, Moundville, Alabama

1964

WILLIAM CHRISTENBERRY

Grave with Bed as Marker (View I), near Faunsdale, Alabama

1965

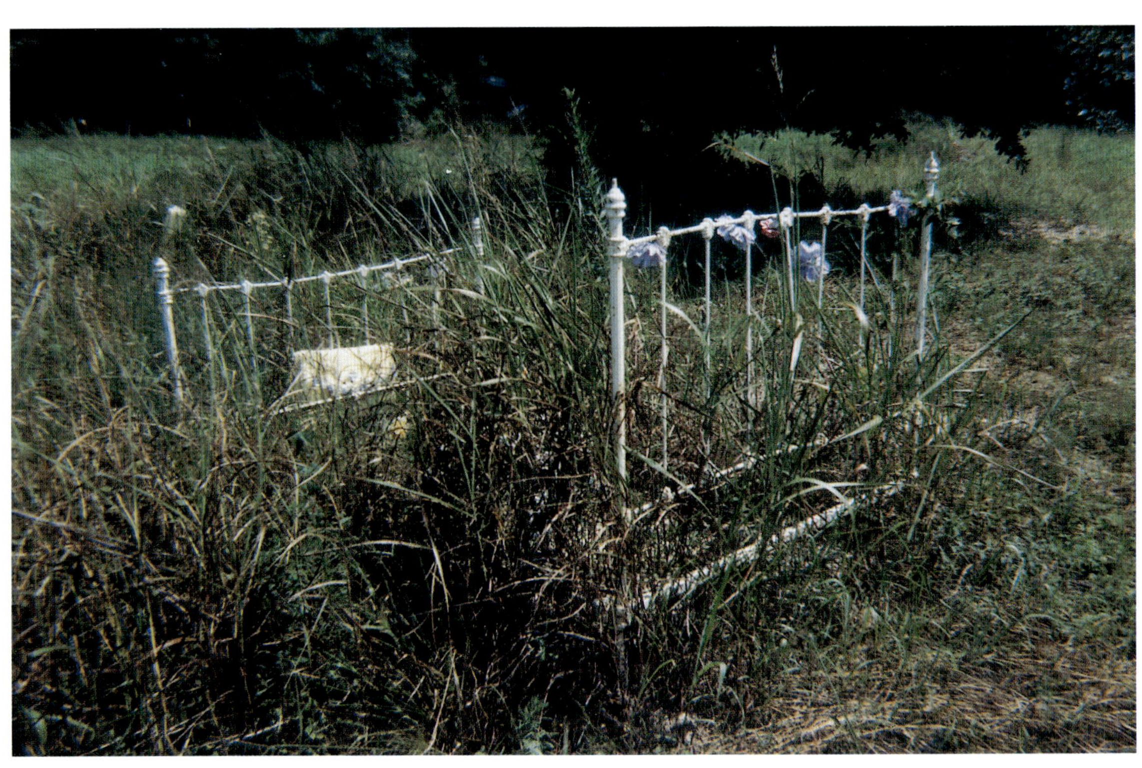

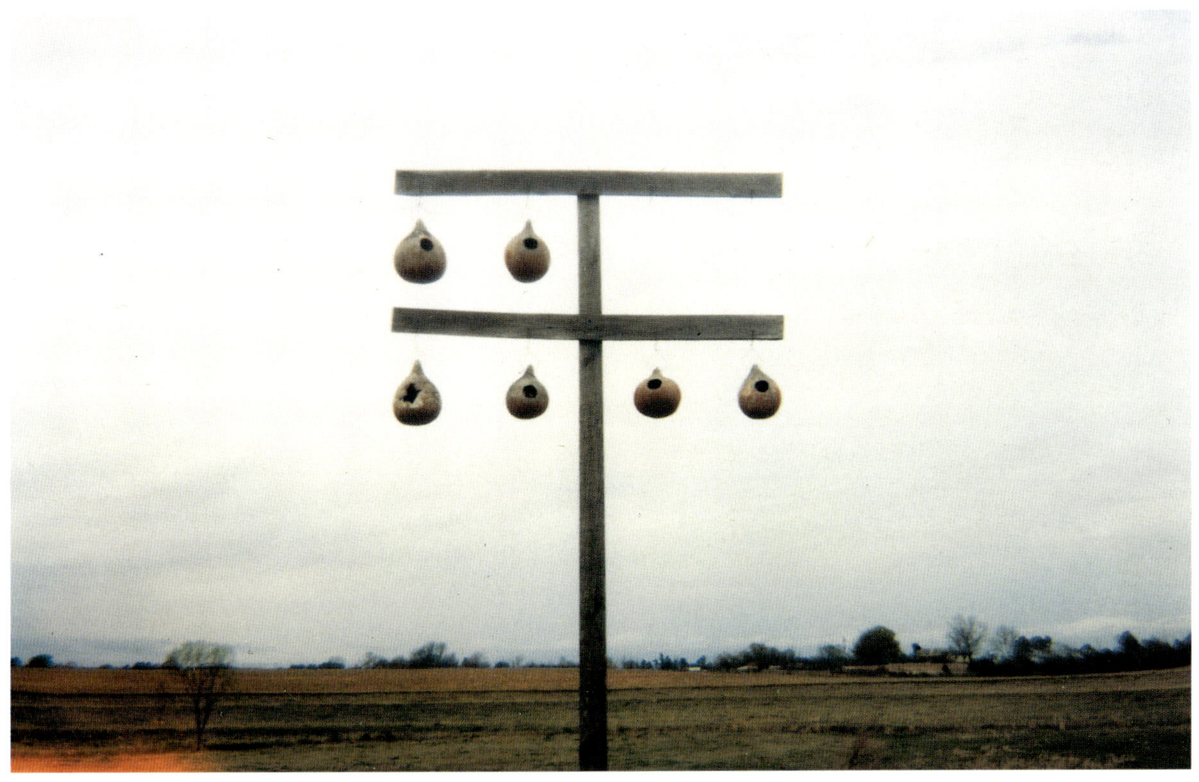

WILLIAM CHRISTENBERRY
Gourd Tree, near Akron, Alabama
1976

WILLIAM CHRISTENBERRY
Church across Early Cotton, Pickinsville, Alabama
1964

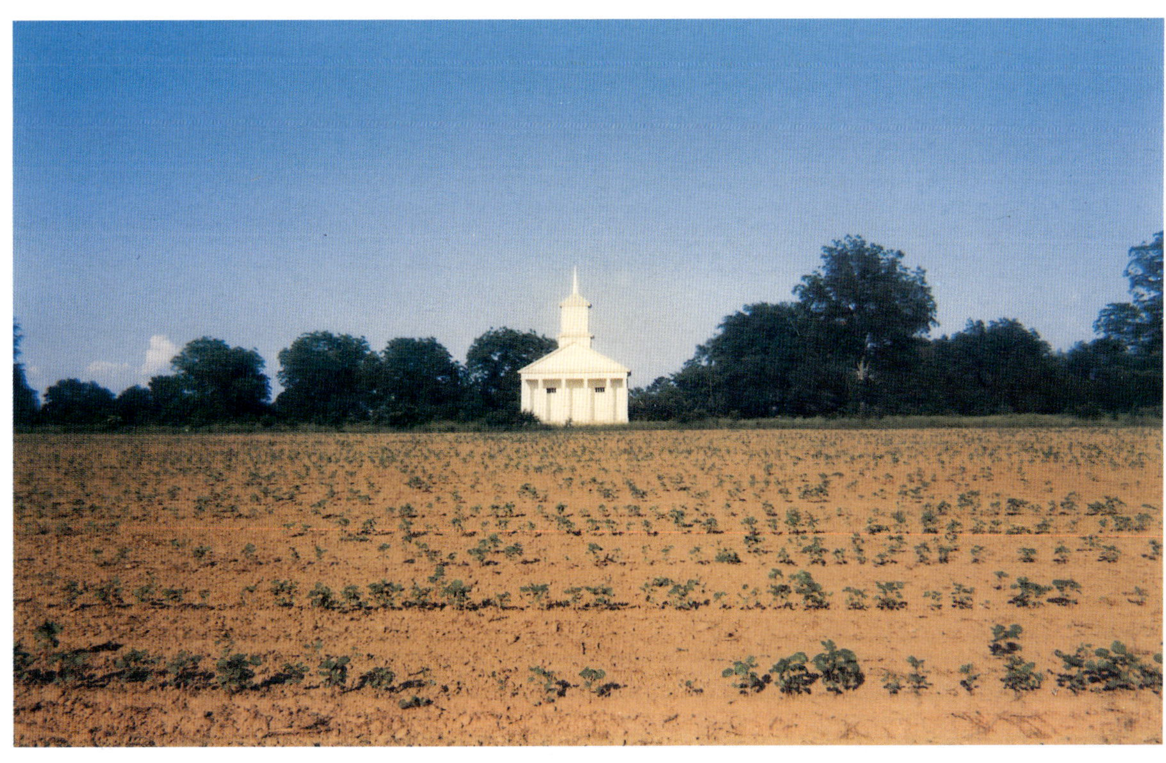

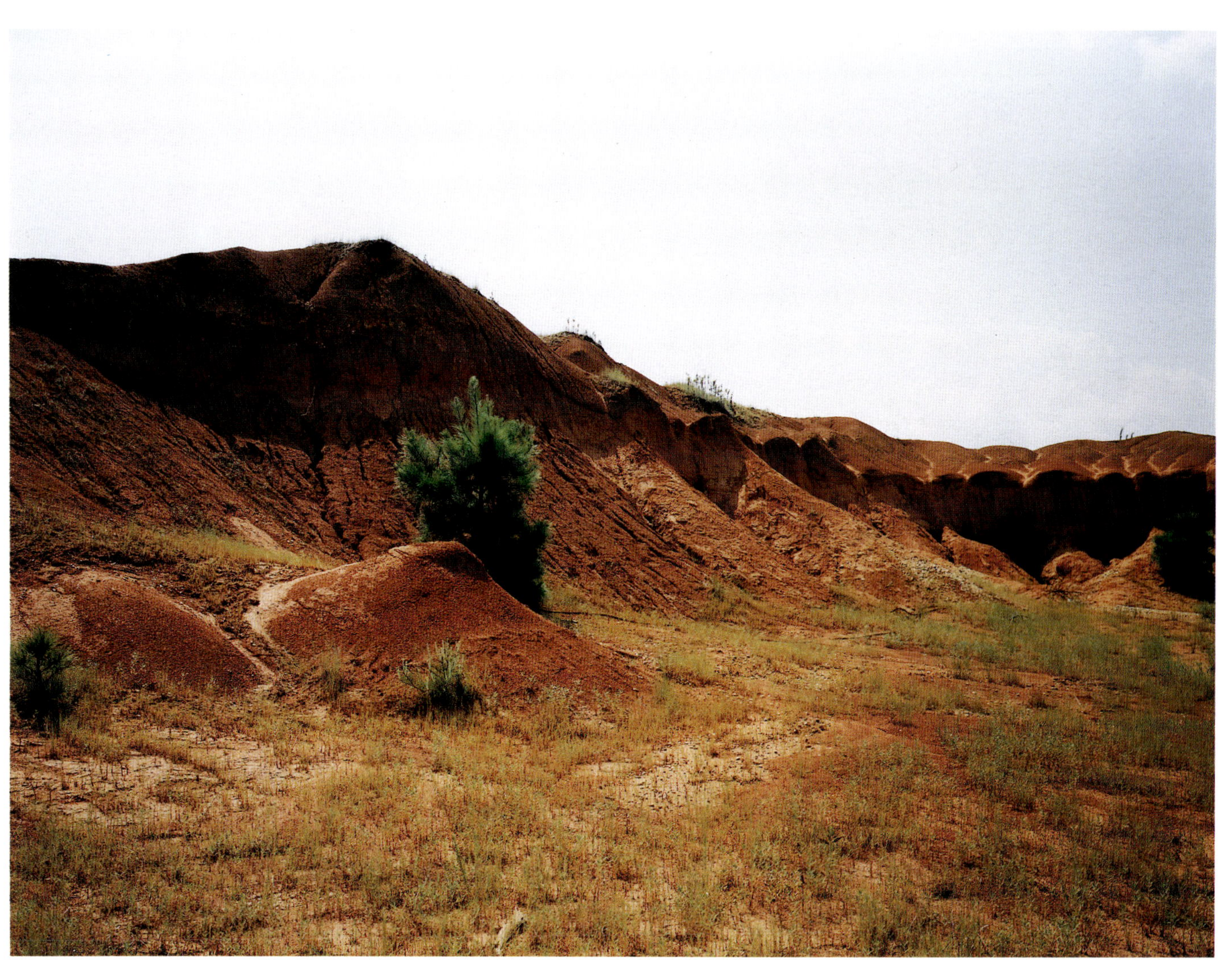

WILLIAM CHRISTENBERRY

Alabama Landscape, near Tuscaloosa, Alabama

1980

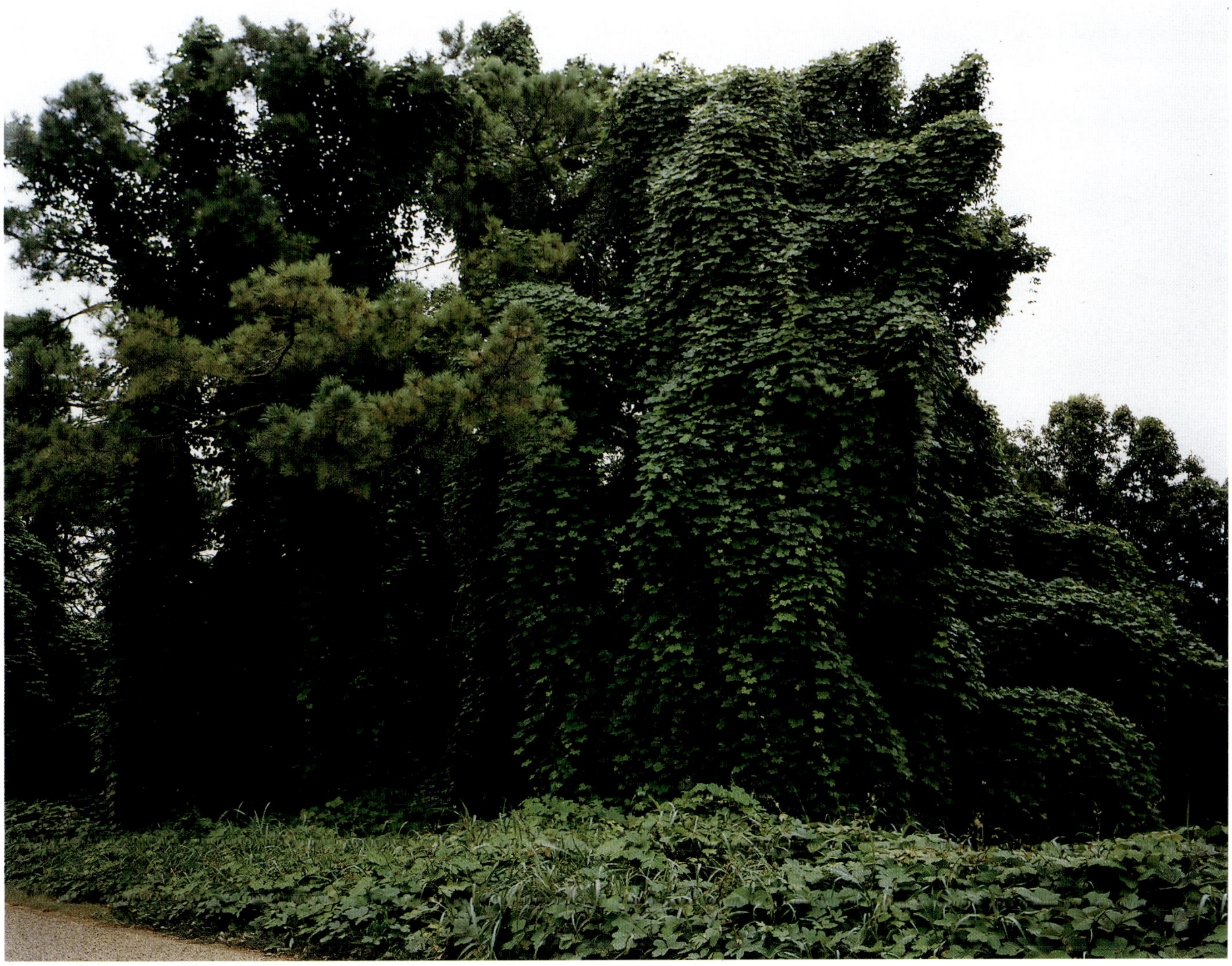

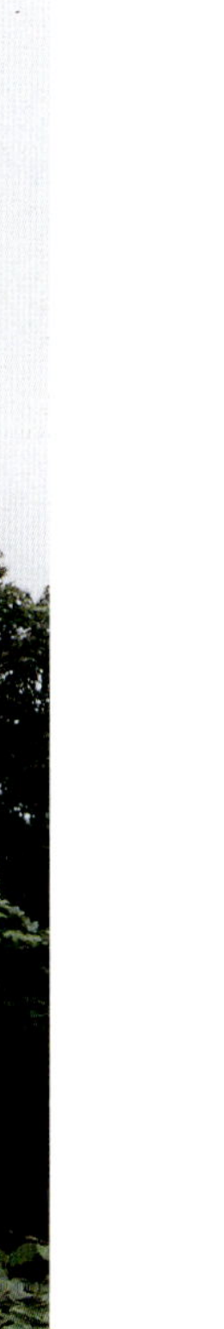

WILLIAM CHRISTENBERRY

High Kudzu, near Akron, Alabama

1978

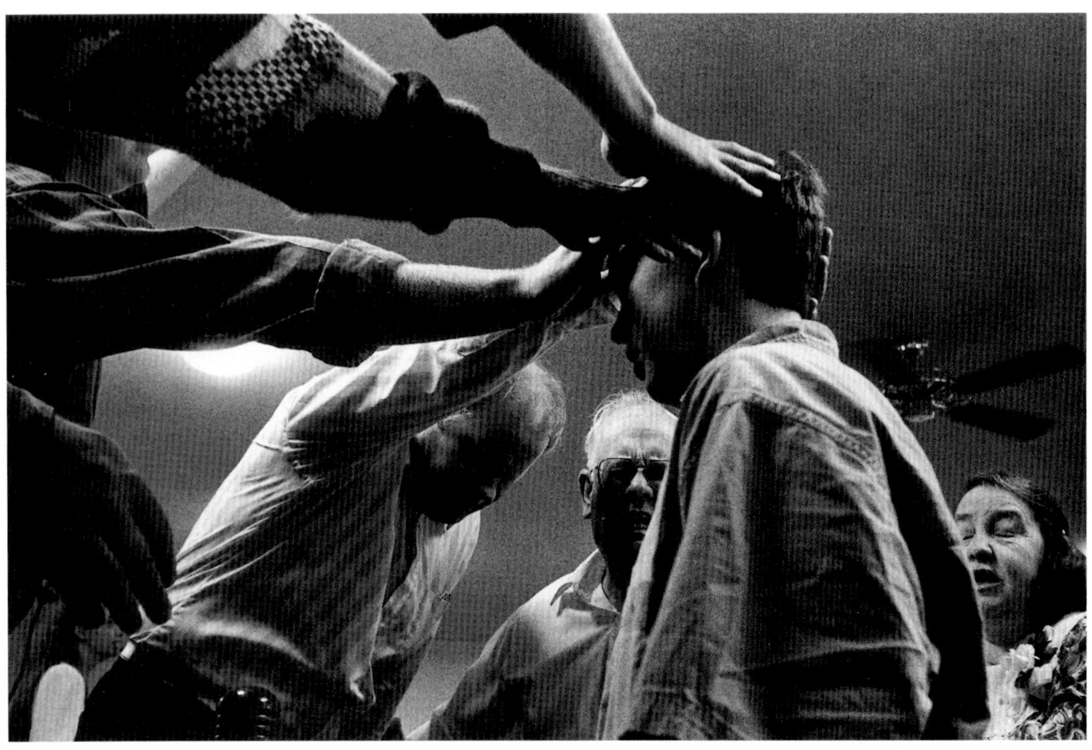

MELISSA SPRINGER

Laying on Hands, Kingston, Georgia from the series "Salvation on Sand Mountain"

1992

MELISSA SPRINGER

The Serpent Handlers, Jolo, West Virginia from the series "Salvation on Sand Mountain"

1992

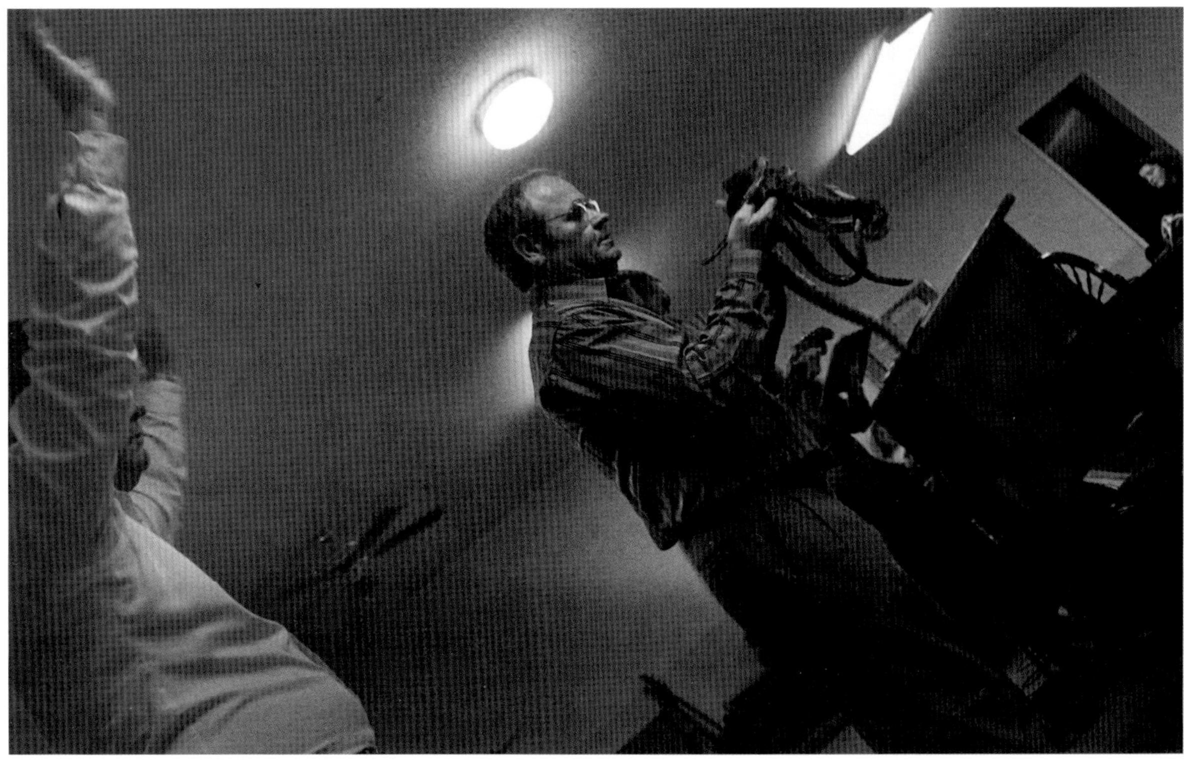

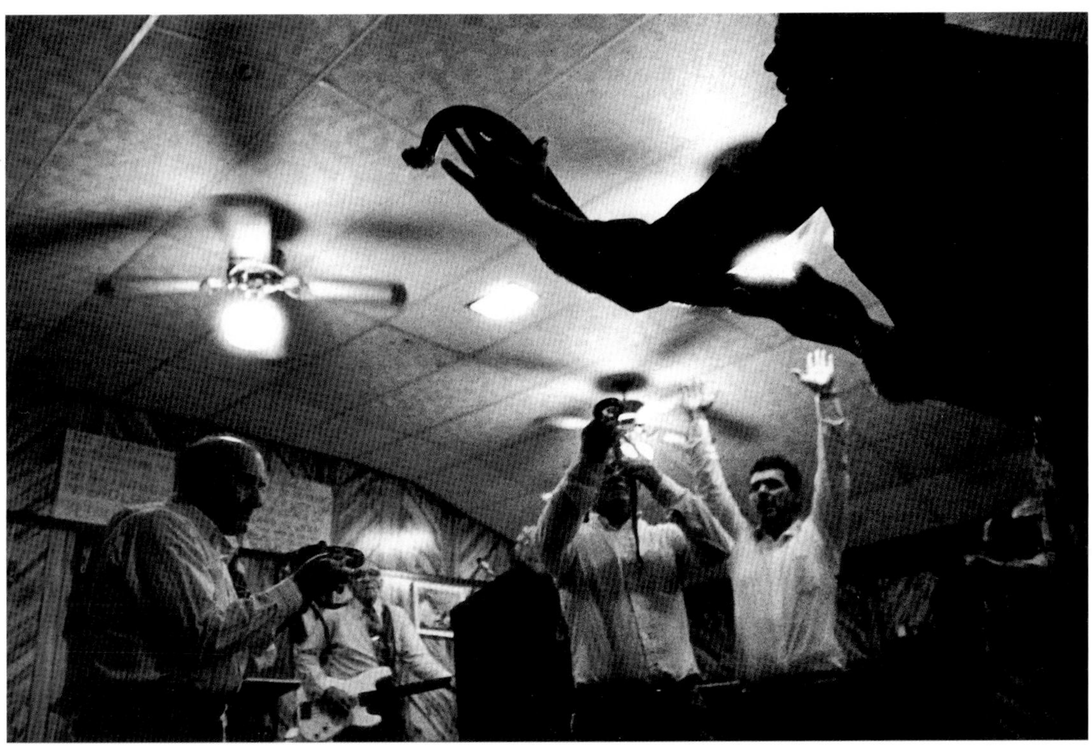

MELISSA SPRINGER

Brother Carl in His Church, Kingston, Georgia from the series "Salvation on Sand Mountain"

1992

MELISSA SPRINGER

Innocents Blessing, Kingston, Georgia from the series "Salvation on Sand Mountain"

1992

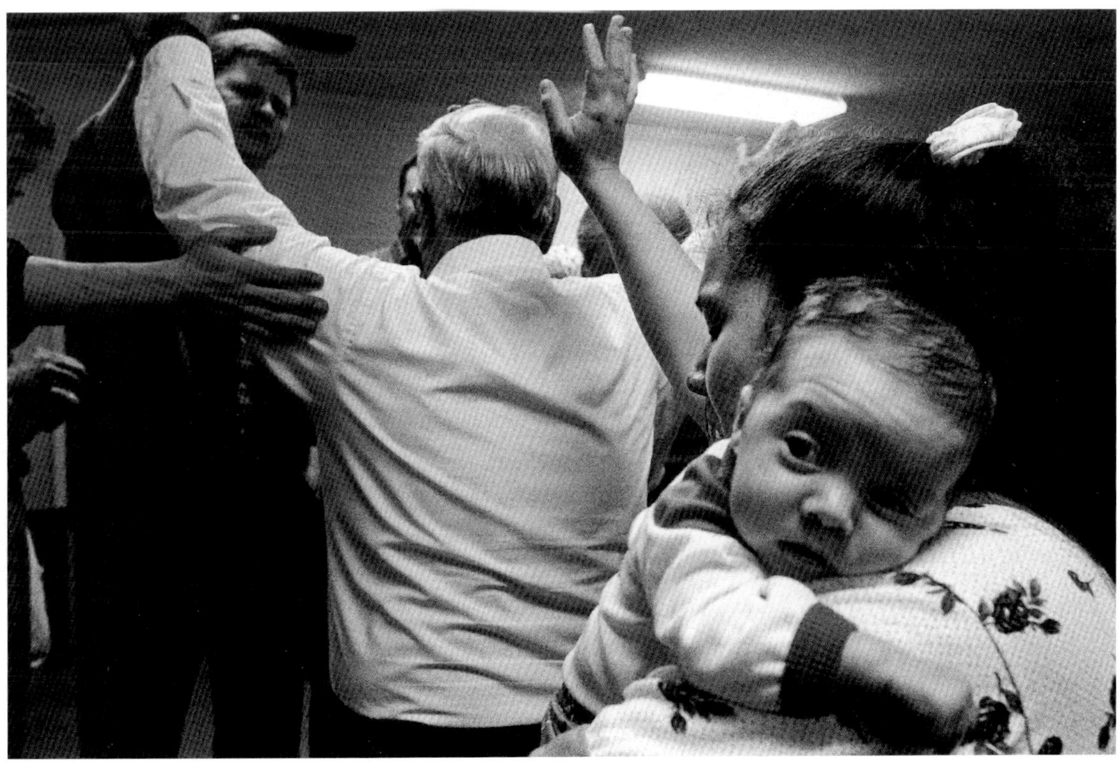

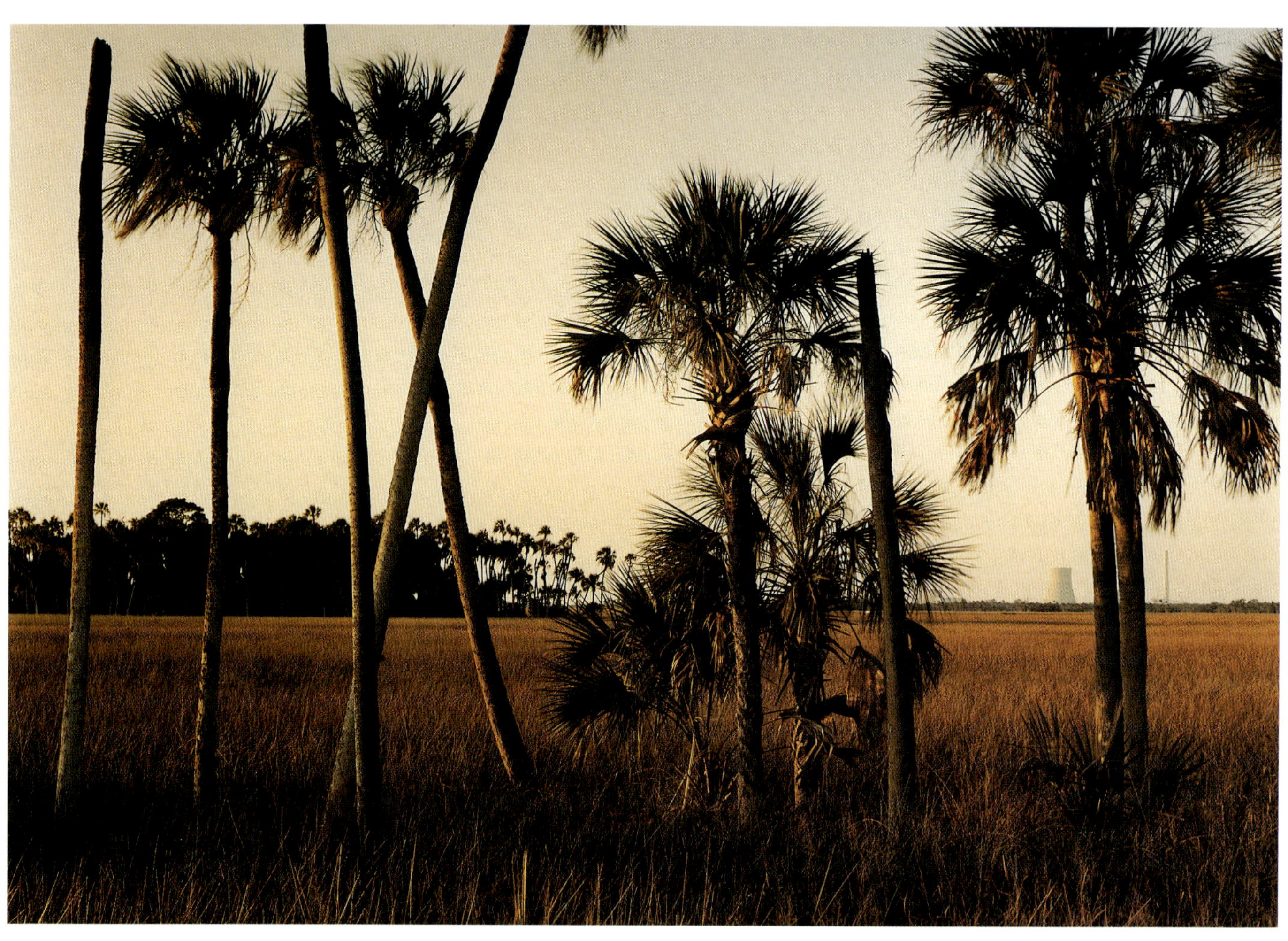

JOHN PFAHL

Crystal River Nuclear Plant (Morning), Crystal River, Florida
from the series "Power Places"
January 1982

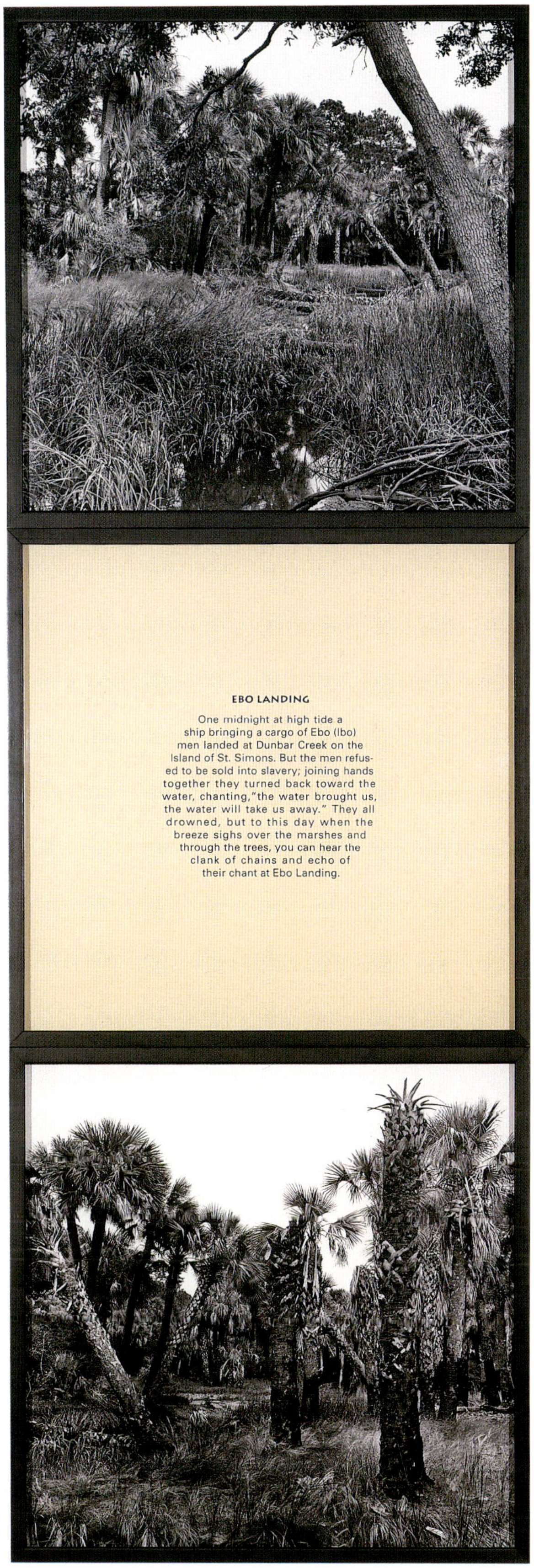

EBO LANDING

One midnight at high tide a
ship bringing a cargo of Ebo (Ibo)
men landed at Dunbar Creek on the
Island of St. Simons. But the men refus-
ed to be sold into slavery; joining hands
together they turned back toward the
water, chanting,"the water brought us,
the water will take us away." They all
drowned, but to this day when the
breeze sighs over the marshes and
through the trees, you can hear the
clank of chains and echo of
their chant at Ebo Landing.

CARRIE MAE WEEMS

Untitled (Ebo Landing) from the "Sea Islands Series"

1992

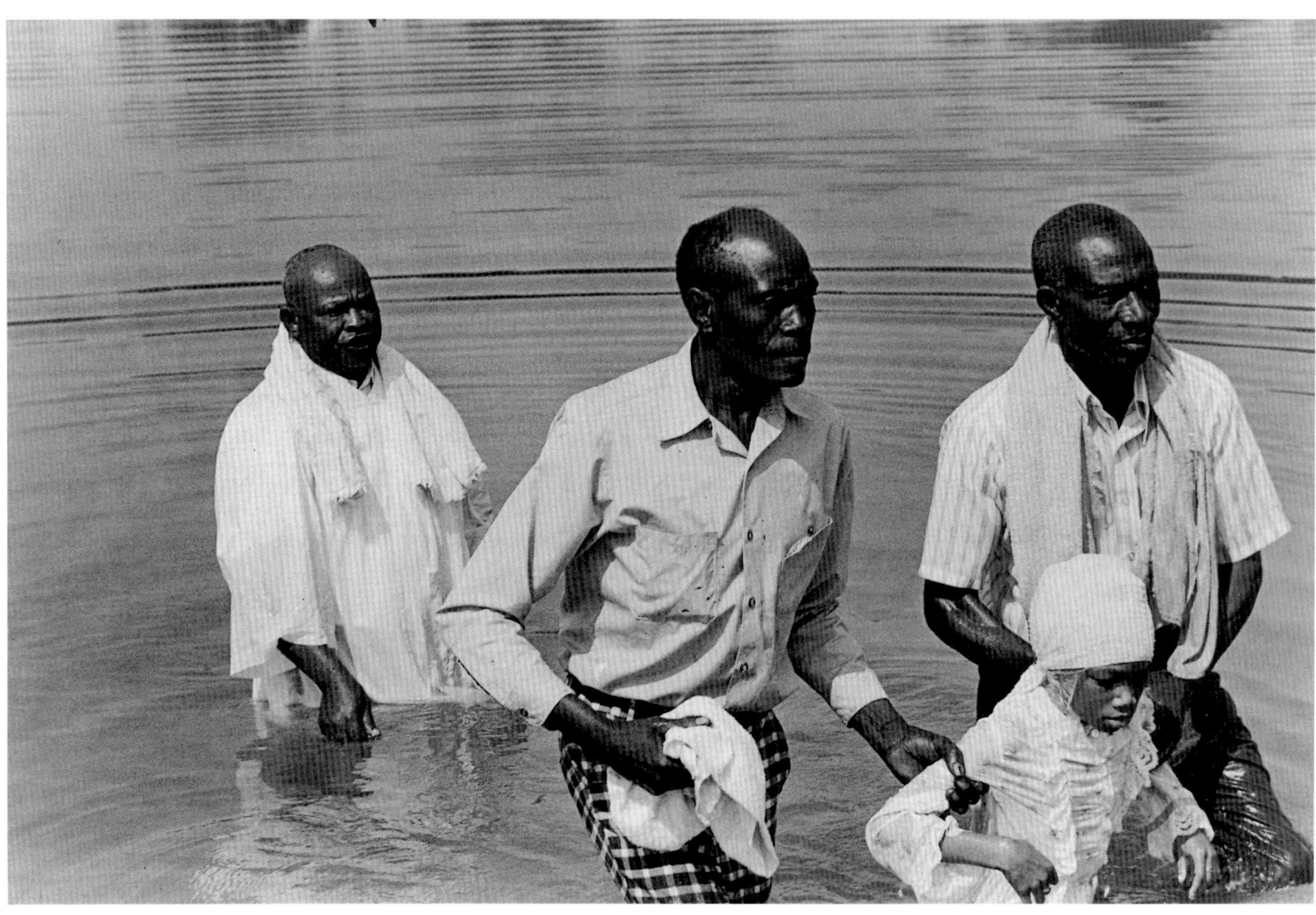

PAUL KWILECKI

Mt. Zuma Baptism at Boat Basin, Flint River.
Reverend E. E. Mitchell Has Just Baptized Lisa Spear
from the series "Religion in Decatur County, Georgia"
1977

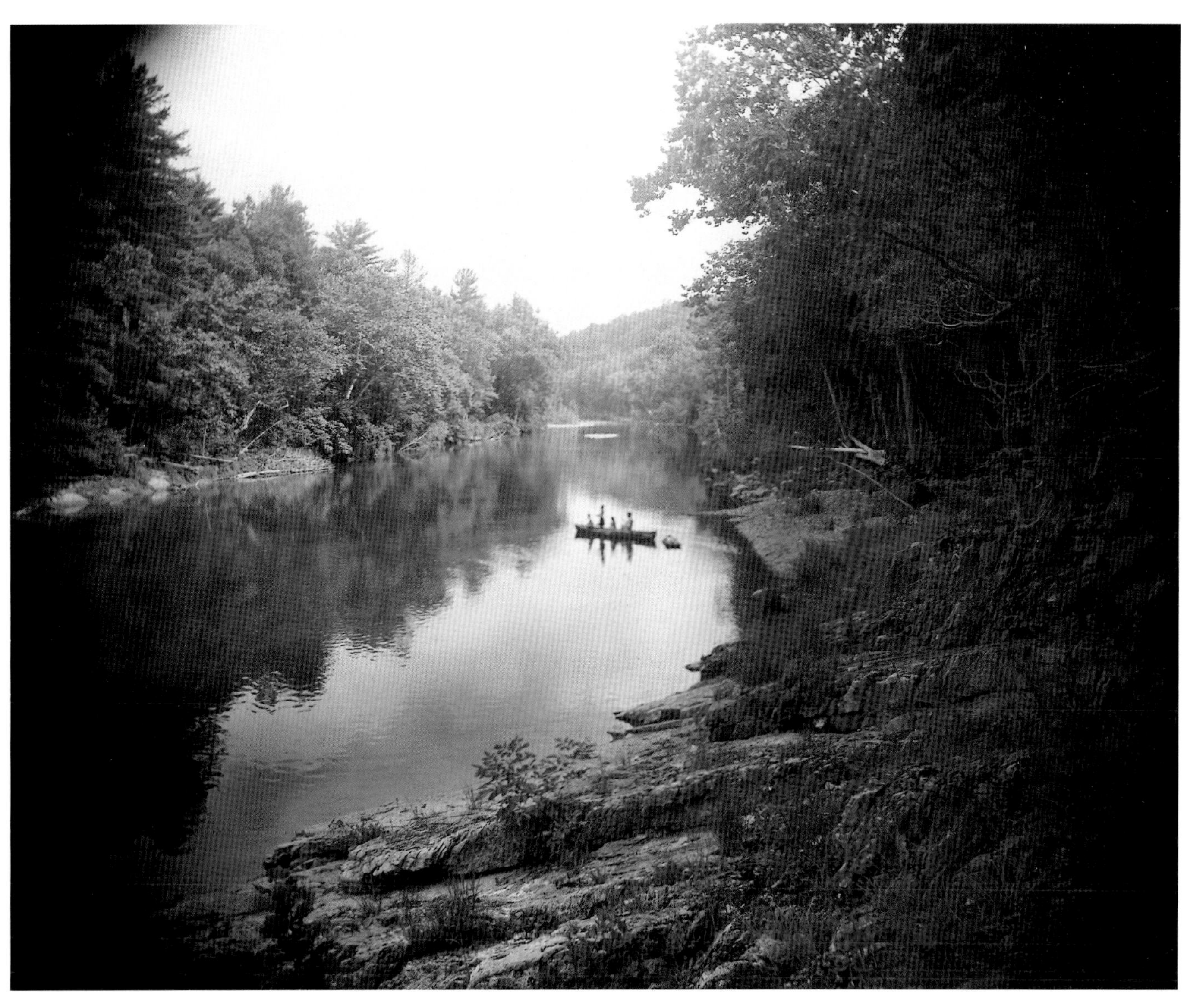

SALLY MANN
Crossing the Maury
1992

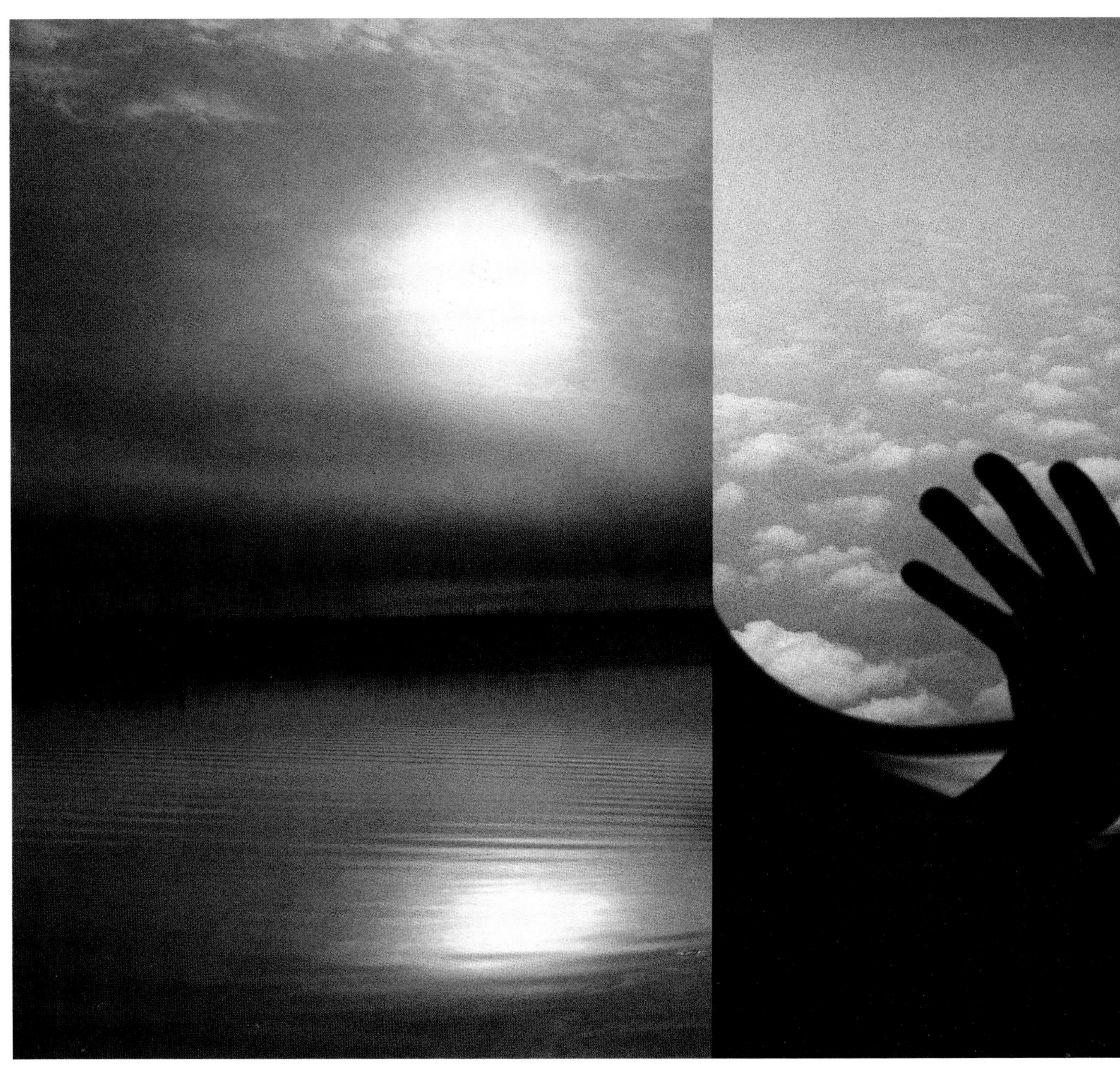

JOHN MCWILLIAMS

Dreams of Future

1995

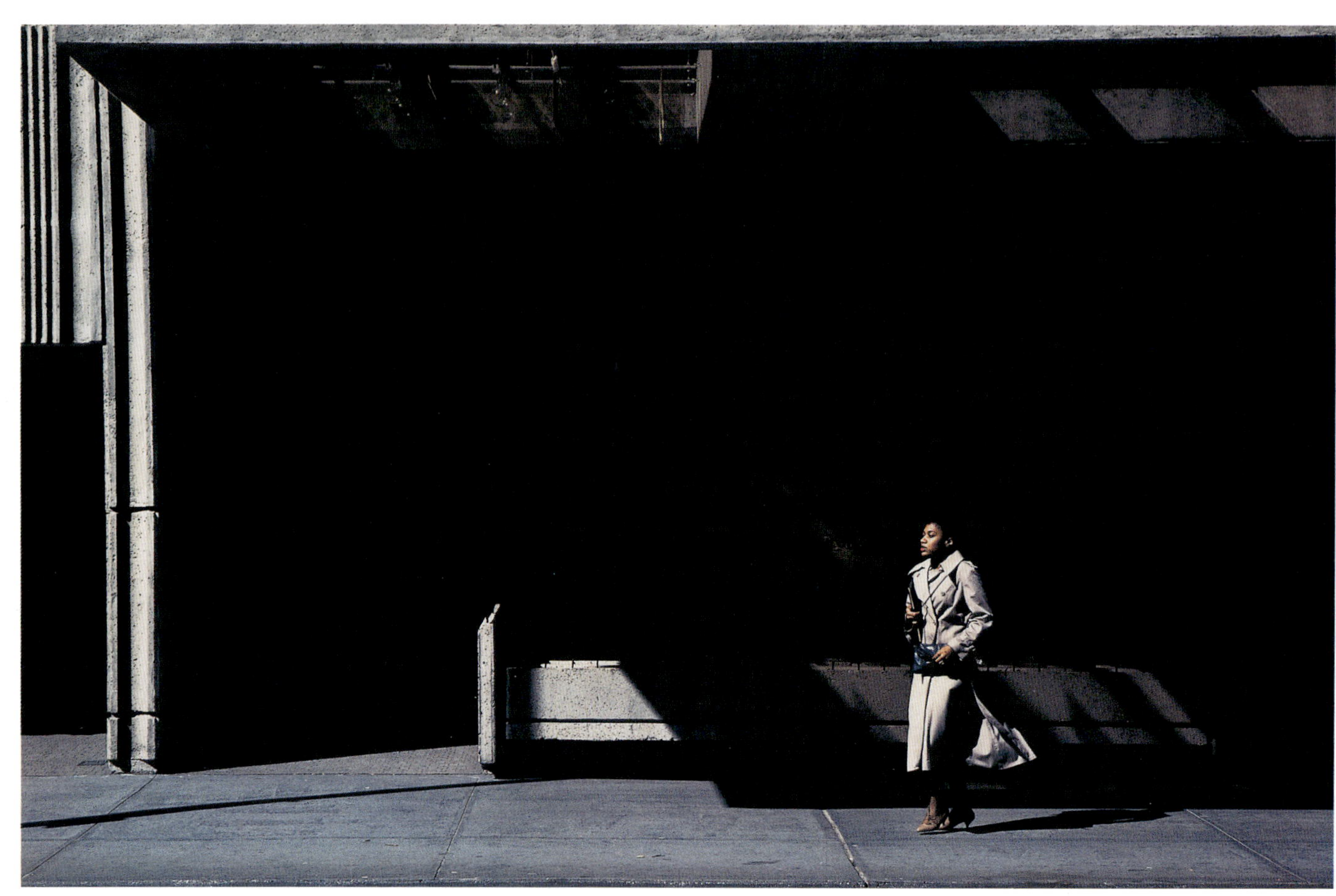

HARRY CALLAHAN
Atlanta
1984

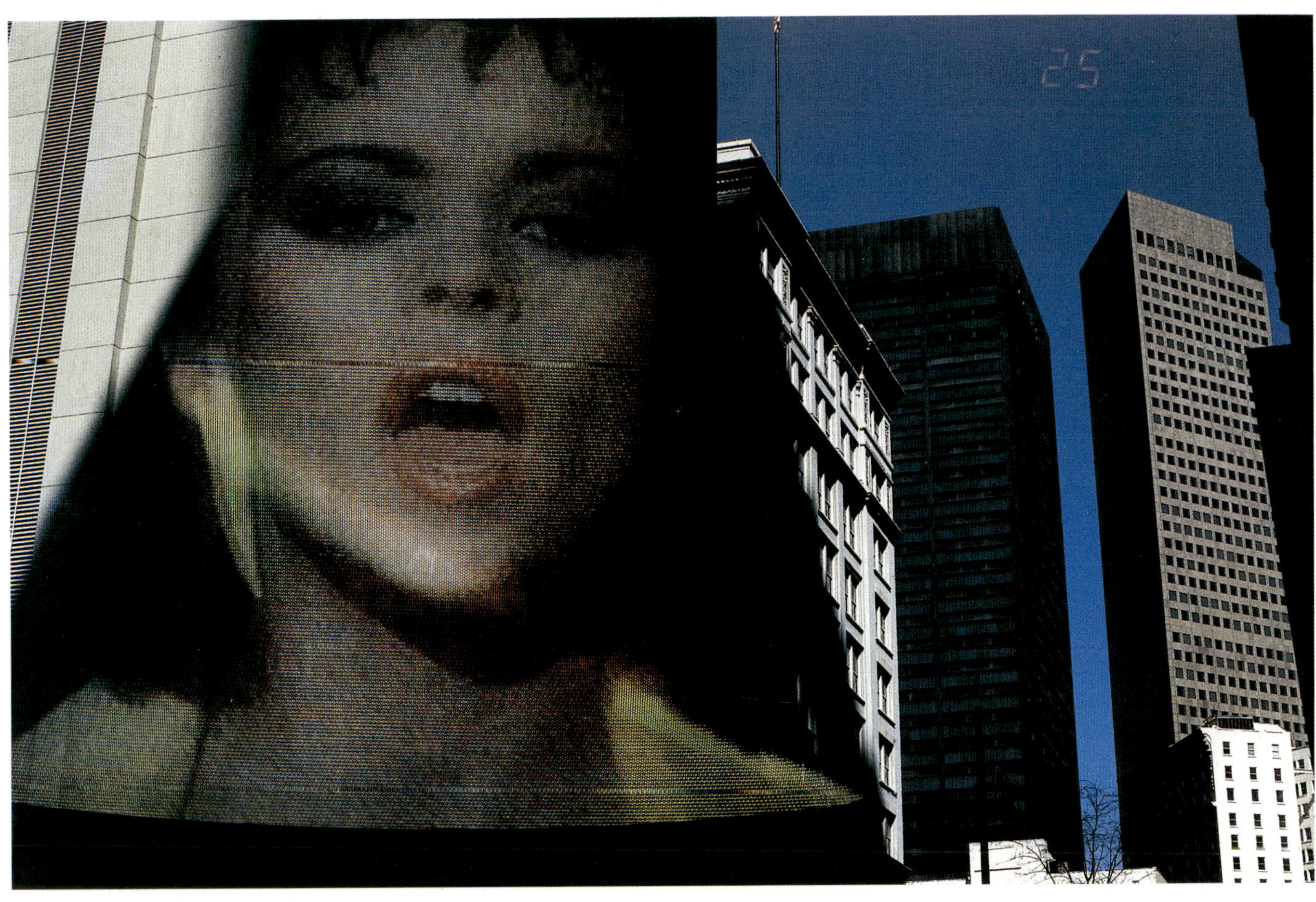

HARRY CALLAHAN
Atlanta
1985

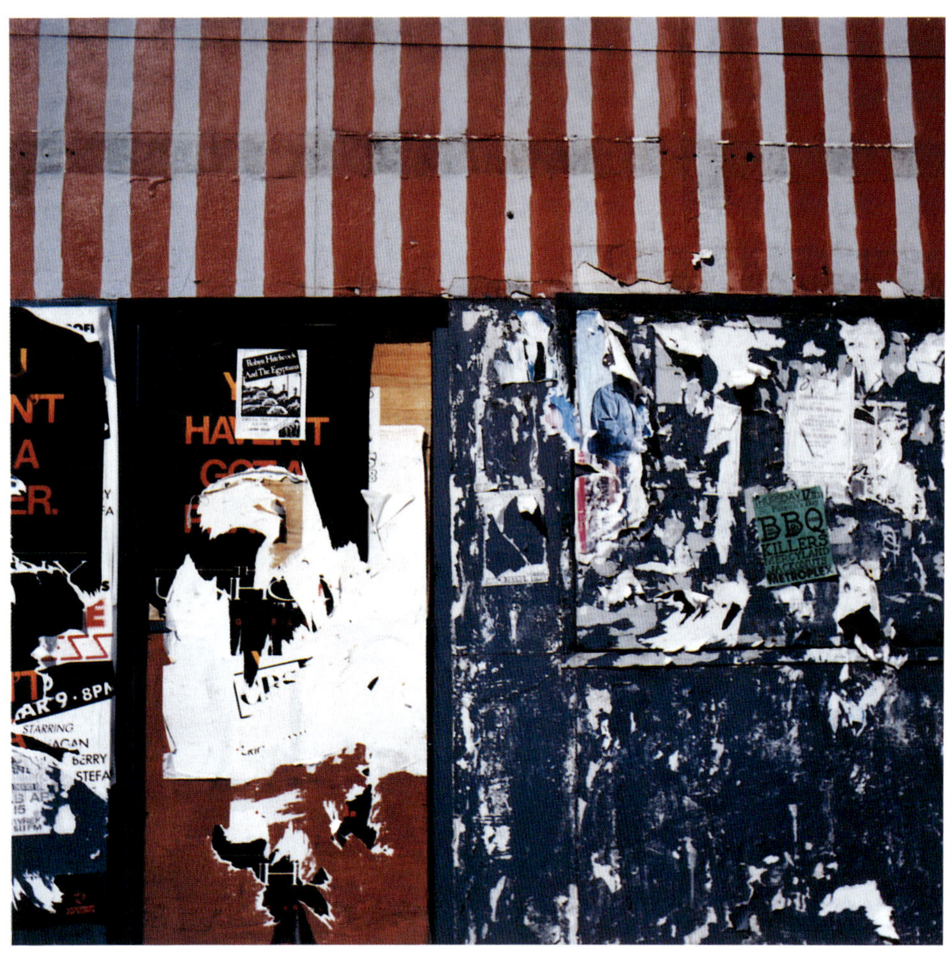

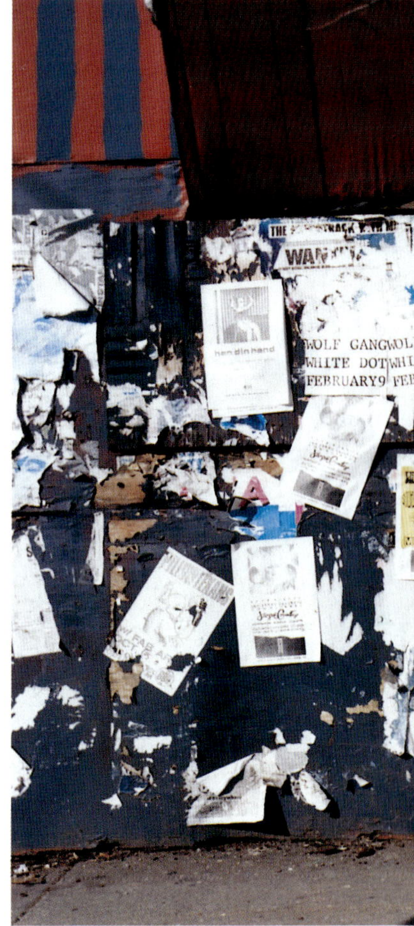

HARRY CALLAHAN

Untitled [Haven't Got a Prayer] from the "Peachtree Series"

1987–90

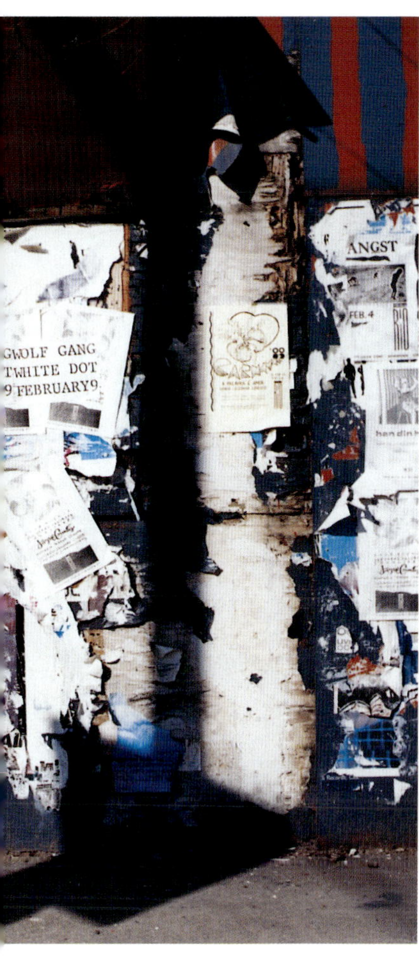
ANGST
WOLF GANG
WHITE DOT
FEBRUARY

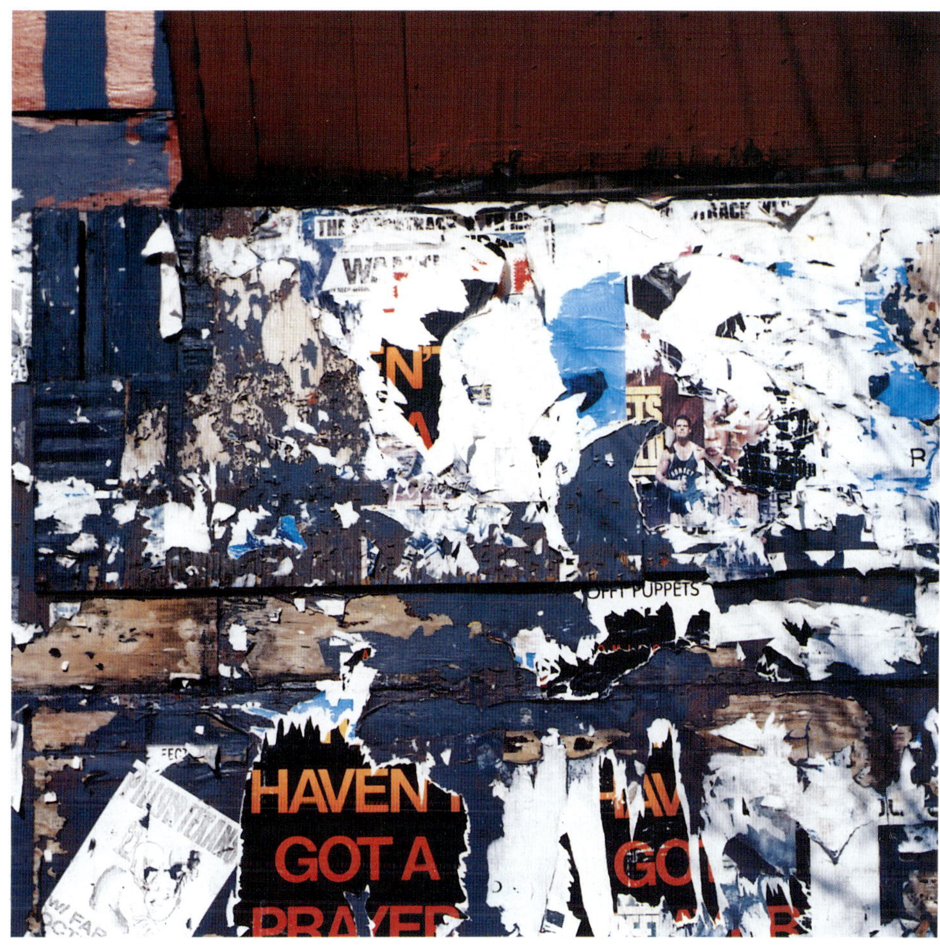
HAVEN
GOT A
PUPPETS

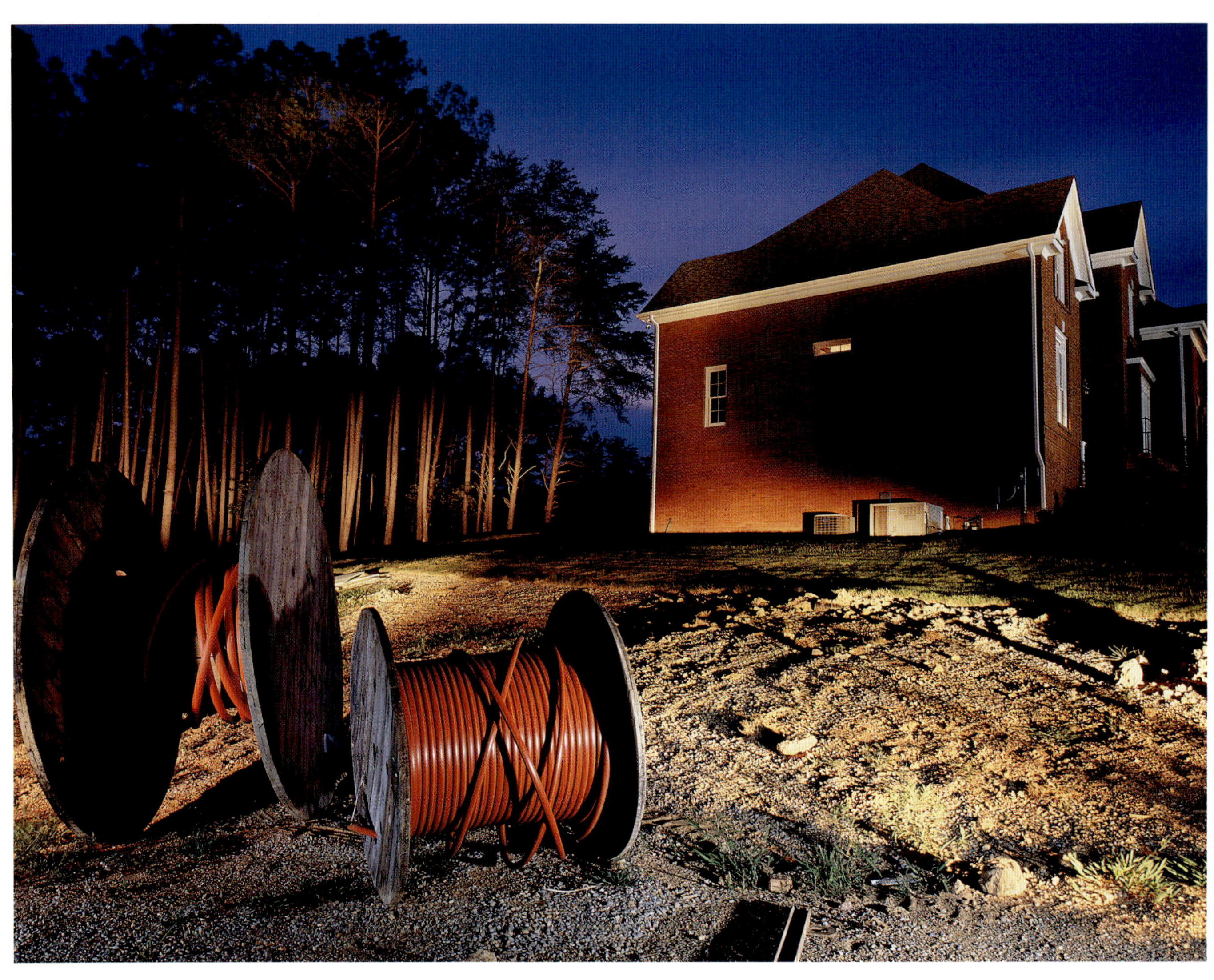

THOMAS TULIS

Construction of Suburbia #22

1993

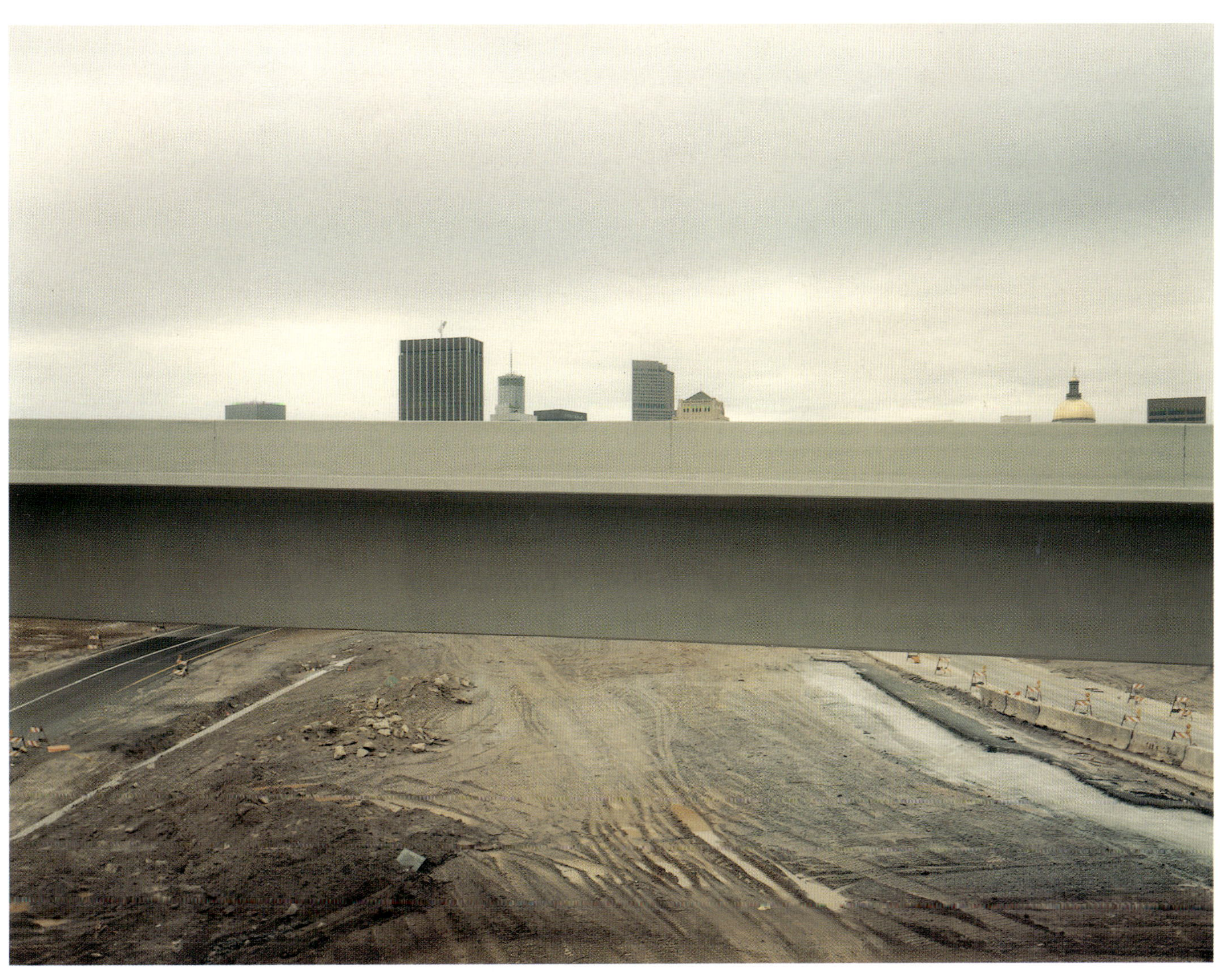

JOEL MEYEROWITZ
Atlanta
1988

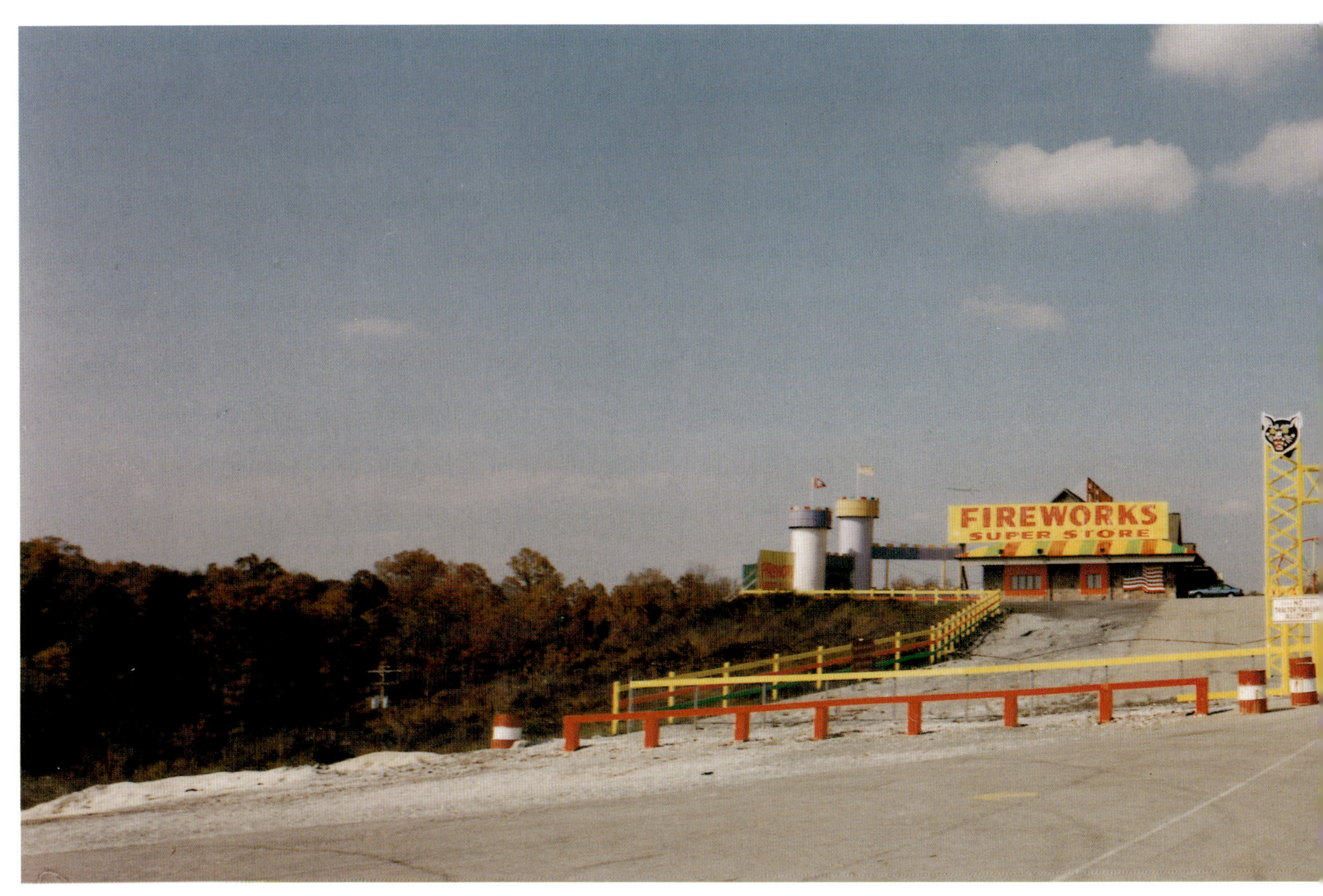

STUART D. KLIPPER

Fireworks Superstore, Exit 144, I-75, Tennessee
from the series "The World in a Few States"
October 23, 1992

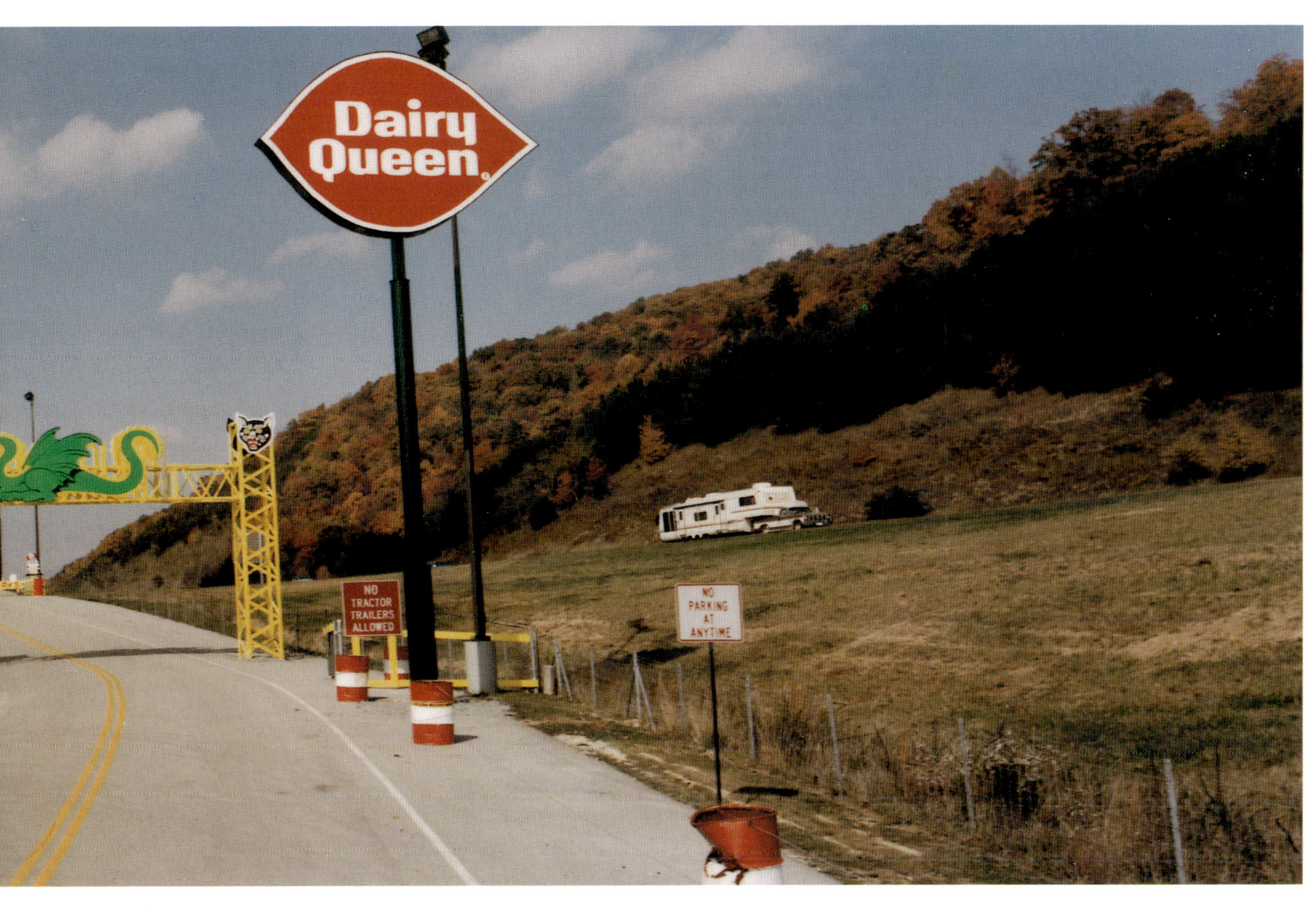
Dairy Queen
NO TRACTOR TRAILERS ALLOWED
NO PARKING AT ANYTIME

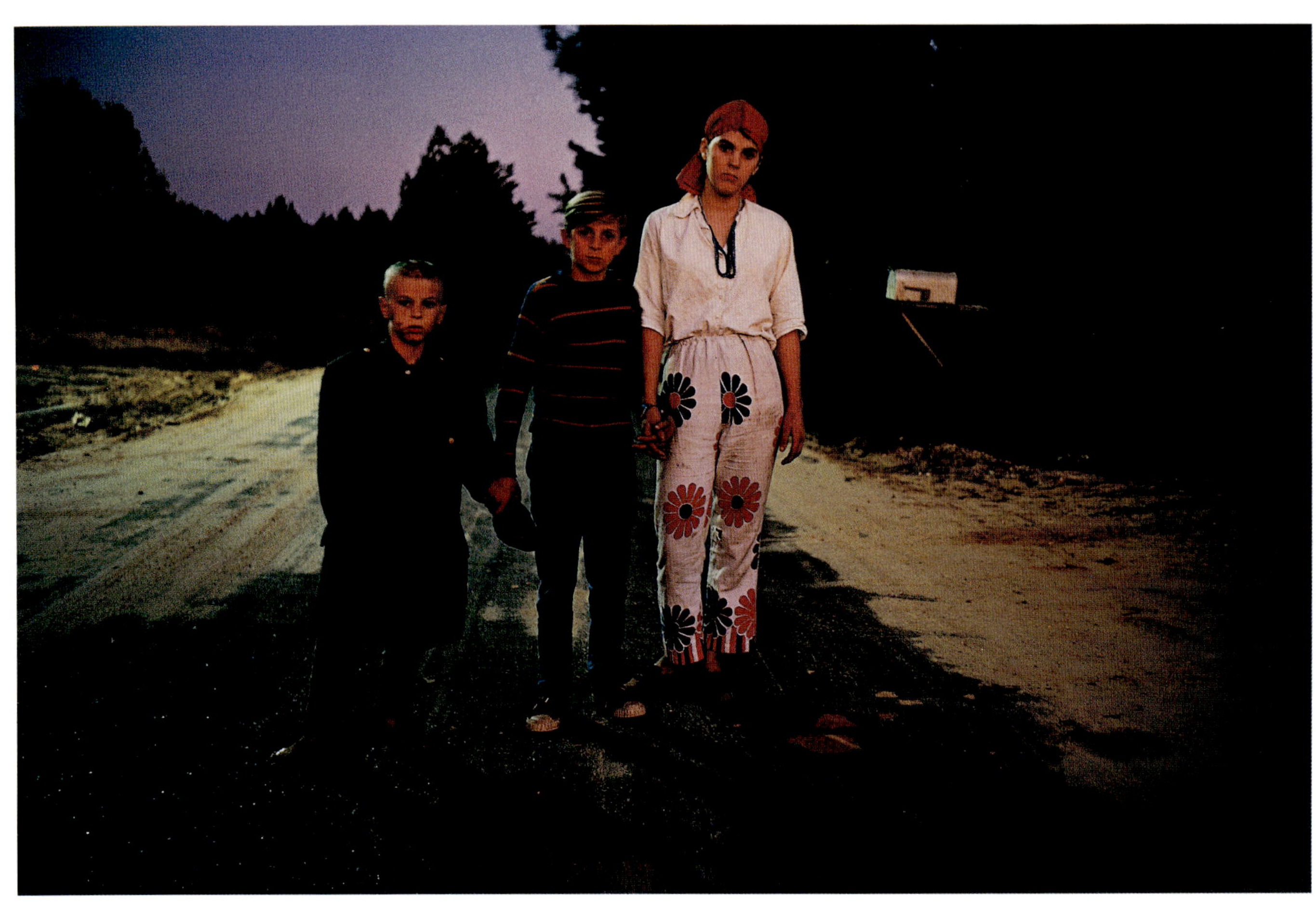

WILLIAM EGGLESTON

Halloween, Outskirts of Morton, Mississippi

1971

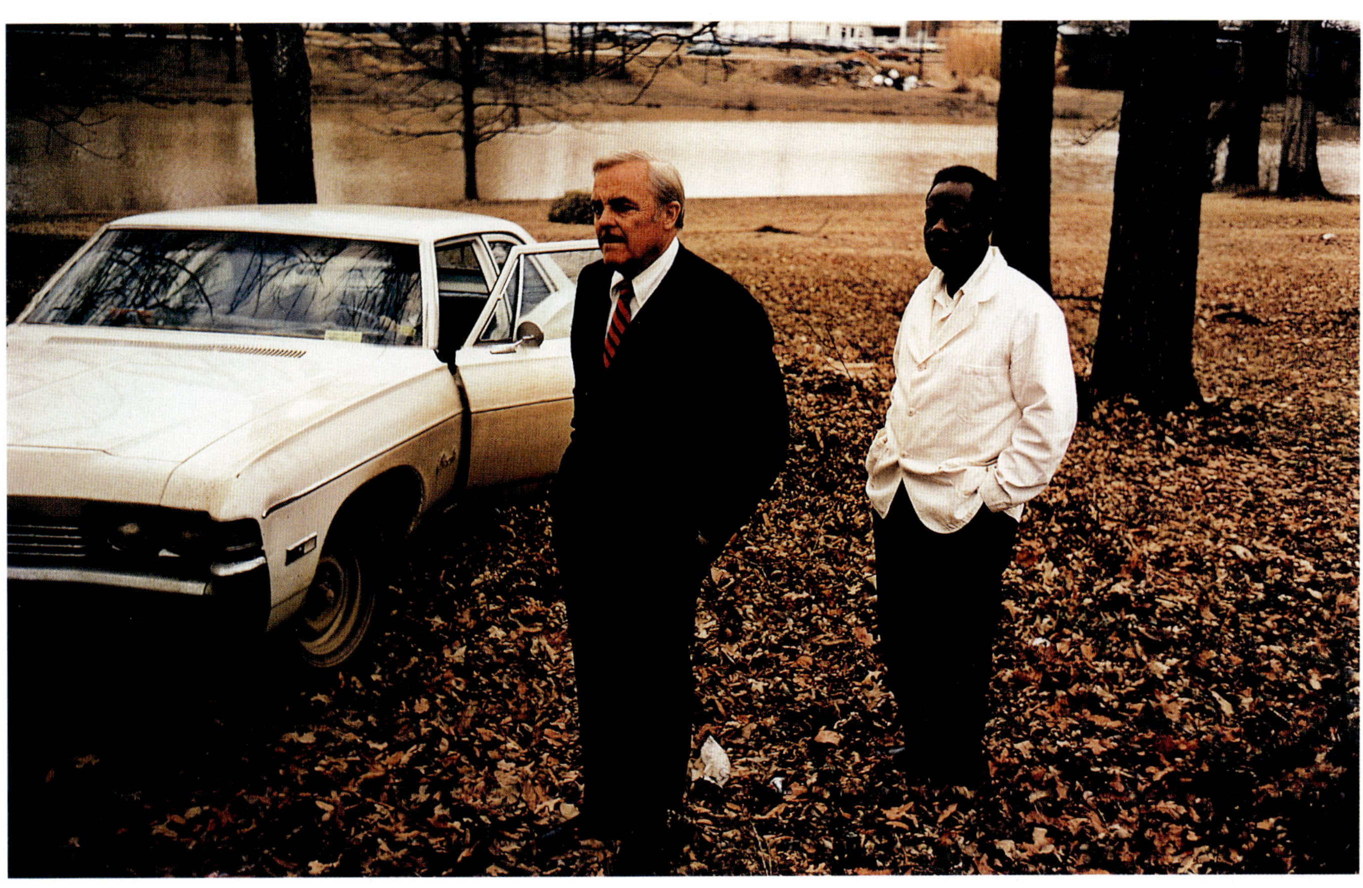

WILLIAM EGGLESTON
Sumner, Mississippi, Cassidy Bayou in Background
1971

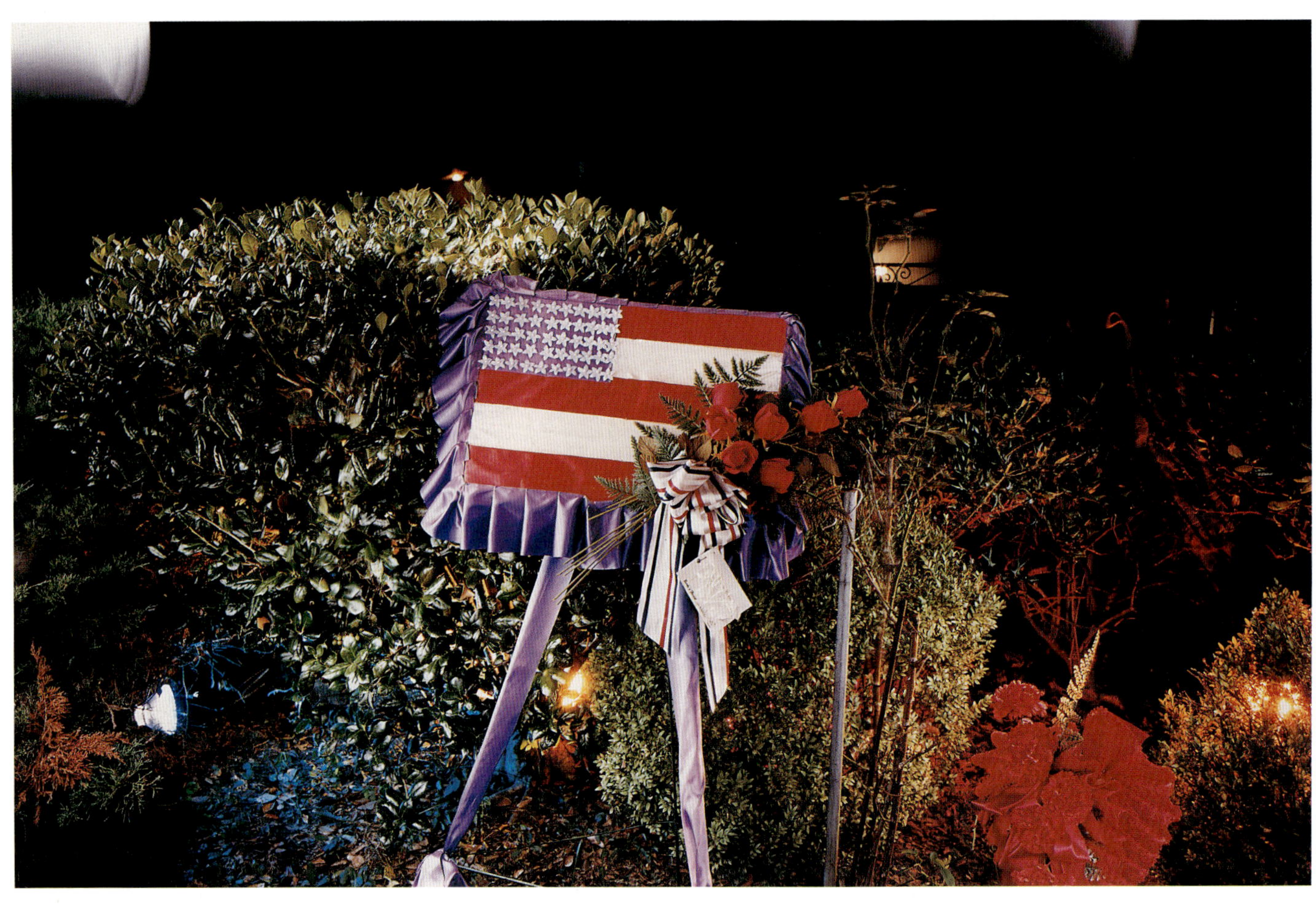

WILLIAM EGGLESTON

Memphis from the portfolio "William Eggleston's Graceland"

1983

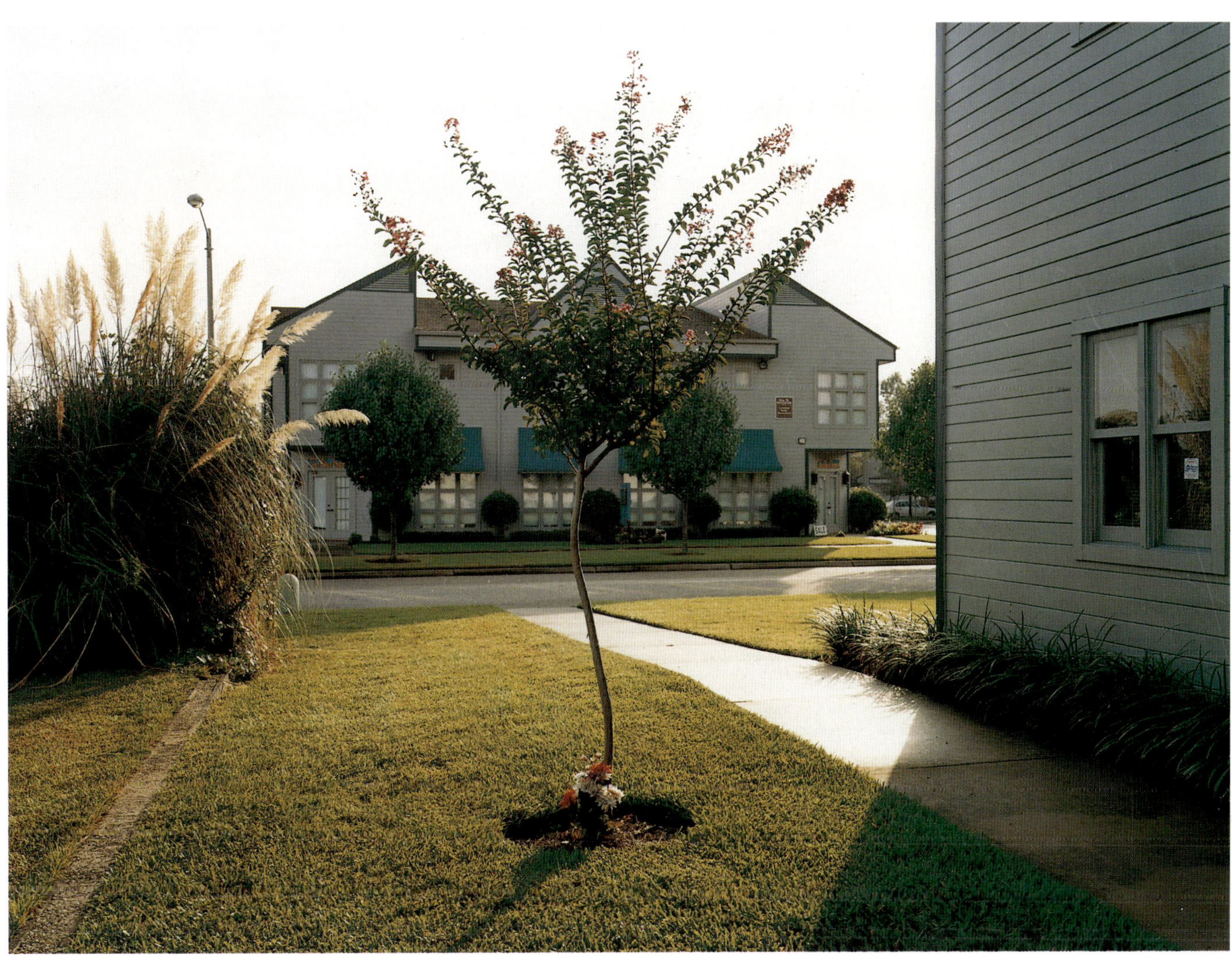

JOEL STERNFELD

Pensacola Women's Medical Services, 4400 Bayou Boulevard, Cordova Square, Pensacola, Florida from the series "On this Site . . ."
August 1993

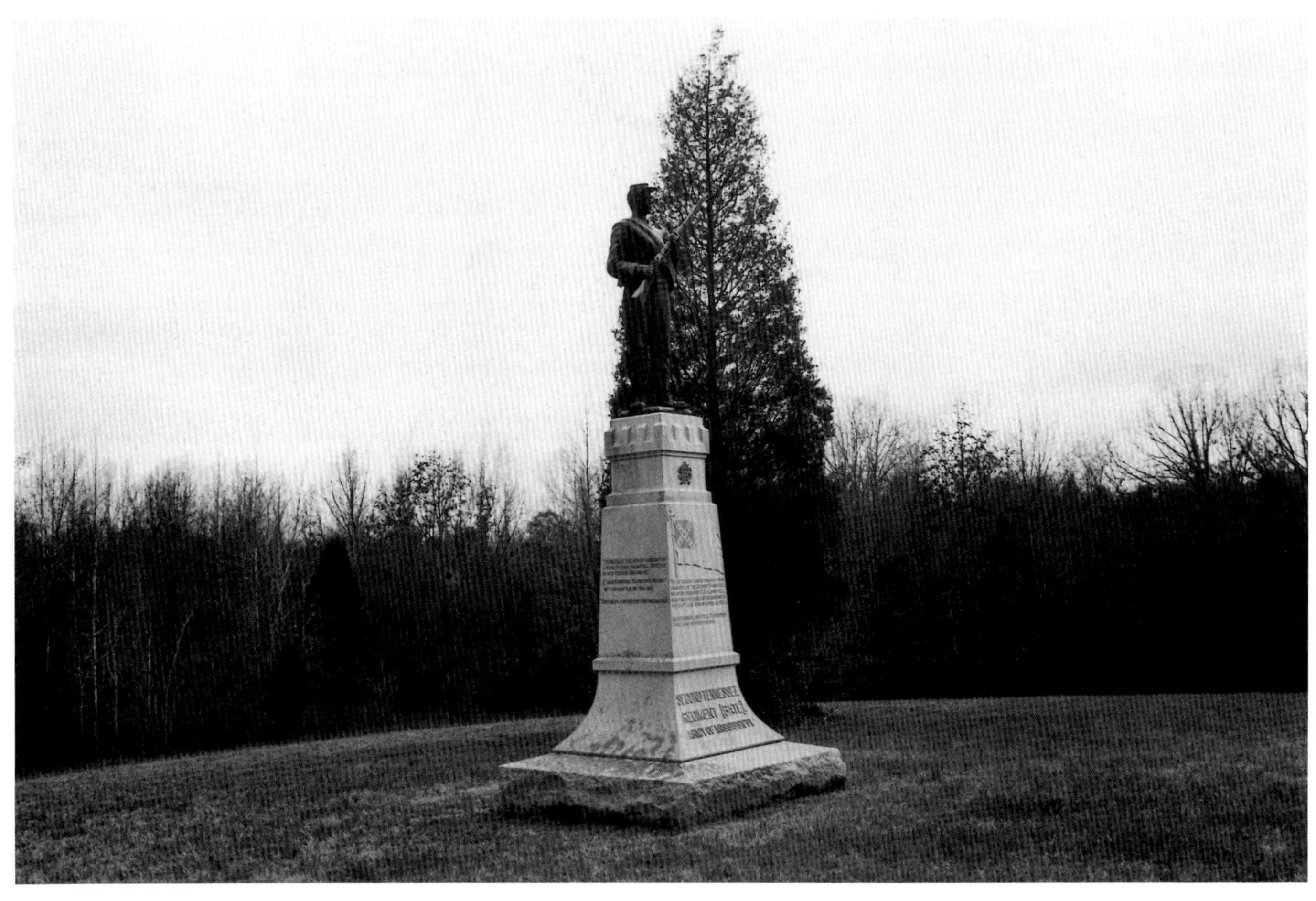

LEE FRIEDLANDER

Shiloh Military National Park from the portfolio "Shiloh"
December 1977

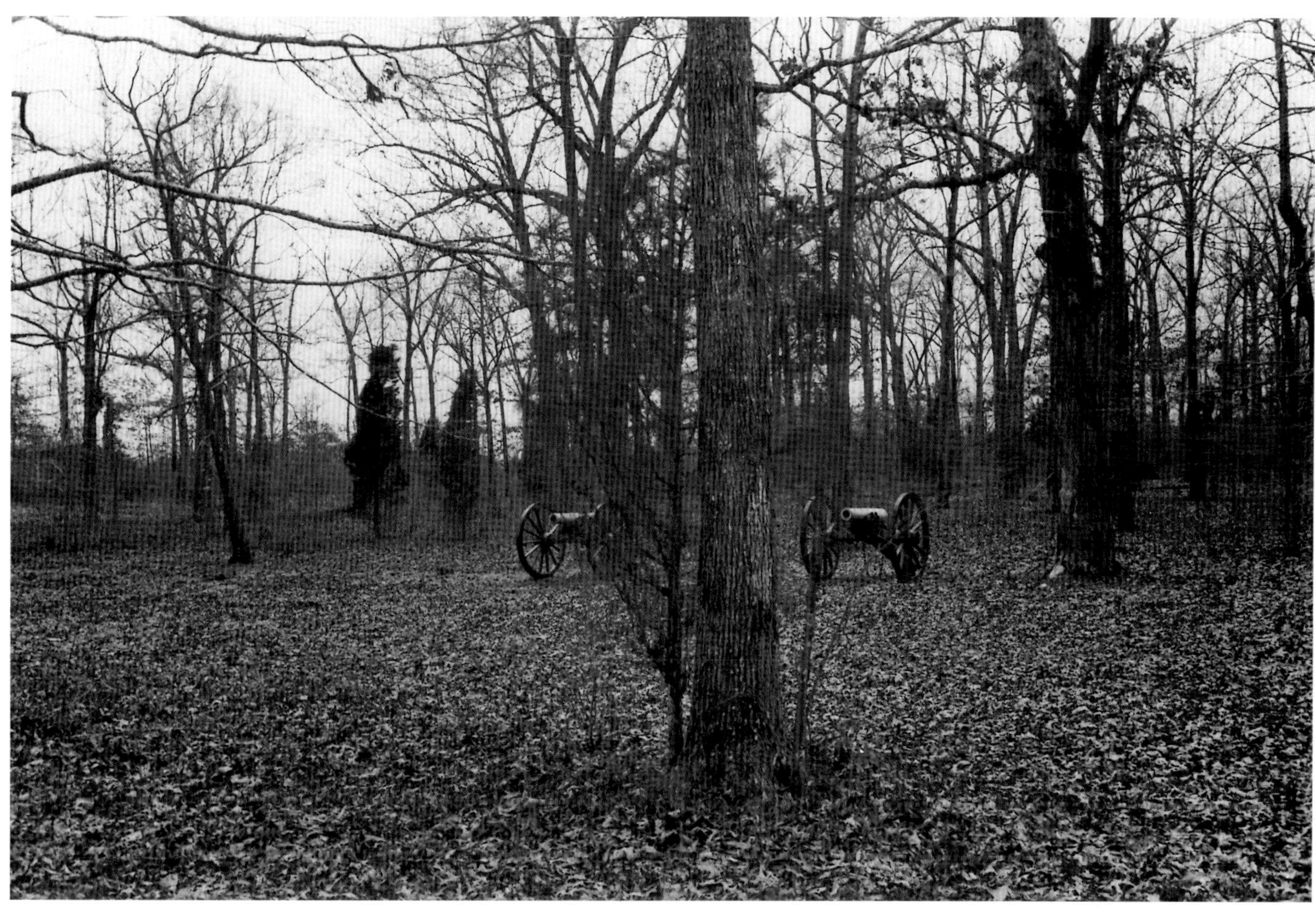

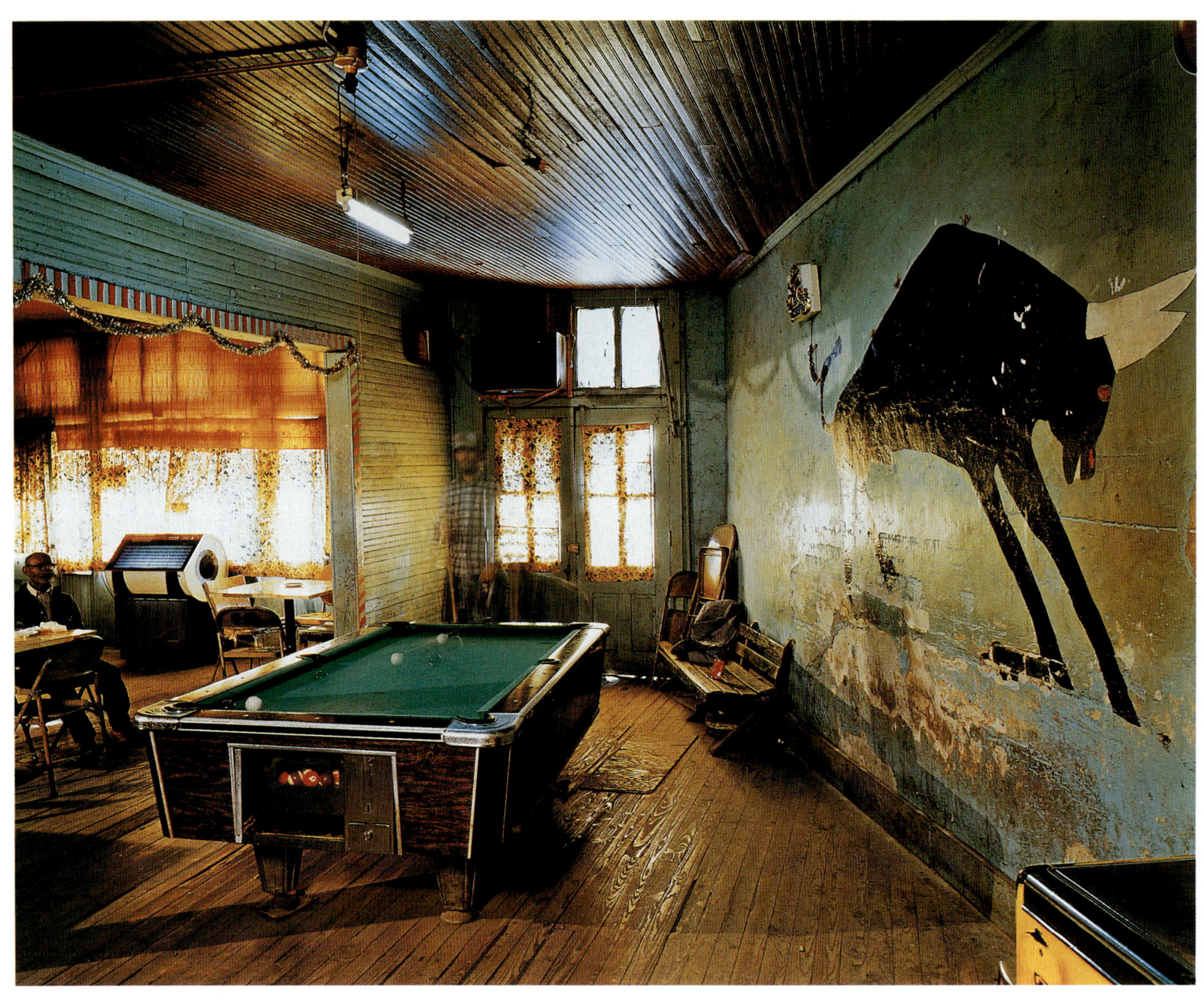

BIRNEY IMES

Riverside Lounge, Shaw, Mississippi

1986

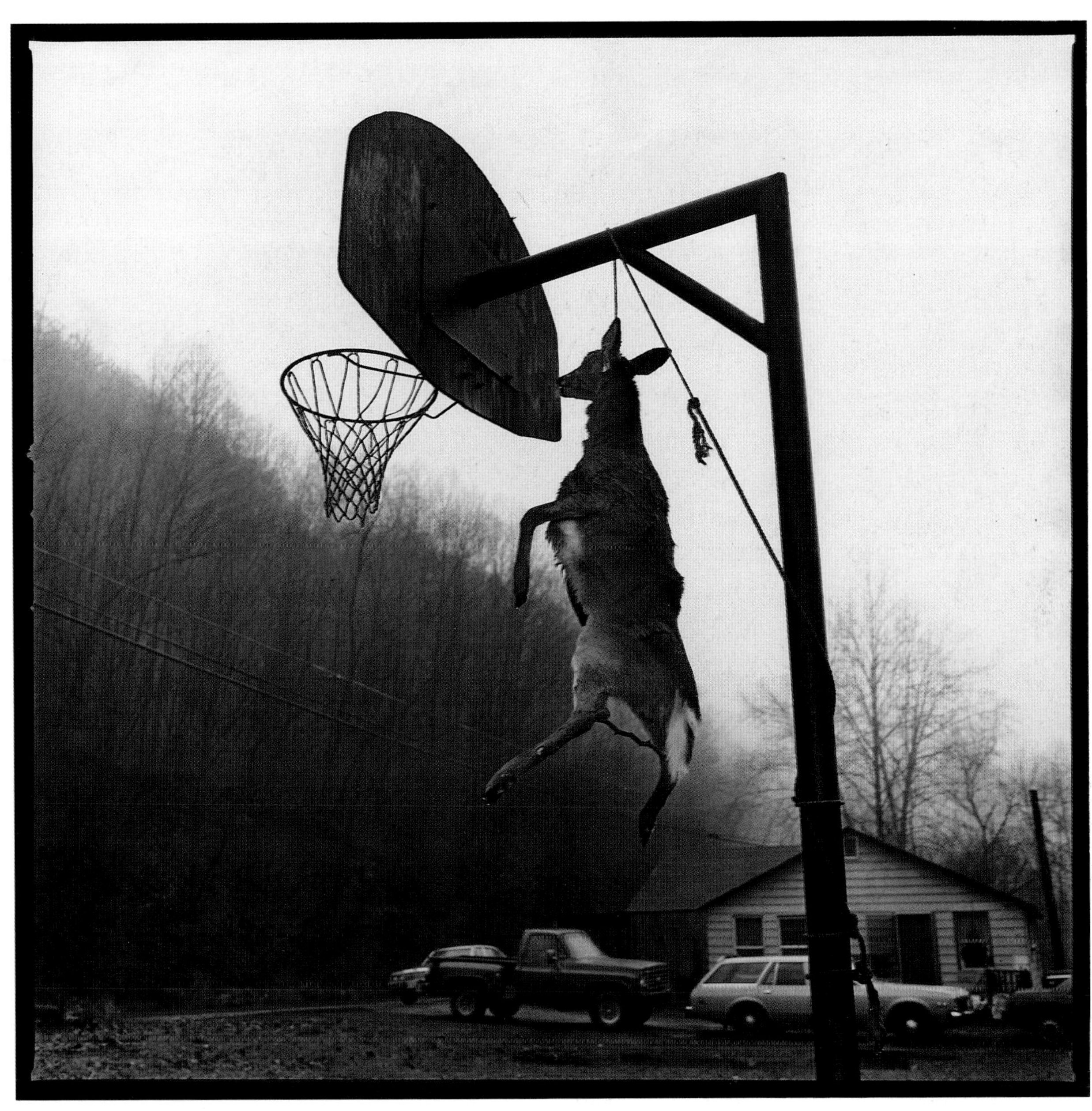

SUSAN LIPPER
Untitled from the "Grapevine Series"
1991

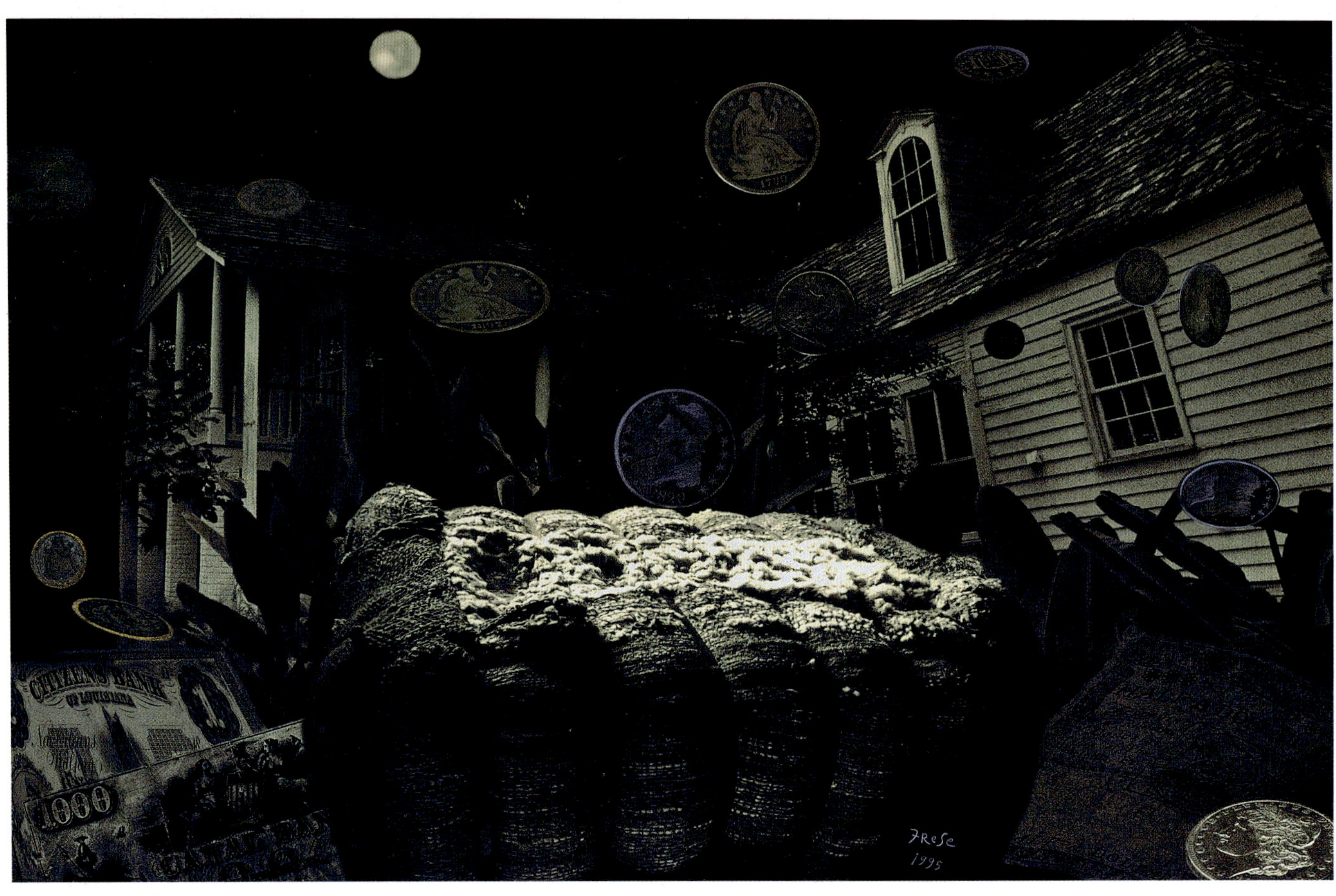

LYNDA FRESE

Prosperity from the series "Reconstituting the Vanished"

1995

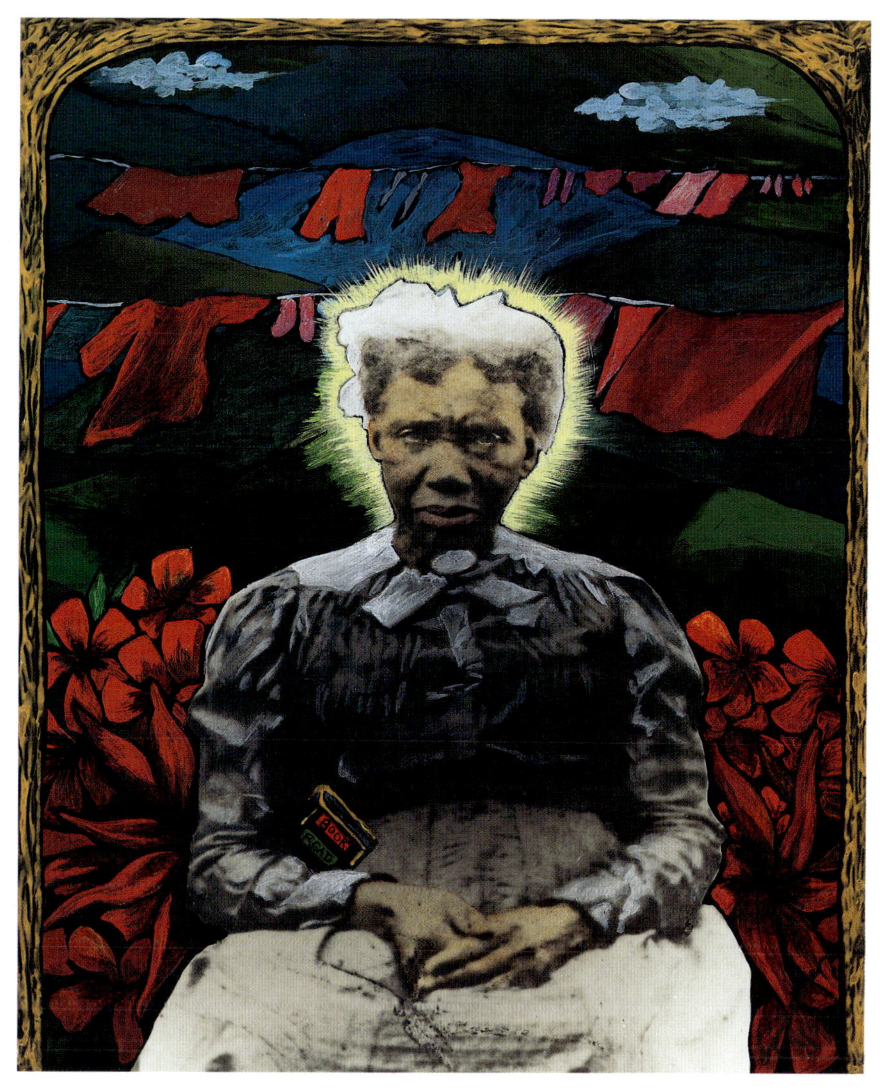

LYNN MARSHALL-LINNEMEIER
On the Peak of Time, Page 1
1995

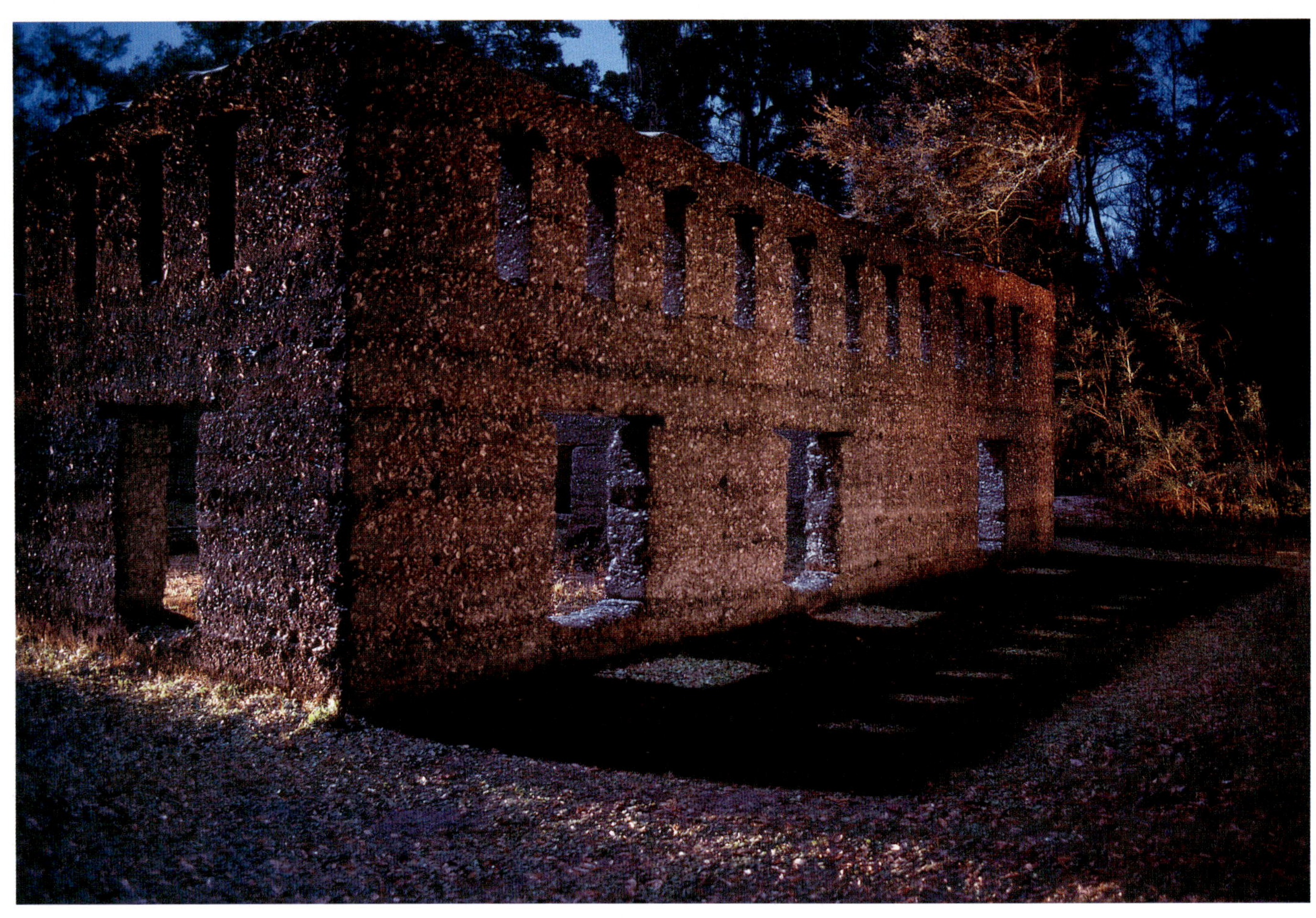

KAREKIN GOEKJIAN

Pandora's Box, St. Mary's, Georgia

1992

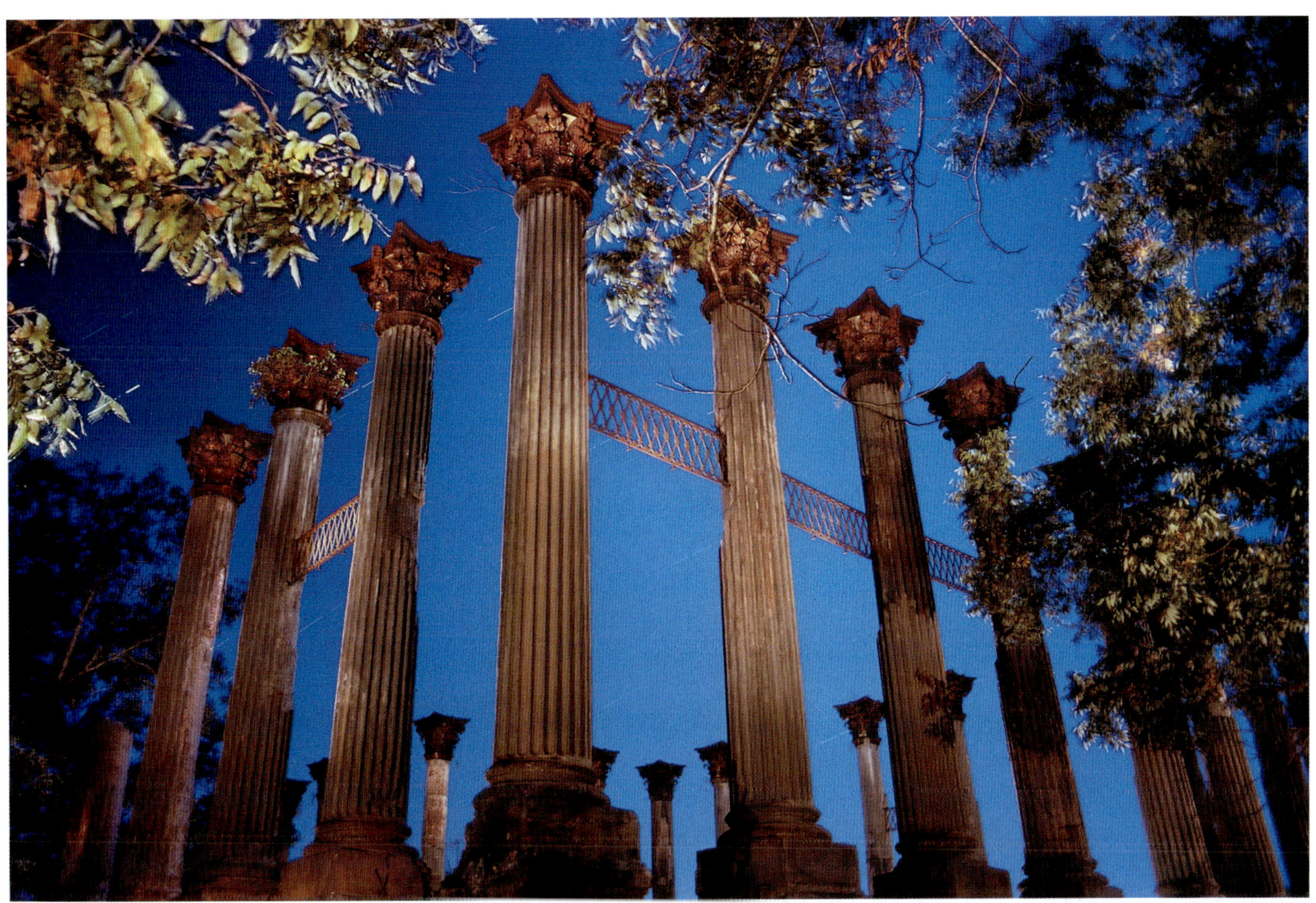

KAREKIN GOEKJIAN

Windsor Columns, Port Gibson, Mississippi

1991

CHECKLIST OF THE EXHIBITION

George Barker (American, 1844–1894)
Oklawaha River, Florida (with bird standing on log), ca. 1886, albumen print, $20\frac{1}{8} \times 16\frac{3}{16}$ inches. Prints and Photographs Division, Library of Congress, Washington, D.C.
PAGE 76

George N. Barnard (American, 1819–1902)
Atlanta, before being burnt by order of General Sherman, from the cupola of the Female Seminary, October 1864, six albumen prints (panorama), overall $3\frac{7}{16} \times 13\frac{7}{8}$ inches. Prints and Photographs Division, Library of Congress, Washington, D.C.

Rebel Works in Front of Atlanta, Georgia, No. 1, 1864, from the album "Photographic Views of Sherman's Campaign," 1866, albumen print, $10\frac{1}{8} \times 14\frac{1}{4}$ inches. High Museum of Art, Atlanta; Gift of Mrs. Everett N. McDonnell
PAGE 45

Ruins in Charleston, South Carolina, 1865 or 1866, from the album "Photographic Views of Sherman's Campaign," 1866, albumen print, $10\frac{1}{8} \times 14\frac{1}{4}$ inches. High Museum of Art, Atlanta; Purchase
PAGE 24

Interior View of Ginning Mills Ginning Sea Island Cotton, on Alex. Knox's Plantation, Mt. Pleasant, near Charleston, South Carolina, ca. 1874, from the series "South Carolina Views," albumen print stereograph, $3\frac{1}{8} \times 6\frac{1}{8}$ inches. The Charleston Museum

Laborers Returning at Sunset from Picking Cotton on Alex. Knox's Plantation, Mt. Pleasant, near Charleston, South Carolina, ca. 1874, from the series "South Carolina Views," albumen print stereograph, $3\frac{1}{8} \times 6\frac{1}{8}$ inches. Collection of George S. Whiteley IV
PAGE 57

Old Maumer Selling Groundnut Candy in the Streets of Charleston, South Carolina, ca. 1874, from the series "South Carolina Views," albumen print stereograph, $3\frac{1}{8} \times 6\frac{1}{8}$ inches. Collection of George S. Whiteley IV

Fifteenth Amendment—A Good Specimen, ca. 1874–75, albumen print stereograph, $3\frac{1}{4} \times 6$ inches. Robert N. Dennis Collection of Stereographic Views, Miriam and Ira D. Wallach Division of Art, Prints and Photographs, The New York Public Library; Astor, Lenox and Tilden Foundations
PAGE 56

Barnard & Gibson (American, active early 1860s)
Departure from the Old Homestead, Centreville, Virginia, 1862, from the series "Brady's Album Gallery," albumen print carte-de-visite, $2\frac{1}{2} \times 3\frac{5}{8}$ inches. The New-York Historical Society
PAGE 42

Cornelius Marion Battey (American, 1873–1927)
Carpentry Class, Tuskegee Institute, Tuskegee, Alabama, ca. 1920, gelatin silver print, $7\frac{7}{16} \times 9\frac{7}{16}$ inches. Photographs and Prints Division, Schomburg Center for Research in Black Culture, The New York Public Library; Astor, Lenox and Tilden Foundations
PAGE 69

Arthur P. Bedou (American, 1882–1966)
Booker T. Washington's Last Tour of Louisiana, 1915, gelatin silver print, $7\frac{1}{8} \times 9\frac{1}{2}$ inches. Xavier University Archives and Special Collections, New Orleans
PAGE 71

Craig School Kinder Band, New Orleans, Louisiana, ca. 1930s, gelatin silver print, $7\frac{1}{8} \times 9\frac{1}{4}$ inches. Xavier University Archives and Special Collections, New Orleans
PAGE 83

Ernest J. Bellocq (American, 1873–1949)
Woman in a White Hat, ca. 1911–13, printed by Lee Friedlander, 1976, gelatin silver printing-out paper print, $9\frac{7}{8} \times 7\frac{15}{16}$ inches. New Orleans Museum of Art; Museum Purchase, 1977 Acquisition Fund
PAGE 80

Samuel T. Blessing (American, 1832–1897)
Cutting Sugar Cane, ca. 1880, albumen print stereograph, $3\frac{11}{16} \times 6\frac{7}{8}$ inches. The Historic New Orleans Collection

Margaret Bourke-White (American, 1904–1971)
At the Time of the Louisville Flood, Louisville, Kentucky, 1936–37, gelatin silver print, $10 \times 13\frac{5}{16}$ inches. George Eastman House, International Museum of Photography and Film, Rochester, New York; Museum Collection
PAGE 124

Maiden Lane, Georgia, 1936–37, from the series "You Have Seen Their Faces," gelatin silver print, $10 \times 13\frac{1}{2}$ inches. Margaret Bourke-White Papers, George Arents Research Library for Special Collections, Syracuse University, Syracuse, New York
PAGE 114

Preacher and Congregation, Exminster, South Carolina, 1936–37, from the series "You Have Seen Their Faces," gelatin silver print, $11 \times 13\frac{7}{8}$ inches. Margaret Bourke-White Papers, George Arents Research Library for Special Collections, Syracuse University, Syracuse, New York

Mathew Brady (American, 1823–1896)
Slave Pens, Alexandria, Virginia, 1862, from the series "Brady's Album Gallery," albumen print carte-de-visite, $2\frac{1}{4} \times 3\frac{3}{4}$ inches. The New-York Historical Society

Attributed to Mathew Brady Studio (American, active 1844–1868)
Ruins of the Willis House, Marye's Heights, Fredericksburg, Virginia, ca. 1864, albumen print, $8\frac{3}{8} \times 12\frac{3}{4}$ inches. The Medford Historical Society, Massachusetts
PAGE 44

Stern J. Bramson (American, 1912–1989)
Rialto Block, 600 S. Fourth Street, Louisville, Kentucky, 1946, gelatin silver print, $18\frac{1}{8} \times 22\frac{11}{16}$ inches. Royal Photographic Collection, Photographic Archives, University of Louisville, Kentucky
PAGE 135

Composite Photo for Newspaper Advertisement, Fourth and Broadway. Client: Howell Furniture Company, Louisville, Kentucky, 1952, gelatin silver print, $14\frac{5}{8} \times 18\frac{5}{16}$ inches. Royal Photographic Collection, Photographic Archives, University of Louisville, Kentucky
PAGE 133

Harry Callahan (American, born 1912)
Atlanta, 1984, dye transfer print, $9\frac{9}{16} \times 14\frac{7}{16}$ inches. Courtesy of the artist, PaceWildensteinMacGill, New York, and Jackson Fine Art, Atlanta
PAGE 194

Atlanta, 1985, dye transfer print, $9\frac{5}{8} \times 14\frac{7}{16}$ inches. Courtesy of the artist, PaceWildensteinMacGill, New York, and Jackson Fine Art, Atlanta
PAGE 195

Untitled [Haven't Got a Prayer], from the "Peachtree Series," 1987–90, three chromogenic development prints (triptych), each 4 × 4 inches, overall 16 × 22 inches. Courtesy of the artist, PaceWildensteinMacGill, New York, and Jackson Fine Art, Atlanta
PAGES 196–97

Henri Cartier-Bresson (French, born 1908)
Hinds County, Mississippi, 1962, gelatin silver print, $6\frac{7}{8} \times 9\frac{1}{4}$ inches. High Museum of Art, Atlanta; Purchase with funds from the Massey Charitable Trust and Lucinda W. Bunnen for the Bunnen Collection
PAGE 166

William Christenberry (American, born 1936)
Church Across Early Cotton, Pickinsville, Alabama, 1964, chromogenic development print, $3\frac{1}{8} \times 4\frac{7}{8}$ inches. Courtesy of the artist and Jackson Fine Art, Atlanta
PAGE 183

Rebel Gasoline Station, Moundville, Alabama, 1964, chromogenic development print, $3\frac{1}{16} \times 3\frac{1}{16}$ inches. Courtesy of the artist and Jackson Fine Art, Atlanta
PAGE 182

Grave with Bed as Marker (View I), near Faunsdale, Alabama, 1965, chromogenic development print, $3\frac{1}{8} \times 4\frac{7}{8}$ inches. Courtesy of the artist and Jackson Fine Art, Atlanta
PAGE 182

Gourd Tree, near Akron, Alabama, 1976, chromogenic development print, $3\frac{1}{8} \times 4\frac{7}{8}$ inches. Courtesy of the artist and Jackson Fine Art, Atlanta
PAGE 183

High Kudzu, near Akron, Alabama, 1978, chromogenic development print, $7\frac{1}{2} \times 9\frac{1}{2}$ inches. Courtesy of the artist and Jackson Fine Art, Atlanta
PAGE 185

Alabama Landscape, near Tuscaloosa, Alabama, 1980, chromogenic development print, $7\frac{7}{16} \times 9\frac{9}{16}$ inches. Courtesy of the artist and Jackson Fine Art, Atlanta
PAGE 184

John Hawley Clarke (American, ca. 1831–1914)
Rebel's Den, 1861, ambrotype, 4 × 5 inches. Louisiana State Museum, New Orleans

Gregory Conniff (American, born 1944)
Cotton Field After Rain, Yazoo County, Mississippi, 1992, gelatin silver print, 28 × 34 inches. Courtesy of the artist

Cotton Field, Lafayette County, Mississippi, 1993, gelatin silver print, 28 × 34 inches. Courtesy of the artist
PAGE 181

George Smith Cook (American, 1819–1902)
"Comrades" (Portrait of W. M. Ellis, Black Body Servant, and T. B. Ellis), ca. 1870s, albumen print, $5\frac{1}{2} \times 3\frac{7}{8}$ inches. The Valentine Museum, Richmond, Virginia
PAGE 50

Emancipation Day Celebration, Richmond, Virginia, 1888, albumen print, $5\frac{1}{16} \times 7$ inches. The Valentine Museum, Richmond, Virginia
PAGE 60

Ralston Crawford (American, born Canada, 1906–1978)
Eureka Brass Band at McDonoghville Cemetery, New Orleans, Louisiana, 1956, gelatin silver print, $6\frac{1}{4} \times 9\frac{5}{8}$ inches. Ralston Crawford Collection of New Orleans Jazz Photographs, William Ransom Hogan Jazz Archive, Tulane University Library
PAGE 139

George H. Dabbs (American, active 1900s)
Coal Opening on the Lurn Drake Farm, Butler County, Kentucky, ca. 1900–1904, from the "Arthur Y. Ford Album," gelatin silver print, $6\frac{1}{2} \times 4\frac{3}{8}$ inches. Photographic Archives, University of Louisville, Kentucky
PAGE 82

Bruce Davidson (American, born 1933)
Arresting Demonstrators, Birmingham, Alabama, 1963, gelatin silver print, $6\frac{5}{16} \times 9\frac{7}{16}$ inches. High Museum of Art, Atlanta; Gift of Howard Greenberg
PAGE 167

Jack Delano (American, born 1935)
Portrait of a Couple, Greene County, Georgia, 1940, gelatin silver print, 8 × 10 inches. Arthur F. Raper Papers, Southern Historical Collection, University of North Carolina Library at Chapel Hill
PAGE 115

Alain Desvergnes (French, born 1931)
Yoknapatawpha, Oxford, Mississippi, 1963, gelatin silver print, 7 × 7 inches. Courtesy of the artist and Catherine Edelman Gallery, Chicago
PAGE 143

Yoknapatawpha, Oxford, Mississippi, 1963, gelatin silver print, 7 × 7 inches. Courtesy of the artist and Catherine Edelman Gallery, Chicago
PAGE 144

Yoknapatawpha, Oxford, Mississippi, 1963, gelatin silver print, 7 × 7 inches. Courtesy of the artist and Catherine Edelman Gallery, Chicago
PAGE 145

Michael Disfarmer (American, 1884–1959)
Woman in Print Dress and Young Boy with Ice Cream Cone, 1939–46, gelatin silver print, $11\frac{3}{4} \times 9\frac{1}{8}$ inches. The Metropolitan Museum of Art; Gift of Julia S. Scully, 1979
PAGE 136

A. J. Earp (American, active 1900s)
Cliff Owen Dairy Farm, Clark County, Kentucky, ca. 1900–1904, from the "Arthur Y. Ford Album," gelatin silver print, $7\frac{3}{16} \times 9\frac{5}{8}$ inches. Photographic Archives, University of Louisville, Kentucky
PAGE 72

William Eggleston (American, born 1939)
Halloween, Outskirts of Morton, Mississippi, 1971, dye transfer print, $11\frac{15}{16} \times 17\frac{3}{4}$ inches. High Museum of Art, Atlanta; Gift of Lucinda W. Bunnen for the Bunnen Collection
PAGE 202

Sumner, Mississippi, Cassidy Bayou in Background, 1971, dye transfer print, $10\frac{3}{4} \times 16\frac{3}{4}$ inches. Collection of Lucinda W. Bunnen
PAGE 203

Memphis, 1983, from the portfolio "William Eggleston's Graceland," 1984, chromogenic development print, $14\frac{3}{4} \times 22$ inches. High Museum of Art, Atlanta; Purchase with funds from the Massey Charitable Trust
PAGE 204

Rudolf Eickemeyer, Jr. (American, 1862–1932)
Wash Day on the Plantation, Mt. Meigs, Alabama, ca. 1887, platinum print, $7\frac{1}{8} \times 9\frac{1}{8}$ inches. Prints and Photographs Division, Library of Congress, Washington, D.C.
PAGE 63

Walker Evans (American, 1903–1975)
Breakfast Room at Belle Grove Plantation, White Chapel, Louisiana, 1935, gelatin silver print, $7 \times 8\frac{5}{8}$ inches. The Museum of Modern Art, New York; Anonymous fund
PAGE 111

Levee Seen from Car Window, Vicinity New Orleans, 1935, gelatin silver print, $5\frac{1}{8} \times 8$ inches. The Metropolitan Museum of Art, New York; Gift of the Estate of Walker Evans, 1990
PAGE 89

Stables, Natchez, Mississippi, 1935, gelatin silver print, $8\frac{1}{2} \times 7\frac{1}{4}$ inches. The Museum of Modern Art, New York; Gift of Mr. and Mrs. Alfred H. Barr, Jr.
PAGE 118

Telfair Academy of Arts and Sciences, Savannah, Georgia, 1935, gelatin silver print, $5\frac{9}{16} \times 5\frac{7}{8}$ inches. National Gallery of Art, Washington, D.C.; Gift of Mr. and Mrs. Harry H. Lunn, Jr., in Honor of the 50th Anniversary of the National Gallery of Art
PAGE 110

Allie Mae Burroughs, Wife of a Cotton Sharecropper, Hale County, Alabama, 1936, gelatin silver print, $7\frac{3}{4} \times 5\frac{1}{4}$ inches. The Museum of Modern Art, New York; Purchase
PAGE 104

Battlefield Monument, Vicksburg, Mississippi, 1936, gelatin silver print, 7 15/16 × 7 5/16 inches. Collection of Dr. Benjamin A. Hill
PAGE 95

Houses and Billboards in Atlanta, Georgia, 1936, gelatin silver print, 6 1/2 × 9 1/8 inches. The Museum of Modern Art, New York; Purchase
PAGE 125

Negro Church, South Carolina, 1936, gelatin silver print, 9 1/16 × 6 15/16 inches. The Museum of Modern Art, New York; Gift of Willard Van Dyke
PAGE 96

Photographer's Display Window, Birmingham, Alabama, ca. 1936, gelatin silver print, 9 13/16 × 8 inches. National Gallery of Art, Washington, D.C.; Gift of Mr. and Mrs. Harry H. Lunn, Jr., in Honor of Jacob Kainen and in Honor of the 50th Anniversary of the National Gallery of Art
PAGE 93

Roadside Stand Near Birmingham, Alabama, 1936, gelatin silver print, 7 3/8 × 9 3/8 inches. The Art Institute of Chicago; Gift of Mrs. James Ward Thorne
COVER, PAGE 16

Steel Mill and Workers' Houses, Birmingham, Alabama, 1936, gelatin silver print, 7 1/2 × 9 1/4 inches. High Museum of Art, Atlanta; Purchase with funds from a Friend of the Museum
PAGE 123

Street Scene, Southern City, ca. 1936, gelatin silver print, 6 1/8 × 7 1/8 inches. Collection of Dr. Benjamin A. Hill
PAGE 102

Tupelo, Mississippi, 1936, gelatin silver print, 8 × 9 7/8 inches. National Gallery of Art, Washington, D.C.; Anonymous Gift
PAGE 112

Robert Frank (American, born Switzerland, 1924)

Beaufort, South Carolina, 1955–56, from the series "The Americans," gelatin silver print, 12 7/16 × 18 11/16 inches. Philadelphia Museum of Art; Funds given by Dorothy Norman
PAGE 149

Chattanooga, Tennessee, 1955–56, from the series "The Americans," gelatin silver print, 8 3/4 × 13 1/4 inches. The Art Institute of Chicago; Restricted Gift of Photography Gallery
PAGE 153

Restaurant, U.S. 1, Leaving Columbia, South Carolina, 1955–56, from the series "The Americans," gelatin silver print, 8 3/4 × 13 inches. The Art Institute of Chicago; Photography Gallery Fund
PAGE 152

St. Petersburg, Florida, 1955–56, from the series "The Americans," gelatin silver print, 8 3/4 × 13 inches. George Eastman House, International Museum of Photography and Film, Rochester, New York; Museum Collection
PAGE 150

Trolley, New Orleans, 1955–56, from the series "The Americans," gelatin silver print, 11 × 16 inches. Collection of Dr. and Mrs. Barry S. Ramer, Santa Rosa, California
PAGE 151

Lynda Frese (American, born 1956)

Prosperity, 1995, from the series "Reconstituting the Vanished," 1994–present, digital image with graphite and ink, 26 1/2 × 40 5/8 inches. Courtesy of the artist
PAGE 210

Lee Friedlander (American, born 1934)

New Orleans, Louisiana, 1969, gelatin silver print, 8 × 12 inches. Courtesy of the artist and Fraenkel Gallery, San Francisco
PAGE 174

Versailles, Kentucky, 1976, gelatin silver print, 8 × 11 inches. Courtesy of the artist and Fraenkel Gallery, San Francisco
PAGE 180

Shiloh Military National Park, December 1977, from the portfolio "Shiloh," two gelatin silver prints (diptych), each 7 1/2 × 11 1/8 inches. George Eastman House, International Museum of Photography and Film, Rochester, New York; Purchase with National Endowment for the Arts Support
PAGES 206–07

G. Gable (American, active 1860s)

Summer Scene (The Harry Stephens Family), 1866, albumen print, 2 1/4 × 3 5/8 inches. Gilman Paper Company Collection, New York
PAGE 54

Alexander Gardner (American, born Scotland, 1821–1882)

Ruins of Gallego Flour Mills, Richmond, Virginia, 1865, two albumen prints (panorama), 6 7/8 × 14 1/2 inches overall. The Metropolitan Museum of Art, New York; Harris Brisbane Dick Fund, 1933
PAGES 48–49

Arnold Genthe (American, born Germany, 1869–1942)

Chartres Street, Formerly the Main Shopping Thoroughfare, New Orleans, Louisiana, 1925 or 1926, from the book "Impressions of Old New Orleans," gelatin silver print, 9 1/4 × 7 inches. The Historic New Orleans Collection
PAGE 81

Karekin Goekjian (American, born Lebanon, 1949)

Windsor Columns, Port Gibson, Mississippi, 1991, silver dye bleach print, 13 1/2 × 19 3/4 inches. High Museum of Art, Atlanta; Purchase with funds from Wanda and Lindsey Hopkins III and the Robert Ferst Memorial Fund
PAGE 213

Pandora's Box, St. Mary's, Georgia, 1992, silver dye bleach print, 13 1/2 × 19 3/4 inches. High Museum of Art, Atlanta; Purchase with funds from Wanda and Lindsey Hopkins III and the Robert Ferst Memorial Fund
PAGE 212

John Gutmann (American, born Germany, 1905)

The Game, New Orleans, Louisiana, 1937, gelatin silver print, 13 1/16 × 10 1/2 inches. New Orleans Museum of Art; Museum Purchase
PAGE 101

Ernst Haas (Austrian, 1921–1986)

Martin Luther King, Jr., at Press Conference, Birmingham, Alabama, May 1963, gelatin silver print, 20 × 16 inches. Ernst Haas Studio, New York
PAGE 160

Declan Haun (American, 1937–1994)

Integration Protest, Monroe, North Carolina, August 1961, gelatin silver print, 13 1/2 × 9 inches. High Museum of Art, Atlanta; Purchase with funds from the Massey Charitable Trust and Lucinda W. Bunnen for the Bunnen Collection
PAGE 164

Chester Higgins Jr. (American, born 1946)

Tuskegee Barber Shop, Tuskegee, Alabama, 1972, gelatin silver print, 11 × 14 inches. Courtesy of the artist
PAGE 173

Lewis W. Hine (American, 1874–1940)

Sadie Pfeifer, 48 Inches High. One of Many Small Children at Work, 1908, from the series "Child Labor," gelatin silver print, 9 1/2 × 7 inches. George Eastman House, International Museum of Photography and Film, Rochester, New York; Gift of the Photo League, New York
PAGE 82

The Last Stand of the Confederacy, Mobile, Alabama, 1914, gelatin silver print, 4 1/2 × 6 1/2 inches. George Eastman House, International Museum of Photography and Film, Rochester, New York; Museum Collection
PAGE 61

John Horgan, Jr. (American, 1859–1926)

12 o'Clock in the Deadening, Jas. S. Richardson's Walnut Grove Plantation, Mississippi Valley Route, ca. 1891, albumen print, 17 × 19 1/4 inches. Gilman Paper Company Collection, New York
PAGE 62

Birney Imes (American, born 1951)

Riverside Lounge, Shaw, Mississippi, 1986, chromogenic development print, 38 3/4 × 44 5/8 inches. High Museum of Art, Atlanta; Purchase
PAGE 208

William Henry Jackson (American, 1843–1942)

Horse Races on Ormond Beach, ca. 1900, albumen print, 7 1/2 × 11 1/8 inches. George Eastman House, International Museum of Photography and Film, Rochester, New York; Gift of Harvard University
PAGE 78

Frances Benjamin Johnston (American, 1864–1952)
Arithmetic. Measuring and Pacing, 1899–1900, from "The Hampton Album," platinum print, 7½ × 9½ inches. The Museum of Modern Art, New York; Gift of Lincoln Kirstein
PAGE 68

Consuelo Kanaga (American, 1894–1978)
Mother and Son or The Question (Florida), 1950, gelatin silver print, 9⅜ × 7⅞ inches. The Brooklyn Museum; Gift of Wallace B. Putnam from the Estate of Consuelo Kanaga
PAGE 136

James H. Karales (American, born 1930)
Selma-to-Montgomery March, Alabama, March 1965, gelatin silver print, 13¾ × 20 inches. High Museum of Art, Atlanta; Purchase with funds from the Massey Charitable Trust and Lucinda W. Bunnen for the Bunnen Collection
PAGE 171

Stuart D. Klipper (American, born 1941)
Fireworks Superstore, Exit 144, I-75, Tennessee, October 23, 1992, from the series "The World in a Few States," 1980–present, chromogenic development print (panorama), 12 × 38 inches. Courtesy of the artist
PAGES 200–01

Ferne Koch (American, born 1913)
"Plutocrat," Blakely, Georgia, 1950, from the "Comic Series," gelatin silver print, 10 × 10 inches. Courtesy of the artist
PAGE 134

William Kuhn (American, active 1867–1900)
Portrait of Harry Stephens, ca. 1875, tintype, 8¼ × 6 inches. Private Collection; Courtesy of Ezra Mack, New York
PAGE 55

Paul Kwilecki (American, born 1928)
Mt. Zuma Baptism at Boat Basin, Flint River. Reverend E. E. Mitchell Has Just Baptized Lisa Spear, 1977, from the series "Religion in Decatur County, Georgia," 1961–present, gelatin silver print, 12⅛ × 17⅞ inches. High Museum of Art, Atlanta; Gift of Lucinda W. Bunnen for the Bunnen Collection
PAGE 190

Dorothea Lange (American, 1895–1965)
Plantation Overseer and His Field Hands, near Clarksdale, Mississippi, 1936, gelatin silver print, 7½ × 9⅜ inches. George Eastman House, International Museum of Photography and Film, Rochester, New York; Gift of the Photographer
PAGE 107

The Families of Evicted Sharecroppers of the Dibble Plantation, near Parkin, Cross County, Arkansas, 1936, gelatin silver print, 7⅝ × 9⅝ inches. The Oakland Museum of California; Gift of Paul S. Taylor
PAGE 117

Aged Cotton Farmer, Greene County, Georgia. He Inherited His Land which is now Heavily Mortgaged, 1937, gelatin silver print, 6⅞ × 8⅝ inches. Roy Stryker Collection, Photographic Archives, University of Louisville, Kentucky

Crossroads Store, Alabama, 1937, gelatin silver print, 13⅞ × 19¼ inches. The Museum of Modern Art, New York; Purchase
PAGE 90

Family on the Road, Oklahoma, 1938, modern gelatin silver print from original negative, 13⅜ × 10⅜ inches. The Oakland Museum of California; Gift of Paul S. Taylor
PAGE 116

Killing Time, Mississippi. The Board that Divides Service to Whites and Blacks, 1938, gelatin silver print, 7 × 4⅜ inches. The Oakland Museum of California; Gift of Paul S. Taylor
PAGE 109

Tennessee, 1938, gelatin silver print, 10¾ × 10½ inches. The Museum of Modern Art, New York; Purchase
PAGE 119

Clarence John Laughlin (American, 1905–1985)
The Mirror of Long Ago, 1946, gelatin silver print, 13$^{5}/_{16}$ × 10⅝ inches. Collection of Virginia Warren Smith
PAGE 129

The Waters of Memory, 1946, gelatin silver print, 10¾ × 13½ inches. High Museum of Art, Atlanta; Bequest of the artist
PAGE 128

The Insect-Headed Tombstone, 1953, gelatin silver print, 13⅝ × 10¼ inches. High Museum of Art, Atlanta; Gift of Lucinda W. Bunnen, 1981
PAGE 130

Jay B. Leviton (American, born 1923)
Elvis Presley, Jacksonville, Florida, August 10, 1956, gelatin silver print, 10 × 16 inches. Courtesy of the artist and Fay Gold Gallery, Atlanta. © Jay: Leviton—Atlanta
PAGE 154

Elvis Presley, New Orleans, Louisiana, August 12, 1956, gelatin silver print, 10 × 16 inches. Courtesy of the artist and Fay Gold Gallery, Atlanta. © Jay: Leviton—Atlanta
PAGE 155

O. Winston Link (American, born 1911)
Main Line on Main Street, Northfork, West Virginia, August 29, 1958, gelatin silver print, 15¼ × 19½ inches. High Museum of Art, Atlanta; Purchase
PAGE 133

E. B. Linn (American, active 1860s)
Cotton on the Steamboat Wave, ca. 1860, ambrotype, 3¾ × 3¼ inches. Alabama Department of Archives and History, Montgomery
PAGE 28

Lynn Marshall-Linnemeier (American, born 1954)
On the Peak of Time, Page 1, 1995, gelatin silver print with acrylic paint, 20 × 16 inches. Courtesy of the artist and The McIntosh Gallery, Atlanta
PAGE 211

Susan Lipper (American, born 1953)
Untitled, 1991, from the "Grapevine Series," 1988–93, gelatin silver print, 12½ × 12½ inches. Courtesy of the artist and Deborah Bell Photographs, New York
PAGE 209

Danny Lyon (American, born 1942)
SNCC Activists Sitting at a Lunch Counter, Atlanta, Georgia, Winter 1963–64, gelatin silver print, 8⅝ × 12$^{15}/_{16}$ inches. High Museum of Art, Atlanta; Purchase with funds from the Massey Charitable Trust and Lucinda W. Bunnen for the Bunnen Collection
PAGE 159

Taylor Washington Arrested at Leb's Delicatessen, Atlanta, Georgia, 1964, gelatin silver print, 13⅜ × 9$^{1}/_{16}$ inches. High Museum of Art, Atlanta; Purchase with funds from the Massey Charitable Trust and Lucinda W. Bunnen for the Bunnen Collection
PAGE 168

Sally Mann (American, born 1951)
Yard Eggs, 1991, gelatin silver print, 20 × 24 inches. High Museum of Art, Atlanta; Purchase with funds from Lucinda W. Bunnen for the Bunnen Collection
PAGE 179

Crossing the Maury, 1992, gelatin silver print, 20 × 24 inches. Courtesy of Houk Friedman, New York
PAGE 191

James "Spider" Martin (American, born 1939)
Barricade at Selma after "Bloody Sunday," March 7, 1965, gelatin silver print, 11 × 14 inches. Courtesy of the artist
PAGE 170

Selma-to-Montgomery March Makes Its Way Through Lowndes County Under Armed Guard, March 1965, gelatin silver print, 11 × 14 inches. Courtesy of the artist
PAGE 171

State Trooper Gives Marchers Two-Minute Warning, Selma, Alabama, March 7, 1965, gelatin silver print, 11 × 14 inches. Courtesy of the artist
PAGE 170

Kate Matthews (American, 1870–1956)
Mother and Child, ca. 1900, from the "Kate Matthews Family Album," platinum print, 6⅞ × 4½ inches. Photographic Archives, University of Louisville, Kentucky

A Snowy Morning, Ashwood Avenue, Pewee Valley, Kentucky, ca. 1900, from the "Kate Matthews Family Album," platinum print, 5⅜ × 3¼ inches. Photographic Archives, University of Louisville, Kentucky
PAGE 79

J. S. Mayer (American, active 1860s)
Free Woman of Color, New Orleans, Louisiana, 1850–60, ambrotype, 3⅜ × 2³⁄₁₆ inches. Collection of Derrick Joshua Beard
PAGE 31

Archibald Crossland McIntyre (American, 1832–1891)
Hannah McIntyre Cozart and Toccoa Cozart, ca. 1859–60, ambrotype, 2¾ × 2½ inches. Alabama Department of Archives and History, Montgomery

First Inauguration of Jefferson Davis as President of the Confederate States of America at Montgomery, Alabama, February 18, 1861, salt print, 7⅞ × 5¾ inches. Boston Athenaeum
PAGE 36

John McWilliams (American, born 1941)
Dreams of Future, 1995, accordion-folded book with sixteen gelatin silver print panels mounted on board, 12 × 8 inches closed, three-dimensional presentation opens to cover an area 3 feet square. Courtesy of the artist
PAGES 192–93

Ralph Eugene Meatyard (American, 1925–1972)
Untitled, 1954–56, gelatin silver print, 6¼ × 10⁷⁄₁₆ inches. Courtesy of the Estate of Ralph Eugene Meatyard
PAGE 178

Untitled, 1961, gelatin silver print, 6½ × 6¹³⁄₁₆ inches. Courtesy of the Estate of Ralph Eugene Meatyard

Joel Meyerowitz (American, born 1938)
Atlanta, 1988, chromogenic development print, 19 × 23 inches. Courtesy of the artist and Bonni Benrubi Gallery, New York
PAGE 199

Michael Miley (American, 1841–1918)
General Robert E. Lee on Traveller, 1867, printed ca. 1870s, platinum print, 14¼ × 17¼ inches. Collection of Peter and Judy Wach, Wach Gallery, Cleveland, Ohio
PAGE 58

Leigh Richmond Miner (American, 1864–1935)
Alfred Graham, The First Teacher of Basketry at Penn, Brought the Craft from Africa as a Boy, 1909, modern gelatin silver print from original glass negative, 9 × 7 inches. Penn School Collection, Penn Center, Inc., St. Helena, South Carolina
PAGE 84

Charles Moore (American, born 1931)
Martin Luther King, Jr., Arrested, Montgomery, Alabama, 1958, gelatin silver print, 9⅛ × 13⅜ inches. High Museum of Art, Atlanta; Purchase with funds from Lucinda W. Bunnen for the Bunnen Collection
PAGE 158

Firemen Blasting Demonstrators, Birmingham, Alabama, May 3, 1963, gelatin silver print, 9¼ × 13½ inches. High Museum of Art, Atlanta; Purchase with funds from Lucinda W. Bunnen for the Bunnen Collection
PAGE 165

Henry P. Moore (American, 1833–1911)
Planting Sweet Potatoes, James Hopkinson's Plantation, Edisto Island, South Carolina, 1862, albumen print, 6 × 8 inches. Memphis Brooks Museum of Art, Memphis; Gift of Mr. and Mrs. J. Hubert Kiersky, Mr. and Mrs. Robert T. Goldsmith, Mr. and Mrs. Edward M. Marks, Mrs. Carol B. Hinchin, Mrs. A. W. Frederick, Jr., and the Photographic Circle in Honor of Shelby Foote
PAGE 35

George François Mugnier (American, born Switzerland, ca. 1857–1938)
Sugar Mill Payday, ca. 1900, gelatin silver print, 8 × 10 inches. Louisiana State Museum, New Orleans

Osborn's Gallery (American, active early 1860s)
Negro Church, Goose Creek, South Carolina, 1860–65, albumen print carte-de-visite, 2⅜ × 3⅛ inches. The New-York Historical Society

The Evacuation of Ft. Sumter, April 1861, albumen print cartes-de-visite album, overall album dimensions (open) 4¹¹⁄₁₆ × 6¾ inches. Gilman Paper Company Collection, New York

Timothy O'Sullivan (American, born Ireland, 1840–1882)
Fugitive Slaves Fording the Rappahannock River, Virginia, 1862, albumen print, 3⅜ × 4¼ inches. High Museum of Art, Atlanta; Purchase
PAGE 43

Marion Palfi (American, born Germany, 1907–1978)
To the Colored Waiting Room, Florida, 1945–49, gelatin silver print, 13½ × 10⅜ inches. High Museum of Art, Atlanta; Purchase with funds from the Massey Charitable Trust and Lucinda W. Bunnen for the Bunnen Collection
PAGE 146

Fred A. Parrish (American, 1893–1980)
Vivien Leigh as Scarlett O'Hara Ascending the Staircase at Twelve Oaks in "Gone With the Wind," 1939, modern gelatin silver print from original negative, 8 × 10 inches. Courtesy of Turner Entertainment Company, Los Angeles
PAGE 126

John Pfahl (American, born 1939)
Crystal River Nuclear Plant (Morning), Crystal River, Florida, January 1982, from the series "Power Places," 1981–84, chromogenic development print, 16 × 20 inches. Courtesy of the artist
PAGE 188

Prentice H. Polk (American, 1898–1984)
Charles Turner at His Cabin, 1930, gelatin silver print, 7¼ × 9¾ inches. Collection of Paul R. Jones
PAGE 85

Portrait of Mr. and Mrs. T. M. Campbell and Their Children, ca. 1932, gelatin silver print, 9 × 7½ inches. High Museum of Art, Atlanta; Purchase
PAGE 86

Charmian Reading (American, born Canada, 1930)
Fannie Lou Hamer Singing, March Against Fear, Mississippi, 1966, gelatin silver print, 10½ × 13⁷⁄₁₆ inches. High Museum of Art, Atlanta; Purchase with funds from the Massey Charitable Trust and Lucinda W. Bunnen for the Bunnen Collection
PAGE 163

Martha McMillan Roberts (American, 1919–1992)
Farmer Jack Wade, Quebie Town, South Carolina, 1948, gelatin silver print, 11⁹⁄₁₆ × 10⁹⁄₁₆ inches. High Museum of Art, Atlanta; Purchase with funds from Powell, Goldstein, Frazer & Murphy
PAGE 137

Richard Samuel Roberts (American, 1880–1936)
Portrait of Hilliard and James Hopkins, ca. 1920s, modern gelatin silver print from original glass negative, 13¹¹⁄₁₆ × 9⅜ inches. Courtesy of the Estate of Richard Samuel Roberts, Washington, D.C.
PAGE 87

Thomas Roche (American, 1826–1895)
A Dead Rebel Soldier in the Trenches of Fort Mahone, Petersburg, Virginia, April 2, 1865, from the series "Photographic History—The War for the Union," albumen print stereograph, 3⅛ × 6¼ inches. The New-York Historical Society

Arthur Rothstein (American, 1915–1987)
Aletta Bendolph in Log Cabin, Gee's Bend, Alabama, 1937, gelatin silver print, 9 × 12 inches. Howard Greenberg Gallery, New York
PAGE 103

Louis Rousseau (French, active 1860s)
Portrait of Marie Lassus, New Orleans, 1860, albumen print, 6⅞ × 4¼ inches. New Orleans Museum of Art; Museum Purchase, Clarence John Laughlin Photographic Society Funds
PAGE 31

Edward Ruscha (American, born 1937)
Knox Less, Oklahoma City, Oklahoma, 1962, from the portfolio "Twenty-Six Gasoline Stations," gelatin silver print, 19½ × 23 inches. Courtesy of the artist and James Corcoran Gallery

Andrew Joseph Russell (American, 1830–1902)
Slave Pen, Alexandria, Virginia, ca. 1863, albumen print, 10⅛ × 14⅜ inches. Gilman Paper Company Collection, New York
PAGE 33

Flip Schulke (American, born 1930)

Governor George Wallace Reading The Birmingham News, 1963, gelatin silver print, $12\frac{3}{8} \times 8\frac{1}{4}$ inches. Courtesy of the artist and James Danziger Gallery, New York
PAGE 161

Myrlie Evers and Her Children at the Casket of Medgar Evers, Jackson, Mississippi, June 1963, gelatin silver print, $12\frac{7}{8} \times 8\frac{3}{16}$ inches. Courtesy of the artist and James Danziger Gallery, New York
PAGE 162

White Students in Montgomery Demonstrate against Integration in Their High School, Montgomery, Alabama, September 1963, gelatin silver print, $12\frac{5}{8} \times 8\frac{1}{4}$ inches. Courtesy of the artist and James Danziger Gallery, New York
PAGE 157

Ben Shahn (American, born Lithuania, 1898–1969)

Watching a Medicine Show, Huntingdon, Tennessee, 1935, gelatin silver print, $7\frac{13}{16} \times 9\frac{3}{4}$ inches. Fogg Art Museum, Harvard University Art Museums, Cambridge, Massachusetts; Gift of Mrs. Bernarda Bryson Shahn
PAGE 98

Watching a Medicine Show, Huntingdon, Tennessee, 1935, gelatin silver print, $6\frac{3}{4} \times 9\frac{5}{8}$ inches. Fogg Art Museum, Harvard University Art Museums, Cambridge, Massachusetts; Gift of Mrs. Bernarda Bryson Shahn
PAGE 98

Watching a Medicine Show, Huntingdon, Tennessee, 1935, gelatin silver print, $6\frac{5}{8} \times 9\frac{3}{4}$ inches. Fogg Art Museum, Harvard University Art Museums, Cambridge, Massachusetts; Gift of Mrs. Bernarda Bryson Shahn
PAGE 99

Watching a Medicine Show, Huntingdon, Tennessee, 1935, gelatin silver print, $6\frac{5}{8} \times 9\frac{5}{8}$ inches. Fogg Art Museum, Harvard University Art Museums, Cambridge, Massachusetts; Gift of Mrs. Bernarda Bryson Shahn
PAGE 99

Watching a Medicine Show, Huntingdon, Tennessee, 1935, gelatin silver print, $7\frac{1}{2} \times 9\frac{3}{4}$ inches. Fogg Art Museum, Harvard University Art Museums, Cambridge, Massachusetts; Gift of Mrs. Bernarda Bryson Shahn
PAGE 100 (TOP)

Watching a Medicine Show, Huntingdon, Tennessee, 1935, gelatin silver print, $7\frac{13}{16} \times 9\frac{3}{4}$ inches. Roy Stryker Collection, Photographic Archives, University of Louisville, Kentucky
PAGE 100 (BOTTOM)

Moneta Sleet, Jr. (American, born 1926)

Rain-Soaked Woman Singing During Selma March, March 1965, gelatin silver print, $16\frac{15}{16} \times 13\frac{9}{16}$ inches. The St. Louis Art Museum; Gift of the Johnson Publishing Company

Two Teenaged Supporters of the Selma March, March 1965, gelatin silver print, $17 \times 11\frac{1}{2}$ inches. The St. Louis Art Museum; Gift of the Johnson Publishing Company
PAGE 169

W. Eugene Smith (American, 1918–1978)

Ku Klux Klan Meeting, North Carolina, 1951, gelatin silver print, $10\frac{1}{2} \times 12\frac{3}{4}$ inches. Center for Creative Photography, University of Arizona, Tucson
PAGE 148

Untitled [Maude attending patient, assistant looking on with clasped hands], 1951, from the series "Nurse Midwife. Maude Callen Eases Pain of Birth, Life and Death," *Life,* vol. 31, no. 23, December 3, 1951, gelatin silver print, $10\frac{1}{2} \times 13\frac{1}{4}$ inches. Center for Creative Photography, University of Arizona, Tucson
PAGE 138

Melissa Springer (American, born 1956)

Innocents Blessing, Kingston, Georgia, 1992, from the series "Salvation on Sand Mountain," gelatin silver print, $11\frac{1}{2} \times 16$ inches. Courtesy of the artist
PAGE 187

Laying on Hands, Kingston, Georgia, 1992, from the series "Salvation on Sand Mountain," gelatin silver print, $11\frac{1}{2} \times 16$ inches. Courtesy of the artist
PAGE 186

The Serpent Handlers, Jolo, West Virginia, 1992, from the series "Salvation on Sand Mountain," gelatin silver print, $11\frac{1}{2} \times 16$ inches. Courtesy of the artist
PAGE 186

Brother Carl in His Church, Kingston, Georgia, 1993, from the series "Salvation on Sand Mountain," gelatin silver print, $11\frac{1}{2} \times 16$ inches. Courtesy of the artist
PAGE 187

Mother St. Croix (American, born France, 1854–1940)

Girls around the Statue of the Sacred Heart of Jesus, Ursuline Convent Academy, New Orleans, Louisiana, ca. 1905, modern gelatin silver print from original glass negative, $16 \times 19\frac{7}{8}$ inches. New Orleans Museum of Art; Museum Purchase, 1975 Acquisition Fund
PAGE 83

Joel Sternfeld (American, born 1944)

Pensacola Women's Medical Services, 4400 Bayou Boulevard, Cordova Square, Pensacola, Florida, August 1993, from the series "On this Site . . . ," 1992–93, chromogenic development print and text, $18\frac{3}{4} \times 23\frac{1}{2}$ inches. Courtesy of the artist and PaceWildensteinMacGill, New York

Dr. David Gunn, the founder of this clinic, was shot in the back three times as he walked to the rear entrance of the building during an anti-abortion demonstration on March 10, 1993. He fell beneath this small tree and died two hours later in surgery. Michael Griffen, the assailant, walked to the front of the clinic and surrendered to the police.
PAGE 205

Thomas Sully (American, 1855–1939)

Portrait of Two Hunters, ca. 1890, gelatin silver print, $5 \times 7\frac{7}{8}$ inches. Thomas Sully Collection, Southeastern Architectural Archive, Tulane University Library, New Orleans; Gift of Jeanne Sully West
PAGE 77

Reverend Lonzie Odie Taylor (American, 1900–1977)

Tri-State Bank Opening, Memphis, ca. 1946, gelatin silver print, 8×10 inches. Center for Southern Folklore, Memphis
PAGE 137

Thomas Tulis (American, born 1961)

Construction of Suburbia #22, 1993, silver dye bleach print, 19×23 inches. Courtesy of the artist and Agnes Gallery, Birmingham, Alabama
PAGE 198

Unidentified Photographer (American, active ca. 1860s)

Portrait of a Slave Child with Master's Children, Virginia, ca. 1858–60, ambrotype, $3\frac{1}{4} \times 4\frac{1}{4}$ inches. Collection of Derrick Joshua Beard

Unidentified Photographer (American, active ca. 1850s–1860s)

Portrait of a Planter's Family and Slave, New Market, Virginia, ca. 1859–64, tintype with applied color, $3\frac{1}{4} \times 4\frac{1}{4}$ inches. Collection of William A. Turner
PAGE 32

Unidentified Photographer (American, active ca. 1860s)

Slave with Inventory Number, ca. 1860, albumen print carte-de-visite, $4 \times 2\frac{1}{2}$ inches. Stanley B. Burns, M.D., and The Burns Archive, New York
PAGE 29

Unidentified Photographer (American, active ca. 1860s)

Hamilton, a Slave at the Legare Plantation, Capers Island, South Carolina, ca. 1860–63, albumen print carte-de-visite, $2\frac{3}{8} \times 3\frac{1}{8}$ inches. The New-York Historical Society
PAGE 27

Unidentified Photographer (American, active ca. 1860s)

Negro Quarters, Perseverance Plantation, Goose Creek Parish, South Carolina, ca. 1860–63, albumen print carte-de-visite, $2\frac{3}{8} \times 3\frac{1}{8}$ inches. The New-York Historical Society
PAGE 27

Unidentified Photographer (American, active ca. 1860s)

Negro Quarters, Perseverance Plantation, Goose Creek Parish, South Carolina, ca. 1860–63, albumen print carte-de-viste, $2\frac{3}{8} \times 3\frac{1}{4}$ inches. The New-York Historical Society
PAGE 27

Unidentified Photographer (American, active ca. 1860s)

Portraits of an Unidentified Slave, ca. 1860–63, double tintype, each $4\frac{1}{4} \times 3\frac{1}{4}$ inches. Collection of William A. Turner
PAGE 30

Unidentified Photographer (American, active ca. 1860s)
Slaves Going to Church, Bryan Plantation, Folly Island, South Carolina, ca. 1860–63, albumen print carte-de-visite, 2⅜ × 3⅛ inches. The New-York Historical Society
PAGE 27

Unidentified Photographer (American, active ca. 1860s)
Portrait of an Alabama Infantryman, ca. 1861, tintype, 4¼ × 3¼ inches. Collection of Al and Claudia Niemiec
PAGE 37

Unidentified Photographer (American, active ca. 1860s)
Portrait of Columbus W. Motes, Troup Artillery, 1861–65, stereo ambrotype in Mascher case, 3¼ × 4¼ inches. Collection of Steve Folio
PAGE 37

Unidentified Photographer (American, active ca. 1860s)
Portrait of Henry Figuers and Friend, 1861–65, ambrotype, 2¾ × 3¼ inches. Collection of William A. Turner

Unidentified Photographer (American, active ca. 1860s)
Portrait of Major General William W. Loring, 1861–65, ambrotype with applied color, 5½ × 4¼ inches. The Museum of the Confederacy, Richmond, Virginia

Unidentified Photographer (American, active ca. 1860s)
Portrait of Mrs. Ridgley-Brown, 1861–65, albumen print carte-de-visite with applied color, 4 × 2½ inches. Collection of William A. Turner
PAGE 38

Unidentified Photographer (American, active ca. 1860s)
Portrait of Private Alexander Harris, Parker's Virginia Battery, 1861–65, ambrotype with applied color, 3¼ × 2¾ inches. Collection of William A. Turner
PAGE 40

Unidentified Photographer (American, active ca. 1860s)
Portrait of an Unidentified Woman and a Confederate Cavalryman, 1861–65, tintype, 3 × 2½ inches. Atlanta History Center; DuBose Civil War Collection
PAGE 39

Unidentified Photographer (American, active ca. 1860s)
Post-Mortem Portrait of Charles Bostrick Marshall, Mobile, Alabama, 1861–65, ambrotype with applied color, 4¼ × 3¼ inches. Collection of Willliam A. Turner
PAGE 41

Unidentified Photographer (American, active ca. 1860s)
View of Garden, James E. Seabrook's Plantation, Edisto Island, South Carolina, 1862, from the album "Photographs of the War of the Rebellion (U.S. Navy, Edisto Island, Morris and Folly Island . . .)," gelatin silver print from original glass plate negative, 1926, 5¾ × 7¼ inches. The New-York Historical Society; Gift of the Library of the Military Order of the Loyal Legion of the United States, Commandery of the State of New York

View of Park, James E. Seabrook's Plantation, Edisto Island, South Carolina, 1862, from the album "Photographs of the War of the Rebellion (U.S. Navy, Edisto Island, Morris and Folly Island . . .)," gelatin silver print from original glass plate negative, 1926, 5¾ × 7¼ inches. The New-York Historical Society; Gift of the Library of the Military Order of the Loyal Legion of the United States, Commandery of the State of New York
PAGE 34

Unidentified Photographer (American, active 1860s)
Graveyard and Monument of Hazen's Brigade on Stones River Battleground, ca. 1865, from the "Chattanooga Album," albumen print, 9½ × 11¾ inches. George Eastman House, International Museum of Photography and Film, Rochester, New York; Museum Purchase

Unidentified Photographer (American, active ca. 1860s)
The Wilderness Battlefield, 1865–67, four solarized albumen prints, each approximately 4⅞ × 3⅛ inches. Gilman Paper Company Collection, New York
PAGES 46–47

Unidentified Photographer (American, active ca. 1860s)
Ku Klux Klansman, ca. 1869, tintype, 3¼ × 1⅞ inches. Gilman Paper Company Collection, New York
PAGE 66

Unidentified Photographer (American, active ca. 1880s)
In Memory of Our Confederate Dead, ca. 1880s, albumen print, 7⅜ × 9⅝ inches. Collection of George S. Whiteley IV
PAGE 59

Unidentified Photographer (American, active ca. 1880s)
Members of the Henry McCall and Meta McCall Diesback Families and Their Servants at Evan Hall Plantation, Donaldsonville, Louisiana, 1888, eight gelatin silver prints, each approximately 2½ inches in diameter. The Historic New Orleans Collection; Gift of James L. McCall, Jr.
PAGES 64–65

Unidentified Photographer (American, active ca. 1890s)
Men Guarding Prisoners, Campbell County, Georgia, ca. 1890, albumen print, 7¾ × 9⅝ inches. Collection of Derrick Joshua Beard
PAGE 67

Unidentified Photographer (American, active ca. 1900)
Untitled, ca. 1900, from the "Calhoun School and Settlement Album, Calhoun, Alabama," platinum print, 4¼ × 6⅝ inches. The Daniel Cowin Collection of African American History, International Center of Photography, New York
PAGE 70

Unidentified Photographer (American, active ca. 1900s)
Reunion of Nathaniel Burwell's Slaves at Sherwood Plantation near Salem, in Roanoke County, Virginia, 1903, gelatin silver printing-out paper print, 10 × 7½ inches. The Virginia Historical Society, Richmond
PAGE 53

John Vachon (American, 1914–1975)
A Day in Court, Rustburg, Virginia, 1941, modern gelatin silver print from original negative, 11 × 14 inches. Prints and Photographs Division, Library of Congress, Washington, D.C.
PAGE 113

Todd Webb (American, born 1906)
Louisiana Oil Field, 1947 or 1948, gelatin silver print, 10½ × 13½ inches. The Historic New Orleans Collection
PAGE 132

Carrie Mae Weems (American, born 1953)
Untitled (Ebo Landing), 1992, from the "Sea Islands Series," two gelatin silver prints and one text panel, each 20 × 20 inches, overall 60 × 20 inches. Courtesy of the artist and P·P·O·W, Inc., New York
PAGE 189

Dan Weiner (American, 1919–1959)
White Rider during Bus Boycott, Montgomery, Alabama, 1956, gelatin silver print, 8¾ × 13⁵⁄₁₆ inches. High Museum of Art, Atlanta; Purchase with funds from the Massey Charitable Trust and Lucinda W. Bunnen for the Bunnen Collection
PAGE 140

Eudora Welty (American, born 1909)
Preacher and Leaders of Holiness Church, Jackson, Mississippi, 1939, gelatin silver print, 13¹⁵⁄₁₆ × 10¼ inches. Collection of Virginia Warren Smith; Promised Gift to the High Museum of Art, Atlanta
PAGE 97

Political Rally on the Courthouse Grounds, Pontotoc, Mississippi, 1930s, gelatin silver print, 17¼ × 12½ inches. The Roger Houston Ogden Collection
PAGE 94

Edward Weston (American, 1886–1958)
Union Station, Nashville, Tennessee, 1941, gelatin silver print, 7⁷⁄₁₆ × 9½ inches. Henry E. Huntington Library and Art Gallery, San Marino, California
PAGE 132

William Edmondson's Sculpture, Nashville, Tennessee, 1941, gelatin silver print, 7½ × 9⅝ inches. Center for Creative Photography, University of Arizona, Tucson
PAGE 131

Fonville Winans (American, 1911–1992)

Cajun Fare (Fat of the Land, Morgan City, Louisiana), 1939, gelatin silver print, 16 × 20 inches. The Roger Houston Ogden Collection
PAGE 121

Uncle Earl Long Skins a Polecat, 1940, gelatin silver print, 16 × 20 inches. Louisiana State Museum, New Orleans

Ernest C. Withers (American, born 1922)

"No White People Allowed in Zoo Today," 1950s, gelatin silver print, 15 × 18 inches. Courtesy of the artist and Panopticon Gallery, Boston
PAGE 147

Desegregation of Central High School by "Little Rock Nine," Little Rock, Arkansas, 1957, gelatin silver print, 15 × 18 inches. Courtesy of the artist and Panopticon Gallery, Boston
PAGE 156

Supporters of the Volunteer Ticket Welcome Dr. Martin Luther King, Jr., to Memphis, Tennessee, March 1959, gelatin silver print, 18 × 15 inches. Courtesy of the artist and Panopticon Gallery, Boston

I Am A Man (Sanitation Workers Assemble in Front of Clayborn Temple for a Solidarity March, Memphis, Tennessee), March 28, 1968, gelatin silver print, 10⅞ × 18⅞ inches. High Museum of Art, Atlanta; Purchase with funds from the Massey Charitable Trust and Lucinda W. Bunnen for the Bunnen Collection
PAGE 172

Marion Post Wolcott (American, 1910–1990)

Arranging Tobacco in Baskets Before Auction in Warehouse, Mebane, North Carolina, 1939, gelatin silver print, 8 × 10 inches. Howard W. Odum Subregional Photographic Study Papers, Southern Historical Collection, University of North Carolina Library at Chapel Hill
PAGE 108

Cashiers Paying Off Cotton Pickers in Marcella Plantation Store, Mileston, Mississippi, 1939, gelatin silver print, 8½ × 11⅞ inches. The Art Institute of Chicago; Gift of Michael D. Wolcott
PAGE 106

Making Biscuits for Dinner on Corn Husking Day. The Fred Wilkens Farm near Tallyho, North Carolina, 1939, gelatin silver print, 8⅞ × 12 inches. The Art Institute of Chicago; Gift of Michael D. Wolcott
PAGE 105

Negro Man Entering a Movie Theatre by "Colored" Entrance, Belzoni, Mississippi, 1939, gelatin silver print, 16 × 20 inches. The Roger Houston Ogden Collection
PAGE 127

Two Couples in Booth at Juke Joint, Moorehaven, Florida, 1939, gelatin silver print, 12 × 8⅞ inches. The Art Institute of Chicago; Gift of Michael D. Wolcott
PAGE 120

Union Members Waiting for the Strike-Breaking Scabs to Come Out of the Copper Mines, Ducktown, Tennessee, 1939, gelatin silver print, 8¾ × 11⅞ inches. The Art Institute of Chicago; Gift of Michael D. Wolcott
PAGE 122

Bayard Wootten (American, 1875–1959)

Sunset across the Ashley from the Battery, Charleston, South Carolina, ca. 1935, gelatin silver print, 10¹¹⁄₁₆ × 13⅝ inches. North Carolina Collection, University of North Carolina Library at Chapel Hill
PAGE 88

PHOTOGRAPHIC CREDITS

Photographs reproduced in this volume have been provided, in the majority of cases, by the owners or custodians of the works, who are indicated in the captions, except for the following:

Ben Blackwell: 151

Robert M. Fouts: 28

Bruno Joachim: 30, 32, 38, 40, 41

Mike McKelvey: 31, 67, 85, 95, 97, 102, 128, 129, 130, 137, 178, 182, 183, 184, 185, 194, 195, 196, 197, 210

Mary Carolyn Pindar: 45, 154, 155, 203

George S. Whiteley, IV: 57, 59

The following list, keyed to page numbers, applies to photographs for which a separate acknowledgment is due.

© 1995, The Art Institute of Chicago: 105, 106, 120, 122

"Gone With the Wind" © 1939 Turner Entertainment Company, All rights reserved: 126

© Estate of Clarence John Laughlin, courtesy The Historic New Orleans Collection: 128, 129, 130

© Black Star, Inc.: 158, 165

© Magnum Photos, Inc.: 159, 167, 168

© Harry Callahan, courtesy PaceWildensteinMacGill and Jackson Fine Art: 194, 195, 196–97

© Johnson Publishing Company: 169

© Walker Evans Archives, courtesy The Metropolitan Museum of Art: cover, 16, 89, 93, 102, 110, 111, 112, 118, 123

© President and Fellows, Harvard College, Harvard University Art Museums: 98, 99, 100 (top)

© Estate of Fonville Winans: 121

© Estate of Dan Weiner: 140

© Joel Sternfeld, courtesy PaceWildensteinMacGill: 205

© Henri Cartier-Bresson, courtesy Helen Wright: 166

© Estate of Margaret Bourke-White: 114, 124

© James H. Karales: 171 (bottom)

© Ernst Haas, courtesy Ernst Haas Studio, Inc.: 160

© Chester Higgins Jr., All rights reserved: 173

© Sally Mann, courtesy Houk Friedman: 179, 191

© Robert Frank, courtesy PaceWildensteinMacGill: 149, 150, 151, 152, 153

© Estate of Declan Haun: 164

© Gregory Conniff: 181

© Eudora Welty Collection, Mississippi Department of Archives and History: 94, 97

© Lee Friedlander, courtesy Fraenkel Gallery: 174, 180, 206–7

© The Dorothea Lange Collection, The Oakland Museum of California, The City of Oakland: 109, 116, 117

Courtesy Linda Wolcott-Moore: 105, 106, 108, 120, 122, 127

© 1982 The Heirs of W. Eugene Smith: 138, 148

© James "Spider" Martin: 170, 171 (top)

Courtesy New York Public Library, Astor, Lenox and Tilden Foundations: 56, 69

© Jay: Leviton—Atlanta: 154, 155

© Ralston Crawford Collection of New Orleans Jazz Photographs, William Ransom Hogan Jazz Archive, Tulane University Library: 139

© Estate of Arthur Rothstein, courtesy Howard Greenberg Gallery: 103

© Charmian Reading: 163

© Ernest C. Withers, courtesy Panopticon Gallery: 147, 156, 172

© Penn School Collection, Penn Center, Inc., courtesy Southern Historical Collection, University of North Carolina Library at Chapel Hill: 84

© 1981 Center for Creative Photography, Arizona Board of Regents: 131, 132 (bottom)

© William Eggleston, courtesy Robert Miller Gallery: 202, 203, 204

© William Christenberry, courtesy PaceWildensteinMacGill: 182, 183, 184, 185

© Flip Schulke, courtesy James Danziger Gallery: 157, 161, 162

NOTES ON WRITERS

William Baldwin lives with his wife in McClellanville, South Carolina. He has degrees in History and English Literature from Clemson University. He designs and builds houses. In the past he's taught school, been a magistrate, and worked as a screenwriter. In addition to two nonfiction books, he wrote the novel *The Hard To Catch Mercy*, which won the Lillian Smith Award and the DLB Yearbook Award for first fiction. His second novel, *The Fennel Family Papers*, has recently been published.

Ellen Dugan is Curator of Photography at the High Museum of Art. She has organized numerous exhibitions and is the author of *First Person Singular: Self-Portrait Photography, 1840–1987* and *This Sporting Life, 1878–1991*.

Clyde Edgerton has taught most recently in North Carolina, Georgia, and Mississippi. He is the author of six novels: *Raney*, *Walking Across Egypt*, *The Floatplane Notebooks*, *Killer Diller*, *In Memory of Junior*, and *Redeye, A Western*. He is also a member of the Tarwater Band, a folk and bluegrass group.

Josephine Humphreys won the Ernest Hemingway Foundation award for her first novel, *Dreams of Sleep*. She is also the author of *Rich in Love* and *The Fireman's Fair*. She lives in Charleston, South Carolina, with her husband and children.

Bobbie Ann Mason was born and raised in Kentucky. Her stories have appeared in *The New Yorker*, *The Atlantic*, *Harper's*, and *The Paris Review*. She is the author of *In Country*, *Spence + Lila*, *Shiloh and Other Stories*, and *Feather Crowns*.

Willie Morris was born in Jackson, Mississippi, and raised in Yazoo City. At the age of thirty-two, he became editor-in-chief of *Harper's*, the nation's oldest magazine. From 1980 to 1990 Morris was writer-in-residence at the University of Mississippi. His books include *North Toward Home*, *Good Old Boy*, *Faulkner's Mississippi*, and *New York Days*. He lives with his wife in Jackson.

A. J. Verdelle was born and raised in Washington, D.C. She holds an MA in Applied Statistics from the University of Chicago and an MFA from Bard College. She has studied at the Whitney Museum of American Art and lives in Brooklyn, New York. Her first novel, *The Good Negress*, was published in 1995.

Charles Reagan Wilson, born in Tennessee and raised in Texas, has taught at the University of Mississippi since 1981. Coeditor of the *Encyclopedia of Southern Culture*, Wilson teaches History and Southern Studies. His most recent book, published in 1995, is *Judgment and Grace in Dixie: Southern Faiths from Faulkner to Elvis*.